MORAL PROBLEMS

MORAL PROBLEMS

a collection of philosophical essays

second edition

.

edited by

James Rachels

University of Miami

HARPER & ROW, Publishers
New York   Evanston   San Francisco   London

Sponsoring Editor: Walter H. Lippincott, Jr.
Project Editor: Holly Detgen
Designer: T. R. Funderburk
Production Supervisor: Stefania J. Taflinska

Moral Problems: A Collection of Philosophical Essays, *Second Edition*

Library of Congress Cataloging in Publication Data
Rachels, James, Date–   comp.
    Moral problems: a collection of philosophical essays.

    CONTENTS: Sex: Nagel, T.   Sexual perversion.
Ruddick, S.   On sexual morality.—Abortion: Ramsey, P.
The morality of abortion.   Foot, P.   The problem of
abortion and the doctrine of the double effect.
Wertheimer, R.   Understanding the abortion argument.
Thomson, J. J.   A defense of abortion.—Prejudice and
discrimination: Wasserstrom, R.   Rights, human rights,
and racial discrimination. [etc.] Selected bibliography
(p.   )
    1.   Social ethics.   I.   Title.
HM216.R24   1975   170'.8   74–18035
ISBN 0–06–045307–9

contents

preface

One of the most exciting developments in recent philosophy has been the revival of interest in practical moral issues. Until a few years ago there was very little work being done by philosophers on such issues as abortion, war, and racial or sexist prejudice. Moral philosophers were preoccupied with other, very different matters, such as the nature of evaluative language or the question of whether it is possible to derive evaluative conclusions from purely factual premises. If practical problems of conduct were mentioned at all, it was only by way of illustrating a more theoretical point. There were exceptions, of course, but this was the general state of the subject.

This lack of concern for practical issues was connected with a certain conception of the nature of moral philosophy shared by many philosophers. According to this conception, moral philosophy is concerned mainly with "metaethics," which is the study of questions *about* morality as opposed to questions that arise *within* morality. Metaethical issues are usually characterized as issues of meaning or logical analysis: What does it mean to say that an action is right? What is the role of principles in moral decision making? What is the nature of *moral* rules as opposed to legal or religious rules? And so on. Metaethics is contrasted with "normative ethics," the attempt to say which actions are right and which are wrong. Some questions of normative ethics were included within the domain of philosophy, but only the very general ones. It was thought to be the philosopher's business, for example, to critically scrutinize general theories of right and wrong, such as the theory that actions are right when they produce more happiness than misery and wrong when they produce more misery than happiness. But it was not thought to be the philosopher's job to investigate *particular* moral issues, such as the issue of whether (or when) abortion is justified. As one writer put it, "A philosopher is not a parish priest or Universal Aunt or Citizens' Advice Bureau" (P. H. Nowell-Smith, *Ethics* [Harmondsworth, Middlesex: Penguin, 1954], p. 12). Philosophers have no greater expertise in practical matters than anyone else. These matters are the concern of everyone; and, therefore, they are not the special business of philosophers.

The events of recent years have prompted many philosophers to reject this conception of their subject as too narrow and restricted. The Vietnam war caused some to turn their attention to questions concerning the morality of war. The civil rights movement, the black power movement, and the women's liberation movement took philosophical questions about social justice, which were formerly only of academic interest, and made them the subject of urgent public discussion. The national debate over legalized abortion posed some old, philosophical questions in a new and challenging form. For example, moral philosophers usually agreed that normal adult persons have a right to life, and for that reason it is wrong to kill them. But this is so uncontroversial as to be uninteresting. However, the question of whether a *fetus* is a person and whether *it* has a right to life is another matter: Here, the philosopher may have something to say of immediate, practical importance.

Thus, within the past few years philosophers have begun to produce a body of literature focusing on specific moral issues in which particular moral claims and arguments are analyzed from a philosophical point of view. This book presents a selection of the new literature.

It should not be thought, however, that the essays included in this book represent an entirely new emphasis in moral philosophy. There is a long tradition of normative ethical reflection among philosophers: Hume and Kant, for example, both had interesting things to say about suicide; the justification of punishment has been vigorously debated since the utilitarian reformers of the nineteenth century challenged the traditional retributivist view that punishment is justified as "paying back" the offender for his evil deed; and the question of our duty to obey the law has always come up whenever political philosophers have tried to define the proper relation between government and citizen. However, there has been more work by philosophers on these subjects during the past fifteen years than during the previous sixty years combined; and, in my judgment at least, this new work is superior to anything that philosophers have ever before produced on these topics.

I continue to be indebted to the three people who gave generous advice and help when I was preparing the first edition of this book: Kai Nielsen, William Ruddick, and Steven Cahn. In preparing the second edition I have benefited very much from several suggestions by Peter Singer, to whom I am most grateful.

J.R.

1

SEX

sexual perversion*

thomas nagel

There is something to be learned about sex from the fact that we possess a concept of sexual perversion. I wish to examine the concept, defending it against the charge of unintelligibility and trying to say exactly what about human sexuality qualifies it to admit of perversions. Let me make some preliminary comments about the problem before embarking on its solution.

Some people do not believe that the notion of sexual perversion makes sense, and even those who do disagree over its application. Nevertheless I think it will be widely conceded that, if the concept is viable at all, it must meet certain general conditions. First, if there are any sexual perversions, they will have to be sexual desires or practices that can be plausibly described as in some sense unnatural, though the explanation of this natural/unnatural distinction is of course the main problem. Second, certain practices will be perversions if anything is, such as shoe fetishism, bestiality, and sadism; other practices, such as unadorned sexual intercourse, will not be; about still others there is controversy. Third, if there are perversions, they will be unnatural sexual *inclinations* rather than merely unnatural practices adopted not from inclination but for other reasons. I realize that this is at

From the *Journal of Philosophy*, vol. 66 (1969). Reprinted by permission of the author and the *Journal of Philosophy*.

*My research was supported in part by the National Science Foundation.

variance with the view, maintained by some Roman Catholics, that contraception is a sexual perversion. But although contraception may qualify as a deliberate perversion of the sexual and reproductive functions, it cannot be significantly described as a *sexual* perversion. A sexual perversion must reveal itself in conduct that expresses an unnatural *sexual* preference. And although there might be a form of fetishism focused on the employment of contraceptive devices, that is not the usual explanation for their use.

I wish to declare at the outset my belief that the connection between sex and reproduction has no bearing on sexual perversion. The latter is a concept of psychological, not physiological interest, and it is a concept that we do not apply to the lower animals, let alone to plants, all of which have reproductive functions that can go astray in various ways. (Think of seedless oranges.) Insofar as we are prepared to regard higher animals as perverted, it is because of their psychological, not their anatomical similarity to humans. Furthermore, we do not regard as a perversion every deviation from the reproductive function of sex in humans: sterility, miscarriage, contraception, abortion.

Another matter that I believe has no bearing on the concept of sexual perversion is social disapprobation or custom. Anyone inclined to think that in each society the perversions are those sexual practices of which the community disapproves, should consider all the societies that have frowned upon adultery and fornication. These have not been regarded as unnatural practices, but have been thought objectionable in other ways. What is regarded as unnatural admittedly varies from culture to culture, but the classification is not a pure expression of disapproval or distaste. In fact it is often regarded as a *ground* for disapproval, and that suggests that the classification has an independent content.

I am going to attempt a psychological account of sexual perversion, which will depend on a specific psychological theory of sexual desire and human sexual interactions. To approach this solution I wish first to consider a contrary position, one which provides a basis for skepticism about the existence of any sexual perversions at all, and perhaps about the very significance of the term. The skeptical argument runs as follows:

"Sexual desire is simply one of the appetites, like hunger and thirst. As such it may have various objects, some more common than others perhaps, but none in any sense 'natural.' An appetite is identified as sexual by means of the organs and erogenous zones in which its satisfaction can be to some extent localized, and the special sensory pleasures which form the core of that satisfaction. This enables us to recognize widely divergent goals, activities,

and desires as sexual, since it is conceivable in principle that anything should produce sexual pleasure and that a nondeliberate,
sexually charged desire for it should arise (as a result of condi-
tioning, if nothing else). We may fail to empathize with some of
these desires, and some of them, like sadism, may be objectionable
on extraneous grounds, but once we have observed that they meet
the criteria for being sexual, there is nothing more to be said on
that score. Either they are sexual or they are not: sexuality does
not admit of imperfection, or perversion, or any other such qualification—it is not that sort of affection.''

This is probably the received radical position. It suggests that
the cost of defending a psychological account may be to deny that
sexual desire is an appetite. But insofar as that line of defense is
plausible, it should make us suspicious of the simple picture of
appetites on which the skepticism depends. Perhaps the standard
appetites, like hunger, cannot be classed as pure appetites, in
that sense either, at least in their human versions.

Let us approach the matter by asking whether we can imagine
anything that would qualify as a gastronomical perversion. Hunger and eating are importantly like sex in that they serve a biological function and also play a significant role in our inner lives.
It is noteworthy that there is little temptation to describe as perverted an appetite for substances that are not nourishing. We
should probably not consider someone's appetites as *perverted* if
he liked to eat paper, sand, wood, or cotton. Those are merely
rather odd and very unhealthy tastes: they lack the psychological
complexity that we expect of perversions. (Coprophilia, being
already a sexual perversion, may be disregarded.) If on the other
hand someone liked to eat cookbooks, or magazines with pictures
of food in them, and preferred these to ordinary food—or if when
hungry he sought satisfaction by fondling a napkin or ashtray
from his favorite restaurant—then the concept of perversion might
seem appropriate (in fact it would be natural to describe this as a
case of gastronomical fetishism). It would be natural to describe as
gastronomically perverted someone who could eat only by having
food forced down his throat through a funnel, or only if the meal
were a living animal. What helps in such cases is the peculiarity of
the desire itself, rather than the inappropriateness of its object to
the biological function that the desire serves. Even an appetite, it
would seem, can have perversions if in addition to its biological
function it has a significant psychological structure.

In the case of hunger, psychological complexity is provided
by the activities that give it expression. Hunger is not merely a
disturbing sensation that can be quelled by eating; it is an attitude

toward edible portions of the external world, a desire to relate to them in rather special ways. The method of ingestion: chewing, savoring, swallowing, appreciating the texture and smell, all are important components of the relation, as it is the passivity and controllability of the food (the only animals we eat live are helpless mollusks). Our relation to food depends also on our size: we do not live upon it or burrow into it like aphids or worms. Some of these features are more central than others, but any adequate phenomenology of eating would have to treat it as a relation to the external world and a way of appropriating bits of that world, with characteristic affection. Displacements or serious restrictions of the desire to eat could then be described as perversions, if they undermined that direct relation between man and food which is the natural expression of hunger. This explains why it is easy to imagine gastronomical fetishism, voyeurism, exhibitionism, or even gastronomical sadism and masochism. Indeed some of these perversions are fairly common.

If we can imagine perversions of an appetite like hunger, it should be possible to make sense of the concept of sexual perversion. I do not wish to imply that sexual desire is an appetite—only that being an appetite is no bar to admitting of perversions. Like hunger, sexual desire has as its characteristic object a certain relation with something in the external world; only in this case it is usually a person rather than an omelet, and the relation is considerably more complicated. This added complication allows scope for correspondingly complicated perversions.

The fact that sexual desire is a feeling about other persons may tempt us to take a pious view of its psychological content. There are those who believe that sexual desire is properly the expression of some other attitude, like love, and that when it occurs by itself it is incomplete and unhealthy—or at any rate subhuman. (The extreme Platonic version of such a view is that sexual practices are all vain attempts to express something they cannot in principle achieve: this makes them all perversions, in a sense.) I do not believe that any such view is correct. Sexual desire is complicated enough without having to be linked to anything else as a condition for phenomenological analysis. It cannot be denied that sex may serve various functions—economic, social, altruistic—but it also has its own content as a relation between persons, and it is only by analyzing that relation that we can understand the conditions of sexual perversion.

I believe it is very important that the object of sexual attraction is a particular individual, who transcends the properties that make him attractive. When different persons are attracted to a single person for different reasons: eyes, hair, figure, laugh, intelligence —we feel that the object of their desire is nevertheless the same, namely that person. There is even an inclination to feel that this is so if the lovers have different sexual aims, if they include both men and women, for example. Different specific attractive characteristics seem to provide enabling conditions for the operation of a single basic feeling, and the different aims all provide expressions of it. We approach the sexual attitude toward the person through the features that we find attractive, but these features are not the objects of that attitude.

This is very different from the case of an omelet. Various people may desire it for different reasons, one for its fluffiness, another for its mushrooms, another for its unique combination of aroma and visual aspect; yet we do not enshrine the transcendental omelet as the true common object of their affections. Instead we might say that several desires have accidentally converged on the same object: any omelet with the crucial characteristics would do as well. It is not similarly true that any person with the same flesh distribution and way of smoking can be substituted as object for a particular sexual desire that has been elicited by those characteristics. It may be that they will arouse attraction whenever they recur, but it will be a new sexual attraction with a new particular object, not merely a transfer of the old desire to someone else. (I believe this is true even in cases where the new object is unconsciously identified with a former one.)

The importance of this point will emerge when we see how complex a psychological interchange constitutes the natural development of sexual attraction. This would be incomprehensible if its object were not a particular person, but rather a person of a certain *kind.* Attraction is only the beginning, and fulfillment does not consist merely of behavior and contact expressing this attraction, but involves much more.

The best discussion of these matters that I have seen appears in part III of Sartre's *Being and Nothingness.*[1] Since it has influenced my own views, I shall say a few things about it now. Sartre's treatment of sexual desire and of love, hate, sadism, masochism, and further attitudes toward others, depends on a general theory of consciousness and the body which we can neither expound nor assume here. He does not discuss perversion, and this is partly because he regards sexual desire as one form of the perpetual attempt of an embodied consciousness to come to terms with the existence of others, an attempt that is as doomed to fail in this

---

[1]Translated by Hazel E. Barnes (New York: Philosophical Library, 1956).

form as it is in any of the others, which include sadism and masochism (if not certain of the more impersonal deviations) as well
as several nonsexual attitudes. According to Sartre, all attempts to
incorporate the other into my world as another subject, i.e., to
apprehend him at once as an object for me and as a subject for
whom I am an object, are unstable and doomed to collapse into
one or other of the two aspects. Either I reduce him entirely to an
object, in which case his subjectivity escapes the possession or
appropriation I can extend to that object; or I become merely an
object for him, in which case I am no longer in a position to appropriate his subjectivity. Moreover, neither of these aspects is
stable; each is continually in danger of giving way to the other.
This has the consequence that there can be no such thing as a
successful sexual relation, since the deep aim of sexual desire cannot in principle be accomplished. It seems likely, therefore, that
the view will not permit a basic distinction between successful
or complete and unsuccessful or incomplete sex, and therefore
cannot admit the concept of perversion.

I do not adopt this aspect of the theory, nor many of its metaphysical underpinnings. What interests me is Sartre's picture of
the attempt. He says that the type of possession that is the object
of sexual desire is carried out by "a double reciprocal incarnation"
and that this is accomplished, typically in the form of a caress, in
the following way: "I make myself flesh in order to impel the
Other to realize *for herself* and *for me* her own flesh, and my
caresses cause my flesh to be born for me in so far as it is for the
Other *flesh causing her to be born as flesh*" (391; italics Sartre's).
The incarnation in question is described variously as a clogging
or troubling of consciousness which is inundated by the flesh in
which it is embodied.

The view I am going to suggest, I hope in less obscure language, is related to this one, but it differs from Sartre's in allowing
sexuality to achieve its goal on occasion and thus in providing the
concept of perversion with a foothold.

Sexual desire involves a kind of perception, but not merely a
single perception of its object, for in the paradigm case of mutual
desire there is a complex system of superimposed mutual perceptions—not only perceptions of the sexual object, but perceptions
of oneself. Moreover, sexual awareness of another involves considerable self-awareness to begin with—more than is involved in
ordinary sensory perception. The experience is felt as an assault
on oneself by the view (or touch, or whatever) of the sexual object.

Let us consider a case in which the elements can be separated.
For clarity we will restrict ourselves initially to the somewhat arti-

ficial case of desire at a distance. Suppose a man and a woman, whom we may call Romeo and Juliet, are at opposite ends of a cocktail lounge, with many mirrors on the walls which permit unobserved observation, and even mutual unobserved observation. Each of them is sipping a martini and studying other people in the mirrors. At some point Romeo notices Juliet. He is moved, somehow, by the softness of her hair and the diffidence with which she sips her martini, and this arouses him sexually. Let us say that X *senses* Y whenever X regards Y with sexual desire. (Y need not be a person, and X's apprehension of Y can be visual, tactile, olfactory, etc., or purely imaginary; in the present example we shall concentrate on vision.) So Romeo senses Juliet, rather than merely noticing her. At this stage he is aroused by an unaroused object, so he is more in the sexual grip of his body than she of hers.

Let us suppose, however, that Juliet now senses Romeo in another mirror on the opposite wall, though neither of them yet knows that he is seen by the other (the mirror angles provide three-quarter views). Romeo then begins to notice in Juliet the subtle signs of sexual arousal: heavy-lidded stare, dilating pupils, faint flush, et cetera. This of course renders her much more bodily, and he not only notices but senses this as well. His arousal is nevertheless still solitary. But now, cleverly calculating the line of her stare without actually looking her in the eyes, he realizes that it is directed at him through the mirror on the opposite wall. That is, he notices, and moreover senses, Juliet sensing him. This is definitely a new development, for it gives him a sense of embodiment not only through his own reactions but through the eyes and reactions of another. Moreover, it is separable from the initial sensing of Juliet; for sexual arousal might begin with a person's sensing that he is sensed and being assailed by the perception of the other person's desire rather than merely by the perception of the person.

But there is a further step. Let us suppose that Juliet, who is a little slower than Romeo, now senses that he senses her. This puts Romeo in a position to notice, and be aroused by, her arousal at being sensed by him. He senses that she senses that he senses her. This is still another level of arousal, for he becomes conscious of his sexuality through his awareness of its effect on her and of her awareness that this effect is due to him. Once she takes the same step and senses that he senses her sensing him, it becomes difficult to state, let alone imagine, further iterations, though they may be logically distinct. If both are alone, they will presumably turn to look at each other directly, and the proceedings will continue on another plane. Physical contact and intercourse are perfectly natural extensions of this complicated visual exchange, and mutual touch can involve all the complexities of awareness present in the visual case, but with a far greater range of subtlety and acuteness.

Ordinarily, of course, things happen in a less orderly fashion —sometimes in a great rush—but I believe that some version of this overlapping system of distinct sexual perceptions and interactions is the basic framework of any full-fledged sexual relation and that relations involving only part of the complex are significantly incomplete. The account is only schematic, as it must be to achieve generality. Every real sexual act will be psychologically far more specific and detailed, in ways that depend not only on the physical techniques employed and on anatomical details, but also on countless features of the participants' conceptions of themselves and of each other, which become embodied in the act. (It is a familiar enough fact, for example, that people often take their social roles and the social roles of their partners to bed with them.)

The general schema is important, however, and the proliferation of levels of mutual awareness it involves is an example of a type of complexity that typifies human interactions. Consider aggression, for example. If I am angry with someone, I want to make him feel it, either to produce self-reproach by getting him to see himself through the eyes of my anger, and to dislike what he sees—or else to produce reciprocal anger or fear, by getting him to perceive my anger as a threat or attack. What I want will depend on the details of my anger, but in either case it will involve a desire that the object of that anger be aroused. This accomplishment constitutes the fulfillment of my emotion, through domination of the object's feelings.

Another example of such reflexive mutual recognition is to be found in the phenomenon of meaning, which appears to involve an intention to produce a belief or other effect in another by bringing about his recognition of one's intention to produce that effect. (That result is due to H. P. Grice,[2] whose position I shall not attempt to reproduce in detail.) Sex has a related structure: it involves a desire that one's partner be aroused by the recognition of one's desire that he or she be aroused.

It is not easy to define the basic types of awareness and arousal of which these complexes are composed, and that remains a lacuna in this discussion. I believe that the object of awareness is the same in one's own case as it is in one's sexual awareness of another, although the two awarenesses will not be the same, the difference being as great as that between feeling angry and experiencing the anger of another. All stages of sexual perception are

---

[2] "Meaning," *Philosophical Review*, LXVI, 3 (July 1957): 377–388.

varieties of identification of a person with his body. What is perceived is one's own or another's *subjection* to or *immersion* in his body, a phenomenon which has been recognized with loathing by St. Paul and St. Augustine, both of whom regarded "the law of sin which is in my members" as a grave threat to the dominion of the holy will.[3] In sexual desire and its expression the blending of involuntary response with deliberate control is extremely important. For Augustine, the revolution launched against him by his body is symbolized by erection and the other involuntary physical components of arousal. Sartre too stresses the fact that the penis is not a prehensile organ. But mere involuntariness characterizes other bodily processes as well. In sexual desire the involuntary responses are combined with submission to spontaneous impulses: not only one's pulse and secretions but one's actions are taken over by the body; ideally, deliberate control is needed only to guide the expression of those impulses. This is to some extent also true of an appetite like hunger, but the takeover there is more localized, less pervasive, less extreme. One's whole body does not become saturated with hunger as it can with desire. But the most characteristic feature of a specifically sexual immersion in the body is its ability to fit into the complex of mutual perceptions that we have described. Hunger leads to spontaneous interactions with food; sexual desire leads to spontaneous interactions with other persons, whose bodies are asserting their sovereignty in the same way, producing involuntary reactions and spontaneous impulses in *them*. These reactions are perceived, and the perception of them is perceived, and that perception is in turn perceived, at each step the domination of the person by his body is reinforced, and the sexual partner becomes more possessible by physical contact, penetration, and envelopment.

Desire is therefore not merely the perception of a preexisting embodiment of the other, but ideally a contribution to his further embodiment which in turn enhances the original subject's sense of himself. This explains why it is important that the partner be aroused, and not merely aroused, but aroused by the awareness of one's desire. It also explains the sense in which desire has unity and possession as its object: physical possession must eventuate in creation of the sexual object in the image of one's desire, and not merely in the object's recognition of that desire, or in his or her own private arousal. (This may reveal a male bias: I shall say something about that later.)

To return, finally, to the topic of perversion: I believe that

[3] See Romans, VII, 23; and the *Confessions*, Book 8, V.

various familiar deviations constitute truncated or incomplete versions of the complete configuration, and may therefore be regarded as perversions of the central impulse.

In particular, narcissistic practices and intercourse with animals, infants, and inanimate objects seem to be stuck at some primitive version of the first stage. If the object is not alive, the experience is reduced entirely to an awareness of one's own sexual embodiment. Small children and animals permit awareness of the embodiment of the other, but present obstacles to reciprocity, to the recognition by the sexual object of the subject's desire as the source of his (the object's) sexual self-awareness.

Sadism concentrates on the evocation of passive self-awareness in others, but the sadist's engagement is itself active and requires a retention of deliberate control which impedes awareness of himself as a bodily subject of passion in the required sense. The victim must recognize him as the source of his own sexual passivity, but only as the active source. De Sade claimed that the object of sexual desire was to evoke involuntary responses from one's partner, especially audible ones. The infliction of pain is no doubt the most efficient way to accomplish this, but it requires a certain abrogation of one's own exposed spontaneity. All this, incidentally, helps to explain why it is tempting to regard as sadistic an excessive preoccupation with sexual technique, which does not permit one to abandon the role of agent at any stage of the sexual act. Ideally one should be able to surmount one's technique at some point.

A masochist on the other hand imposes the same disability on his partner as the sadist imposes on himself. The masochist cannot find a satisfactory embodiment as the object of another's sexual desire, but only as the object of his control. He is passive not in relation to his partner's passion but in relation to his nonpassive agency. In addition, the subjection to one's body characteristic of pain and physical restraint is of a very different kind from that of sexual excitement: pain causes people to contract rather than dissolve.

Both of these disorders have to do with the second stage, which involves the awareness of oneself as an object of desire. In straightforward sadism and masochism other attentions are substituted for desire as a source of the object's self-awareness. But it is also possible for nothing of that sort to be substituted, as in the case of a masochist who is satisfied with self-inflicted pain or of a sadist who does not insist on playing a role in the suffering that arouses him. Greater difficulties of classification are presented

12

by three other categories of sexual activity: elaborations of the sexual act; intercourse of more than two persons; and homosexuality.

If we apply our model to the various forms that may be taken by two-party heterosexual intercourse, none of them seem clearly to qualify as perversions. Hardly anyone can be found these days to inveigh against oral-genital contact, and the merits of buggery are urged by such respectable figures as D. H. Lawrence and Norman Mailer. There may be something vaguely sadistic about the latter technique (in Mailer's writings it seems to be a method of introducing an element of rape), but it is not obvious that this has to be so. In general, it would appear that any bodily contact between a man and a woman that gives them sexual pleasure, is a possible vehicle for the system of multi-level interpersonal awareness that I have claimed is the basic psychological content of sexual interaction. Thus a liberal platitude about sex is upheld.

About multiple combinations, the least that can be said is that they are bound to be complicated. If one considers how difficult it is to carry on two conversations simultaneously, one may appreciate the problems of multiple simultaneous interpersonal perception that can arise in even a small-scale orgy. It may be inevitable that some of the component relations should degenerate into mutual epidermal stimulation by participants otherwise isolated from each other. There may also be a tendency toward voyeurism and exhibitionism, both of which are incomplete relations. The exhibitionist wishes to display his desire without needing to be desired in return; he may even fear the sexual attentions of others. A voyeur, on the other hand, need not require any recognition by his object at all: certainly not a recognition of the voyeur's arousal.

It is not clear whether homosexuality is a perversion if that is measured by the standard of the described configuration, but it seems unlikely. For such a classification would have to depend on the possibility of extracting from the system a distinction between male and female sexuality; and much that has been said so far applies equally to men and women. Moreover, it would have to be maintained that there was a natural tie between the type of sexuality and the sex of the body, and also that two sexualities of the same type could not interact properly.

Certainly there is much support for an aggressive-passive distinction between male and female sexuality. In our culture the male's arousal tends to initiate the perceptual exchange, he usually makes the sexual approach, largely controls the course of the act, and of course penetrates whereas the woman receives. When two

13

men or two women engage in intercourse they cannot both adhere to these sexual roles. The question is how essential the roles are to an adequate sexual relation. One relevant observation is that a good deal of deviation from these roles occurs in heterosexual intercourse. Women can be sexually aggressive and men passive, and temporary reversals of role are not uncommon in heterosexual exchanges of reasonable length. If such conditions are set aside, it may be urged that there is something irreducibly perverted in attraction to a body anatomically like one's own. But alarming as some people in our culture may find such attraction, it remains psychologically unilluminating to class it as perverted. Certainly if homosexuality is a perversion, it is so in a very different sense from that in which shoe-fetishism is a perversion, for some version of the full range of interpersonal perceptions seems perfectly possible between two persons of the same sex.

In any case, even if the proposed model is correct, it remains implausible to describe as perverted every deviation from it. For example, if the partners in heterosexual intercourse indulge in private heterosexual fantasies, that obscures the recognition of the real partner and so, on the theory, constitutes a defective sexual relation. It is not, however, generally regarded as a perversion. Such examples suggest that a simple dichotomy between perverted and unperverted sex is too crude to organize the phenomena adequately.

I should like to close with some remarks about the relation of perversion to good, bad, and morality. The concept of perversion can hardly fail to be evaluative in some sense, for it appears to involve the notion of an ideal or at least adequate sexuality which the perversions in some way fail to achieve. So, if the concept is viable, the judgment that a person or practice or desire is perverted will constitute a sexual evaluation, implying that better sex, or a better specimen of sex, is possible. This in itself is a very weak claim, since the evaluation might be in a dimension that is of little interest to us. (Though, if my account is correct, that will not be true.)

Whether it is a moral evaluation, however, is another question entirely—one whose answer would require more understanding of both morality and perversion than can be deployed here. Moral evaluation of acts and of persons is a rather special and very complicated matter, and by no means all our evaluations of persons and their activities are moral evaluations. We make judgments about people's beauty or health or intelligence which are evaluative without being moral. Assessments of their sexuality may be similar in that respect.

14

Furthermore, moral issues aside, it is not clear that unperverted sex is necessarily *preferable* to the perversions. It may be that sex which receives the highest marks for perfection *as sex* is less enjoyable than certain perversions; and if enjoyment is considered very important, that might outweigh considerations of sexual perfection in determining rational preference.

That raises the question of the relation between the evaluative content of judgments of perversions and the rather common *general* distinction between good and bad sex. The latter distinction is usually confined to sexual acts, and it would seem, within limits, to cut across the other: even someone who believed, for example, that homosexuality was a perversion could admit a distinction between better and worse homosexual sex, and might even allow that good homosexual sex could be better *sex* than not very good unperverted sex. If this is correct, it supports the position that, if judgments of perversion are viable at all, they represent only one aspect of the possible evaluation of sex, even *qua sex*. Moreover it is not the only important aspect: certainly sexual deficiencies that evidently do not constitute perversions can be the object of great concern.

Finally, even if perverted sex is to that extent not so good as it might be, bad sex is generally better than none at all. This should not be controversial: it seems to hold for other important matters, like food, music, literature, and society. In the end, one must choose from among the available alternatives, whether their availability depends on the environment or on one's own constitution. And the alternatives have to be fairly grim before it becomes rational to opt for nothing.

on sexual morality

sara ruddick

Why do we think that there is a specifically sexual morality? We
have become accustomed to speaking of a sexual morality because,
until the advent of psychologically acceptable and biologically
effective contraception, we have had to regulate sexual desires in
the interest of the well-being of children. The morality that resulted has a good deal to do with property, the division of labor,
and power, but is only indirectly relevant to our sexual lives. Sexual experiences, like the experiences of driving automobiles, render us liable to special moral situations. As drivers we must guard
against infantile desires for revenge and excitement. As lovers, we
must guard against cruelty and betrayal, for we know sexual experiences provide special opportunities for each. We drive soberly
because, before we get into a car, we believe that, except in morally unusual circumstances, it is wrong to be careless of life. We
resist temptations to adultery because we believe it wrong to betray trust, whether it is a parent, a sexual partner, or a political
colleague who is betrayed. As lovers and drivers, we act on principles which are particular applications of general moral principles.
There seems to be no specifically sexual morality.

Given the superstitions from which sexual experience has suffered, it is tempting to free ourselves, as lovers, from any moral
concerns other than those we bring, as human beings, to a sexual
situation. When pressed, however, the analogy with driving fails
us. Unburdened of "sexual" morality, we do not find it easy to
apply general moral principles to our sexual lives. The "morally

average" lover can be cruel, violate trust, and neglect social duties with less opprobrium precisely because he is a lover. Only political passions and psychological or physical deprivation serve as well as sexual desire to excuse what would otherwise be seriously and clearly immoral acts. (Occasionally, sexual desire is itself conceived of as a deprivation, an involuntary lust. And there is, of course, a tradition that sees sexual morality as a way of controlling those unable to be sexless: "It is better to marry than to burn.") Often, in our sexual lives, we neither flout nor simply apply general moral principles. Rather, the values of sexual experience themselves figure in the construction of moral dilemmas. The conflict between "better sex" (more complete, natural, and pleasurable sex acts) and, say, social duty, is not seen as a conflict between the immoral and compulsive on the one hand and the morally good on the other, but between alternative morally good acts.

How do we evaluate sexual experiences? Upon reflection, should we endorse these evaluations? These are the questions whose answers should constitute a specifically sexual morality. In attempting to answer them, I shall use the familiar moral concepts of *virtue* and *obligation* and the less familiar one of *benefit*. An intrinsic benefit is minimally an experience or relation which an "ideal observer" would wish for any human being who lives and wants anything.[1] "Benefits" may not appear moral to the person who enjoys them, if for him morality is contrasted with the enjoyable. A benefit may alternatively be described as an experience or relation which anyone who properly cares for another is morally obliged to attempt to secure for him. Criteria for the virtue of care[2] and for benefit are reciprocally determined, the virtue consisting in part in recognizing and attempting to secure benefits for the person cared for, the identification of benefit depending on its recognition by those already seen to be properly caring.

In this paper I shall be looking at our sexual lives from the vantage point of hope, not of fear. The principal interlocutor may be considered as a child asking what he should rightly and reasonably hope for in living, rather than as a potential criminal questioning conventional restraints. The specific questions the child may be imagined to ask can now be put: In what way is "better sex" intrinsically beneficial or conducive to experiences or rela-

[1]See Philippa Foot, "Moral Beliefs," *Proceedings of the Aristotelian Society*, 1958–1959. "Hands and eyes, like ears and legs, play a part in so many operations that a man could only be said not to need them if he had no wants at all. That such people exist, in asylums, is not to the present purpose at all; the proper use of his limbs is something a man has reason to want if he wants anything."
[2]On the virtue of care see Erik Erikson, *Insight and Responsibility*, New York: Norton, 1964, ch. IV.

tions which are beneficial? How, if at all, is the enjoyment of "better sex" relevant to social obligation? Which virtues, if any, are promoted by the enjoyment of better sex?

I wish to consider three characteristics that distinguish better from inferior sex acts—greater pleasure, completeness, and naturalness. Other characteristics may be relevant to evaluating sex acts, but these three are central. If and only if they have moral significance will better sex be morally preferable to inferior sex.

SEXUAL PLEASURE

Sensual experiences give rise to sensations and experiences which are paradigms of what is pleasant. Hedonism, in both its psychological and ethical forms, has blinded us to the nature and to the benefits of sensual pleasure by overextending the word "pleasure" to cover anything enjoyable or even agreeable.[3] The paradigmatic type of pleasure is sensual. Pleasure is a temporally extended, more or less intense quality of particular experiences. Pleasure is enjoyable independently of any function pleasurable activity fulfills. The infant who continues to suck well after he is nourished, expressing evident pleasure in doing so, gives us a *demonstration* of the nature of pleasure.[4]

As we learn more about pleasant experiences we not only apply but also extend and attenuate the primary notion of "pleasure." But if pleasure is to have any nonsophistical psychological or moral interest, it must retain its connections with those paradigm instances of sensual pleasure that give rise to it. We may, for example, extend the notion of "pleasure" so that particular episodes in the care of children give great pleasure, but the long-term activity of caring for children, however intrinsically rewarding, is not an experience of pleasure or unpleasure.

Sexual pleasure is a species of sensual pleasure with its own conditions of arousal and satisfaction. Sexual acts vary considerably in pleasure, the limiting case being a sexual act where no one experiences pleasure even though someone may experience affection or "relief of tension" through orgasm. Sexual pleasure can be considered either in a context of deprivation and its relief or in

[3]This may be a consequence of the tepidness of the English "pleasant." It would be better to speak of lust and its satisfactions if our suspicion of pleasure had not been written into that part of our language.
[4]The example is from Sigmund Freud, *Three Essays on Sexuality*, standard ed., vol. VII, London, Hogarth, 1963, p. 182. The concept of pleasure I urge here is narrower, but also I think more useful than the popular one. It is a concept, to paraphrase Wittgenstein, we (could) learn when we learn the language. The idea of paradigmatic uses and subsequent more or less divergent, more or less "normal" uses also is derived from Wittgenstein.

one of satisfaction. Psychological theories have tended to emphasize the frustrated state of sexual desire and to construe sexual pleasure as a relief from that state. There are, however, alternative accounts of sexual pleasure which correspond more closely with our experience. Sexual pleasure is "a primary distinctively poignant pleasure experience that manifests itself from early infancy on. . . . Once experienced it continues to be savored. . . ."[5] Sexual desire is not experienced as frustration but as part of sexual pleasure. Normally, sexual desire transforms itself gradually into the pleasure that appears, misleadingly, to be an aim extrinsic to it. The natural structure of desire, not an inherent quality of frustration, accounts for the pain of an aroused but unsatisfied desire.

Sexual pleasure, like addictive pleasure generally, does not, except very temporarily, result in satiety. Rather, it increases the demand for more of the same, while sharply limiting the possibility of substitutes. The experience of sensual pleasures, and particularly of sexual pleasures, has a pervasive effect on our perceptions of the world. We find bodies inviting, social encounters alluring, smells, tastes, and sights resonant, because our perception of them includes their sexual significance. Merleau-Ponty has written of a patient for whom "perception had lost its erotic structure, both temporally and physically."[6] As a result of a brain injury, his capacity for sexual desire and pleasure (though not his capacity for performing sexual acts) was impaired. He no longer sought sexual intercourse of his own accord, was left indifferent by the sights and smells of available bodies, and if in the midst of sexual intercourse, his partner turned away, he showed no signs of displeasure. The capacity for sexual pleasure upon which the erotic structure of perception depends can be accidentally damaged. With greater biochemical and psychiatric knowledge, we shall presumably be able to manipulate it at will.[7] The question Merleau-Ponty's patient mutely raises is whether it would be desirable to interfere with this capacity in a more systematic way than we now do. And if so, toward what end should we interfere? Is the capacity for sexual pleasure a benefit, and if so, how? I shall return to this question after describing the other two characteristics of "better sex"— completeness and naturalness.

[5]George Klein, "Freud's Two Theories of Sexuality," in L. Berger (ed.), *Clinical-Cognitive Psychology: Models and Integrations*, Englewood Cliffs: Prentice-Hall, 1969, pp. 131–181. This essay gives a clear idea of alternative psychological accounts of sexual pleasure.

[6]Maurice Merleau-Ponty, *Phenomenology of Perception*, Colin Smith (trans.), London: Routledge & Kegan Paul, 1962, p. 156.

[7]See Kurt Vonnegut, Jr., "Welcome to the Monkey House," in *Welcome to the Monkey House*, Dell, 1968, which concerns both the manipulation and the benefit of sexual pleasure.

COMPLETE SEX ACTS

The completeness of a sexual act depends upon the relation of the participants to their own and each others' desire. A sex act is complete if each partner (1) allows himself to be "taken over" by desire, which (2) is desire not merely for the other's body but also for *his* desire, and (3) where each desire is occasioned by a response to the partner's desire. "Completeness" is hard to characterize, though complete sex acts are at least as natural as any others—especially, it seems, among those people who take them casually for granted. The notion of "completeness" (as I shall call it) has figured under various guises in the work of Sartre, Merleau-Ponty, and more recently Thomas Nagel. "The being which desires is consciousness *making itself body*."[8] "What we try to possess, then, is not just a body, but a body brought to life by consciousness."[9] "It is important that the partner be aroused, and not merely aroused, but aroused by the awareness of one's desire."[10]

The precondition of complete sex acts is the "embodiment" of the participants. Each participant submits to sexual desires which take over consciousness and direct action. It is sexual desire and not a separable satisfaction of it (for example, orgasm) which is important here. Indeed, Sartre finds pleasure external to the essence of desire, and Nagel gives an example of embodiment in which the partners do not touch each other. Desire is pervasive and "overwhelming," but it does not make its subject its involuntary victim (as it did the Boston Strangler, we are told), nor does it, except at its climax, alter capacities for ordinary perceptions, memories, and inferences. Nagel's embodied partners can presumably get themselves from bar stools to bed while their consciousness is "clogged" with desire. With what then is embodiment contrasted?

Philosophers make statements which, when intended literally, are evidence of pathology: "Human beings are automata," "I never really see physical objects," "I can never know what another person is feeling." The clearest statement of disembodiment I know is Stace's claim: "I become aware of my body in the end chiefly because it insists on accompanying me wherever I go."[11] What just accompanies me can also stay away. "When my body leaves me/

[8] Jean-Paul Sartre, *Being and Nothingness*, Hazel E. Barnes (trans.), New York: Philosophical Library, 1956, p. 389.
[9] Merleau-Ponty, op. cit., p. 167.
[10] Thomas Nagel, "Sexual Perversion," *The Journal of Philosophy*, January 16, 1969, p. 13. [Reprinted in this volume, pp. 3–15].
[11] W. T. Stace, "Solipsism," from *The Theory of Knowledge and Existence*. Reprinted in Tillman, Berofsky, and O'Connor (eds.), *Introductory Philosophy*, New York: Harper & Row, 1967, p. 113.

I'm lonesome for it./ . . . body/ goes away I don't know where/ and it's lonesome to drift/ above the space it/fills when it's here."[12] If "the body is felt more as one object among other objects in the world than as the core of the individual's own being"[13] what appears to be bodily can be dissociated from the "real" self. Both a generalized separation of "self" from body and particular disembodied experiences have had their advocates. The attempt at disembodiment has also been seen as conceptually confused and psychologically disastrous.

We may often experience ourselves as relatively disembodied, observing or "using" our bodies to fulfill our intentions. On some occasions, however, such as in physical combat, sport, physical suffering, or danger, we "become" our bodies, our consciousness is bodily experience of bodily activity.[14] Sexual acts are such occasions for embodiment, which may, however, fail for a variety of reasons, for example, because of pretense or an excessive need of self-control. If someone is embodied by sexual desire, he submits to its direction. Spontaneous impulses of desire become his movements—some involuntary, like gestures of "courting behavior" or physical expressions of intense pleasure, some deliberate. His *consciousness* or "mind" is taken over by desire and the pursuit of its object, in the way that at other times it may be taken over by an intellectual problem or by obsessive fantasies. But unlike the latter takeovers, this one is bodily. A desiring consciousness is flooded with specifically sexual feelings which eroticize all perception and movement. Consciousness "becomes flesh."

Granted the precondition of embodiment, complete sex acts occur when each partner's embodying desire is a response to the other's. This second aspect of complete sex constitutes a "reflexive mutual recognition" of desire by desire.[15]

Nagel compares sexual desire to anger. If I am angry, I wish to hurt the person who angers me. I may simply arrange for him to be hurt without letting him know of my anger. But usually this is unsatisfying. I want my *anger* to make a difference to him. I want him to be aroused by the recognition of my feeling. Imperviousness to anger is the deepest defense against it, for it refuses to recognize

[12]Denise Levertov, "Gone Away," in *O Taste and See*, New York: New Directions, 1962, p. 59. Copyright © by Denise Levertov Goodman, New Directions Publishing Corporation, New York.
[13]R. D. Laing, *The Divided Self*, Pelican Books, 1965, p. 69.
[14]We *need* not become our bodies on such occasions. Pains, muscular feelings, and emotions can be reduced to mere "sensations" which may impinge on "me" but which I attempt to keep at a distance. Laing describes the case of a man who, when beaten up, felt that any damage to his *body* could not really hurt *him*. Laing, op. cit., p. 68.
[15]Nagel, op. cit., p. 12.

the feeling. Research on families whose members tend to become schizophrenic has shown us how such imperviousness can force a vulnerable attacker to deny or to obscure the nature of his feelings. Imperviousness deprives even a relatively invulnerable attacker of his efficacy, of "the fulfillment of (his) emotions, through the domination of the object's feelings."[16] The particular demand that our feelings elicit a response appropriate to them, is part of a general demand that *we* be recognized, allowed to make a difference.

Sexual desire is comparable to anger. Just as the angry person wishes to arouse his partner by his anger, so the desiring person wishes to arouse his partner by his desire. There are many ways of appropriately responding to sexual desire—countless forms of resistance and submission. Complete sex involves a recognition of desire that returns it with desire.

Sexual acts can be partly incomplete. A necrophiliac may be taken over by desire, and a frigid woman may respond to her lover's desire without being embodied by her own. Partners whose sexual activities are accompanied by private fantasies engage in an incomplete sex act. Consciousness is used by desire but remains apart from it, providing it with stimulants and controls. Neither partner is responding to the other's desire though each may appear to. Sartre's "dishonest masturbator" for whom masturbation is the sex act of choice engages in a paradigmatically incomplete sex act.

> . . . He asks only to be slightly distanced from his own body, only for there to be a light coating of otherness over his flesh and over his thoughts. His personae are melting sweets. . . . The masturbator is enchanted at never being able to feel himself sufficiently another, and at producing for himself alone the diabolic appearance of a couple that fades away when one touches it. . . . Masturbation is the derealisation of the world and of the masturbator himself.[17]

Completeness is more difficult to describe than incompleteness, for it turns on precise but subtle ways of responding to a *particular* person's desire with specific expressions of impulse, which are both spontaneous and responsive.

According to Nagel, complete sex requires more than mutually embodied responsive desire. Both anger and sex involve "a desire that one's partner be aroused by the recognition of one's *desire*

[16]Ibid.
[17]Jean-Paul Sartre, *Saint Genet*, New York: Braziller, 1963, p. 398. Cited and translated by R. D. Laing, *Self and Others*, New York: Pantheon, 1969, pp. 39–40.

that he or she be aroused."[18] As a statement of the typical case, this seems wrong for both anger and desire. We wish our partner to respond to our anger or to our desire, but not to respond to our desire that he respond. Occasionally, especially in seduction (Nagel's case) or first sexual encounters between acquaintances, another person's desire may be the most arousing feature about him. But even when this is the case, it is the other person's desire for sexual enjoyment or his desire for oneself that is arousing, very rarely the desire that one be aroused (which has a slightly sadistic sound).

There are many possible sex acts that are pleasurable but not complete. Sartre, Nagel and Merleau-Ponty each suggest that the desire for the responsive desire of one's partner is the "central impulse" of sexual desire.[19] The desire for a sleeping woman, for example, is possible only "in so far as this sleep appears on the ground of consciousness."[20] This seems too strong. Some lovers desire that their partners resist, others like them coolly controlled, others prefer them asleep. We would not say that there was anything abnormal or less fully sexual about their desire. Whether or not complete sex is preferable to incomplete sex (the question to which I shall turn shortly), incompleteness does not disqualify a sex act from being fully sexual.

SEXUAL PERVERSION

The final characteristic of better sex is that it is "natural" rather than perverted. The *ground* for classifying sexual acts into the natural and unnatural is that the former serve or could serve the evolutionary and biological function of sexuality—viz., reproduction. "Natural" sexual desire has as its "object" living persons of the opposite sex and in particular their postpubertal genitals. The "aim" of "natural" sexual desire—that is, the act that "naturally" completes it—is genital intercourse. Perverse sex acts are deviations from the "natural" object (for example, homosexuality, fetishism) or from the standard aim (for example, voyeurism, sadism). Among the variety of objects and aims of sexual desire, I can see no other ground for selecting some as natural, except that they are of the type that can lead to reproduction.[21]

The connection of sexual desire with reproduction gives us the

[18]Nagel, op. cit., p. 12.
[19]Ibid., p. 13.
[20]Jean-Paul Sartre, *Being and Nothingness,* op. cit., p. 386.
[21]See, in support of this point, Sigmund Freud, *Introductory Lectures on Psychoanalysis,* standard ed., vol. XVI, London: Hogarth, 1963, chs. XX and XXI.

criterion but not the motive of the classification. The concept of perversion depends upon a disjointedness between our *experience* of sexual desire from infancy on and its *function*, viz., reproduction. In our collective experience of sexuality, perverse desires are as "natural" as nonperverse ones. The sexual desires of the "polymorphously perverse" child has many objects—for example, breasts, anus, mouth, and genitals—and many aims, autoerotic or other-directed looking, smelling, touching, hurting. From the social and developmental point of view, "natural" sex is an *achievement*, partly biological, partly conventional, consisting in a dominant *organization* of sexual desires in which perverted aims or objects are subordinate to "natural" ones. The concept of perversion reflects the vulnerability as much as the evolutionary warrant of this organization.

The connection of sexual desire with reproduction is not sufficient to yield the concept of perversion but it is surely necessary. Nagel thinks otherwise. There are, he points out, many sexual acts that do not lead to reproduction but that we are not even inclined to call perverse—for example, sexual acts between partners who are sterile. Perversion, according to him, is a psychological concept while reproduction is (only?) a physiological one. (Incidentally, this view of reproduction seems to me the clearest instance of male bias in Nagel's paper.)

Nagel is right about our judgments of particular acts, but he draws the wrong conclusions from those judgments. The perversity of sex acts does not depend upon whether they are intended to achieve reproduction. "Natural" sexual desire is for heterosexual genital activity, not for reproduction. The *ground* for classifying that desire as natural is that it is so organized that it *could* lead to reproduction in normal physiological circumstances. The "reproductive" organization of sexual desires gives us a *criterion* of "naturalness," but the *virtue* of which it is a criterion is the "naturalness" itself, not reproduction. Our vacillating attitude toward the apparently "perverse" acts of animals reflects our shifting from criterion to virtue. If, when confronted with a perverse act of animals, we withdraw the label "perverted" from our own similar acts rather than extend it to theirs, we are relinquishing the reproductive criterion of naturalness, while retaining the virtue. Animals cannot be "unnatural." If, on the other hand, we "discover" that animals can be perverts too, we are maintaining our criterion, but giving a somewhat altered sense to the "naturalness" of which it is a criterion.

Nagel's alternative attempt to classify acts as natural or perverted on the basis of their completeness fails. "Perverted" and

Sara Ruddick

"complete" are evaluations of an entirely different order. The completeness of a sex act depends upon qualities of the participants' experience and upon qualities of their relation, qualities of which they are the best judge. To say a sex act is perverted is to pass a conventional judgment about characteristics of the act, which could be evident to any observer. As one can pretend to be angry but not to shout, one can pretend to a complete but not to a natural sex act (though one may, of course, conceal desires for perverse sex acts or shout in order to mask one's feelings). As Nagel himself sees, judgments about particular sex acts clearly differentiate between perversion and completeness. Unadorned heterosexual intercourse where each partner has his private fantasies is clearly "natural" and clearly "incomplete," but there is nothing *prima facie* incomplete about exclusive oral-genital intercourse or homosexual acts. If many perverse acts are incomplete, as Nagel claims, this is an important *fact* about perversion, but it is not the basis upon which we judge its occurrence.

THE MORAL SUPERIORITY OF "BETTER SEX"

"Better sex" is, then, more pleasurable, complete, and natural than inferior sex. What is the moral significance of this evaluation? In answering this question, official sexual morality sometimes appeals to the social consequences of particular types of better sex acts. For example, since dominantly perverse organizations of sexual impulses limit reproduction, the merits of perversion depend upon the need to limit or increase population. Experience of sexual pleasure may be desirable if it promotes relaxation and communication in an acquisitive society, undesirable if it limits the desire to work or, in armies, to kill. The social consequences of complete sex have not received particular attention, partly because the quality of sexual experience has been of little interest to moralists. It *might* be found that those who had complete sexual relations were more cooperative, less amenable to political revolt. If so, complete sexual acts would be desirable in just and peaceable societies, undesirable in unjust societies requiring revolution.

The social desirability of types of sexual acts depends on particular social conditions and independent criteria of social desirability. It may be interesting and important to assess particular claims about the social desirability of sex acts, but this is not a concern of a specifically sexual morality. What *is* of concern is the extent to which we will allow our judgments of sexual worth to be influenced by social considerations. But this issue cannot even be raised until we have a better sense of sexual *worth*.

25

THE BENEFIT OF SEXUAL PLEASURE

To say that an experience is pleasant is to give a self-evident, terminal reason for seeking it. We can sometimes "see" that an experience is pleasant. When, for example, we observe someone's sensual delight in eating, his behavior can expressively characterize pleasure. We can only question the benefit of such an experience by referring to other goods with which it might conflict. Though sensual pleasures may not be sufficient to warrant giving birth or to deter suicide, so long as we live they are self-evidently benefits to us.

The most eloquent detractors of sexual experience have admitted that it provides sensual pleasures so poignant that once experienced they are repeatedly, almost addictively, sought after. Yet, unlike other appetites such as hunger, sexual desire can be permanently resisted and resistance has been advocated. How can the *prima facie* benefits of sexual pleasure appear deceptive?

There are several grounds for complaint. Sexual pleasure is ineradicably "mixed," frustration being part of every sexual life. The capacity for sexual pleasure is unevenly distributed, cannot be voluntarily acquired, and diminishes through no fault of its subject. If such a pleasure were an intrinsic benefit, benefit would in this case be independent of moral effort. Sexual pleasures are not serious. Enjoyment of them is one of life's greatest recreations, but none of its business. And finally, sexual desire has the defects of its strengths. Before satisfaction, it is, at the least, distracting, in satisfaction it "makes one little roome, an everywhere." Like psychosis, sexual desire turns us from "reality"—whether the real be God, social justice, children, or intellectual endeavor. This turning away is more than a social consequence of desire, though it is that. Lovers themselves feel that their sexual desires are separate from their "real" political, domestic, ambitious, social selves.

If the moralist is taken to argue that sensual pleasures are not the sole benefits and that the acquisition of them cannot be a duty, he is right. And in emphasizing the social, private nature of sexual experiences he is emphasizing a morally important characteristic of them. But his case against desire, as I have sketched it, is surely overstated. The "mixed," partly frustrated character of any desire is not particularly pronounced for sexual desire, which is in fact especially "plastic" or adaptable to changes (provided perverse sex acts have not been ruled out). Inhibition, social deprivation, or disease make our sexual lives unpleasant, but that is because they interfere with sexual desire, not because the desire is by its nature frustrating. More than other well-known desires (for example, de-

26

sire for knowledge, success, or power) sexual desire is simply and completely satisfied upon attaining its object. Partly for this reason, even if we are overtaken by desire during sexual experience, our sexual experiences do not overtake us. Lovers turn away from the world while loving, but return—sometimes all too easily—when loving is done. The moralist rightly perceives sexual pleasure as a recreation, and those who upon realizing its benefits make a business of its pursuit appear ludicrous. The capacity for recreation, however, is surely a benefit which any human being rightly hopes for who hopes for anything. Indeed, in present social and economic conditions we are more likely to lay waste our powers in work than in play. Thus, though priest, revolutionary, and parent are alike in fearing sexual pleasure, this fear should inspire us to psychological and sociological investigation of the fearing, rather than to moral doubt about the benefit of sexual pleasure.

Let us agree, then, that the capacity for sexual pleasure is a benefit. Let us also assume, as psychiatrists have told us, that this capacity, though "normal," is fragile. It morally behooves us to protect the sexual capacities of those we care for against overorganization, moral superstition, premature "sublimation," and conditions of social life inimical to sexual pleasure.

THE MORAL SIGNIFICANCE OF PERVERSION

What is the moral significance of the perversity of a sexual act? Next to none, so far as I can see. Though perverted sex may be "unnatural" both from an evolutionary and developmental perspective, there is no connection, inverse or correlative, between what is natural and what is good. Perverted sex is sometimes said to be less pleasurable than natural sex. We have little reason to believe this claim is true and no clear idea on what kind of evidence it would be based. In any case, to condemn perverse acts for lack of pleasure is to recognize the worth of *pleasure*, not of naturalness.

There are many other claims about the nature and consequences of perversity. Some merely restate "scientific" facts in morally tinged terminology. Perverse acts are, by definition and by psychiatric theory, "immature" and "abnormal," since natural sex acts are selected by criteria of "normal" sexual function and "normal" and "mature" psychological development. But there is no greater connection of virtue with maturity and normality than there is of virtue with nature. The elimination of a village by an invading army would be no less evil if it were the expression of controlled, "normal," "natural," and "mature" aggression.

Nagel claims that many perverted sex acts are incomplete, and in making his point, gives the most specific arguments I have read for the inferiority of perverted sex. But as he points out, there is no reason to think an act consisting solely of oral-genital intercourse is incomplete; it is doubtful whether homosexual acts and acts of buggery are especially liable to be incomplete; and the incompleteness of sexual intercourse with animals is a relative matter depending upon their limited consciousness. And again, the alleged inferiority is not a consequence of perversity but of incompleteness which can afflict natural sex as well.

Perverted acts might be thought to be inferior because they cannot result in children. Whatever the benefits and moral significance of the procreation and care of children (and I believe they are extensive and complicated), the virtue of proper care for children neither requires nor follows from biological parenthood. Even if it did, only a sexual life consisting *solely* of perverse acts rules out conception.

If perverted sex acts did rule out normal sex acts, if one were *either* a pervert *or* a natural, then certain kinds of sexual relations would be denied some perverts, relations that are benefits to those who enjoy them. It seems that sexual relations with the living and the human would be of greater benefit than those with the dead or with animals. But there is no reason to think that heterosexual relations are of greater benefit than homosexual ones. It might be that children can only be raised by heterosexual couples who perform an abundance of natural sex acts. If so (though it seems unlikely), perverts will be denied the happiness of parenthood. This would be an *indirect* consequence of perverted sex and might yield a moral dilemma: how to choose between the benefits of children and the benefits of more pleasurable, more complete sex acts?

Some perversions are immoral on independent grounds. Sadism is the obvious example, though sadism practiced with a consenting masochist is far less evil than other, more familiar, forms of aggression. Voyeurism may seem immoral because, since it must be secret to be satisfying, it violates others' rights to privacy.[22] Various kinds of rape can constitute perversion if rape, rather than genital intercourse, is the aim of desire. Rape is seriously immoral, a vivid violation of respect for persons. Sometimes doubly perverse rape is doubly evil (the rape of a child), but other times (the rape of a pig) its evil is halved. In any case, though rape is always wrong it is only perverse when raping becomes the aim, not the means, of desire.

Someone can be dissuaded from acting on his perverse de-

[22]I am indebted to Dr. Leo Goldberger for this example.

Sara Ruddick

sires either from moral qualms or from social fears. Although there may be ample basis for the latter, I can find none for the former except the possible indirect loss of the benefits of child care. I am puzzled about this, since reflective people who do not usually attempt to legislate the preferences of others think differently. There is no doubt that preferences in these matters involve deep emotions which should be respected. But for those who do in fact have perverted desires, the first concern will be to satisfy them, not to divert or to understand them. For sexual pleasure is intrinsically a benefit and complete sex acts, which depend upon expressing the desires one in fact has, are both beneficial and conducive to virtue. Therefore, barring extrinsic moral or social considerations, perverted sex acts are preferable to natural ones if the latter are less· pleasurable or less complete.

THE MORAL SIGNIFICANCE OF COMPLETENESS

Complete sex consists in mutually embodied responsive desire. Both embodiment and mutual responsiveness are instrumentally beneficial because they are conducive to our psychological well-being which is an intrinsic benefit. The alleged pathological consequences of disembodiment are more specific and better documented than those of perversity.[23] To dissociate oneself from one's actual body, either by creating a delusory body or by rejecting the bodily, is to court a variety of ill-effects ranging from self-disgust, to diseases of the will, to faulty mental development, to the destruction of a recognizable "self," and finally to madness. It is difficult to assess psychiatric claims outside their theoretical context, but in this case, I believe that they are justified. Relative embodiment is a stable, *normal* condition which is not confined to cases of complete embodiment. But psychiatrists tell us that exceptional physical occasions of embodiment seem to be required in order to balance tendencies to reject or to falsify the body. Sexual acts are not the only such occasions, but they do provide an immersion of consciousness in the bodily which is pleasurable and especially conducive to correcting experiences of shame and

[23]See, for example, R. D. Laing, *The Divided Self*, op. cit.; D. W. Winnicott, "Transitional Objects and Transitional Phenomena," *International Journal of Psychoanalysis*, 34 (1953), 89–97; Paul Federn, *Ego Psychology and the Psychoses*, New York: Basic Books, 1952; Phyllis Greenacre, *Trauma, Growth, and Personality*, New York: International Universities Press, 1969; Paul Schilder, *The Image and Appearance of the Human Body*, International Universities Press, 1950; Moses Laufer, "Body Image and Masturbation in Adolescence," *The Psychoanalytic Study of the Child*, XXIII (1968), 114–146. Laing's work is most specific about both the nature and consequences of disembodiment, but the works cited, and others similar to them, give the clinical evidence upon which much of Laing's work depends.

29

disgust which work toward disembodiment. The mutual responsiveness of complete sex is also instrumentally beneficial. It satisfies a general desire to be recognized as a particular "real" person and to make a difference to other particular "real" people. The satisfaction of this desire in sexual experience is especially rewarding, its thwarting especially cruel.[24]

In addition to being instrumentally beneficial, complete sex acts are likely to have three characteristics relevant to their moral worth. They tend to resolve tensions fundamental to moral life, they involve the preeminently moral virtue, respect for persons, and they are conducive to emotions, which if they become stable and dominant, are in turn conducive to the virtue of loving.

In one of its aspects morality is opposed to the private and untamed. Morality is "civilization," social and regulating, desire is "discontent" resisting the regulation. Obligation rather than benefit is the notion central to morality so conceived, and the virtues required of a moral person are directed to preserving right relations and social order. Both the insistence on natural sex and the encouragement of complete sex can be looked at as attempts to make sexual desire more amenable to regulation. But whereas the regulation of perverted desires is extrinsic to them, those of completeness modify the desires themselves. The desiring sensual body which, in our social lives we may laugh away or disown, becomes our "self" and enters into a social relation. Narcissism and altruism are satisfied in complete sex acts in which one gives what one receives by receiving it. Social and private "selves" are unified in an act in which impersonal spontaneous impulses govern an action that is responsive to a particular person. For this to be true, we must surmount our social "roles" as well as our sexual "techniques," though we incorporate rather than surmount our social selves. We must also surmount regulations imposed in the name of naturalness if *our* desires are to be spontaneously expressed. Honestly spontaneous first love gives us back our private desiring selves while allowing us to see the desiring self of another. Mutually responding partners confirm each others' desires and declare them good. Such occasions, when we are "moral" without cost, may reconcile us to our moral being and to the usual mutual exclusion between our social and private lives.

Sartre has emphasized that complete sex acts attempt to preserve a respect for persons, each person remaining a "subject" rather than an "object" both for himself and for his partner. Respect for persons is a principle virtue in many aspects of moral-

[24]See R. D. Laing, *Self and Other, passim;* and Erik Erikson, *Childhood and Society,* New York: Norton, 1950, especially ch. 7.

ity,[25] and has different requirements depending upon the phenomena under discussion. In sex acts respect for persons requires that *actual, present* partners participate, partners whose desires are recognized and endorsed. Respect for persons typically requires taking a distance both from one's own demands and those of others. But in sexual acts the demands of desire take over and equal distance is replaced by mutual responsiveness. Respect typically requires refusing to treat another person merely as a means to fulfilling demands. In sexual acts another person is so clearly a means to satisfaction that he is always on the verge of becoming merely a means ("Intercourse counterfeits masturbation"). In complete sex acts, instrumentality vanishes only because it is mutual and mutually satisfying. Respect requires encouraging or at least protecting the autonomy of another. In complete sex acts autonomy of will is recruited by desire, and freedom from others is replaced by a frank dependence on another person's desire. Again, the respect consists in the reciprocity of desiring dependence, which bypasses rather than violates autonomy. Sartre is not alone in believing that complete sex, just because it involves respect for persons, is impossible. Completeness is surely threatened by pervasive tendencies to fantasy, possessiveness, and controlling domination. But a complete sex act as I (and, apparently, Merleau-Ponty and Nagel) see it is not a difficult accomplishment but a normal mode of sexual activity expressing the natural structure and impulses of sexual desire.

The connection between sex and certain emotions—particularly love, jealousy, fear, and anger—is as evident as it is obscure. Complete sex acts seem more likely than incomplete pleasurable ones to lead toward affection and away from fear and anger, since any guilt and shame will be extrinsic to the act and meliorated by it. It is clear that we need not feel any affection for someone beyond that required by respect for persons in order to participate with him in a complete sex act. However, it is equally clear that sexual pleasure, especially as experienced in complete sex acts, is conducive to many feelings—gratitude, tenderness, pride, appreciation, dependency, and others. These feelings magnify their object who occasioned them, making him unique among men. ("Women don't have friends, they have lovers. Others are people they just happen to meet.") When these magnifying feelings become stable and habitual they are conducive to love—not universal. love, of course, but love of a particular sexual partner. However,

[25]See for example Rawls on the duty of "fair play" where respect for persons takes a different form: "Justice as Fairness," *Philosophical Review*, 67 (1958) 164–194; "The Sense of Justice," *Philosophical Review*, 72 (1963) 281–305.

even "selfish" love is a virtue, a disposition to care for someone as *his* interests and demands would dictate. Neither the best sex nor the best love require each other, but they go together more often than reason would expect—often enough to count the virtue of loving as one of the rewards of the capacity for sexual pleasure exercised in complete sex acts.

It might be argued that the coincidence of sex acts and several valued emotions is a cultural matter. It is notoriously difficult to make judgments about the emotional, and particularly the sexual, lives of others, especially culturally alien others. There is, however, some anthropological evidence which at first glance relativizes the connection between good sex and valued emotion. For example, among the Manus of New Guinea, it seems that relations of affection and love are encouraged primarily among brother and sister, while easy familiarity, joking, and superficial sexual play is expected only between cross cousins. Sexual intercourse is, however, forbidden between siblings and cross cousins but required of married men and women who are as apt to hate as to care for each other and often seem to consider each other strangers. It seems, however, that the Manus do not value or experience complete or even pleasurable sex. Both men and women are described as "puritanical" and the sexual life of women seems blatantly unrewarding. Moreover, their emotional life is generally impoverished. This impoverishment, in conjunction with an unappreciated and unrewarding sexual life dissociated from love or affection, would argue *for* a connection between better sex and valued emotions. If, as Peter Winch suggests, cultures provide their members with particular possibilities of making sense of their lives, and thereby with possibilities of good and evil, the Manus might be said to deny themselves one possibility both of sense and of good—namely the coincidence of good sex and of affection and love. Other cultures, including our own, allow this possibility, whose realization is encouraged in varying degrees by particular groups and members of the culture.[26]

In sum, then, I suggest that complete sex is superior to less complete sex because it is conducive to psychological well-being, involves a particular type of respect for persons, and is frequently coincident with valued emotions which are productive of virtue.

To say that complete sex is superior to incomplete sex is not to say that we should avoid incompleteness. There are degrees of

[26]The evidence about the life of the Manus comes from Margaret Mead, *Growing Up in New Guinea* (Harmondsworth: Penguin Books, 1942). Peter Winch's discussion can be found in his "Understanding a Primitive Society," *American Philosophical Quarterly*, I (1964), 307–324.

completeness, relative completeness being better than none. Any sexual act that is pleasurable is *prima facie* good, though the more incomplete it is—the more private, essentially autoerotic, unresponsive, unembodied, and imposed—the more likely it is to be harmful to someone.

ON SEXUAL MORALITY: CONCLUDING REMARKS

There are many questions we have neglected to consider because we have not been sufficiently attentive to the quality of sexual lives. For example, we know little about the ways of achieving better sex. When we must choose between inferior sex and abstinence, how and when will our choice of inferior sex damage our capacity for better sex? Does, for example, the repeated experience of controlled sexual disembodiment ("desire which takes over will take you too far") which we urge (or used to urge) on adolescents damage their capacity for complete sex? The answers to this and similar questions are not obvious, though unfounded opinions are always ready to hand.

Some of the traditional sexual vices might be condemned on the ground that they are inimical to better sex. Obscenity, or repeated public exposure to sexual acts, might impair our capacity for pleasure or for response to desire. Promiscuity might undercut the tendency of complete sex acts to promote emotions that magnify their object. Some of the traditional virtues that govern our sexual lives are not justified by their relation to better sex but by reference to other, possibly conflicting, benefits or obligations. Fidelity, for example, is probably neither conducive nor inimical to complete sex acts. The obligation of fidelity has many sources, one of which may be a past history of shared complete sex acts during the course of which exclusive intimacy was promised. But promises are as apt to conflict with as to accord with the demand for better sex. I have said nothing about how such a conflict would be settled, only that there is a moral claim on both sides.

There is a tendency when thinking about moral matters to look for a "summum bonum," "an end of action which is desired for its own sake, while everything else is desired for the sake of it."[27] Sexual pleasure experienced in complete sex acts is clearly not such a summum bonum. There are many other intrinsic benefits besides better sex—good health, personal affection, and esthetic enjoyment being obvious ones. Moreover, benefit, a relative of happiness (the traditional summum bonum) is not the only end of moral action. Moral action also aims at fulfilling obligations, in-

[27]Aristotle, *Nichomachean Ethics*, 1094 a19.

suring justice, achieving excellence, and protecting the vulnerable (Marcel's "metaphysics of hospitality"[28]). These, and possibly other moral aims, cannot be assimilated to each other. They are general moral aims which organize moral phenomena in different ways. Particular virtues—that is, the dispositions to attempt and the strengths to succeed in being moral—may be appropriate to some moral aim but conflict with another. (For example, kindness is central to protection of the vulnerable but may conflict with demands of justice and may be inimical to requirements for particular excellences.) Some virtues, like respect for persons, are central to several moral aims, but vary according to the particular moral context—for example, as respect for persons differs when speaking of fair play and when speaking of better sex. There are high-order moral conflicts when the ends of action which justify our particular moral decisions themselves conflict, when any virtue will require neglect of some others, when what is just is merciless and mediocre, when fulfilling our obligations would deprive us of our benefits. It is tempting to resolve this conflict by *a priori* fiat—for example, by arguing that fulfilling any moral aim will be a benefit or conducive to excellence, or by denying that some moral aims are really "moral." But the order procured by these maneuvers distorts our moral lives.

The pursuit of more pleasurable and more complete sex acts, is only one among many moral activities. Since our sexual lives are very important to us, this pursuit rightly engages our moral reflections. But it is not, and should never become, the dominating aim of moral activity. Equally, it should not be relegated to the immoral or to the "merely" prudent.

[28]Gabriel Marcel, *The Mystery of Being*, Chicago: Henry Regnery, 1951, *passim*.

2

ABORTION

the morality of abortion

paul ramsey

POSSIBLE MEANINGS OF "ANIMATION"

Almost everyone has a proposal to make concerning when in the course of its prenatal or postnatal development embryonic life becomes "human." At one extreme are the views of those who hold that life is not human until the individual is a personal subject or has reason in exercise. If to be human *means* to be a person, to be a self-conscious subject of experience, or if it means to be rational, this state of affairs does not come to pass until a long while after the birth of a baby. A human infant acquires its personhood and self-conscious subjective identity through "Thou–I" encounters with other selves; and a child acquires essential rationality even more laboriously. If life must be human in these senses before it has any sanctity and respect or rights due it, infanticide would seem to be justified under any number of conditions believed to warrant it as permissible behavior or as a social policy. In any case, those who identify being human with personhood or rationality adopt a modern form of an ancient theological position called "creationism." According to this view, the unique, never-to-be-repeated individual human being (the "soul" is the religious word for him) comes into existence by a process of humanization or socialization in interaction with the persons around him. In the traditional religious language, he is "created" and

From Daniel H. Labby (ed.), *Life or Death: Ethics and Options* (Seattle, Washington: University of Washington Press, 1968). Reprinted by permission of the author and the University of Washington Press. Revised by the author for this volume.

"infused" into the already existing organism—sometime, gradually, after physical birth.

At the other extreme is the latest scientific view, that of modern genetics. Indeed, microgenetics seems to have demonstrated what religion never could; and biological science, to have resolved an ancient theological dispute. The human individual comes into existence first as a minute informational speck, drawn at random from many other minute informational specks his parents possessed out of the common human gene pool. This took place at the moment of impregnation. There were, of course, an unimaginable number of combinations of specks on his paternal and maternal chromosomes that did not come to be when they were refused and he began to be. Still (with the single exception of identical twins), no one else in the entire history of the human race has ever had or will ever have exactly the same genotype. Thus, it can be said that the individual is whoever he is going to become from the moment of impregnation. Thereafter, his subsequent development may be described as a process of becoming the one he already is. Genetics teaches that we were from the beginning what we essentially still are in every cell and in every human and individual attribute. This scientific account is a modern form of the ancient theological viewpoint called "traducianism." According to this view, the unique, never-to-be-repeated individual human being (the "soul") was drawn forth from his parents at the time of conception.[1]

[1] In order to take care of the case of identical twins (and also to account for the special ways in which our already unique combination of genetic determiners develops over a lifetime), it is necessary, of course, to bring in the modern version of "creationism" to which I have referred. Identical twins have the same genotype. They arise from the same informational speck. Yet each is and knows he is a unique, unrepeatable human person. He is something that he never was by virtue of his genes. He became something, at some time and in some manner, that he was not already, from the fission following that original conception. It is the environment who is the maker of all twin differences and the creator of a twin person's unsharable individual being; after they were born the environment "infused" this into those two blobs of identical hereditary material, which contained not only an incalculable number of powers distinguishing them as human blobs but also an incalculable number of the features of the individual beings each is to spend a whole lifetime becoming and exhibiting.

The case of identical twins does, however, suggest a significant modification of any "proof" from genotype. If we are seeking to locate a moment in the development of nascent life subsequent to impregnation and prior to birth (or graduation from Princeton) at which it would be reasonable to believe that an individual life *begins* to be inviolate, it is at least *arguable* that this takes place at the stage of *blastocyst*. In the blastocyst there appears a "primitive streak" across the hollow cluster of developing cells that signals the separation of the same genotype into identical twins. This segmentation is completed by about the time of implantation, i.e., on the seventh or eighth day after ovulation. It might be asserted that at blastocyst, not earlier, not later, these two products of human generation become "animate," each a unique individual "soul." This is *not* to say that any credit is

What is this but to say that we are all fellow fetuses? That from womb to tomb ours is a nascent life? That we are in essence congeners from the beginning? What is this but a rather antiseptic way of saying that the Creator has beset us behind and before? While we know only the light of our particular span of conscious existence, this light and that darkness whence we came and toward which we go are both alike to the One who laid his hands upon us, covered us in the womb, and by whom we were fearfully and wonderfully made.

Between the extremes of "traducianism" at conception and "creationism" gradually after birth, there are other accounts of when the human being originates and thus becomes a subject worthy of respect, rights, sanctity. No one of the positions yet to be mentioned is quite as up-to-date and scientific as the genetic account of the origin of human individuality. Among these are religious and legal viewpoints that seem always to be based on prescientific notions and "superstitions." Anglo-American law, for example, takes the moment of birth to be the moment after which there is a "man alive" (for which the evidence is air in the lungs) and before which there was no human life, separable from the mother's, that could be murdered. When it is born a "man alive," the child is from that moment already the one it ever thereafter becomes; not before, as genetics teaches. After it is born a "man alive," a child is then and then only a possible victim of the crime of "murder."

Where "abortion" is defined as a criminal offense in our legal systems, this creates another category of proscribed actions. It is not because the fetus is regarded as having sanctity or integrity or an independent right to life such as the law presupposes in the case of a "man alive." The legal reason for prohibiting abortion is not because it is believed to be a species of murder; it is the religious tradition, we shall see, and not the law which inculcates the latter view. The law's presumption is only that society has a stake in the prehuman material out of which the unique indi-

---

to be given to those self-serving arguments that "implantation" is the first moment of "life" having claims upon our respect. These are, in the worst sense of the word, mere rationalizations currently offered for the purpose of rejecting out of hand the proofs that interuterine devices (the "loop") are abortifacient, and that the "morning after" or retroactive pill (which will be available in a year or so) will directly abort a human life. Still, blastocyst (which, as it happens, is roughly coincident with implantation) affords serious moralists a fact concerning nascent life (and not only concerning its location) that may and must be taken into account when dealing with the morality of using interuterine devices or a retroactive "contraceptive" pill. This may have bearing on whether the question raised by these scientific applications is one of abortion or contraception only, or of an attack upon prehuman organic matter.

vidual is to be born. Or it may be that the law exhibits a belief that as a matter of public policy society has an interest in *men* and *women*, who have an interest in and by their actions take responsibility for the prehuman material out of which an individual human being is to be brought forth a man alive.

This brings us to the theories advanced by theologians and by church-law—all doubtless to be classed, along with the law, as "superstitious" and prescientific in comparison with the genetic account of the arrival of the essential constitutive features of a human individual. The theologians propose an analysis of the prenatal development of the fetus. This means that they assert that the fetus *before* birth may be the victim of the sin of "murder." But this does not immediately entail that *all* destruction of fetal life should be classified as murder. Only modern genetics seems to lead to that conclusion, with its teaching about the unrepeatability or at least the never-to-be-repeated character of that first informational speck each of us once was and still is in every cell and attribute. Theology, however, is premicrobiology! The theologians debate the question, *when* between conception and birth the unique not-to-be-repeated individual human being has arrived on the scene. Wherever the line is drawn, the direct destruction of a fetus after that point will, by definition, be murder, while before that point its direct destruction would fall under some other species of sin or grave violation.

In the prenatal development of the fetus, "animation" is the point between conception and birth that is usually taken to be crucial, although as we shall see animation may have more than one meaning. If animation and not impregnation or birth is the moment when an individual offspring first begins to be what he is to become and launches on a course of thereafter becoming what he already is, then direct abortion after animation would be to kill a man alive. It would be—morally, not legally—a species of murder. Then, on this view, to define a direct abortion before animation as an offense would require that such an action be understood to fall within a class of less serious violations. In no case would the destruction of a preanimate fetus raise questions regarding the respect due or the rights and sanctity of another distinct human life. The fetus is then not yet human; it is still only a part of the mother's body, even though there may be a special responsibility for this prehuman material out of which is to come, at animation, a man alive.

The term "animation" may be understood in two different ways, and from this follows two different views concerning when in the course of the development of a fetus its direct abortion

40

would be murder. "Animation" may most obviously be taken to indicate the moment fetal life becomes an independent source of movement in the womb, and modern thought would define animation in terms of physical motion. This should perhaps be called "quickening," the better to distinguish it from the second, the classical and more philosophical interpretation.

It was once commonly believed that there were forty days for the male and eighty days for the female between impregnation and the time, long before quickening, when the fetus became animate in this other sense. The second and more fundamental meaning of "animation" is derived not from motion but from *anima* (soul). The controlling philosophical doctrine was one which held that the soul is the *form of the body*. Thus *fetus animatus = fetus humanus = fetus formatus*. This did not entail another purely physical determination of when there was a formed fetus, or a fetus in human form or shape, on the scene. That would be earlier, of course, than when the fetus quickens. The meaning of the soul as the form of the body was too subtle a notion for that. It entailed a belief that there is a living human fetus, possibly much earlier than when there is either discernible motion or discernible human shape.

But the point to be noted here is that in theoretical speculation there has never been a certain or unanimous opinion among theologians to the effect that a *fetus humanus/fetus animatus* begins to be at the very moment of conception. In the controversies among theologians past and present, there has always been allowed a period of time between conception and "animation." "Scientifically" or at the level of theory or doctrine, one cannot speak with certainty of a human fetus before the lapse, some say, of six days. [2]

[2] Many of the themes and distinctions in the text above are exhibited in the remarks of a much-used commentary on the Code of Canon Law of 1917, specifically upon Canon 985, in reference to actions which after baptism would incur for a man "irregularity by delict" and render him unworthy of entering the clerical state or of exercising the orders he may have already received. The paragraph is as follows:

> Those who perform an abortion on a human being incur irregularity, provided, of course, the act is committed, not accidentally or unawares, but intentionally or through grievous culpability, even though by accident. The aborted fetus must be a *fetus humanus*, and is generally added, *animatus*, i.e., a living human fetus. We were surprised to see no reference, among Card. Gasparri's quotations, to the Constitution of Gregory XIV, "Sedes Apostolica," of May 31, 1591, which restricted irregularity and penalties to the *fetus animatus*, as the old law had it. However, said Constitution is quoted under can. 2350, §1. We believe that the unanimous teaching of the school should not be set aside, especially since the wording *fetus humanus* can only signify a living fetus. Animation, as stated before, takes place within the first week after conception. Theologians as well as canonists admit that the old theory concerning animation may still be held as far as the incurring of penalties and irregularities is concerned. This theory is that between the conception and the animation of a male fetus forty days, and of a female fetus, eighty days elapse. As long as no authentic

It is the modern science of genetics and not theology that theoretically closes this gap completely (unless segmentation in the case of identical twins is taken to be some sort of *rebutting* scientific evidence for identifying the moment of animation).

In any case, the older theologians distinguished between a formed fetus and a quickened fetus, and between nutritive, animal, and intellectual parts of the soul. They did not go so far as to say that all this was created and infused at impregnation. By the intellectual or human soul informing the fetus and by the doctrine that the soul is the "form" of the body, they meant an immanent constitutive element, not "form" in the sense of physical shape. Their reasoning entailed a distinction between *fetus formatus/fetus animatus* and a quickened fetus. This meant, of course, that the embryo became essentially human very early in its development —much earlier than could be concluded from form or animation in the gross physical senses of these terms.

In a remarkable way, modern genetics also teaches that there are "formal causes," immanent principles, or constitutive elements long before there is any shape or motion or discernible size. These minute formal elements are already determining the organic life to be the uniquely individual human being it is to be. According to this present-day scientific equivalent of the doctrine that the soul is the "form" or immanent *entelechy* of the body, it can now be asserted—not unreasonably—for the first time in the history of "scientific" speculation upon this question that who one is and is to be is present from the moment the ovum is impregnated.[3]

One can, of course, allow this and still refuse to affirm that the

---

declaration has been issued, the strict interpretation applied to penal laws may be followed here, and the period of forty, respectively eighty days be admitted. At any rate, we cannot scientifically speak of a human fetus before the lapse of six days after conception.

Roger John Huser, *The Crime of Abortion in Canon Law* (Washington, D.C.: Catholic University of America, 1942), quoted by Eugene Quay, "Justifiable Abortion," *Georgetown Law Journal XLIX*, no. 3 (Spring, 1961), 438.

[3]That is, on the assumption that the morality of abortion is—at least to some degree—a science-based issue. After attributing to the present writer the view that "the biological and genetic criteria are the *only* practical way of resolving the problem," Charles E. Curran goes on to point out (with a degree of approval) that "the problem exists precisely because some people will not accept the biological and genetic criteria for *establishing* the beginning of human life" ["Natural Law and Contemporary Moral Theology," in Charles E. Curran, ed., *Contraception: Authority and Dissent* (New York: Herder and Herder, 1969), p. 164 and n. 24, italics added]. It is in place here simply to point out that one cannot arbitrarily have it both ways. One cannot appeal to those paper popes—medical and socioscientific research papers, or scientific findings in general—when in agreement with them in some matters and then disavow the relevance of biological data when one wants to mount a moral argument loosed from such considerations.

embryo is as yet in any sense the bearer of human rights. In that case, however, one would have to provide himself with some account (perhaps drawn from these ancient and contemporary accounts of the prenatal and postnatal development of human personhood) of how by stages or degrees a human offspring approaches sacredness, and he would have to say when a child probably attains life that has sanctity. One could, for example, take "viability" and not impregnation or animation or quickening or actual birth or one year of age as the point in time when nascent life becomes subject to the protections due to any human life. Glanville Williams has recently proposed another place to draw the line, this time in between quickening and viability. "One might take," he writes, "the time at which the fetal brain begins to function," which can be determined by electrodes detecting the electric potentials or "brain waves" that are discernible in the seventh month or shortly before the time of viability, to be the beginning of justifiable protection for the fetus.[4]

Of all these demarcations, the time of birth would in many ways seem the least likely account of the beginning of life that has dignity and sanctity. A newborn baby is not noticeably much more human than before. It can, of course, do its own breathing; but before it could within limits do its own moving, and it could very definitely do its own dying. While its independence of its mother's body is relatively greater, even dramatically greater, a born baby is still a long, long way from being able to do its own praying, from being a "subject," an "I," or from being rational.

THE SANCTITY AND PROTECTION OF LIFE

Having begun with all these distinctions and theories about when germinating life becomes human, it is now necessary for me to

[4]Glanville Williams, *The Sanctity of Life and the Criminal Law* (New York: Knopf, 1957), p. 231. On the assumption that men are *rational* animals even when they are discussing controversial moral questions and controverted public questions such as abortion, we can demand a degree of consistency between their views of when a human life begins and when a human life ends. If EEG is to determine the moment of death, EEG should be decisive in determining the moment of life's beginning. If spontaneous heartbeat still counts as a vital sign for the terminal patient, it would seem also to be a good candidate for inclusion among the vital signs of when the fetus becomes alive among us. If respiration should ever be dismissed as an indication that a brain-damaged patient is still alive, why then should respiration at birth be given such importance? If the achievement of brain and heart and lung function are all to be counted at the first of life as necessary for an individual to qualify as a being deserving respect and protection, why should not the cessation of all three be required before we cease to protect that same individual when he comes to the end of his life?

say that from an authentic religious point of view none of them matters very much.

Strictly speaking, it is far more crucial for contemporary thought than it is for any religious viewpoint to *say when* there is on the scene enough of the actuality of a man who is coming to be for there to be any sacredness in or any rights attached to his life. This is the case because in modern world views the sanctity of life can rest only on something inherent in man. It is, therefore, important to determine when proleptically he already essentially is all else that he will ever become in the course of a long life. Respect for life in the first of it, if this has any sacredness, must be an overflow backward from or in anticipation of something—some capability or power—that comes later to be a man's inherent possession.

One grasps the religious outlook upon the sanctity of human life only if he sees that this life is asserted to be *surrounded* by sanctity that need not be in a man; that the most dignity a man ever possesses is a dignity that is alien to him. From this point of view it becomes *relatively* unimportant to say exactly when among the products of human generation we are dealing with an organism that is human and when we are dealing with organic life that is not yet human (despite all the theological speculations upon this question). A man's dignity is an overflow from God's dealings with him, and not primarily an anticipation of anything he will ever be by himself alone.

This is why in our religious traditions fetal life was so *certainly* surrounded with protections and prohibitions. This is why fetal life was surrounded by protections for the time before anyone supposed that a "man alive" *assuredly* existed, and even when, in opinions then current, there was a great degree of probability that he did not. "When nature is in deliberation about the man,"[5] Christians through the ages knew that God was in deliberation about the man. This took some of the weight off of analyzing the stages in the course of nature's deliberations, and off of the proofs from nature and from reason that were nevertheless used.

The value of a human life is ultimately grounded in the value God is placing on it. Anyone who can himself stand imaginatively even for a moment within an outlook where everything is referred finally to God—who, from things that are not, brings into being the things that are—should be able to see that God's deliberations about the man need have only begun. If there is anything incredible here, it is not the science, but the pitch of faith which no science proves, disproves, or confirms.

[5]Tertullian *Apologia* ix. 6–7.

44

According to the religious outlooks and "on-looks" that have been traditioned to us, man is a sacredness *in* human biological processes no less than he is a sacredness in the human social or political order. That sacredness is not composed by observable degrees of relative worth. A life's sanctity consists not in its worth *to* anybody. What life is in and of itself is most clearly to be seen in situations of naked equality of one life with another, and in the situation of congeneric helplessness which is the human condition in the first of life. No one is ever much more than a fellow fetus; and in order not to become confused about life's primary value, it is best not to concentrate on degrees of relative worth we may later acquire.

The Lord did not set his love upon you, nor choose you, because you were already intrinsically more than a blob of tissue in the uterus or greater in size than the period at the end of this sentence. Even so, the writer of Deuteronomy proclaimed to the children of Israel:

> The Lord did not set his love upon you, nor choose you, because you were more in number than any people; for you were the fewest of all people.
>
> But because the Lord loved you, and because he would keep the oath which he had sworn unto your fathers, hath the Lord brought you out with a mighty hand . . . [7:7, 8a].

Not only the prophet Jeremiah, but anyone who has a glimmer of what it means to be a religious man, should be able to repeat after him: "Before I formed thee in the belly I knew thee; and before thou camest forth out of the womb I sanctified thee; and I ordained thee . . ." (1:5). Or after the Psalmist:

> O Lord, thou hast searched me, and known me.
>
> . . .
>
> Thou has beset me behind and before, and laid thy hand upon me.
>
> . . .
>
> Behold . . . the darkness and the light are both alike to thee.
> For thou hast possessed my reins:
> Thou hast covered me in my mother's womb.
> I will praise thee; for I am fearfully and wonderfully made:
> Marvelous are thy works: and that my soul knoweth right well [139:1, 5, 12b, 13, 14].

Thus, every human being is a unique, unrepeatable opportunity to praise God. His life is entirely an ordination, a loan, and a stewardship. His essence is his existence before God and to God, as it is from Him. His dignity is "an *alien* dignity," an evaluation that is not of him but placed upon him by the divine decree.

In regard to the respect to be accorded this generic, nascent, and dying life of ours, it does not matter much which of several religious formulations is chiefly invoked. This may be the doctrine concerning the origin of a human life, or man's creation in the image of God. It may be the biblical doctrine of God's covenant with his people and thence with all mankind, with the standard this provides for the mercy to be extended in every human relation. It may be the doctrine concerning man's ultimate destination. Nor does it matter much whether it is man's life from God, before God, or toward God that is most stressed in a religious philosophy of life, whether it is supernatural faith or divine charity or supernatural hope that bestows the value. In all these cases it is hardly possible to exclude what is nowadays narrowly called "nascent life" from our purview or from the blessing and sanctity and protection which—a religious man is convinced—God places over all human lives. *Sub specie Dei* human procreation is pro-creation. That is the most fundamental "pro" word in our vocabulary. This means procreation in God's behalf. *Sub specie Dei,* it was not because it could be proved that after a certain point in our pre- or even our postnatal development we became discernibly "human" and thus a bearer of rights and deserving of respect, while before that we were not; it was rather because the Lord loved us even while we were yet microscopic and sent forth his call upon us and brought forth from things that are not the things that are. *Sub specie Dei,* it is precisely the little ones who have hardly any human claims who are sought out and covered by his mercy. *Sub specie Dei,* it is precisely when all reasonable natural grounds for hope are gone that one needs hope and may hope in God, even as when all hope was gone Abraham hoped on in faith; and in this perspective it is hardly possible to exclude from the meaning of nascent life God's call sent forth among men that once again they have hope beyond and beneath the limits reason might set.

These Biblical themes resound throughout Karl Barth's writings on respect for life and the protection of life. For the greatest Protestant theologian of this generation, the congeneric human situation is that ours is a "fellow humanity" held in trust. Respect for life means that a man should "treat as a loan both the life of all men with his own and his own with that of all men." [6] "Respect" is indeed too pale a term to use for the attitude and response of those who "handle life as a divine loan" (p. 338). Or rather—since

---

[6] Karl Barth, *Church Dogmatics* (Edinburg: T. and T. Clark, 1961), vol. III/4, para. 55, p. 335. All parenthetical references in the text are to this work.

Barth uses the term—we must allow the word "respect" to be filled full of the meaning and awe derived from the fact that whenever a man's life is in question the primary affirmation to be made about it is that from all eternity God resolved not even to be God without this particular human life.

> Respect is man's astonishment, humility and awe at a fact in which he meets something superior—majesty, dignity, holiness, a mystery which compels him to withdraw and keep his distance, to handle it modestly, circumspectly and carefully. . . . When man in faith in God's Word and promise realizes how God from eternity has maintained and loved him in his little life, and what He has done for him in time, in this knowledge of human life he is faced by a majestic, dignified and holy fact. In human life itself he meets something superior. . . . [The incarnation of Jesus Christ, the Word of God made *man*] unmistakably differentiates human life from everything that is and is done in heaven and earth. This gives it even in its most doubtful form the character of something singular, unique, unrepeatable and irreplaceable. This decides that it is an advantage and something worthwhile to be as man. This characterizes life as the incomparable and non-recurrent opportunity to praise God [p. 339].

Respect means to treat human life with "holy awe" (p. 344).

Respect for life does not mean that a man must live and let live from some iron law of necessity, or even that there is a rational compulsion to do this, or a decisive rational ground for doing so. It is rather that because God has said "Yes" to life, man's "Yes" should echo His. First and foremost, this means that man can and may live; he can and may respect the lives of others with his own. Into the darkness of the void before creation, or of the suicide's despair, or of a woman's womb, went forth the Divine utterance, "Thou mayest live." Because of God's decree and election, a man, in his own case, can and may live; he should ("must") accept his life as a trust superior to his own determination. Because the "can" and "may" that went forth also to summon every other life together with his own came from the same God and not from any human source, he can and may and must say the only human word that is appropriate or in accord with God's Yea-saying: "Thou, too, mayest live."

It is obviously because of this understanding of the meaning of life's sanctity that Barth can write, as it were, from above about nascent life, and not because of some pseudo science or even a correct science describing prenatal life from the underside:

> The unborn child is from the very first a child. It is still developing and has no independent life. But it is a man and not a thing, nor a

47

mere part of the mother's body. . . . He who destroys germinating life kills a man and thus ventures the monstrous thing of decreeing concerning the life and death of a fellow-man whose life is given by God and therefore, like his own, belongs to Him [pp. 415–416].

It is precisely because *it is only nascent* life, weak and helpless and with no intrinsic reason for claiming anything by inherent right, that Barth can say: "This child is a man for whose life the Son of God has died. . . . The true light of the world shines already in the darkness of the mother's womb" (p. 416). Or again: "Those who live by mercy will always be disposed to practice mercy, especially to a human being which is so dependent on the mercy of others as the unborn child" (p. 418).

Because it is the Lord who has beset him behind and before, the child is a bit of sacredness in the temporal and biological order —whether it is in the womb of the mother, in the arms of its father, playing hopscotch on the sidewalk, a professional football player, or a scientist at work in his laboratory (or whichever one you value most). Each has the same title to life immediately from God.

SPECIFIC PROBLEMS

Nothing in the foregoing solves any problems. In these meager times, it is first necessary to create the problem; and this, I venture to believe, is more important than solutions to the problem— namely, the problems arising from the sanctity of life in the first of it.

Nevertheless, by endorsing a religious understanding of the sanctity of nascent life, I have made myself responsible for offering some minimal comment upon the direction and the ingredients of actual moral decisions in the matter of abortion.

1. Roman Catholic theologians do *not* in principle teach that absolute preference is to be given to the child's life over that of the mother in cases of fatal conflict between them. This may seem to be the case in practice only because of an extraordinary effort to do nothing that denies them *equal* rights and *equal* protection. Protestant Christians and everyone of whatever profound religious outlook must join our Roman Catholic brethren in experiencing extraordinary anguish in the face of situations that throw life against nascent life, each of whom has *equal* title to protection.

My first comment is that we must adopt the main "rule of practice," which Roman Catholicism unfolds for the charitable protection of human life in cases of irremediable conflict of equals. This is the distinction between *direct* and *indirect* abortion. To abort the fetus may be the foreknown, anticipated, and permitted result of surgical or other emergency action whose *primary thrust* is directed to the end of saving the mother's life. An action may in its *primary thrust* be to save the mother's life, while it is foreknown that the fetus will or will likely die or be killed in the course of thus giving medical attention to the mother. Alternatively, if the fetus is viable, the primary thrust of the medical action may be to save the nascent life, while it is foreknown that the mother will or will likely die or be killed as a secondary consequence of trying to save her child's life. My language distinguishing between the primary and the secondary *thrust* of an action may be a peculiar Americanism. If so, it has to be invented in these times and among Protestants and other Americans who have so far reduced the meaning of "the intention of an act" that it has come to mean only the motives of the agent. Today we seem able to analyze play acting better than we can analyze moral action, in that we can distinguish the "intention" of a drama from the motives and meaning the author may have had in mind, but are scarcely able to grasp the fact that the intention of moral action is not exactly the same as the subjective motives of the man who is the agent. (These, too, should be righteous.)

It is in these terms that Catholics distinguish between direct and indirect, intended and unintended, abortion. The latter can be justified but the former cannot; and, of course, neither death should be subjectively *wanted*. This rule of moral practice seems to be both a logical and a charitable extension of ethical deliberation impelled by respect for the *equal* sanctity of both the lives that are in mortal conflict, and both of whom one wants to save.

Only a moment of reflection is required to see that a woman's psychological or mental life would be equally overriding—provided her unborn child is *as certain* a threat to that. If proof were offered that this is the case, the structure of the traditional Christian argument would surely yield the point. The fact is, however, that in the present age we have proceeded to abort for psychological reasons generally without demonstrating the necessity. There are four possibilities in the case of the so-called "psychological" indices for abortion: The woman on the brink of psychological destruction may (1) abort and then (a) go to pieces or (b) hold together, or (2) bring the child to term and either (a) go to pieces or (b) hold together. Presently there is considerable evidence that the psychologists not only do not know how to *predict* these eventualities but also that they cannot *retrospectively* diagnose why what took place! Their psychological diagnosis becomes secure only after adding in a socioeconomic factor. In any case, the point here to be made is simply this: The life of the mother always prevails over the life of the unborn when both equals are in mortal conflict and she alone can be saved. There is no reason for not extending this to encompass mental or personal life as well as physical life, if the facts or our knowledge of the facts were sufficient to sustain an extension of this moral judgment to such cases.

2. My second comment addresses cases that cannot be covered by the justification of indirect abortion only. The conflict situation may be one in which the mother's life cannot be saved and both will die unless the main thrust of the medical action is to kill the fetus. I do not know how many *sorts* of birth-room emergencies fall under this classification. I suspect there are fewer of this *kind* or of these *kinds* of cases than is ordinarily supposed by persons who do not know Roman Catholic medical ethics, and therefore do not know how far this has gone in resolving one type of case after another (including ectopic pregnancy) so as to permit the action to be taken that alone will save the one life that can be saved while allowing the fetus to die. Nor do I know how often unique, individual cases may arise, even under *kinds* of medical difficulties where ordinarily indirect abortion will save the mother's life, in which a conscientious physician must judge that, taking everything into account, more positive and direct action must be taken in *this* situation or else both will die. I suspect that the number of instances in which medical practice limited to indirect abortion would be a law that kills, or rather one that allows both to die, is greater than Roman Catholic moralists suppose.

It seems altogether likely, however, whether by reason of some critical *kind* or *kinds* of medical situations or by reason of unique situations falling under any of these kinds in all their individual features, that there is need for taking up the question of the possible justification of *direct* abortion in cases of mortal conflict between a mother's life and a nascent life where only the mother can be saved. In cases in which both will die together unless the mother's life is saved by an act of direct abortion, does the person who secures or performs this operation do something *wrong* that good may come of it?

I think not. This would be to do the *right* thing as means (where no other means are available), and not only to seek a good end. It is permissible, nay, it is even morally obligatory to kill the fetus directly if, without this, both mother and child will die together.

The usual arguments for this practice, however, are quite inadequate. There needs to be Christian, rational, moral reflection penetrating the act of justifiable direct abortion itself, and not only its justifying circumstances or good results. In particular, if we are serious about ethics, the Protestant Christian should wrestle with his Catholic brother over the verdict each delivers upon this proposed action in the course of his deliberations upon the Christian moral life. It is not sufficient for the Protestant simply to *assert* arbitrarily that direct abortion is the right action to be performed, and then fix his attention on the results of such conduct, on the life that is saved by this means. The goodness of this result was never in question. No one doubts that the action in question respects the sanctity of the mother's life. The question that was raised, and the question every Christian must face, is whether direct abortion is not in every way incompatible with any remaining regard of the sanctity of the nascent life.

What can and may and must be said about direct abortion insofar as this is an action brought upon the child? If Roman Catholicism is incorrect in prohibiting this as a choice-worthy means for saving the mother's life (which is only of *equal* value), then it must be possible for ethical reflection to penetrate the action proposed for situations of mortal conflict in a fashion that is, morally, significantly distinguishable from the Catholic moral penetration of it. It helps not at all to say that we should do what love requires in the consequences, since the question was whether every shred of respect for the sanctity of nascent life must not be abandoned ever to do such a thing *to the child* for the sake of those consequences. No one ever doubted that the proposed action in its effects would be charitable to the mother. It is therefore no argument to say that it is.

The first thing that should be said concerning a forced choice of justifiable direct abortion is that the *motives* of the agent toward the child should not be any different from his motives toward the mother's life. To want to save her, it is not necessary for him to *want* the death of the fetus. In fact, the death of the fetus can and should be radically *unwanted*. A person should perform or procure a direct abortion in the midst of a mortal conflict of life with life, while not *wanting* the death of either. To this degree and in the motivational realm, a person does not altogether deny the equality of these two lives to God, or direct his own human love upon the one and not the other.

If it is objected that the fetus will be dead anyway, and moreover by an act of direct aggression on his life, the answer has to be that the motives of moral agents constitute a part, but only a part, of the meaning of righteousness, along with the intention and direction of action, the consequences, and so forth. It should also be said that the requirement that in the agent's *motives* the death of the fetus be never *wanted* (which I grant has no practical consequence in the case of direct abortion to save the mother's life) may be among the *deciding* factors in assessing proposals that abortion is justifiable under other circumstances. Just so, the distinction between direct and indirect abortion, between killing and allowing to die, has no practical consequences at all in cases in which medically it is possible to save the one life that can be saved only by direct action. Still, ethical deliberation must traverse this ground and clarify this distinction, if for no other reason than that it is likely to prove to be among the deciding factors or to be definitive of the action to be adopted in other cases or circumstances.

Having said this about the moral agent's not *wanting* motivationally the death of the child which he encompasses, one has then to ask if anything more can be said about justifiable direct abortion. Can *the action itself* and *its intention* be further penetrated by Christian moral reflection, and not only the heart of the moral agent? Certainly, if there is more to be said, this should be traced out.

We must side with Karl Barth[7] against reducing ethics to motivation alone, and especially against reducing it to motivations that have in regard only the mother's life and have already put empty room in the place of nascent life.

As regards the intentionality and the direction of the act of direct abortion which we are discussing, the following analysis seems to me to be decisive ethically. The intention of the action, and in this sense its direction, is not upon the *death* of the fetus, any more than are the motives of the agent. The intention of the action is directed toward the *incapacitation* of the fetus from doing what it is doing to the life of the mother, and is not directed toward the death of the fetus, as such, even in the killing of it. The child, of course, is only doing what comes naturally, i.e., growing and attempting to be born. But this, objectively and materially, is aggressing upon the life of its mother. Her life, which alone can be saved, can be saved only if this is stopped; and to incapacitate the fetus from doing this can be done only, we are supposing, by a direct act of killing nascent life. Still, in this situation it is correct to say that the intention of this action is not the killing, not the death of the fetus, but the incapacitation of it from carrying out the material aggression that it is effecting upon the life of the mother.

This is the way that the Protestant Christian should wrestle with his fellow Catholic moralist for the verdict approving direct abortion as a means. Of course, the child is innocent; it is not

[7]Ibid., p. 425.

"formally" or deliberately and culpably an aggressor. It is, however, a most unchristian line of reasoning that makes so much of a distinction between guilt and innocence in measuring out sanctity and respect to life. If this is true, then finding a guilty one cannot be the basic justification for ever killing a man. Catholicism simply stakes too much on an autonomous natural justice in every one of its judgments about when a formally guilty aggressor forfeits his right to life (and the same applies to everything said about the fact that the fetus has done nothing to forfeit its right to life). The determination of right conduct simply should not stop at the distinction between the "innocent" and the "aggressor," if our reflection upon righteousness has in any significant measure been invaded by the righteousness of God, who makes rain to fall upon the just and the unjust and has surrounded not only microscopic life but also ungodly lives with sanctity and protection.

We must argue, therefore, that precisely the fact and the effects of *material* aggression of life upon life should be the main concern in our attempts to penetrate the meaning of the Christian life, not waiting to find a guilty aggressor before we are permitted ever to take one life in order to save another in a mortal conflict of lives and values. Just so, in warfare it is not guilty aggressors but material aggression that ever warrants the taking of life to stop the action that is going on. Moreover, a proper analysis of the intentionality and direction of an act of war in killing an enemy soldier is exactly that proposed here in the case of justifiable abortion. It is the incapacitation of the soldier and not his death that is the intention of the action.[8] If a combatant surrenders and incapacitates himself, the just and the actual objective in ever killing him has been secured; and nothing would then justify his death. The fact that he, as materially the bearer of the force that should be stopped, cannot otherwise be incapacitated than by death or surrender is the tragedy of war. The fact that the nascent life cannot incapacitate itself from materially bearing its force against the only life that can be saved, in the case we are supposing, is the tragedy of abortion. But in neither case is wickedness done. These actions are not *morally* evil, either in the motives of the agent or in the intention of the action, because the agent need not *want* the death of another human being nor by his action does he *intend* this. He wants and his action intends rather the incapacitation of a life

[8] No less an authority than Thomas Aquinas can be cited in support of this analysis of an act of justifiable killing, in his original formulation of the rule of "double effect" (*Summa Theologica*, II–II, Q. 64, art. 7). After much derision of Catholic moral analysis, Glanville Williams makes this same point in *The Sanctity of Life*, p. 204.

that is exerting materially aggressive fatal force upon the life of another. The stopping of materially aggressive action is the highest possible warrant for the killing of men by men (if life cannot otherwise be saved), not the aggressor-innocent distinction.

Quite possibly even a tradition-minded Catholic can agree with the foregoing analysis of acts of justifiable abortion in which the physical force of the action is directed upon the unborn child. He would point to Thomas Aquinas' justification (cited above) of any killing of man by man if and only if this is indirect in the sense of stopping an assault and not for the purpose of killing *him*. He would quite properly call attention to the fact that traditional moralists spoke not of the physical target of the destructive action but of the "directly *voluntary*" and the "indirectly *voluntary*." This allows that the physical force of the action may be directed upon the unborn child and yet that his death is only indirectly *willed* as an aspect of the action whose objective is to stop the child's material aggression upon the life of the mother.[9]

We are concerned, however, with the moral analysis and the reasoning to this sort of justifiable abortion, and not with who (Catholic or Protestant) accepts it. Despite the niceties and validity of the distinction just mentioned, there may be some point in still calling this (in the meaning of the action's physical force or target) *direct* justifiable abortion. There are some conservative moralists who before agreeing that such an abortion is ever right would require that the *description* of the physical action be something like "emptying the uterus" (from which the death of the child unavoidably results) and not "killing the baby" to stop its destruction of the mother. At the same time there are a growing number of liberal moralists who, embattled against all such physical descriptions, have apparently forgotten that the heart and soul of the "rule of double effect" and its true origin is in a charitable attention to and respect for the two *personal* termini of a single action that to save one life must kill another.

3. My final comment concerns the principal value to be derived from steadfastly maintaining the verdicts that can be reached in ethical justification or prohibition from a religious understanding of the sanctity of life and also of nascent life. This is not always or primarily the praise or blame of individual actions or agents. These may, for a variety of reasons, be *excusable* even for wrongdoing, and the judgment of blameworthiness may fall elsewhere, e.g., upon the moral ethos of an entire society or epoch

[9]See Richard A. McCormick, S.J., "Past Church Teaching on Abortion," *Proceedings of the Catholic Theological Society of America*, vol. 23 (1968), pp. 131–151, especially pp. 137–140.

Paul Ramsey

We need, therefore, to look to the fundamental moral premises of contemporary society in order to see clearly what is at stake in the survival or demise of a religious evaluation of nascent life.

This is an abortifacient society. Women readily learn to "loop before you leap," but they forget to ask whether interuterine devices prevent conception or abort germinating life. They do both. A significant part of the efficiency of the loop arises from the fact that it is not only a contraceptive, but also an abortifacient. The pills that prevent ovulation are more totally effective than the combined capacities of the loop, and this fact alone in an abortifacient civilization will lead to preference for the pill in the practice of birth control.

American women who can afford to do so go to Sweden to avail themselves of more liberal legal regulations concerning abortion; but Swedish women go to Poland, which is at the moment the real paradise for legal abortions. Sweden's is a middle way between American rigidity and Polish unlimited permissiveness. The stated reason why Sweden does not go further and adopt still more liberal practices in regard to legal abortion is because of the fear that, as one doctor put it, where abortion is altogether easy, people will not take care to practice birth control.[10] Abortion is therefore a contraceptive device in this age. Doubtless, it is not the most choice-worthy means or a means frequently chosen, but it is an alternative means. Loop before you leap, abort before you birth! The evidence seems to be that the latter may not be merely a last resort, but is actually an option for contraceptive purposes. If quite freely available, abortion may relieve the moral and psychological pressures that are exerted upon their freedom to copulate by the remaining regard that men and women have for possible nascent life. Just as surely as this is a contraceptive society, it is also abortifacient.

We are not concerned here with what the criminal law should be in regard to abortion. Not everything that is legal is right, nor should every wrong be legally prohibited; and nothing that is right is right *because* it is legal. Perhaps the penal code regarding abortion should be reformed in directions that will lead to less evil being done than is done under our present more stringent laws.[11] However, in comprehending the meaning of describing this age as an abortifacient civilization (in contrast to societies

[10]"Abortion and the Law," *CBS Reports,* April 5, 1965.
[11]Note that I say, "lead to less evil being done than is *done*," not "to less evil *happening* than now occurs." This is to say that a primary legislative purpose of law and of the reform of law in this area should remain a moral one. The goal of law is the regulation of human *conduct*, and not only the prevention of certain consequences.

55

based at all on a religious comprehension of the sanctity of life), it is illuminating to notice what happens when legal prohibitions of abortion are "liberalized." Glanville Williams[12] has this to say about the Swedish experiment: "There is convincing evidence that it is to a large extent an entirely new clientele that is now granted legal abortion, that is to say women who would not have had an illegal abortion if they had been refused the legal one." Thereupon Williams states and endorses the value judgment upon these abortifacient trends that are characteristic of the contemporary period: "Although the social result is rather to add the total of legal abortions to the total of illegal abortions than to reduce the number of illegal abortions, a body of medical opinion refuses to regret the legal abortions on this account." That judgment is, of course, in no sense a "medical opinion."

The foregoing analysis of our society as in its ethos abortifacient is pertinent to the question concerning the moral justification of (direct) abortion of a fetus that is likely to be gravely defective physically or mentally. The answer to this question seems obvious indeed to a simple and sincere humanitarianism. It is not at all obvious. A first step in throwing doubt upon the proposal is to ask what was forgotten in the discussion of the blindness and deformities that will result from a woman's contracting rubella, especially in early pregnancy. It is often hard to tell whether a woman has rubella; yet her child may be gravely damaged. Moreover, it is hard to tell whether an individual case of measles is rubella; this can be determined with a great degree of certainty only in the case of *epidemics* of rubella. It is proposed that women who have rubella while pregnant should be able to secure a legal abortion, and it is affirmed that under these circumstances fetal euthanasia is not only ethically permissible but may even be morally obligatory for the sake of the child.

We are interested primarily in the ethical question. The proposal, as I understand it, is based on a kind of *interims ethik;* direct abortion is justified at least until medical science develops a *vaccine* against these measles and a reliable *test* of whether a woman has or has had the German measles. In our abortifacient culture, however, it is forgotten, or if mentioned it does not sink into the consciousness of men and women today, that there is an alternative to adopting the widespread medical practice and legal institution of fetal euthanasia. This optional social practice of medicine would be equally or more preventive of damage to nascent life from rubella. The *disease itself* gives complete immunization to contracting rubella again. The popular belief that

[12]Williams, *The Sanctity of Life,* p. 242.

56

a woman can have several cases of German measles is an "old wives' tale," my pediatrician tells me, which arises from the fact that it is almost impossible to tell one sort of measles from another, except in epidemics. But there is one way to be certain of this, and to obtain immunization against the disease in the future. The virus itself, the disease itself, can be used, as it were, to "vaccinate" against itself

Why is it not proposed that for the interim between now and the perfection of a more convenient, reliable vaccine, all girl children be *given* the German measles?[13] Would this not be a more choice-worthy *interims ethik*? The answer to this question can only be found in the complete erosion of religious regard for nascent life in a technological and abortifacient era. Abortion when the mother contracts rubella is another example of the "American way of death." In this instance, the darkness of the womb makes unnecessary resort to a mortician's art to cover the grim reality. As long as we do not see the deaths inflicted or witness the dying, the direct killing of nascent life has only to be compared with the greater or less inconvenience of other solutions in an antiseptic society where the prevention of disease at all cost is the chief light upon our conscious paths. But that darkness and this light are both alike to the Lord of nascent and conscious life. Upon this basis it would not be possible to choose actions and practices that deliberately abort over an interim social practice of deliberate disease giving. At least in the problem of rubella-induced fetal damage, it is not mercy or charity but some other motivation in regard to sentient life that can look with favor upon the practice of euthanasia for the child's sake.

The real situation in which our ethical deliberations should proceed cannot be adequately defined short of the location of moral agency and the action under consideration in the context of the lives of all mankind and the general social practices most apt to exhibit righteousness or to make for good. Moreover, our ethical deliberations cannot disregard the fact that the *specific* contemporary context must include the erosion of the moral bond between moments in a single individual life without which there can be no enduring covenants of life with life—the erosion of the moral bonds between life and life, between soul and bodily life, and between conscious life and nascent life—which has

---

[13]There are sometimes, of course, serious effects from having German measles. Still, it is arguable that these effects would be far less serious than the destruction of both damaged and undamaged nascent lives which, it is said, ought now systematically to be inflicted while we await the perfection and widespread use of a vaccine.

brought about the divorcing, contraceptive, and abortifacient ethos of the present day.

A chief business of ethics is to distinguish between venereal freedom and the meaning of venereal responsibility in such a fashion that it is barely possible (or at least that this possibility is not methodologically excluded) that from the reflections of moralists there may come clear direction for the structural changes needed to address the structural defects of this age. If this is so, I suggest that a strong case can be made for every effort to re-vitalize a religious understanding of the integrity and sanctity of life, for unfolding from this at the outmost limits the distinction between direct killing and allowing to die and the distinction be-tween intending to kill and intending to incapacitate the fetus to save the mother's life, and for retaining in the order of ethical jus-tification the prohibition of the direct killing of nascent life. This would be to keep needed moral pressures upon ourselves in many areas where a proper regard for life threatens to be dissolved, or has already been dissolved. This would be to endeavor to reverse the trends of a scientific and a secular age that have already gone far in emptying our culture of any substantive morality.

The first order of business would be to strengthen an ethics that contains some remaining sense of the sanctity of life against the corrosive influence of the view that what *should* be done is largely a function of what *technically can* be done, and against the view that morality is entirely a matter of engineering the conse-quences for the conscious span of our lives. Moreover, if we do not confuse ethical justification with moral excusability, compas-sion can still encompass the possibility and the reality of indi-vidual moral excusability for a wrong that had to be done or was done in a particular situation in this world where sin (especially the sin in social structures) begets sin.

the problem of abortion and the doctrine of the double effect

philippa foot

One of the reasons why most of us feel puzzled about the problem of abortion is that we want, and do not want, to allow to the unborn child the rights that belong to adults and children. When we think of a baby about to be born it seems absurd to think that the next few minutes or even hours could make so radical a difference to its status; yet as we go back in the life of the foetus we are more and more reluctant to say that this is a human being and must be treated as such. No doubt this is the deepest source of our dilemma, but it is not the only one. For we are also confused about the general question of what we may and may not do where the interests of human beings conflict. We have strong intuitions about certain cases; saying, for instance, that it is all right to raise the level of education in our country, though statistics allow us to predict that a rise in the suicide rate will follow, while it is not all right to kill the feeble-minded to aid cancer research. It is not easy, however, to see the principles involved, and one way of throwing light on the abortion issue will be by setting up parallels involving adults or children once born. So we will be able to isolate the "equal rights" issue, and should be able to make some advance.

From the *Oxford Review*, No. 5 (1967). Reprinted by permission of the author.

I shall not, of course, discuss all the principles that may be used in deciding what to do where the interest or rights of human beings conflict. What I want to do is to look at one particular theory, known as the "doctrine of the double effect" which is invoked by Catholics in support of their views on abortion but supposed by them to apply elsewhere. As used in the abortion argument this doctrine has often seemed to non-Catholics to be a piece of complete sophistry. In the last number of the *Oxford Review* it was given short shrift by Professor Hart.[1] And yet this principle has seemed to some non-Catholics as well as to Catholics to stand as the only defence against decisions on other issues that are quite unacceptable. It will help us in our difficulty about abortion if this conflict can be resolved.

The doctrine of the double effect is based on a distinction between what a man foresees as a result of his voluntary action and what, in the strict sense, he intends. He intends in the strictest sense both those things that he aims at as ends and those that he aims at as means to his ends. The latter may be regretted in themselves but nevertheless desired for the sake of the end, as we may intend to keep dangerous lunatics confined for the sake of our safety. By contrast a man is said not strictly, or directly, to intend the foreseen consequences of his voluntary actions where these are neither the end at which he is aiming nor the means to this end. Whether the word "intention" should be applied in both cases is not of course what matters: Bentham spoke of "oblique intention," contrasting it with the "direct intention" of ends and means, and we may as well follow his terminology. Everyone must recognize that some such distinction can be made, though it may be made in a number of different ways, and it is the distinction that is crucial to the doctrine of the double effect. The words "double effect" refer to the two effects that an action may produce: the one aimed at, and the one foreseen but in no way desired. By "the doctrine of the double effect" I mean the thesis that it is sometimes permissible to bring about by oblique intention what one may not directly intend. Thus the distinction is held to be relevant to moral decision in certain difficult cases. It is said for instance that the operation of hysterectomy involves the death of the foetus as the foreseen but not strictly or directly intended consequence of the surgeon's act, while other operations kill the child and count as the direct intention of taking an innocent life, a distinction that has evoked particularly bitter reactions on the part of non-Catholics. If

[1]H. L. A. Hart, "Intention and Punishment," *Oxford Review*, number 4, Hilary 1967. I owe much to this article and to a conversation with Professor Hart, though I do not know whether he will approve of what follows.

you are permitted to bring about the death of the child, what does it matter how it is done? The doctrine of the double effect is also used to show why in another case, where a woman in labour will die unless a craniotomy operation is performed, the intervention is not to be condoned. There, it is said, we may not operate but must let the mother die. We foresee her death but do not directly intend it, whereas to crush the skull of the child would count as direct intention of its death.[2]

This last application of the doctrine has been queried by Professor Hart on the ground that the child's death is not strictly a means to saving the mother's life and should logically be treated as an unwanted but foreseen consequence by those who make use of the distinction between direct and oblique intention. To interpret the doctrine in this way is perfectly reasonable given the language that has been used; it would, however, make nonsense of it from the beginning. A certain event may be desired under one of its descriptions, unwanted under another, but we cannot treat these as two different events, one of which is aimed at and the other not. And even if it be argued that there are here two different events— the crushing of the child's skull and its death—the two are obviously much too close for an application of the doctrine of the double effect. To see how odd it would be to apply the principle like this we may consider the story, well known to philosophers, of the fat man stuck in the mouth of the cave. A party of potholers have imprudently allowed the fat man to lead them as they make their way out of the cave, and he gets stuck, trapping the others behind him. Obviously the right thing to do is to sit down and wait until the fat man grows thin; but philosophers have arranged that flood waters should be rising within the cave. Luckily (luckily?) the trapped party have with them a stick of dynamite with which they can blast the fat man out of the mouth of the cave. Either they use the dynamite or they drown. In one version the fat man, whose head is *in* the cave, will drown with them; in the other he will be rescued in due course.[3] Problem: may they use the dynamite or not? Later we will find parallels to this example. Here it is introduced for light relief and because it will serve to show how ridiculous one version of the doctrine of the double effect would be. For suppose that the trapped explorers were to argue that the death of the fat man might be taken as a merely foreseen consequence of the act of blowing him up. ("We didn't want to kill him . . . only to blow him into small pieces" or even ". . . . only to blast him out of

[2] For discussions of the Catholic doctrine on abortion see Glanville Williams, *The Sanctity of Life and the Criminal Law* (New York, 1957); also N. St. John Stevas, *The Right to Life* (London, 1963).
[3] It was Professor Hart who drew my attention to this distinction.

the mouth of the cave.'') I believe that those who use the doctrine of the double effect would rightly reject such a suggestion, though they will, of course, have considerable difficulty in explaining where the line is to be drawn. What is to be the criterion of "closeness" if we say that anything very close to what we are literally aiming at counts as if part of our aim?

Let us leave this difficulty aside and return to the arguments for and against the doctrine, supposing it to be formulated in the way considered most effective by its supporters, and ourselves bypassing the trouble by taking what must on any reasonable definition be clear cases of "direct" or "oblique" intention.

The first point that should be made clear, in fairness to the theory, is that no one is suggesting that it does not matter what you bring about as long as you merely foresee and do not strictly intend the evil that follows. We might think, for instance, of the (actual) case of wicked merchants selling, for cooking, oil they knew to be poisonous and thereby killing a number of innocent people, comparing and contrasting it with that of some unemployed gravediggers, desperate for custom, who got hold of this same oil and sold it (or perhaps *they* secretly gave it away) in order to create orders for graves. They strictly (directly) intend the deaths they cause, while the merchants could say that it was not part of their *plan* that anyone should die. In morality, as in law, the merchants, like the gravediggers, would be considered as murderers; nor are the supporters of the doctrine of the double effect bound to say that there is the least difference between them in respect of moral turpitude. What they are committed to is the thesis that *sometimes* it makes a difference to the permissibility of an action involving harm to others that this harm, although foreseen, is not part of the agent's direct intention. An end such as earning one's living is clearly not such as to justify *either* the direct or oblique intention of the death of innocent people, but in certain cases one is justified in bringing about knowingly what one could not directly intend.

It is now time to say why this doctrine should be taken seriously in spite of the fact that it sounds rather odd, that there are difficulties about the distinction on which it depends, and that it seemed to yield one sophistical conclusion when applied to the problem of abortion. The reason for its appeal is that its opponents have often *seemed* to be committed to quite indefensible views. Thus the controversy has raged around examples such as the following. Suppose that a judge or magistrate is faced with rioters demanding that a culprit be found for a certain crime and threatening otherwise to take their own bloody revenge on a particular section of the community. The real culprit being unknown, the judge sees himself as able to prevent the bloodshed only by framing some innocent person and having him executed. Beside this example is placed another in which a pilot whose aeroplane is about to crash is deciding whether to steer from a more to a less inhabited area. To make the parallel as close as possible it may rather be supposed that he is the driver of a runaway tram which he can only steer from one narrow track on to another; five men are working on one track and one man on the other; anyone on the track he enters is bound to be killed. In the case of the riots the mob have five hostages, so that in both the exchange is supposed to be one man's life for the lives of five. The question is why we should say, without hesitation, that the driver should steer for the less occupied track, while most of us would be appalled at the idea that the innocent man could be framed. It may be suggested that the special feature of the latter case is that it involves the corruption of justice, and this is, of course, very important indeed. But if we remove that special feature, supposing that some private individual is to kill an innocent person and pass him off as the criminal we still find ourselves horrified by the idea. The doctrine of the double effect offers us a way out of the difficulty, insisting that it is one thing to steer towards someone foreseeing that you will kill him and another to aim at his death as part of your plan. Moreover there is one very important element of good in what is here insisted. In real life it would hardly ever be certain that the man on the narrow track would be killed. Perhaps he might find a foothold on the side of the tunnel and cling on as the vehicle hurtled by. The driver of the tram does *not* then leap off and brain him with a crowbar. The judge, however, needs the death of the innocent man for his (good) purposes. If the victim proves hard to hang he must see to it that he dies another way. To choose to execute him is to choose that this evil *shall come about*, and this must therefore count as a *certainty* in weighing up the good and evil involved. The distinction between direct and oblique intention is crucial here, and is of great importance in an uncertain world. Nevertheless this is no way to defend the doctrine of the double effect. For the question is whether the difference between aiming at something and obliquely intending it is *in itself* relevant to moral decisions; not whether it is important when correlated with a difference of certainty in the balance of good and evil. Moreover we are particularly interested in the application of the doctrine of the double effect to the question of abortion, and no one can deny that in medicine there are sometimes certainties so complete that it would be a mere quibble to speak of the "probable outcome" of this course of action or that. It is not, therefore, with a merely philo-sophical interest that we should put aside the uncertainty and scrutinize the examples to test the doctrine of the double effect. Why can we not argue from the case of the steering driver to that of the judge?

Another pair of examples poses a similar problem. We are about to give to a patient who needs it to save his life a massive dose of a certain drug in short supply. There arrive, however, five other patients each of whom could be saved by one-fifth of that dose. We say with regret that we cannot spare our whole supply of the drug for a single patient, just as we should say that we could not spare the whole resources of a ward for one dangerously ill in-dividual when ambulances arrive bringing in the victims of a mul-tiple crash. We feel bound to let one man die rather than many if that is our only choice. Why then do we not feel justified in killing people in the interests of cancer research or to obtain, let us say, spare parts for grafting on to those who need them? We can sup-pose, similarly, that several dangerously ill people can be saved only if we kill a certain individual and make a serum from his dead body. (These examples are not over fanciful considering present controversies about prolonging the life of mortally ill patients whose eyes or kidneys are to be used for others.) Why cannot we argue from the case of the scarce drug to that of the body needed for medical purposes? Once again the doctrine of the double effect comes up with an explanation. In one kind of case but not the other we aim at the death of the innocent man.

A further argument suggests that if the doctrine of the double effect is rejected this has the consequence of putting us hopelessly in the power of bad men. Suppose for example that some tyrant should threaten to torture five men if we ourselves would not tor-ture one. Would it be our duty to do so, supposing we believed him, because this would be no different from choosing to rescue five men from his tortures rather than one? If so anyone who wants us to do something we think wrong has only to threaten that other-wise he himself will do something we think worse. A mad mur-derer, known to keep his promises, could thus make it our duty to kill some innocent citizen to prevent him from killing two. From this conclusion we are again rescued by the doctrine of the double effect. If we refuse, we foresee that the greater number will be killed but we do not intend it: it is he who intends (that is strictly or directly intends) the death of innocent persons; we do not.

At one time I thought that these arguments in favour of the doctrine of the double effect were conclusive, but I now believe that the conflict should be solved in another way. The clue that

Philippa Foot

we should follow is that the strength of the doctrine seems to lie in the distinction it makes between what we *do* (equated with direct intention) and what we allow (thought of as obliquely intended). Indeed it is interesting that the disputants tend to argue about whether we are to be held responsible for what we allow as we are for what we do.[4] Yet it is not obvious that this is what they should be discussing, since the distinction between what one does and what one allows to happen is not the same as that between direct and oblique intention. To see this one has only to consider that it is possible *deliberately* to allow something to happen, aiming at it either for its own sake or as part of one's plan for obtaining something else. So one person might want another person dead, and deliberately allow him to die. And again one may be said to *do* things that one does not aim at, as the steering driver would kill the man on the track. Moreover there is a large class of things said to be brought about rather than either done or allowed, and either kind of intention is possible. So it is possible to *bring about* a man's death by getting him to go to sea in a leaky boat, and the intention of his death may be either direct or oblique.

Whatever it may, or may not, have to do with the doctrine of the double effect, the idea of *allowing* is worth looking into in this context. I shall leave aside the special case of giving permission, which involves the idea of authority, and consider the two main divisions into which cases of allowing seem to fall. There is firstly the allowing which is forbearing to prevent. For this we need a sequence thought of as somehow already in train, and something that the agent could do to intervene. (The agent must be able to intervene, but does not do so.) So, for instance, he could warn someone, but *allows* him to walk into a trap. He could feed an animal but *allows* it to die for lack of food. He could stop a leaking tap but *allows* the water to go on flowing. This is the case of allowing with which we shall be concerned, but the other should be mentioned. It is the kind of allowing which is roughly equivalent to *enabling;* the root idea being the removal of some obstacle which is, as it were, holding back a train of events. So someone may remove a plug and *allow* water to flow; open a door and *allow* an animal to get out; or give someone money and *allow* him to get back on his feet.

The first kind of allowing requires an omission, but there is no other general correlation between omission and allowing, commission and bringing about or doing. An actor who fails to turn up

[4]See, e.g., J. Bennett, "Whatever the Consequences," *Analysis*, January 1966; and G. E. M. Anscombe's reply in *Analysis*, June 1966. See also Miss Anscombe's "Modern Moral Philosophy" in *Philosophy*, January 1958.

65

for a performance will generally spoil it rather than allow it to be spoiled. I mention the distinction between omission and commission only to set it aside.

Thinking of the first kind of allowing (forebearing to prevent), we should ask whether there is any difference, from the moral point of view, between what one does or causes and what one merely allows. It seems clear that on occasions one is just as bad as the other, as is recognized in both morality and law. A man may murder his child or his aged relatives, by allowing them to die of starvation as well as by giving poison; he may also be convicted of murder on either account. In another case we would, however, make a distinction. Most of us allow people to die of starvation in India and Africa, and there is surely something wrong with us that we do; it would be nonsense, however, to pretend that it is only in law that we make a distinction between allowing people in the underdeveloped countries to die of starvation and sending them poisoned food. There is worked into our moral system a distinction between what we owe people in the form of aid and what we owe them in the way of non-interference. Salmond, in his *Jurisprudence*, expressed as follows the distinction between the two.

> A positive right corresponds to a positive duty, and is a right that he on whom the duty lies shall do some positive act on behalf of the person entitled. A negative right corresponds to a negative duty, and is a right that the person bound shall refrain from some act which would operate to the prejudice of the person entitled. The former is a right to be positively benefited; the latter is merely a right not to be harmed.[5]

As a general account of rights and duties this is defective, since not all are so closely connected with benefit and harm. Nevertheless for our purposes it will do well. Let us speak of negative duties when thinking of the obligation to refrain from such things as killing or robbing, and of the positive duty, e.g., to look after children or aged parents. It will be useful, however, to extend the notion of positive duty beyond the range of things that are strictly called duties, bringing acts of charity under this heading. These are owed only in a rather loose sense, and some acts of charity could hardly be said to be *owed* at all, so I am not following ordinary usage at this point.

Let us now see whether the distinction of negative and positive duties explains why we see differently the action of the steering driver and that of the judge, of the doctors who withhold the scarce drug and those who obtain a body for medical purposes, of

[5]J. Salmond, *Jurisprudence*, 11th edition, p. 283.

those who choose to rescue the five men rather than one man from torture and those who are ready to torture the one man themselves in order to save five. In each case we have a conflict of duties, but what kind of duties are they? Are we, in each case, weighing positive duties against positive, negative against negative, or one against the other? Is the duty to refrain from injury, or rather to bring aid?

The steering driver faces a conflict of negative duties, since it is his duty to avoid injuring five men and also his duty to avoid injuring one. In the circumstances he is not able to avoid both, and it seems clear that he should do the least injury he can. The judge, however, is weighing the duty of not inflicting injury against the duty of bringing aid. He wants to rescue the innocent people threatened with death but can do so only by inflicting injury himself. Since one does not *in general* have the same duty to help people as to refrain from injuring them, it is not possible to argue to a conclusion about what he should do from the steering driver case. It is interesting that, even where the strictest duty of positive aid exists, this still does not weigh as if a negative duty were involved It is not, for instance, permissible to commit a murder to bring one's starving children food. If the choice is between inflicting injury on one or many there seems only one rational course of action; if the choice is between aid to some at the cost of injury to others, and refusing to inflict the injury to bring the aid, the whole matter is open to dispute. So it is not inconsistent of us to think that the driver must steer for the road on which only one man stands while the judge (or his equivalent) may not kill the innocent person in order to stop the riots. Let us now consider the second pair of examples, which concern the scarce drug on the one hand and on the other the body needed to save lives. Once again we find a difference based on the distinction between the duty to avoid injury and the duty to provide aid. Where one man needs a massive dose of the drug and we withhold it from him in order to save five men, we are weighing aid against aid. But if we consider killing a man in order to use his body to save others, we are thinking of doing him injury to bring others aid. In an interesting variant of the model, we may suppose that instead of killing someone we deliberately let him die. (Perhaps he is a beggar to whom we are thinking of giving food, but then we say "No, they need bodies for medical research ") Here it does seem relevant that in allowing him to die we are aiming at his death, but presumably we are inclined to see this as a violation of negative rather than positive duty. If this is right, we see why we are unable in either case to argue to a conclusion from the case of the scarce drug.

In the examples involving the torturing of one man or five men, the principle seems to be the same as for the last pair. If we are bringing aid (rescuing people about to be tortured by the tyrant), we must obviously rescue the larger rather than the smaller group. It does not follow, however, that we would be justified in inflicting the injury, or getting a third person to do so, in order to save the five. We may therefore refuse to be forced into acting by the threats of bad men. To refrain from inflicting injury ourselves is a stricter duty than to prevent other people from inflicting injury, which is not to say that the other is not a very strict duty indeed.

So far the conclusions are the same as those at which we might arrive following the doctrine of the double effect, but in others they will be different, and the advantage seems to be all on the side of the alternative. Suppose, for instance, that there are five patients in a hospital whose lives could be saved by the manufacture of a certain gas, but that this inevitably releases lethal fumes into the room of another patient whom for some reason we are unable to move. His death, being of no use to us, is clearly a side effect, and not directly intended. Why then is the case different from that of the scarce drug, if the point about that is that we foresaw but did not strictly intend the death of the single patient? Yet it surely is different. The relatives of the gassed patient would presumably be successful if they sued the hospital and the whole story came out. We may find it particularly revolting that someone should be *used* as in the case where he is killed or allowed to die in the interest of medical research, and the fact of *using* may even determine what we would decide to do in some cases, but the principle seems unimportant compared with our reluctance to bring such injury for the sake of giving aid.

My conclusion is that the distinction between direct and oblique intention plays only a quite subsidiary role in determining what we say in these cases, while the distinction between avoiding injury and bringing aid is very important indeed. I have not, of course, argued that there are no other principles. For instance it clearly makes a difference whether our positive duty is a strict duty or rather an act of charity: feeding our own children or feeding those in far away countries. It may also make a difference whether the person about to suffer is one thought of as uninvolved in the threatened disaster, and whether it is his presence that constitutes the threat to the others. In many cases we find it very hard to know what to say, and I have not been arguing for any general conclusion such as that we may never, whatever the balance of good and evil, bring injury to one for the sake of aid to others, even when this injury amounts to death. I have only tried to show that even if we reject the doctrine of the double effect we are not forced to the conclusion that the size of the evil must always be our guide.

Let us now return to the problem of abortion, carrying out our plan of finding parallels involving adults or children rather than the unborn. We must say something about the different cases in which abortion might be considered on medical grounds.

First of all there is the situation in which nothing that can be done will save the life of child and mother, but where the life of the mother can be saved by killing the child. This is parallel to the case of the fat man in the mouth of the cave who is bound to be drowned with the others if nothing is done. Given the certainty of the outcome, as it was postulated, there is no serious conflict of interests here, since the fat man will perish in either case, and it is reasonable that the action that will save someone should be done. It is a great objection to those who argue that the direct intention of the death of an innocent person is never justifiable that the edict will apply even in this case. The Catholic doctrine on abortion must here conflict with that of most reasonable men. Moreover we would be justified in performing the operation whatever the method used, and it is neither a necessary nor a good justification of the special case of hysterectomy that the child's death is not directly intended, being rather a foreseen consequence of what is done. What difference could it make as to how the death is brought about?

Secondly we have the case in which it is possible to perform an operation which will save the mother and kill the child or kill the mother and save the child. This is parallel to the famous case of the shipwrecked mariners who believed that they must throw someone overboard if their boat was not to founder in a storm, and to the other famous case of the two sailors, Dudley and Stephens, who killed and ate the cabin boy when adrift on the sea without food. Here again there is no conflict of interests so far as the decision to act is concerned; only in deciding whom to save. Once again it would be reasonable to act, though one would respect someone who held back from the appalling action either because he preferred to perish rather than do such a thing or because he held on past the limits of reasonable hope. In real life the certainties postulated by philosophers hardly ever exist, and Dudley and Stephens were rescued not long after their ghastly meal. Nevertheless if the certainty were absolute, as it might be in the abortion case, it would seem better to save one than none. Probably we should decide in favour of the mother when weighing her life against that of the unborn child, but it is interesting that, a few years later, we might easily decide it the other way.

The worst dilemma comes in the third kind of example where to save the mother we must kill the child, say by crushing its skull, while if nothing is done the mother will perish but the child can be safely delivered after her death. Here the doctrine of the double effect has been invoked to show that we may not intervene, since the child's death would be directly intended while the mother's would not. On a strict parallel with cases not involving the unborn we might find the conclusion correct though the reason given was wrong. Suppose, for instance, that in later life the presence of a child was certain to bring death to the mother. We would surely not think ourselves justified in ridding her of it by a process that involved its death For in general we do not think that we can kill one innocent person to rescue another, quite apart from the special care that we feel is due to children once they have prudently got themselves born. What we would be prepared to do when a great many people were involved is another matter, and this is probably the key to one quite common view of abortion on the part of those who take quite seriously the rights of the unborn child. They probably feel that if *enough* people are involved one must be sacrificed, and they think of the mother's life against the unborn child's life as if it were many against one. But of course many people do not view it like this at all, having no inclination to accord to the foetus or unborn child anything like ordinary human status in the matter of rights. I have not been arguing for or against these points of view but only trying to discern some of the currents that are pulling us back and forth. The levity of the examples is not meant to offend.

understanding the abortion argument

roger wertheimer

At what stage of fetal development, if any, and for what reasons, if any, is abortion justifiable? Each part of the question has received diverse answers, which in turn have been combined in various ways.

According to the liberal, the fetus should be disposable upon the mother's request until it is viable; thereafter it may be destroyed only to save the mother's life. To an extreme liberal the fetus is always like an appendix, and may be destroyed upon demand anytime before its birth. A moderate view is that until viability the fetus should be disposable if it is the result of felonious intercourse, or if the mother's or child's physical or mental health would probably be gravely impaired. This position is susceptible to wide variations. The conservative position is that the fetus may be aborted before quickening but not after, unless the mother's life is at stake. For the extreme conservative, the fetus, once conceived, may not be destroyed for any reason short of saving the mother's life.

This last might be called the Catholic view, but note that it, or some close variant of it, is shared by numerous Christian sects,

This is a shortened version of "Understanding the Abortion Argument" by Roger Wertheimer, *Philosophy and Public Affairs*, vol. 1, no. 1 (copyright © 1971 by Princeton University Press), pp. 67–95. Reprinted by permission of Princeton University Press.

and is or was maintained by Jews, by Indians of both hemispheres, by a variety of tribes of diverse geographical location and cultural level, and even by some contemporary atheistical biochemists who are political liberals. Much the same can be said of any of the listed positions. I call attention to such facts for two reasons. First, they suggest that the abortion issue is in some way special, since, given any position on abortion and any position on any other issue, you can probably find a substantial group of people who have simultaneously held both. Second, these facts are regularly denied or distorted by the disputants. Thus, liberals habitually argue as though extreme conservatism were an invention of contemporary scholasticism with a mere century of popish heritage behind it. This in the face of the fact that that position has had the force of law in most American states for more than a century, and continues to be law even in states where Catholicism is without influence. We shall see that these two points are not unrelated.

Now, it is commonly said that the crux of the controversy is a disagreement as to the *value* of fetal life in its various stages. But I submit that this subtly but seriously misdescribes the actual arguments, and, further, betrays a questionable understanding of morality and perhaps a questionable morality as well. Instead, I suggest, we had best take the fundamental question to be: When does a human life begin?

First off I should note that the expressions "a human life," "a human being," "a person" are virtually interchangeable in this context. As I use these expressions, except for monstrosities, every member of our species is indubitably a person, a human being at the very latest at birth. The question is whether we are human lives at any time before birth. Virtually everyone, at least every party to the current controversy, *actually* does agree to this. However, we should be aware that in this area both agreement and disagreement are often merely verbal and therefore only apparent. For example, many people will say that it takes a month or even more after birth for the infant to become a person, and they will explain themselves by saying that a human being must have self-consciousness, or a personality. But upon investigation this disagreement normally turns out to be almost wholly semantic, for we can agree on all the facts about child development, and furthermore we can agree, at least in a general way, in our moral judgments on the care to be accorded the child at various stages. Thus, though they deny that a day-old infant is a person, they admit that its life cannot be forfeited for any reason that would not equally apply to a two-year-old.

On the other hand, significant disagreements can be masked

by a merely verbal agreement. Sometimes a liberal will grant that a previable fetus is a human being, but investigation reveals that he means only that the fetus is a potential human being. Or he may call it human to distinguish it from canine and feline fetuses, and call it alive or living in opposition to dead or inert. But the sum of these parts does not equal what he means when he uses the phrase "a human life" in connection with himself and his friends, for in that extended sense he could equally apply that expression to human terata, and, at least in extreme cases, he is inclined to deny that they are human lives, and to dispose of them accordingly.

Implicit in my remarks is the suggestion that one way to find out how someone uses the expression "human being" and related ones is by looking at his moral judgments. I am suggesting that this is a way, sometimes the only way, of learning both what someone means by such expressions and what his conception of a human being is. It seems clear enough that given that a man has a certain set of desires, we can discern his conception of something, X, by seeing what kinds of behavior he takes to be appropriate regarding X. I am saying that we may have to look at his *moral* beliefs regarding X, especially if X is a human being. And I want to say further that while some moral judgments are involved in determining whether the fetus is a human being, still, the crucial question about the fetus is not "How much is it worth?" but "What is it?"

The defense of the extreme conservative position runs as follows. The key premise is that a human fetus is a human being, not a partial or potential one, but a full-fledged, actualized human life. Given that premise, the entire conservative position unfolds with a simple, relentless logic, every principle of which would be endorsed by any sensible liberal. Suppose human embryos are human beings. Their innocence is beyond question, so nothing could justify our destroying them except, perhaps, the necessity of saving some other innocent human life. That is, since similar cases must be treated in similar ways, some consideration would justify the abortion of a prenatal child if and only if a comparable consideration would justify the killing of a postnatal child.

This is a serious and troubling argument posing an objection in principle to abortion. It is the *only* such argument. Nothing else could possibly justify the staggering social costs of the present abortion laws.

It should be unmistakably obvious what the Catholic position is. Yet, and this deserves heavy emphasis, liberals seem not to understand it, for their arguments are almost invariably infelicitous. The Catholic defense of the status quo is left unfazed, even untouched, by the standard liberal critique that consists of an inventory of the calamitous effects of our abortion laws on mother and child, on family, and on society in general. Of course, were it not for those effects we would feel no press to be rid of the laws—nor any *need* to retain them. That inventory does present a conclusive rebuttal of any of the piddling objections conservatives often toss in for good measure. But still, the precise, scientific tabulations of grief do not add up to an argument here, for sometimes pain, no matter how considerable and how undesirable, may not be avoidable, may not stem from some injustice. I do not intend to understate that pain; the tragedies brought on by unwanted children are plentiful and serious—but so too are those brought on by unwanted parents, yet few liberals would legalize parricide as the final solution to the massive social problem of the permanently visiting parent who drains his children's financial and emotional resources. In the Church's view, these cases are fully analogous: the fetus is as much a human life as is the parent; they share the same moral status. Either can be a source of abiding anguish and hardship for the other—and sometimes there may be no escape. In this, our world, some people get stuck with the care of others, and sometimes there may be no way of getting unstuck, at least no just and decent way. Taking the other person's life is not such a way.

The very elegance of the Catholic response is maddening. The ease with which it sweeps into irrelevance the whole catalogue of sorrow has incited many a liberal libel of the Catholic clergy as callous and unfeeling monsters, denied domestic empathy by their celibacy and the simplest human sympathies by their unnatural asceticism. Of course, slander is no substitute for argument—that's what the logic books say—and yet, we cast our aspersions with care, for they must deprive the audience of the *right* to believe the speaker. What wants explanation, then, is why the particular accusation of a *warped sensibility* seems, to the liberal, both just and pertinent. I shall come back to this. For the moment, it suffices to record that the liberal's accusation attests to a misunderstanding of the Catholic defense, for it is singularly inappropriate to label a man heartless who wants only to protect innocent human lives at all costs.

There is a subsidiary approach, a peculiarly liberal one, which seeks to disarm the Catholic position not by disputing it, but by conceding the Catholic's right to believe it and act accordingly. The liberal asks only that Catholics concede him the same freedom, and thus abandon support of abortion laws. The Catholic must retort that the issue is not, as the liberal supposes, one of religious ritual and self-regarding behavior, but of minority rights, the minority being not Catholics but the fetuses of all faiths, and the right being the right of an innocent human being to life itself. The liberal's proposal is predicated on abortion being a crime without a victim, but in the Catholic view the fetus is a full-scale victim and is so independent of the liberal's recognition of that fact. Catholics can no more think it wrong for themselves but permissible for Protestants to destroy a fetus than liberals can think it wrong for themselves but permissible for racists to victimize blacks. Given his premise, the Catholic is as justified in employing the power of the state to protect embryos as the liberal is to protect blacks. I shall be returning to this analogy, because the favored defense of slavery and discrimination takes the form of a claim that the subjugated creatures are by nature inferior to their masters, that they are *not fully human.*

Now, why do liberals, even the cleverest ones, so consistently fail to make contact with the Catholic challenge? After all, as I have made plain, once premised that the fetus is a person, the entire conservative position recites the common sense of any moral man. The liberal's failure is, I suggest, due to that premise. He doesn't know how to respond to the argument, because he cannot *make sense* of that premise. To him, it is not simply false, but wildly, madly false, it is nonsense, totally unintelligible, literally unbelievable. Just look at an embryo. It is an amorphous speck of apparently coagulated protoplasm. It has no eyes or ears, no head at all. It can't walk or talk; you can't dress it or wash it. Why, it doesn't even qualify as a Barbie doll, and yet millions of people call it a human being, just like one of us. It's as though someone were to look at an acorn and call it an oak tree, or, better, it's as though someone squirted a paint tube at a canvas and called the outcome a painting, a work of art—and people believed him. The whole thing is precisely that mad—and just that sane. The liberal is befuddled by the conservative's argument, just as Giotto would be were he to assess a Pollock production as a *painting.* If the premises make no sense, then neither will the rest of the argument, except as an exercise in abstract logic.

The Catholic claim would be a joke were it not that millions of people take it seriously, and millions more suffer for their solemnity. Liberals need an explanation of how it is possible for the conservatives to believe what they say, for after all, conservatives are not ignorant or misinformed about the facts here—I mean, for example, the facts of embryology. So the liberal asks, "How *can* they believe what they say? How *can* they even make sense of it?" The question is forced upon the liberal because his conception of rationality is jeopardized by the possibility that a normal, unbiased observer of the relevant facts could really accept the conservative claim. It is this question, I think, that drives the liberal to attribute the whole antiabortion movement to Catholicism and to the Roman clergy in particular. For it is comforting to suppose that the conservative beliefs could take root only in a mind that had been carefully cultivated since infancy to support every extravagant dogma of an arcane theology fathered by the victims of unnatural and unhealthy lives. But, discomforting though it may be, people, and not just Catholics, can and sometimes do agree on all the facts about embryos and still disagree as to whether they are persons. Indeed, apparently people can agree on *every* fact and still disagree on whether it is a fact that embryos are human beings. So now one might begin to wonder: What sort of fact is it?

I hasten to add that not only can both parties agree on the scientific facts, they need not disagree on any supernatural facts either. The conservative claim does not presuppose that we are invested with a soul, some sort of divine substance, at or shortly after our conception. No doubt it helps to have one's mind befogged by visions of holy hocus-pocus, but it's not necessary, since some unmuddled atheists endorse a demythologized Catholic view. Moreover, since ensoulment is an unverifiable occurrence, the theologian dates it either by means of some revelation—which, by the way, the Church does not (though some of its parishioners may accept the humanity of embryos on the Church's say-so)—or by means of the same scientifically acceptable data by which his atheistical counterpart gauges the emergence of an unbesouled human life (e.g., that at such and such a time the organism is capable of independent life, or is motile).

The religious position derives its plausibility from independent secular considerations. It serves as an expression of them, not as a substitute for them. In brief, here as elsewhere, talk about souls involves an unnecessary shuffle. Yet, though unnecessary, admittedly it is not without effect, for such conceptions color our perceptions and attitudes toward the world and thereby give sense and substance to certain arguments whose secular translations lack appeal. To take a pertinent instance, the official Church position (not the one believed by most of the laity or used against the liberals, but the official position) is that precisely because ensoulment is an unverifiable occurrence, we can't locate it with certainty, and hence abortion at any stage involves the *risk* of destroying a human life. But first off, it is doubtful whether this claim can support the practical conclusions the Catholic draws. For even if it is true, is abortion an *unwarrantable* risk? Always? Is it morally indefensible to fire a pistol into an uninspected barrel? After all, a child *might* be hiding in it. Secondly, though this argument has no attractive secular version, still, it derives its appeal from profane considerations. For what is it that so much as makes it seem that a blastocyst *might* be a person? If the conception of being besouled is cut loose from the conception of being human *sans* soul, then a human soul might reside in anything at all (or at least any living thing), and then the destruction of anything (or any living thing) would involve the risk of killing someone.

I have said that the argument from risk has no secular counterpart. But why not? Well, for example, what sense would it make to the liberal to suppose that an embryo *might* be a person? Are there any discoveries that are really (not just logically) possible which would lead him to admit he was mistaken? It is not a *hypothesis* for the liberal that embryos are not persons; *mutatis mutandis* for the conservative.

At this juncture of the argument, a liberal with a positivistic background will announce that it's just a matter of definition whether the fetus is a person. If by this the liberal means that the question "Is a fetus a person?" is equivalent to "Is it proper to call a fetus a person?"—that is, "Is it true to say of a fetus, 'It is a person'?"—then the liberal is quite right and quite unhelpful. But he is likely to add that we can define words any way we like. And that is either true and unhelpful or flatly false. For note, both liberals and conservatives think it wrong to kill an innocent person except when other human lives would be lost. So neither party will reform its speech habits regarding the fetus unless that moral principle is reworded in a way that vouchsafes its position on abortion. Any stipulated definition can be recommended only by appealing to the very matters under dispute. Any such definition will therefore fail of universal acceptance and thus only mask the real issues, unless it is a mere systematic symbol switch. In brief, agreement on a definition will be a consequence of, not a substitute for, agreement on the facts.

A more sophisticated liberal may suggest that fetuses are borderline cases. Asking whether fetuses are persons is like asking whether viruses are living creatures; the proper answer is that they are like them in some ways but not in others; the rules of the language don't dictate one way or the other, so you can say what you will. Yet this suggests that we share a single concept of a human being, one with a fuzzy or multifaceted boundary that would make any normal person feel indecision about whether a fetus is a human being, and would enable that person, however he decided, to understand readily how someone else might decide otherwise. But at best this describes only the minds of moderates. Liberals and conservatives suffer little indecision, and, further, they are enigmatic to one another, both intellectually and as whole persons. And finally, precisely because with the virus you can say what you will, it is unlike the fetus. As regards the virus, scientists can manage nicely while totally ignoring the issue. Not so with the fetus, because deciding what to call it is tantamount to a serious and unavoidable moral decision.

This last remark suggests that the fetus' humanity is really a moral issue, not a factual one at all. But I submit that if one insists on using that raggy fact-value distinction, then one ought to say that the dispute is over a matter of fact in the sense in which it is a fact that the Negro slaves were human beings. But it would be better to say that this dispute calls that distinction into question. To see this, let us look at how people actually argue about when a human life begins.

The liberal dates hominization from birth or viability. The choice of either stage is explicable by reference to some obvious considerations. At birth the child leaves its own private space and enters the public world. And he can be looked at and acted upon and interacted with. And so on. On the other hand, someone may say viability is the crucial point, because it is then that the child has the capacity to do all those things it does at birth; the sole difference is a quite inessential one of geography.

Now note about both of these sets of considerations that they are not used as proofs or parts of proofs that human life begins at birth or at viability. What would the major premise of such a proof be? The liberal does not—nor does anyone else—have a rule of the language or a definition of "human life" from which it follows that if the organism has such and such properties, then it is a human life. True, some people have tried to state the essence of human life and argue from that definition, but the correctness of any such definition must first be tested against our judgments of particular cases, and on some of those judgments people disagree; so the argument using such a definition which tries to settle that disagreement can only beg the question. Thus, it seems more accurate to say simply that the kinds of considerations I have mentioned explain why the liberal chooses to date human life in a certain way. More accurately still, I don't think the liberal chooses or decides at all; rather, he looks at certain facts and he responds in a particular way to those facts: he dates human life from birth or from viability—and he acts and feels accordingly. There is nothing surprising in such behavior, nor anything irrational or illegitimate.

All this can be said of any of the considerations that have been used to mark the beginning of a human life.

Liberals always misplace the attractions of fertilization as the critical date when they try to argue that if you go back that far, you could just as well call the sperm or the egg a human being. But people call the zygote a human life not just because it contains the DNA blueprint which determines the physical development of the organism from then on, and not just because of the potential inherent in it, but also because it and it alone can claim to be the beginning of the spatio-temporal-causal chain of the physical object that is a human body. And though I think the abortion controversy throws doubt on the claim that bodily continuity is the *sole* criterion of personal identity, I think the attractions of that philosophical thesis are of a piece with the attractions of fertilization as the point marking the start of a person. Given our conceptual framework, one can't go back further. Neither the sperm nor the egg could be, by itself, a human being, any more than an atom of sodium or an atom of chlorine could by itself properly be called salt. One proof of this is that *no one* is in the least inclined to call a sperm or an egg a human life, a fact acknowledged by the liberal's very argument, which has the form of a *reductio ad absurdum*.

These are some of the considerations, but how are they actually presented? What, for example, does the liberal say and do? Note that his arguments are usually formulated as a series of rhetorical questions. He points to certain facts, and then, quite understandably, he expects his listeners to respond in a particular way—and when they don't, he finds their behavior incomprehensible. First he will point to an infant and say, "Look at it! Aren't you inclined to say that it is one of us?" And then he will describe an embryo as I did earlier, and say, "Look at the difference between it and us! Could you call that a human being?" All this is quite legitimate, but notice what the liberal is doing. First, he has us focus our attention on the *earliest stages* of the fetus, where the contrast with us is greatest. He does not have us look at the fetus shortly before viability or birth, where the differences between it and what he is willing to call a human being are quite minimal. Still, this is not an unfair tactic when combating the view that the fertilized egg is a human life. The other side of this maneuver is that he has us compare the embryo with *us adults*. This seems fair in that we are our own best paradigms of a person. If you and I aren't to be called human beings, then what is? And yet the liberal would not say that a young child or a neonate or even a viable fetus is to be called a human life only in an extended sense. He wants to say that the infant at birth or the viable fetus is a one hundred percent human being, but, again, the differences between a neonate and a viable fetus or between a viable fetus and a soon-to-be-viable fetus are not impressive.

The liberal has one other arrow in his meager quiver. He will say that if you call an embryo a human life, then presumably you think it is a valuable entity. But, he adds, what does it have that is of any value? Its biochemical potential to become one of us doesn't ensure that it itself is of any real value, especially if neither the mother nor any other interested party wants it to fulfill that potential.

When liberals say that an embryo is of no value if no one has a good reason to want to do anything but destroy it, I think they are on firm ground. But the conservative is not saying that the embryo has some really nifty property, so precious that it's a horrid waste to destroy it. No, he is saying that the embryo is a human being and it is wrong to kill human beings, and that is why you must not destroy the embryo. The conservative realizes that, unless he uses religious premises, premises inadmissible in the court of common morality, he has no way of categorically condemning the killing of a fetus except by arguing that a fetus is a person. And he doesn't call it a human being because its properties are valuable. The properties it has which make it a human being may be valuable, but he does not claim that it is their value which makes it a human being. Rather he argues that it is a human being by turning the liberal's argument inside out.

The conservative points, and keeps pointing, to the similarities between each set of successive stages of fetal development, instead of pointing, as the liberal does, to the gross differences between widely separated stages. Each step of his argument is persuasive, but if this were all there was to it, his total argument would be no more compelling than one which traded on the fuzziness of the boundaries of baldness and the arbitrariness of any sharp line of demarcation to conclude that Richard M. Nixon is glabrous. If this were the whole conservative argument, then it would be open to the liberal's *reductio* argument, which says that if you go back as far as the zygote, the sperm and the egg must also be called persons. But in fact the conservative can stop at the zygote; fertilization does seem to be a nonarbitrary point marking the inception of a particular object, a human body. That is, the conservative has independent reasons for picking the date of conception, just like the liberal who picks the date of birth or viability, and unlike the sophist who concludes that Nixon is bald.

But we still don't have the whole conservative argument, for on the basis of what has been said so far the conservative should also call an acorn an oak tree, but he doesn't, and the reason he uses is that, as regards a human life, it would be *morally* arbitrary to use any date other than that of conception. That is, he can ask liberals to name the earliest stage at which they are willing to call the organism a human being, something which may not be killed for any reason short of saving some other human life. The conservative will then take the stage of development immediately preceding the one the liberals choose and challenge them to point to a difference between the two stages, a difference that is a morally relevant difference.

Suppose the liberal picks the date of birth. Yet a newborn infant is only a fetus that has suffered a change of address and some physiological changes like respiration. A neonate delivered in its twenty-fifth week lies in an incubator physically less well developed and no more independent than a normal fetus in its thirty-seventh week in the womb. What difference is there that can be used to justify killing the prenatal child where it would be wrong to kill the postnatal child?

Or suppose the liberal uses the date of viability. But the viability of a fetus is its capacity to survive outside the mother, and *that* is totally relative to the state of the available medical technology. In principle, eventually the fetus may be deliverable at any time, perhaps even at conception. The problems this poses for liberals are obvious, and in fact one finds that either a liberal doesn't understand what viability really is, so that he takes it to be necessarily linked to the later fetal stages; or he is an extreme liberal in disguise, who is playing along with the first kind of liberal for political purposes; or he has abandoned the viability criterion and is madly scurrying about in search of some other factor in the late fetal stages which might serve as a nonarbitrary cutoff point. But I am inclined to suppose that the conservative is right, that going back stage by stage from the infant to the zygote one will not find any differences between successive stages significant enough to bear the enormous moral burden of allowing wholesale slaughter at the earlier stage while categorically denying that permission at the next stage.

The full power and persuasiveness of the conservative argument is still not revealed until we uncover its similarities to and connections with any of the dialectical devices that have been used to widen a man's recognition of his fellowship with all the members of his biological species. It is a matter of record that men of good will have often failed to recognize that a certain class of fellow creatures were really human beings just like themselves.

To take but one example, the history of Negro slavery includes among the white oppressors men who were, in all other regards, essentially just and decent. Many such men sincerely defended their practice of slavery with the claim that the Negro was not a member of the moral community of men. Not only legally, but also conceptually, for the white master, the Negro was property, livestock. He would be inclined to, and actually did, simply point to the Negroes and say: "Look at them! Can't you see the differences between them and us?" And the fact is that at one time that argument had an undeniable power, as undeniable as the perceptual differences it appealed to. Check your own perceptions. Ask yourself whether you really, in a purely phenomenological sense, *see* a member of another race in the same way you see a member of your own. Why is it that all Chinamen look alike and are so inscrutable? Add to the physiological facts the staggering cultural disparities dividing slave and master, and you may start to sense the force of the master's argument. What has been the rebuttal? We point to the similarities between Negro and white, and then step by step describe the differences and show about each one that it is not a morally relevant difference, not the kind of difference that warrants discriminating against a Negro.

The parallels with the abortion controversy are palpable. Let me extend them some more. First, sometimes a disagreement over a creature's humanity does turn on beliefs about subsidiary matters of fact—but it need not. Further, when it does not, when the disagreement develops from differing responses to the same data, the issue is still a factual one and not a matter of taste. It is not that one party prefers or approves of or has a favorable attitude or emotion toward some property, while the other party does not. Our response concerns what the thing is, not whether we like it or whether it is good. And when I say I don't *care* about the color of a man's skin, that it's not *important* to me, I am saying something quite different than when I say I don't care about the color of a woman's hair. I am saying that this property cannot be used to justify discriminatory behavior or social arrangements. It cannot be so used because it is irrelevant; neither black skin nor white skin is, in and of itself, of any value. The slaveholder's response is not that white skin is of intrinsic value. Rather, he replies that people with naturally black skin are niggers, and that is an inferior kind of creature. So too, the liberal does not claim that infants possess some intrinsically valuable attribute lacked by prenatal children. Rather, he says that a prenatal child is a fetus, not a human being.

Roger Wertheimer

In brief, when seen in its totality the conservative's argument *is* the liberal's argument turned completely inside out. While the liberal stresses the differences between disparate stages, the conservative stresses the resemblances between consecutive stages. The liberal asks, "What has a zygote got that is valuable?" and the conservative answers, "Nothing, but it's a human being, so it is wrong to abort it." Then the conservative asks, "What does a fetus lack that an infant has that is so valuable?" and the liberal answers, "Nothing, but it's a fetus, not a human being, so it is all right to abort it." The arguments are equally strong and equally weak, for they are the *same* argument, an argument that can be pointed in either of two directions. The argument does not itself point in either direction: it is *we* who must point it, and we who are led by it. If you are led in one direction rather than the other, that is not because of logic, but because you respond in a certain way to certain facts.

Recall that the arguments are usually formulated in the interrogative, not the indicative, mood. Though the answers are supposed to be absolutely obvious, they are not comfortably assertible. Why? Because an assertion is a truth claim which invites a request for a proof, but here any assertible proof presupposes premises which beg the question. If one may speak of proof here, it can lie only in the audience's response, in their acceptance of the answer and of its obviousness. The questions convince by leading us to appreciate familiar facts. The conclusion is validated not through assertible presuppositions, but through our acknowledgement that the questions are *rhetorical*. You might say that the conclusion is our seeing a certain aspect: e.g., we see the embryo as a human being. But this seems an unduly provocative description of the situation, for what is at issue is whether such an aspect is there to be seen.

Evidently, we have here a paradigm of what Wittgenstein had in mind when he spoke of the possibility of two people agreeing on the application of a rule for a long period, and then, suddenly and quite inexplicably, diverging in what they call going on in the same way. This possibility led him to insist that linguistic communication presupposes not only agreement in definitions, but also agreement in judgments, in what he called forms of life—something that seems lacking in the case at hand. Apparently, the conclusion to draw is that it is not true that the fetus is a human being, but it is not false either. Without an agreement in judgments, without a common response to the pertinent data, the assertion that the fetus is a human being cannot be assigned a genuine truth-value.

Yet, we surely want to say that Negroes are and always have been full-fledged human beings, no matter what certain segments of mankind may have thought, and no matter how numerous or unanimous those segments were. The humanity of the slaves seems unlike that of the fetus, but not because by now a monolithic majority recognizes—however grudgingly—the full human status of Negroes, whereas no position regarding the fetus commands more than a plurality. The mere fact of disagreement in judgments or forms of life would not render unsettleable statements about the humanity of fetuses, otherwise the comparable statements about Negroes, or for that matter whites, would meet a similar fate. What seems special about the fetus is that, apparently, we have no vantage point from which to criticize opposing systems of belief.

It will be said by some that a form of life is something not really criticizable by or from an opposing form of life. In this instance the point is without practical relevance, since the differences between the disputants are not so systematic and entire as to block every avenue of rational discussion. Clearly, their communality is very great, their differences relatively isolated and free-floating.

At this stage of the dispute over a creature's humanity, I stand to the slaveholder in roughly the same relation I stand to the color-blind man who judges this sheet of paper to be gray. Our differing color judgments express our differing immediate responses to the same data. But his color judgment is mistaken because his vision is defective. I criticize his judgment by criticizing him, by showing him to be abnormal, deviant—which is not the same as being in the minority. In a like manner we criticize those basic beliefs and attitudes which sanction and are sustained by the slaveholder's form of life. We argue that his form of life is, so to speak, an accident of history, explicable by reference to special socio-psychological circumstances that are inessential to the natures of blacks and whites. The fact that Negroes *can* and, special circumstances aside, naturally *would* be regarded and treated no differently than Caucasians is at once a necessary and a sufficient condition for its being right to so regard and treat them. Thus, while we may in large measure understand the life-style of the slaveholder and perhaps withhold condemnation of the man, we need not and should not condone his behavior.

Liberals and conservatives rail at each other with this same canonical schema. And if, for example, antiabortionism required the perverting of natural reason and normal sensibilities by a system of superstitions, then the liberal could discredit it—but it doesn't, so he can't. As things stand, it is not at all clear what, if anything, is the normal or natural or healthy response toward the fetus; it is not clear what is to count as the special historical and social circumstances, which, if removed, would leave us with the appropriate way to regard and treat the fetus. And I think that the unlimited possibility of natural *responses* is simply the other side of the fact of severely limited possibilities of natural *relationships* with the fetus. After all, there isn't much we can do with a fetus; either we let it out or we do it in. I have little hope of seeing a justification for doing one thing or the other unless this situation changes. As things stand, the range of interactions is so minimal that we are not compelled to regard the fetus in any particular way. For example, respect for a fetus cannot be wrung from us as respect for a Negro can be and is, unless we are irretrievably warped or stunted.

We seem to be stuck with the indeterminateness of the fetus' humanity. This does not mean that, whatever you believe, it is true or true for you if you believe it. Quite the contrary, it means that, whatever you believe, it's not true—but neither is it false. You believe it, and that's the end of the matter.

But obviously that's not the end of the matter; the same urgent moral and political decisions still confront us. But before we run off to make our existential leaps over the liberal-conservative impasse, we might meander through the moderate position. I'll shorten the trip by speaking only of features found throughout the spectrum of moderate views. For the moderate, the fetus is not a human being, but it's not a mere maternal appendage either; it's a human fetus, and it has a separate moral status just as animals do. A fetus is not an object that we can treat however we wish, neither is it a person whom we must treat as we would wish to be treated in return. Thus, *some* legal prohibitions on abortions *might* be justified in the name of the fetus *qua* human fetus, just as we accord some legal protection to animals, not for the sake of the owners, but for the benefit of the animals themselves.

Ultimately, most liberals and conservatives are, in a sense, only extreme moderates. Few liberals really regard abortion, at least in the later stages, as a bit of elective surgery. Suppose a woman had her fifth-month fetus aborted purely out of curiosity as to what it looked like, and perhaps then had it bronzed. Who among us would not deem both her and her actions reprehensible? One might refuse to outlaw the behavior, but still, clearly we do not respond to this case as we would to the removal of an appendix or a tooth. Similarly, in my experience few of even the staunchest conservatives consistently regard the fetus, at least in the earlier stages, in the same way as they do a fellow adult. When the cause of grief is a miscarriage, the object of grief is the mother; rarely does anyone feel pity or sorrow for the embryo itself. Nevertheless, enough people give enough substance to the liberal and conservative positions to justify describing them as I have done as views differing in kind rather than degree.

The moderate position is as problematic as it is popular. The moderate is driven in two directions, liberalism and conservatism, by the very same question: Why do you make these exceptions and not those?

The difficulty here is comparable to that regarding animals. There are dogs, pigs, mosquitoes, worms, bacteria, etc., and we kill them for food, clothing, ornamentation, sport, convenience, and out of simple irritation or unblinking inadvertence. We allow different animals to be killed for different reasons, and there are enormous differences between people on all of this. In general, for most of us, the higher the evolutionary stage of the species or the later the developmental stage of the fetus, the more restricted our permission to kill. But it is far more complicated than that, and anyone with a fully consistent, let alone principled, system of beliefs on these matters is usually thought fanatical by the rest of us.

To stabilize his position, the moderate would have to *invent* a new set of moral categories and principles. A happy amalgamation of the ones we have won't do, because our principles of justice apply solely to the relations between persons. But *how* is one to invent new categories and principles? I'm not sure it can be done, especially with the scanty building materials available. Again, our interactions with fetuses are extremely limited and peripheral, which is why our normative conceptual machinery in this area is so abbreviated, unformed, and up for grabs.

But perhaps this could be otherwise. Close your eyes for a moment and imagine that, due to advances in medical technology or mutation caused by a nuclear war, the relevant cutaneous and membranous shields became transparent from conception to parturition, so that when a mother put aside her modesty and her clothing the developing fetus would be in full public view. Or suppose instead, or in addition, that anyone could at any time pluck a fetus from its womb, air it, observe it, fondle it, and then stick it back in after a few minutes. And we could further suppose that this made for healthier babies, and so maybe laws would be passed requiring that it be done regularly. And we might also imagine that gestation took nine days rather than nine months. What then would we think of aborting a fetus? What would *you* think of aborting it? And what does that say about what you *now* think?

In my experience, when such imaginative exercises are properly presented, people are often, not always, moved by them, different people by different stories. They begin to talk about all of it somewhat differently than they had before, and less differently from each other. However, the role of such conjectures in or as arguments is far from clear. I don't think we discover the justifications for our beliefs by such a procedure. A liberal who is disturbed by the picture of a transparent womb may be acquiring some self-knowledge; he may come to realize how much power being visible and being hidden have for us and for him, and he may make a connection between this situation and the differing experiences of an infantryman and a bombardier. But surely the fetus' being hidden was not the liberal's *reason* for thinking it expendable.

Nor is it evident that such *Gedanken* experiments reveal the causes of our beliefs. Their results seem too unreliable to provide anything but the grossest projections as to how we would in fact react in the imagined situations. When I present myself with such science fiction fantasies, I am inclined to respond as I do to a question posed by Hilary Putnam:[1] If we build robots with a psychology isomorphic with ours and a physical structure comparable to ours, should we award them civil rights? In contrast to Putnam, who thinks we can now give a more disinterested and hence objective answer to this question, I would say that our present answer, whatever it is, is so disinterested as to count for nothing. It seems to me that such questions about the robot or the fetus can't be answered in advance. This seems so for much the same reason that some things, especially regarding moral matters, can't be told to a child. A child can of course hear the words and operate with them, but he will not really understand them without undergoing certain experiences, and maybe not even then. Odd as it may sound, I want to know exactly what the robot looks like and what it's like to live with it. I want to know how in fact we—how I—look at it, respond to it, and feel toward it. Hypothetical situations of this sort raise questions which seem answerable only when the situation is realized, and perhaps then there is no longer a real question.

I am suggesting that what our natural response to a thing is, how we naturally react to it cognitively, affectively, and behaviorally, is partly definitive of that thing, and is therefore partly definitive of how we ought to respond to that thing. Often only an actual confrontation will tell us what we need to know, and

[1]Hilary Putnam, "Robots: Machines or Artificially Created Life?" The *Journal of Philosophy* 61, no. 21 (1964): 668–691.

sometimes we may each respond differently, and thus have differing understandings.

Moreover, the relation of such hypothetical situations to our actual situation is problematic. My hunch is that if the fetal condition I described were realized, fewer of us would be liberals and more of us would be conservatives and moderates. But suppose that in fact we would all be hidebound conservatives and that we knew that now. Would a contemporary liberal be irrational, unjustified, or wicked if he remained adamant? Well, if a slaveholder with a conscience were shown why he feels about Negroes as he does, and that he would regard them as his equals if only he had not been reared to think otherwise, he might change his ways, and if he didn't I would unhesitatingly call him irrational and his behavior unjustified and wicked.

But now suppose that dogs or chimps could and did talk so that they entered our lives in more significant roles than those of experimental tools, friendly playthings, or faithful servants, and we enacted antivivisectionist legislation. If we discovered all this now, the news might deeply stir us, but would we necessarily be wrong if we still used animals as we do? Here, so I am inclined to think, we might sensibly maintain that in the hypothetical case the animals and their relations with us are essentially and relevantly different from what they now are. The capacities may exist now, but their realization constitutes a crucial change like that from an infant to an adult, and unlike that from a slave to a citizen. We would no more need to revise our treatment of animals than we need to apply the same principles of reciprocity to children and adults.

In the abortion case my instincts are similar but shakier. Yet I think that the adamant liberal could reply that what is special about fetuses, what distinguishes them from babies, slaves, animals, robots, and the rest, is that they essentially are and relate to us as bundles of potentialities. So, obviously, if their potentialities were actualized, not singly or partially, but in sufficient number and degree, we would feel differently. But to make them and their situation in respect to us different enough so that we would naturally regard them as human beings, they would have to become what they can become: human beings. In the hypothetical situation, they are babies in a biological incubator, and therefore that situation is irrelevant to our situation. In brief, an argument based on such a situation only restates the conservative's original argument with imaginary changes instead of the actual set of changes which transforms the fetus into a human child.

a defense of abortion[1]

judith jarvis thomson

Most opposition to abortion relies on the premise that the fetus is a human being, a person, from the moment of conception. The premise is argued for, but, as I think, not well. Take, for example, the most common argument. We are asked to notice that the development of a human being from conception through birth into childhood is continuous; then it is said that to draw a line, to choose a point in this development and say "before this point the thing is not a person, after this point it is a person" is to make an arbitrary choice, a choice for which in the nature of things no good reason can be given. It is concluded that the fetus is, or anyway that we had better say it is, a person from the moment of conception. But this conclusion does not follow. Similar things might be said about the development of an acorn into an oak tree, and it does not follow that acorns are oak trees, or that we had better say they are. Arguments of this form are sometimes called "slippery slope arguments"—the phrase is perhaps self-explanatory—and it is dismaying that opponents of abortion rely on them so heavily and uncritically.

From Judith Jarvis Thomson, "A Defense of Abortion," *Philosophy and Public Affairs*, vol. 1, no. 1 (copyright © 1971 by Princeton University Press), pp. 47–66. Reprinted by permission of Princeton University Press.

[1] I am very much indebted to James Thomson for discussion, criticism, and many helpful suggestions.

I am inclined to agree, however, that the prospects for "drawing a line" in the development of the fetus look dim. I am inclined to think also that we shall probably have to agree that the fetus has already become a human person well before birth. Indeed, it comes as a surprise when one first learns how early in its life it begins to acquire human characteristics. By the tenth week, for example, it already has a face, arms and legs, fingers and toes; it has internal organs, and brain activity is detectable.[2] On the other hand, I think that the premise is false, that the fetus is not a person from the moment of conception. A newly fertilized ovum, a newly implanted clump of cells, is no more a person than an acorn is an oak tree. But I shall not discuss any of this. For it seems to me to be of great interest to ask what happens if, for the sake of argument, we allow the premise. How, precisely, are we supposed to get from there to the conclusion that abortion is morally impermissible? Opponents of abortion commonly spend most of their time establishing that the fetus is a person, and hardly any time explaining the step from there to the impermissibility of abortion. Perhaps they think the step too simple and obvious to require much comment. Or perhaps instead they are simply being economical in argument. Many of those who defend abortion rely on the premise that the fetus is not a person, but only a bit of tissue that will become a person at birth; and why pay out more arguments than you have to? Whatever the explanation, I suggest that the step they take is neither easy nor obvious, that it calls for closer examination than it is commonly given, and that when we do give it this closer examination we shall feel inclined to reject it.

I propose, then, that we grant that the fetus is a person from the moment of conception. How does the argument go from here? Something like this, I take it. Every person has a right to life. So the fetus has a right to life. No doubt the mother has a right to decide what shall happen in and to her body; everyone would grant that. But surely a person's right to life is stronger and more stringent than the mother's right to decide what happens in and to her body, and so outweighs it. So the fetus may not be killed; an abortion may not be performed.

It sounds plausible. But now let me ask you to imagine this. You wake up in the morning and find yourself back to back in bed with an unconscious violinist. A famous unconscious violinist. He

---

[2]Daniel Callahan, *Abortion: Law, Choice and Morality* (New York, 1970), p. 373. This book gives a fascinating survey of the available information on abortion. The Jewish tradition is surveyed in David M Feldman, *Birth Control in Jewish Law* (New York, 1968), part 5, the Catholic tradition in John T. Noonan, Jr., "An Almost Absolute Value in History," in *The Morality of Abortion*, ed. John T. Noonan, Jr. (Cambridge, Mass., 1970).

has been found to have a fatal kidney ailment, and the Society of Music Lovers has canvassed all the available medical records and found that you alone have the right blood type to help. They have therefore kidnapped you, and last night the violinist's circulatory system was plugged into yours, so that your kidneys can be used to extract poisons from his blood as well as your own. The director of the hospital now tells you, "Look, we're sorry the Society of Music Lovers did this to you—we would never have permitted it if we had known. But still, they did it, and the violinist now is plugged into you. To unplug you would be to kill him. But never mind, it's only for nine months. By then he will have recovered from his ailment, and can safely be unplugged from you." Is it morally incumbent on you to accede to this situation? No doubt it would be very nice of you if you did, a great kindness. But do you *have* to accede to it? What if it were not nine months, but nine years? Or longer still? What if the director of the hospital says, "Tough luck, I agree, but you've now got to stay in bed, with the violinist plugged into you, for the rest of your life. Because remember this. All persons have a right to life, and violinists are persons. Granted you have a right to decide what happens in and to your body, but a person's right to life outweighs your right to decide what happens in and to your body. So you cannot ever be unplugged from him." I imagine you would regard this as outrageous, which suggests that something really is wrong with that plausible-sounding argument I mentioned a moment ago.

In this case, of course, you were kidnapped; you didn't volunteer for the operation that plugged the violinist into your kidneys. Can those who oppose abortion on the ground I mentioned make an exception for a pregnancy due to rape? Certainly. They can say that persons have a right to life only if they didn't come into existence because of rape; or they can say that all persons have a right to life, but that some have less of a right to life than others, in particular, that those who came into existence because of rape have less. But these statements have a rather unpleasant sound Surely the question of whether you have a right to life at all, or how much of it you have, shouldn't turn on the question of whether or not you are the product of a rape. And in fact the people who oppose abortion on the ground I mentioned do not make this distinction, and hence do not make an exception in case of rape.

Nor do they make an exception for a case in which the mother has to spend the nine months of her pregnancy in bed. They would agree that would be a great pity, and hard on the mother; but all the same, all persons have a right to life, the fetus is a person, and so on. I suspect, in fact, that they would not make an exception for a case in which, miraculously enough, the pregnancy went on for nine years, or even the rest of the mother's life.

Some won't even make an exception for a case in which continuation of the pregnancy is likely to shorten the mother's life; they regard abortion as impermissible even to save the mother's life. Such cases are nowadays very rare, and many opponents of abortion do not accept this extreme view. All the same, it is a good place to begin: a number of points of interest come out in respect to it.

1. Let us call the view that abortion is impermissible even to save the mother's life "the extreme view." I want to suggest first that it does not issue from the argument I mentioned earlier without the addition of some fairly powerful premises. Suppose a woman has become pregnant, and now learns that she has a cardiac condition such that she will die if she carries the baby to term. What may be done for her? The fetus, being a person, has a right to life, but as the mother is a person too, so has she a right to life. Presumably they have an equal right to life. How is it supposed to come out that an abortion may not be performed? If mother and child have an equal right to life, shouldn't we perhaps flip a coin? Or should we add to the mother's right to life her right to decide what happens in and to her body, which everybody seems to be ready to grant—the sum of her rights now outweighing the fetus' right to life?

The most familiar argument here is the following. We are told that performing the abortion would be directly killing[3] the child, whereas doing nothing would not be killing the mother, but only letting her die. Moreover, in killing the child, one would be killing an innocent person, for the child has committed no crime, and is not aiming at his mother's death. And then there are a variety of ways in which this might be continued. (1) But as directly killing an innocent person is always and absolutely impermissible, an abortion may not be performed. Or, (2) as directly killing an innocent person is murder, and murder is always and absolutely impermissible, an abortion may not be performed.[4] Or, (3) as one's

[3]The term "direct" in the arguments I refer to is a technical one. Roughly, what is meant by "direct killing" is either killing as an end in itself, or killing as a means to some end, for example, the end of saving someone else's life. See note 6, below, for an example of its use.
[4]Cf. *Encyclical Letter of Pope Pius XI on Christian Marriage*, St. Paul Editions (Boston, n.d.), p. 32: "however much we may pity the mother whose health and even life is gravely imperiled in the performance of the duty allotted to her by nature, nevertheless what could ever be a sufficient reason for excusing in any way the direct murder of the innocent? This is precisely what we are dealing with here." Noonan (*The Morality of Abortion*, p. 43) reads this as follows: "What cause can ever avail to excuse in any way the direct killing of the innocent? For it is a question of that."

duty to refrain from directly killing an innocent person is more stringent than one's duty to keep a person from dying, an abortion may not be performed. Or, (4) if one's only options are directly killing an innocent person or letting a person die, one must prefer letting the person die, and thus an abortion may not be performed.[5]

Some people seem to have thought that these are not further premises which must be added if the conclusion is to be reached, but that they follow from the very fact that an innocent person has a right to life.[6] But this seems to me to be a mistake, and perhaps the simplest way to show this is to bring out that while we must certainly grant that innocent persons have a right to life, the theses in (1) through (4) are all false. Take (2), for example. If directly killing an innocent person is murder, and thus is impermissible, then the mother's directly killing the innocent person inside her is murder, and thus is impermissible. But it cannot seriously be thought to be murder if the mother performs an abortion on herself to save her life. It cannot seriously be said that she *must* refrain, that she *must* sit passively by and wait for her death. Let us look again at the case of you and the violinist. There you are, in bed with the violinist, and the director of the hospital says to you, "It's all most distressing, and I deeply sympathize, but you see this is putting an additional strain on your kidneys, and you'll be dead within the month. But you *have* to stay where you are all the same. Because unplugging you would be directly killing an innocent violinist, and that's murder, and that's impermissible." If anything in the world is true, it is that you do not commit murder, you do not do what is impermissible, if you reach around to your back and unplug yourself from that violinist to save your life.

The main focus of attention in writings on abortion has been on what a third party may or may not do in answer to a request from a woman for an abortion. This is in a way understandable. Things being as they are, there isn't much a woman can safely do to abort herself. So the question asked is what a third party may do, and what the mother may do, if it is mentioned at all, is de-

[5]The thesis in (4) is in an interesting way weaker than those in (1), (2), and (3): they rule out abortion even in cases in which both mother *and* child will die if the abortion is not performed. By contrast, one who held the view expressed in (4) could consistently say that one needn't prefer letting two persons die to killing one.
[6]Cf. the following passage from Pius XII, *Address to the Italian Catholic Society of Midwives*: "The baby in the maternal breast has the right to life immediately from God.—Hence there is no man, no human authority, no science, no medical, eugenic, social, economic or moral 'indication' which can establish or grant a valid juridical ground for a direct deliberate disposition of an innocent human life, that is a disposition which looks to its destruction either as an end or as a means to another end perhaps in itself not illicit.—The baby, still not born, is a man in the same degree and for the same reason as the mother" (quoted in Noonan, *The Morality of Abortion*, p. 45)

duced, almost as an afterthought, from what it is concluded that third parties may do. But it seems to me that to treat the matter in this way is to refuse to grant to the mother that very status of person which is so firmly insisted on for the fetus. For we cannot simply read off what a person may do from what a third party may do. Suppose you find yourself trapped in a tiny house with a growing child. I mean a very tiny house, and a rapidly growing child— you are already up against the wall of the house and in a few minutes you'll be crushed to death. The child on the other hand won't be crushed to death; if nothing is done to stop him from growing he'll be hurt, but in the end he'll simply burst open the house and walk out a free man. Now I could well understand it if a bystander were to say, "There's nothing we can do for you. We cannot choose between your life and his, we cannot be the ones to decide who is to live, we cannot intervene." But it cannot be concluded that you too can do nothing, that you cannot attack it to save your life. However innocent the child may be, you do not have to wait passively while it crushes you to death. Perhaps a pregnant woman is vaguely felt to have the status of house, to which we don't allow the right of self-defense. But if the woman houses the child, it should be remembered that she is a person who houses it.

I should perhaps stop to say explicitly that I am not claiming that people have a right to do anything whatever to save their lives. I think, rather, that there are drastic limits to the right of self-defense. If someone threatens you with death unless you torture someone else to death, I think you have not the right, even to save your life, to do so. But the case under consideration here is very different. In our case there are only two people involved, one whose life is threatened, and one who threatens it. Both are innocent: the one who is threatened is not threatened because of any fault, the one who threatens does not threaten because of any fault. For this reason we may feel that we bystanders cannot intervene. But the person threatened can.

In sum, a woman surely can defend her life against the threat to it posed by the unborn child, even if doing so involves its death. And this shows not merely that the theses in (1) through (4) are false; it shows also that the extreme view of abortion is false, and so we need not canvass any other possible ways of arriving at it from the argument I mentioned at the outset.

2. The extreme view could of course be weakened to say that while abortion is permissible to save the mother's life, it may not be performed by a third party, but only by the mother herself. But this cannot be right either. For what we have to keep in mind is

94

that the mother and the unborn child are not like two tenants in a small house which has, by an unfortunate mistake, been rented to both: the mother *owns* the house. The fact that she does adds to the offensiveness of deducing that the mother can do nothing from the supposition that third parties can do nothing. But it does more than this: it casts a bright light on the supposition that third parties can do nothing. Certainly it lets us see that a third party who says "I cannot choose between you" is fooling himself if he thinks this is impartiality. If Jones has found and fastened on a certain coat, which he needs to keep him from freezing, but which Smith also needs to keep him from freezing, then it is not impartiality that says "I cannot choose between you" when Smith owns the coat. Women have said again and again "This body is *my* body!" and they have reason to feel angry, reason to feel that it has been like shouting into the wind. Smith, after all, is hardly likely to bless us if we say to him, "Of course it's your coat, anybody would grant that it is. But no one may choose between you and Jones who is to have it."

We should really ask what it is that says "no one may choose" in the face of the fact that the body that houses the child is the mother's body. It may be simply a failure to appreciate this fact. But it may be something more interesting, namely the sense that one has a right to refuse to lay hands on people, even where it would be just and fair to do so, even where justice seems to require that somebody do so. Thus justice might call for somebody to get Smith's coat back from Jones, and yet you have a right to refuse to be the one to lay hands on Jones, a right to refuse to do physical violence to him. This, I think, must be granted. But then what should be said is not "no one may choose," but only "*I* cannot choose," and indeed not even this, but "*I* will not *act*," leaving it open that somebody else can or should, and in particular that anyone in a position of authority, with the job of securing people's rights, both can and should. So this is no difficulty. I have not been arguing that any given third party must accede to the mother's request that he perform an abortion to save her life, but only that he may.

I suppose that in some views of human life the mother's body is only on loan to her, the loan not being one which gives her any prior claim to it. One who held this view might well think it impartiality to say "I cannot choose." But I shall simply ignore this possibility. My own view is that if a human being has any just, prior claim to anything at all, he has a just, prior claim to his own body. And perhaps this needn't be argued for here anyway, since, as I mentioned, the arguments against abortion we are looking at do grant that the woman has a right to decide what happens in and to her body.

But although they do grant it, I have tried to show that they do not take seriously what is done in granting it. I suggest the same thing will reappear even more clearly when we turn away from cases in which the mother's life is at stake, and attend, as I propose we now do, to the vastly more common cases in which a woman wants an abortion for some less weighty reason than preserving her own life.

3. Where the mother's life is not at stake, the argument I mentioned at the outset seems to have a much stronger pull. "Everyone has a right to life, so the unborn person has a right to life." And isn't the child's right to life weightier than anything other than the mother's own right to life, which she might put forward as ground for an abortion?

This argument treats the right to life as if it were unproblematic. It is not, and this seems to me to be precisely the source of the mistake.

For we should now, at long last, ask what it comes to, to have a right to life. In some views having a right to life includes having a right to be given at least the bare minimum one needs for continued life. But suppose that what in fact *is* the bare minimum a man needs for continued life is something he has no right at all to be given? If I am sick unto death, and the only thing that will save my life is the touch of Henry Fonda's cool hand on my fevered brow, then all the same, I have no right to be given the touch of Henry Fonda's cool hand on my fevered brow. It would be frightfully nice of him to fly in from the West Coast to provide it. It would be less nice, though no doubt well meant, if my friends flew out to the West Coast and carried Henry Fonda back with them. But I have no right at all against anybody that he should do this for me. Or again, to return to the story I told earlier, the fact that for continued life that violinist needs the continued use of your kidneys does not establish that he has a right to be given the continued use of your kidneys. He certainly has no right against you that *you* should give him continued use of your kidneys. For nobody has any right to use your kidneys unless you give him such a right; and nobody has the right against you that you shall give him this right—if you do allow him to go on using your kidneys, this is a kindness on your part, and not something he can claim from you as his due. Nor has he any right against anybody else that *they* should give him continued use of your kidneys. Certainly he had no right against the Society of Music Lovers that they should plug him into you in the first place. And if you now start to unplug yourself, having learned that you will otherwise have to spend nine years in bed with him, there is nobody in the world who must try to prevent you, in order to see to it that he is given something he has a right to be given.

Some people are rather stricter about the right to life. In their view, it does not include the right to be given anything, but amounts to, and only to, the right not to be killed by anybody. But here a related difficulty arises. If everybody is to refrain from killing that violinist, then everybody must refrain from doing a great many different sorts of things. Everybody must refrain from slitting his throat, everybody must refrain from shooting him—and everybody must refrain from unplugging you from him. But does he have a right against everybody that they shall refrain from unplugging you from him? To refrain from doing this is to allow him to continue to use your kidneys. It could be argued that he has a right against us that *we* should allow him to continue to use your kidneys. That is, while he had no right against us that we should give him the use of your kidneys, it might be argued that he anyway has a right against us that we shall not now intervene and deprive him of the use of your kidneys. I shall come back to third-party interventions later. But certainly the violinist has no right against you that *you* shall allow him to continue to use your kidneys. As I said, if you do allow him to use them, it is a kindness on your part, and not something you owe him.

The difficulty I point to here is not peculiar to the right of life. It reappears in connection with all the other natural rights; and it is something which an adequate account of rights must deal with. For present purposes it is enough just to draw attention to it. But I would stress that I am not arguing that people do not have a right to life—quite to the contrary, it seems to me that the primary control we must place on the acceptability of an account of rights is that it should turn out in that account to be a truth that all persons have a right to life. I am arguing only that having a right to life does not guarantee having either a right to be given the use of or a right to be allowed continued use of another person's body—even if one needs it for life itself. So the right to life will not serve the opponents of abortion in the very simple and clear way in which they seem to have thought it would.

4. There is another way to bring out the difficulty. In the most ordinary sort of case, to deprive someone of what he has a right to is to treat him unjustly. Suppose a boy and his small brother are jointly given a box of chocolates for Christmas. If the older boy takes the box and refuses to give his brother any of the chocolates, he is unjust to him, for the brother has been given a right to half

of them. But suppose that, having learned that otherwise it means nine years in bed with that violinist, you unplug yourself from him. You surely are not being unjust to him, for you gave him no right to use your kidneys, and no one else can have given him any such right. But we have to notice that in unplugging yourself, you are killing him; and violinists, like everybody else, have a right to life, and thus in the view we were considering just now, the right not to be killed. So here you do what he supposedly has a right you shall not do, but you do not act unjustly to him in doing it.

The emendation which may be made at this point is this: the right to life consists not in the right not to be killed, but rather in the right not to be killed unjustly. This runs a risk of circularity, but never mind: it would enable us to square the fact that the violinist has a right to life with the fact that you do not act unjustly toward him in unplugging yourself, thereby killing him. For if you do not kill him unjustly, you do not violate his right to life, and so it is no wonder you do him no injustice.

But if this emendation is accepted, the gap in the argument against abortion stares us plainly in the face: it is by no means enough to show that the fetus is a person, and to remind us that all persons have a right to life—we need to be shown also that killing the fetus violates its right to life, i.e., that abortion is unjust killing. And is it?

I suppose we may take it as a datum that in a case of pregnancy due to rape the mother has not given the unborn person a right to the use of her body for food and shelter. Indeed, in what pregnancy could it be supposed that the mother has given the unborn person such a right? It is not as if there were unborn persons drifting about the world, to whom a woman who wants a child says "I invite you in."

But it might be argued that there are other ways one can have acquired a right to the use of another person's body than by having been invited to use it by that person. Suppose a woman voluntarily indulges in intercourse, knowing of the chance it will issue in pregnancy, and then she does become pregnant; is she not in part responsible for the presence, in fact the very existence, of the unborn person inside? No doubt she did not invite it in. But doesn't her partial responsibility for its being there itself give it a right to the use of her body?[7] If so, then her aborting it would be more like the boy's taking away the chocolates, and less like your unplugging yourself from the violinist—doing so would be de-

[7]The need for a discussion of this argument was brought home to me by members of the Society for Ethical and Legal Philosophy, to whom this paper was originally presented.

priving it of what it does have a right to, and thus would be doing it an injustice.

And then, too, it might be asked whether or not she can kill it even to save her own life: If she voluntarily called it into existence, how can she now kill it, even in self-defense?

The first thing to be said about this is that it is something new. Opponents of abortion have been so concerned to make out the independence of the fetus, in order to establish that it has a right to life, just as its mother does, that they have tended to overlook the possible support they might gain from making out that the fetus is *dependent* on the mother, in order to establish that she has a special kind of responsibility for it, a responsibility that gives it rights against her which are not possessed by any independent person—such as an ailing violinist who is a stranger to her.

On the other hand, this argument would give the unborn person a right to its mother's body only if her pregnancy resulted from a voluntary act, undertaken in full knowledge of the chance a pregnancy might result from it. It would leave out entirely the unborn person whose existence is due to rape. Pending the availability of some further argument, then, we would be left with the conclusion that unborn persons whose existence is due to rape have no right to the use of their mothers' bodies, and thus that aborting them is not depriving them of anything they have a right to and hence is not unjust killing.

And we should also notice that it is not at all plain that this argument really does go even as far as it purports to. For there are cases and cases, and the details make a difference. If the room is stuffy, and I therefore open a window to air it, and a burglar climbs in, it would be absurd to say, "Ah, now he can stay, she's given him a right to the use of her house—for she is partially responsible for his presence there, having voluntarily done what enabled him to get in, in full knowledge that there are such things as burglars, and that burglars burgle." It would be still more absurd to say this if I had had bars installed outside my windows, precisely to prevent burglars from getting in, and a burglar got in only because of a defect in the bars. It remains equally absurd if we imagine it is not a burglar who climbs in, but an innocent person who blunders or falls in. Again, suppose it were like this: people-seeds drift about in the air like pollen, and if you open your windows, one may drift in and take root in your carpets or upholstery. You don't want children, so you fix up your windows with fine mesh screens, the very best you can buy. As can happen, however, and on very, very rare occasions does happen, one of the screens is defective; and a seed drifts in and takes root. Does the person-plant who now develops have a right to the use of your house? Surely not—despite the fact that you voluntarily opened your windows, you knowingly kept carpets and upholstered furniture, and you knew that screens were sometimes defective. Someone may argue that you are responsible for its rooting, that it does have a right to your house, because after all you *could* have lived out your life with bare floors and furniture, or with sealed windows and doors. But this won't do—for by the same token anyone can avoid a pregnancy due to rape by having a hysterectomy, or anyway by never leaving home without a (reliable!) army.

It seems to me that the argument we are looking at can establish at most that there are *some* cases in which the unborn person has a right to the use of its mother's body, and therefore *some* cases in which abortion is unjust killing. There is room for much discussion and argument as to precisely which, if any. But I think we should sidestep this issue and leave it open, for at any rate the argument certainly does not establish that all abortion is unjust killing.

5. There is room for yet another argument here, however. We surely must all grant that there may be cases in which it would be morally indecent to detach a person from your body at the cost of his life. Suppose you learn that what the violinist needs is not nine years of your life, but only one hour: all you need do to save his life is to spend one hour in that bed with him. Suppose also that letting him use your kidneys for that one hour would not affect your health in the slightest. Admittedly you were kidnapped. Admittedly you did not give anyone permission to plug him into you. Nevertheless it seems to me plain you *ought* to allow him to use your kidneys for that hour—it would be indecent to refuse.

Again, suppose pregnancy lasted only an hour, and constituted no threat to life or health. And suppose that a woman becomes pregnant as a result of rape. Admittedly she did not voluntarily do anything to bring about the existence of a child. Admittedly she did nothing at all which would give the unborn person a right to the use of her body. All the same it might well be said, as in the newly emended violinist story, that she *ought* to allow it to remain for that hour—that it would be indecent in her to refuse.

Now some people are inclined to use the term "right" in such a way that it follows from the fact that you ought to allow a person to use your body for the hour he needs, that he has a right to use your body for the hour he needs, even though he has not been given that right by any person or act. They may say that it follows also that if you refuse, you act unjustly toward him. This use of the term is perhaps so common that it cannot be called wrong; nevertheless it seems to me to be an unfortunate loosening of what we would do better to keep a tight rein on. Suppose that box of chocolates I mentioned earlier had not been given to both boys jointly, but was given only to the older boy. There he sits, stolidly eating his way through the box, his small brother watching enviously. Here we are likely to say "You ought not to be so mean. You ought to give your brother some of those chocolates." My own view is that it just does not follow from the truth of this that the brother has any right to any of the chocolates. If the boy refuses to give his brother any, he is greedy, stingy, callous—but not unjust. I suppose that the people I have in mind will say it does follow that the brother has a right to some of the chocolates, and thus that the boy does act unjustly if he refuses to give his brother any. But the effect of saying this is to obscure what we should keep distinct, namely the difference between the boy's refusal in this case and the boy's refusal in the earlier case, in which the box was given to both boys jointly, and in which the small brother thus had what was from any point of view clear title to half.

A further objection to so using the term "right" that from the fact that A ought to do a thing for B, it follows that B has a right against A that A do it for him, is that it is going to make the question of whether or not a man has a right to a thing turn on how easy it is to provide him with it; and this seems not merely unfortunate, but morally unacceptable. Take the case of Henry Fonda again. I said earlier that I had no right to the touch of his cool hand on my fevered brow, even though I needed it to save my life. I said it would be frightfully nice of him to fly in from the West Coast to provide me with it, but that I had no right against him that he should do so. But suppose he isn't on the West Coast. Suppose he has only to walk across the room, place a hand briefly on my brow —and lo, my life is saved. Then surely he ought to do it, it would be indecent to refuse. Is it to be said "Ah, well, it follows that in this case she has a right to the touch of his hand on her brow, and so it would be an injustice in him to refuse"? So that I have a right to it when it is easy for him to provide it, though no right when it's hard? It's rather a shocking idea that anyone's rights should fade away and disappear as it gets harder and harder to accord them to him.

So my own view is that even though you ought to let the violinist use your kidneys for the one hour he needs, we should not conclude that he has a right to do so—we should say that if you refuse, you are, like the boy who owns all the chocolates and will give none away, self-centered and callous, indecent in fact, but not unjust. And similarly, that even supposing a case in which a woman pregnant due to rape ought to allow the unborn person to use her body for the hour he needs, we should not conclude that he has a right to do so; we should conclude that she is self-centered, callous, indecent, but not unjust, if she refuses. The complaints are no less grave; they are just different. However, there is no need to insist on this point. If anyone does wish to deduce "he has a right" from "you ought," then all the same he must surely grant that there are cases in which it is not morally required of you that you allow that violinist to use your kidneys, and in which he does not have a right to use them, and in which you do not do him an injustice if you refuse. And so also for mother and unborn child. Except in such cases as the unborn person has a right to demand it—and we were leaving open the possibility that there may be such cases—nobody is morally *required* to make large sacrifices, of health, of all other interests and concerns, of all other duties and commitments, for nine years, or even for nine months, in order to keep another person alive.

6. We have in fact to distinguish between two kinds of Samaritan: the Good Samaritan and what we might call the Minimally Decent Samaritan. The story of the Good Samaritan, you will remember, goes like this:

> A certain man went down from Jerusalem to Jericho, and fell among thieves, which stripped him of his raiment, and wounded him, and departed, leaving him half dead.
>
> And by chance there came down a certain priest that way; and when he saw him, he passed by on the other side.
>
> And likewise a Levite, when he was at the place, came and looked on him, and passed by on the other side.
>
> But a certain Samaritan, as he journeyed, came where he was; and when he saw him he had compassion on him.
>
> And went to him, and bound up his wounds, pouring in oil and wine, and set him on his own beast, and brought him to an inn, and took care of him.
>
> And on the morrow, when he departed, he took out two pence, and gave them to the host, and said unto him, "Take care of him; and whatsoever thou spendest more, when I come again, I will repay thee." (Luke 10:30–35)

The Good Samaritan went out of his way, at some cost to himself, to help one in need of it. We are not told what the options were, that is, whether or not the priest and the Levite could have helped by doing less than the Good Samaritan did, but assuming they could have, then the fact they did nothing at all shows they were not even Minimally Decent Samaritans, not because they were not Samaritans, but because they were not even minimally decent.

These things are a matter of degree, of course, but there is a difference, and it comes out perhaps most clearly in the story of Kitty Genovese, who, as you will remember, was murdered while thirty-eight people watched or listened, and did nothing at all to help her. A Good Samaritan would have rushed out to give direct assistance against the murderer. Or perhaps we had better allow that it would have been a Splendid Samaritan who did this, on the ground that it would have involved a risk of death for himself. But the thirty-eight not only did not do this, they did not even trouble to pick up a phone to call the police. Minimally Decent Samaritanism would call for doing at least that, and their not having done it was monstrous.

After telling the story of the Good Samaritan, Jesus said "Go, and do thou likewise." Perhaps he meant that we are morally required to act as the Good Samaritan did. Perhaps he was urging people to do more than is morally required of them. At all events it seems plain that it was not morally required of any of the thirty-eight that he rush out to give direct assistance at the risk of his own life, and that it is not morally required of anyone that he give long stretches of his life—nine years or nine months—to sustaining the life of a person who has no special right (we were leaving open the possibility of this) to demand it.

Indeed, with one rather striking class of exceptions, no one in any country in the world is *legally* required to do anywhere near as much as this for anyone else. The class of exceptions is obvious. My main concern here is not the state of the law in respect to abortion, but it is worth drawing attention to the fact that in no state in this country is any man compelled by law to be even a Minimally Decent Samaritan to any person; there is no law under which charges could be brought against the thirty-eight who stood by while Kitty Genovese died. By contrast, in most states in this country women are compelled by law to be not merely Minimally Decent Samaritans, but Good Samaritans to unborn persons inside them. This doesn't by itself settle anything one way or the other, because it may well be argued that there should be laws in this country—as there are in many European countries—compelling at least Minimally Decent Samaritanism.[8] But it does show that there is a gross injustice in the existing state of the law. And it shows

[8] For a discussion of the difficulties involved, and a survey of the European experience with such laws, see *The Good Samaritan and the Law*, ed. James M. Ratcliffe (New York, 1966).

also that the groups currently working against liberalization of abortion laws, in fact working toward having it declared unconstitutional for a state to permit abortion, had better start working for the adoption of Good Samaritan laws generally, or earn the charge that they are acting in bad faith.

I should think, myself, that Minimally Decent Samaritan laws would be one thing, Good Samaritan laws quite another, and in fact highly improper. But we are not here concerned with the law. What we should ask is not whether anybody should be compelled by law to be a Good Samaritan, but whether we must accede to a situation in which somebody is being compelled—by nature, perhaps—to be a Good Samaritan. We have, in other words, to look now at third-party interventions. I have been arguing that no person is morally required to make large sacrifices to sustain the life of another who has no right to demand them, and this even where the sacrifices do not include life itself; we are not morally required to be Good Samaritans or anyway Very Good Samaritans to one another. But what if a man cannot extricate himself from such a situation? What if he appeals to us to extricate him? It seems to me plain that there are cases in which we can, cases in which a Good Samaritan would extricate him. There you are, you were kidnapped, and nine years in bed with that violinist lie ahead of you. You have your own life to lead. You are sorry, but you simply cannot see giving up so much of your life to the sustaining of his. You cannot extricate yourself, and ask us to do so. I should have thought that—in light of his having no right to the use of your body—it was obvious that we do not have to accede to your being forced to give up so much. We can do what you ask. There is no injustice to the violinist in our doing so.

7. Following the lead of the opponents of abortion, I have throughout been speaking of the fetus merely as a person, and what I have been asking is whether or not the argument we began with, which proceeds only from the fetus' being a person, really does establish its conclusion. I have argued that it does not.

But of course there are arguments and arguments, and it may be said that I have simply fastened on the wrong one. It may be said that what is important is not merely the fact that the fetus is a person, but that it is a person for whom the woman has a special kind of responsibility issuing from the fact that she is its mother. And it might be argued that all my analogies are therefore irrelevant—for you do not have that special kind of responsibility for that violinist, Henry Fonda does not have that special kind of responsibility for me. And our attention might be drawn to the fact that men and women both *are* compelled by law to provide support for their children.

I have in effect dealt (briefly) with this argument in section 4 above; but a (still briefer) recapitulation now may be in order. Surely we do not have any such "special responsibility" for a person unless we have assumed it, explicitly or implicitly. If a set of parents do not try to prevent pregnancy, do not obtain an abortion, but rather take it home with them, then they have assumed responsibility for it, they have given it rights, and they cannot *now* withdraw support from it at the cost of its life because they now find it difficult to go on providing for it. But if they have taken all reasonable precautions against having a child, they do not simply by virtue of their biological relationship to the child who comes into existence have a special responsibility for it. They may wish to assume responsibility for it, or they may not wish to. And I am suggesting that if assuming responsibility for it would require large sacrifices, then they may refuse. A Good Samaritan would not refuse—or anyway, a Splendid Samaritan, if the sacrifices that had to be made were enormous. But then so would a Good Samaritan assume responsibility for that violinist; so would Henry Fonda, if he is a Good Samaritan, fly in from the West Coast and assume responsibility for me.

8. My argument will be found unsatisfactory on two counts by many of those who want to regard abortion as morally permissible. First, while I do argue that abortion is not impermissible, I do not argue that it is always permissible. There may well be cases in which carrying the child to term requires only Minimally Decent Samaritanism of the mother, and this is a standard we must not fall below. I am inclined to think it a merit of my account precisely that it does *not* give a general yes or a general no. It allows for and supports our sense that, for example, a sick and desperately frightened fourteen-year-old schoolgirl, pregnant due to rape, may of *course* choose abortion, and that any law which rules this out is an insane law. And it also allows for and supports our sense that in other cases resort to abortion is even positively indecent. It would be indecent in the woman to request an abortion, and indecent in a doctor to perform it, if she is in her seventh month, and wants the abortion just to avoid the nuisance of postponing a trip abroad. The very fact that the arguments I have been drawing attention to treat all cases of abortion, or even all cases of abortion in which the mother's life is not at stake, as morally on a par ought to have made them suspect at the outset.

Secondly, while I am arguing for the permissibility of abortion in some cases, I am not arguing for the right to secure the death of the unborn child. It is easy to confuse these two things in that up to a certain point in the life of the fetus it is not able to survive outside the mother's body; hence removing it from her body guarantees its death. But they are importantly different. I have argued that you are not morally required to spend nine months in bed, sustaining the life of that violinist; but to say this is by no means to say that if, when you unplug yourself, there is a miracle and he survives, you then have a right to turn round and slit his throat. You may detach yourself even if this costs him his life; you have no right to be guaranteed his death, by some other means, if unplugging yourself does not kill him. There are some people who will feel dissatisfied by this feature of my argument. A woman may be utterly devastated by the thought of a child, a bit of herself, put out for adoption and never seen or heard of again. She may therefore want not merely that the child be detached from her, but more, that it die. Some opponents of abortion are inclined to regard this as beneath contempt—thereby showing insensitivity to what is surely a powerful source of despair. All the same, I agree that the desire for the child's death is not one which anybody may gratify, should it turn out to be possible to detach the child alive.

At this place, however, it should be remembered that we have only been pretending throughout that the fetus is a human being from the moment of conception. A very early abortion is surely not the killing of a person, and so is not dealt with by anything I have said here.

3

PREJUDICE
AND
DISCRIMINATION

rights, human rights, and racial discrimination

richard wasserstrom

The subject of natural, or human, rights is one that has recently come to enjoy a new-found intellectual and philosophical respectability. This has come about in part, I think, because of a change in philosophical mood—in philosophical attitudes and opinions toward topics in moral and political theory. And this change in mood has been reflected in a renewed interest in the whole subject of rights and duties. In addition, though, this renaissance has been influenced, I believe, by certain events of recent history—notably the horrors of Nazi Germany and the increasingly obvious injustices of racial discrimination in both the United States and Africa. For in each case one of the things that was or is involved is a denial of certain human rights.

This concern over the subject of natural rights, whatever the causes may be, is, however, in the nature of a reinstatement. Certainly there was, just a relatively few years ago, fairly general agreement that the doctrine of natural rights had been thoroughly and irretrievably discredited. Indeed, this was sometimes looked upon as the paradigm case of the manner in which a moral and political doctrine could be both rhetorically influential and intel-

From the *Journal of Philosophy*, vol. 61 (1964). Reprinted by permission of the author and the *Journal of Philosophy*.

lectually inadequate and unacceptable. A number of objections, each deemed absolutely disposative, had been put forward: the vagueness of almost every formulation of a set of natural rights, the failure of persons to agree upon what one's natural rights are, the ease with which almost everyone would acknowledge the desirability of overriding or disregarding any proffered natural rights in any one of a variety of readily familiar circumstances, the lack of any ground or argument for any doctrine of natural rights.

Typical is the following statement from J. B. Mabbott's little book, *The State and the Citizens:*[1]

> [T]he niceties of the theory [of natural rights] need not detain us if we can attack it at its roots, and there it is most clearly vulnerable. Natural rights must be self-evident and they must be absolute if they are to be rights at all. For if a right is derivative from a more fundamental right, then it is not natural in the sense intended; and if a right is to be explained or defended by reference to the good of the community or of the individual concerned, then these "goods" are the ultimate values in the case, and their pursuit may obviously infringe or destroy the "rights" in question. Now the only way in which to demonstrate the absurdity of a theory which claims self-evidence for every article of its creed is to make a list of the articles....
>
> Not only are the lists indeterminate and capricious in extent, they are also confused in content. . . .[T]here is no single "natural right" which is, in fact, regarded even by its own supporters as sacrosanct. Every one of them is constantly invaded in the public interest with universal approval (57–58).

Mabbott's approach to the problem is instructive both as an example of the ease with which the subject has been taken up and dismissed, and more importantly, as a reminder of the fact that the theory of natural rights has not been a single coherent doctrine. Instead, it has served, and doubtless may still serve, as a quite indiscriminate collection of a number of logically independent propositions. It is, therefore, at least as necessary here as in many other situations that we achieve considerable precision in defining and describing the specific subject of inquiry.

This paper is an attempt to delineate schematically the form of one set of arguments for natural, or human rights.[2] I do this in the following fashion. First, I consider several important and distinctive features and functions of rights in general. Next, I describe and define certain characteristics of human rights and certain specific

[1]London: Arrow, 1958.
[2]Because the phrase "natural rights" is so encrusted with certain special meanings, I shall often use the more neutral phrase "human rights." For my purposes there are no differences in meaning between the two expressions.

functions and attributes that they have. Then, I delineate and evaluate one kind of argument for human rights, as so described and defined. And finally, I analyze one particular case of a denial of human rights—that produced by the system of racial discrimination as it exists in the South today.

1

If there are any such things as human rights, they have certain important characteristics and functions just because rights themselves are valuable and distinctive moral "commodities." This is, I think, a point that is all too often overlooked whenever the concept of a right is treated as a largely uninteresting, derivative notion —one that can be taken into account in wholly satisfactory fashion through an explication of the concepts of duty and obligation.[3]

Now, it is not my intention to argue that there can be rights for which there are no correlative duties, nor that there can be duties for which there are no correlative rights—although I think that there are, e.g., the duty to be kind to animals or the duty to be charitable. Instead, what I want to show is that there are important differences between rights and duties, and, in particular, that rights fulfill certain functions that neither duties (even correlative duties) nor any other moral or legal concepts can fulfill.

Perhaps the most obvious thing to be said about rights is that they are constitutive of the domain of entitlements. They help to define and serve to protect those things concerning which one can make a very special kind of claim—a claim of right. To claim or to acquire anything as a matter of right is crucially different from seeking or obtaining it as through the grant of a privilege, the receipt of a favor, or the presence of a permission. To have a right to something is, typically, to be entitled to receive or possess or enjoy it now,[4] and to do so without securing the consent of another. As long as one has a right to anything, it is beyond the reach of another properly to withhold or deny it. In addition, to have a right is to be absolved from the obligation to weigh a variety of what would in other contexts be relevant considerations; it is to be entitled to the object of the right—at least *prima facie*— without any more ado. To have a right to anything is, in short, to have a very strong moral or legal claim upon it. It is the strongest kind of claim that there is.

[3]See, for example, S. I. Benn and R. S. Peters, *Social Principles and the Democratic State*, p. 89: "Right and duty are different names for the same normative relation, according to the point of view from which it is regarded."
[4]There are some rights as to which the possession of the object of the right can be claimed only at a future time, e.g., the right (founded upon a promise) to be repaid next week.

Because this is so, it is apparent, as well, that the things to which one is entitled as a matter of right are not usually trivial or insignificant. The objects of rights are things that matter.

Another way to make what are perhaps some of the same points is to observe that rights provide special kinds of grounds or reasons for making moral judgments of at least two kinds. First, if a person has a right to something, he can properly cite that right as the *justification* for having acted in accordance with or in the exercise of that right. If a person has acted so as to exercise his right, he has, without more ado, acted rightly—at least *prima facie*. To exercise one's right is to act in a way that gives appreciable assurance of immunity from criticism. Such immunity is far less assured when one leaves the areas of rights and goes, say, to the realm of the permitted or the nonprohibited.

And second, just as exercising or standing upon one's rights by itself needs no defense, so invading or interfering with or denying another's rights is by itself appropriate ground for serious censure and rebuke. Here there is a difference in emphasis and import between the breach or neglect of a duty and the invasion of or interference with a right. For to focus upon duties and their breaches is to concentrate necessarily upon the person who has the duty; it is to invoke criteria by which to make moral assessments of his conduct. Rights, on the other hand, call attention to the injury inflicted; to the fact that the possessor of the right was adversely affected by the action. Furthermore, the invasion of a right constitutes, as such, a special and independent injury, whereas this is not the case with less stringent claims.

Finally, just because rights are those moral commodities which delineate the areas of entitlement, they have an additional important function: that of defining the respects in which one can reasonably entertain certain kinds of expectations. To live in a society in which there are rights and in which rights are generally respected is to live in a society in which the social environment has been made appreciably more predictable and secure. It is to be able to count on receiving and enjoying objects of value. Rights have, therefore, an obvious psychological, as well as moral, dimension and significance.

2

If the above are some of the characteristics and characteristic functions of rights in general, what then can we say about human rights? More specifically, what is it for a right to be a human right, and what special role might human rights play?

Probably the simplest thing that might be said of a human right is that it is a right possessed by human beings. To talk about human rights would be to distinguish those rights which humans have from those which nonhuman entities, e.g., animals or corporations, might have.

It is certain that this is not what is generally meant by human rights. Rather than constituting the genus of all particular rights that humans have, human rights have almost always been deemed to be one species of these rights. If nothing else about the subject is clear, it is evident that one's particular legal rights, as well as some of one's moral rights, are not among one's human rights. If any right is a *human* right, it must, I believe, have at least four very general characteristics. First, it must be possessed by all human beings, as well as only by human beings. Second, because it is the same right that all human beings possess, it must be possessed equally by all human beings. Third, because human rights are possessed by all human beings, we can rule out as possible candidates any of those rights which one might have in virtue of occupying any particular status or relationship, such as that of parent, president, or promisee. And fourth, if there are any human rights, they have the additional characteristic of being assertable, in a manner of speaking, "against the whole world." That is to say, because they are rights that are not possessed in virtue of any contingent status or relationship, they are rights that can be claimed equally against any and every other human being.

Furthermore, to repeat, if there are any human *rights*, they also have certain characteristics as rights. Thus, if there are any human rights, these constitute the strongest of all moral claims that all men can assert. They serve to define and protect those things which all men are entitled to have and enjoy. They indicate those objects toward which and those areas within which every human being is entitled to act without securing further permission or assent. They function so as to put certain matters beyond the power of anyone else to grant or to deny. They provide every human being with a ready justification for acting in certain ways, and they provide each person with ready grounds upon which to condemn any interference or invasion. And they operate, as well, to induce well-founded confidence that the values or objects protected by them will be readily and predictably obtainable. If there are any human rights, they are powerful moral commodities.

Finally, it is, perhaps, desirable to observe that there are certain characteristics I have not ascribed to these rights. In particular, I have not said that human rights need have either of two features: absoluteness and self-evidence, which Mabbott found to be most suspect. I have not said that human rights are absolute in the sense that there are no conditions under which they can properly be overridden, although I have asserted—what is quite different— that they are absolute in the sense that they are possessed equally without any special, additional qualification by all human beings.[5]

Neither have I said (nor do I want to assert) that human rights are self-evident in any sense. Indeed, I want explicitly to deny that a special manner of knowing or a specific epistemology is needed for the development of a theory of human rights. I want to assert that there is much that can be said in defense or support of the claim that a particular right is a human right. And I want to insist, as well, that to adduce reasons for human rights is consistent with their character as human, or natural, rights. Nothing that I have said about human rights entails a contrary conclusion.

3

To ask whether there are any human, or natural, rights is to pose a potentially misleading question. Rights of any kind, and particularly natural rights, are not like chairs or trees. One cannot simply look and see whether they are there. There are, though, at least two senses in which rights of all kinds can be said to exist. There is first the sense in which we can ask and answer the empirical question of whether in a given society there is intellectual or conceptual acknowledgment of the fact that persons or other entities have rights at all. We can ask, that is, whether the persons in that society "have" the concept of a right (or a human right), and whether they regard that concept as meaningfully applicable to persons or other entities in that society. And there is, secondly, the sense in which we can ask the question, to what extent, in a society that acknowledges the existence of rights, is there general respect for, protection of, or noninterference with the exercise of those rights.[6]

These are not, though, the only two questions that can be

---

[5]For the purposes of this paper and the points I wish here to make, I am not concerned with whether human rights are *prima facie* or absolute. I do not think that anything I say depends significantly upon this distinction. Without analyzing the notion, I will assume, though, that they are *prima facie* rights in the sense that there may be cases in which overriding a human right would be less undesirable than protecting it.

[6]This is an important distinction. Incontinence in respect to rights is a fairly common occurrence. In the South, for example, many persons might acknowledge that Negroes have certain rights while at the same time neglecting or refusing (out of timidity, cowardice, or general self-interest) to do what is necessary to permit these rights to be exercised.

asked. For we can also seek to establish whether any rights, and particularly human rights, ought to be both acknowledged and respected. I want now to begin to do this by considering the way in which an argument for human rights might be developed.

It is evident, I think, that almost any argument for the acknowledgment of any rights as human rights starts with the factual assertion that there are certain respects in which all persons are alike or equal. The argument moves typically from that assertion to the conclusion that there are certain human rights. What often remains unclear, however, is the precise way in which the truth of any proposition about the respects in which persons are alike advances an argument for the acknowledgment of human rights. And what must be supplied, therefore, are the plausible intermediate premises that connect the initial premise with the conclusion.

One of the most careful and complete illustrations of an argument that does indicate some of these intermediate steps is that provided by Gregory Vlastos in an article entitled, "Justice and Equality."[7] Our morality, he says, puts an equal intrinsic value on each person's well-being and freedom. In detail, the argument goes like this:

There is, Vlastos asserts, a wide variety of cases in which all persons are capable of experiencing the same values.

> Thus, to take a perfectly clear case, no matter how A and B might differ in taste and style of life, they would both crave relief from acute physical pain. In that case we would put the same value on giving this to either of them, regardless of the fact that A might be a talented, brilliantly successful person, B "a mere nobody." . . . [I]n all cases where human beings are capable of enjoying the same goods, we feel that the intrinsic value of their enjoyment is the same. In just this sense we hold that (1) *one man's well-being is as valuable as any other's*. . . . [Similarly] we feel that choosing for oneself what one will do, believe, approve, say, read, worship, has its own intrinsic value, the same for all persons, and quite independently of the value of the things they happen to choose. Naturally we hope that all of them will make the best possible use of their freedom of choice. But we value their exercise of the freedom, regardless of the outcome and we value it equally for all. For us (2) *one man's freedom is as valuable as any other's*. . . . [Thus], since we do believe in equal value as to human well-being and freedom, we should also believe in the *prima facie* equality of men's *right* to well-being and to freedom (51–52).

[7]In Richard B. Brandt, ed., *Social Justice* (Englewood Cliffs, N.J.: Prentice-Hall, 1962), pp. 31–72.

As it is stated, I am not certain that this argument answers certain kinds of attack. In particular, there are three questions that merit further attention. First, why should anyone have a right to the enjoyment of any goods at all, and, more specifically, well-being and freedom? Second, for what reasons might we be warranted in believing that the intrinsic value of the enjoyment of such goods is the same for all persons? And third, even if someone ought to have a right to well-being and freedom and even if the intrinsic value of each person's enjoyment of these things is equal, why should all men have the equal right—and hence the human right—to secure, obtain, or enjoy these goods?

I think that the third question is the simplest of the three to answer. If anyone has a right to well-being and freedom and if the intrinsic value of any person's enjoyment of these goods is equal to that of any other's, then all men do have an equal right—and hence a human right—to secure, obtain, or enjoy these goods, just because it would be irrational to distinguish among persons as to the possession of these rights. That is to say, the principle that no person should be treated differently from any or all other persons unless there is some general and relevant reason that justifies this difference in treatment is a fundamental principle of morality, if not of rationality itself. Indeed, although I am not certain how one might argue for this, I think it could well be said that all men do have a "second-order" human right—that is, an absolute right—to expect all persons to adhere to this principle.

This principle, or this right, does not by itself establish that there are any specific human rights. But either the principle or the right does seem to establish that well-being and freedom are human rights if they are rights at all and if the intrinsic value of each person's enjoyment is the same. For, given these premises, it does appear to follow that there is no relevant and general reason to differentiate among persons as to the possession of this right.

I say "seem to" and "appear to" because this general principle of morality may not be strong enough. What has been said so far does not in any obvious fashion rule out the possibility that there is some general and relevant principle of differentiation. It only, apparently, rules out possible variations in intrinsic value as a reason for making differentiations.

The requirement of *relevance* does, I think, seem to make the argument secure. For, if *the reason* for acknowledging in a person a right to freedom and well-being is the intrinsic value of his enjoyment of these goods, then the nature of the intrinsic value of any other person's enjoyment is the only relevant reason for making exceptions or for differentiating among persons as to the possession of these rights.[8]

As to the first question, that of whether a person has a right to well-being and freedom, I am not certain what kind of answer is most satisfactory. If Vlastos is correct in asserting that these enjoyments are *values*, then that is, perhaps, answer enough. That is to say, if enjoying well-being is something *valuable*—and especially if it is intrinsically valuable—then it seems to follow that this is the kind of thing to which one ought to have a right. For if anything ought to be given the kind of protection afforded by a right, it ought surely be that which is valuable. Perhaps, too, there is nothing more that need be said other than to point out that we simply do properly value well-being and freedom.

I think that another, more general answer is also possible. Here I would revert more specifically to my earlier discussion of some of the characteristics and functions of rights. There are two points to be made. First, if we are asked, why ought anyone have a right to anything? or why not have a system in which there are not rights at all? the answer is that such a system would be a morally impoverished one. It would prevent persons from asserting those kinds of claims, it would preclude persons from having those types of expectations, and it would prohibit persons from making those kinds of judgments which a system of rights makes possible.

Thus, if we can answer the question of why have rights at all, we can then ask and answer the question of what things—among others—ought to be protected by *rights*. And the answer, I take it, is that one ought to be able to claim as entitlements those minimal things without which it is impossible to develop one's capabilities and to live a life as a human being. Hence, to take one thing that is a precondition of well-being, the relief from acute physical pain, this is the kind of enjoyment that ought to be protected as a right of some kind just because without such relief there is precious little that one can effectively do or become. And similarly for the opportunity to make choices, examine beliefs, and the like.

To recapitulate. The discussion so far has indicated two things: (1) the conditions under which any specific right would be a hu-

---

[8]See, e.g., Bernard Williams, "The Idea of Equality," in P. Laslett and W. G. Runciman, eds., *Philosophy, Politics and Society*, II (Oxford: Basil Blackwell, 1962), pp. 111–113.

Professor Vlastos imposes a somewhat different requirement which, I think, comes to about the same thing: "An equalitarian concept of justice may admit just inequalities without inconsistency if, and only if, it provides grounds for equal human rights *which are also grounds for unequal rights of other sorts*" (Vlastos, op. cit., p. 40; italics in text).

man right, and (2) some possible grounds for arguing that certain values or enjoyments ought to be regarded as matters of right. The final question that remains is whether there are any specific rights that satisfy the conditions necessary to make them human rights. Or, more specifically, whether it is plausible to believe that there are no general and relevant principles that justify making distinctions among persons in respect to their rights to well-being and freedom.

Vlastos has it that the rights to well-being and freedom do satisfy these conditions, since he asserts that we, at least, do regard each person's well-being and freedom as having equal intrinsic value. If this is correct, if each person's well-being and freedom does have *equal* intrinsic value, then there is no general and relevant principle for differentiating among persons as to these values and, hence, as to their rights to secure these values. But this does not seem wholly satisfactory. It does not give us any reason for supposing that it is plausible to ascribe equal intrinsic value to each person's well-being and freedom.

The crucial question, then, is the plausibility of ascribing intrinsic value to each person's well-being and freedom. There are, I think, at least three different answers that might be given.

First, it might be asserted that this ascription simply constitutes another feature of our morality. The only things that can be done are to point out that this is an assumption that we do make and to ask persons whether they would not prefer to live in a society in which such an assumption is made.

While perhaps correct and persuasive, this does not seem to me to be all that can be done. In particular, there are, I think, two further arguments that may be made.

The first is that there are cases in which all human beings *equally* are capable of enjoying the same goods, e.g., relief from acute physical pain,[9] or that they are capable of deriving equal enjoyment from the same goods. If this is true, then if anyone has a right to this enjoyment, that right is a human right just because there is no rational ground for preferring one man's enjoyment to another's. For, if all persons do have equal capacities of these sorts and if the existence of these capacities is the reason for ascribing these rights to anyone, then all persons ought to have the right to claim equality of treatment in respect to the possession and exercise of these rights.

[9]See, Williams, op. cit., p. 112: "These respects [in which men are alike] are notably the capacity to feel pain, both from immediate physical causes and from various situations represented in perception and in thought; and the capacity to feel affection for others, and the consequences of this, connected with the frustration of this affection, loss of its objects, etc."

The difficulty inherent in this argument is at the same time the strength of the next one. The difficulty is simply that it does seem extraordinarily difficult to know how one would show that all men are equally capable of enjoying any of the same goods, or even how one might attempt to gather or evaluate relevant evidence in this matter. In a real sense, interpersonal comparisons of such a thing as the ability to bear pain seems to be logically as well as empirically unobtainable. Even more unobtainable, no doubt, is a measure of the comparative enjoyments derivable from choosing for oneself.[10] These are simply enjoyments the comparative worths of which, as different persons, there is no way to assess. If this is so, then this fact gives rise to an alternative argument.

We do know, through inspection of human history as well as of our own lives, that the denial of the opportunity to experience the enjoyment of these goods makes it impossible to live either a full or a satisfying life. In a real sense, the enjoyment of these goods differentiates human from nonhuman entities. And therefore, even if we have no meaningful or reliable criteria for comparing and weighing capabilities for enjoyment or for measuring their quantity or quality, we probably know all we need to know to justify our refusal to attempt to grade the value of the enjoyment of these goods. Hence, the dual grounds for treating their intrinsic values as equal for all persons: either these values are equal for all persons, or, if there are differences, they are not in principle discoverable or measurable. Hence, the argument, or an argument, for the human rights to well-being and freedom.

Because the foregoing discussion has been quite general and abstract, I want finally to consider briefly one illustration of a denial of human rights and to delineate both the several ways in which such a denial can occur and some of the different consequences of that denial. My example is that of the way in which Negro persons are regarded and treated by many whites in the South.

The first thing that is obvious is that many white Southerners would or might be willing to accept all that has been said so far and yet seek to justify their attitudes and behavior toward Negroes.

They might agree, for example, that all persons do have a right to be accorded equal treatment unless there is a general and relevant principle of differentiation. They would also surely acknowledge that some persons do have rights to many different things, including most certainly well-being and freedom. But they would

[10]At times, Vlastos seems to adopt this view as well as the preceding one. See, e.g., Vlastos, op. cit., p. 49: "So understood a person's well-being and freedom are aspects of his individual existence as unique and unrepeatable as is that existence itself. . . ."

119

insist, nonetheless, that there exists a general and relevant principle of differentiation, namely, that some persons are Negroes and others are not.

Now, those who do bother to concern themselves with arguments and with the need to give reasons would not, typically, assert that the mere fact of color difference does constitute a general and relevant reason. Rather, they would argue that this color difference is correlated with certain other characteristics and attitudes that are relevant.[11] In so doing, they invariably commit certain logical and moral mistakes.

First, the purported differentiating characteristic is usually not relevant to the differentiation sought to be made; e.g., none of the characteristics that supposedly differentiate Negroes from whites has any relevance to the capacity to bear acute physical pain or to the strength of the desire to be free from it. Indeed, almost all arguments neglect the fact that the capacities to enjoy those things which are constitutive of well-being and freedom are either incommensurable among persons or alike in all persons.

Second, the invocation of these differentiating characteristics always violates the requirement of relevance in another sense. For, given the typical definition of a Negro (in Alabama the legal definition is any person with "a drop of Negro blood"), it is apparent that there could not—under any plausible scientific theory—be good grounds for making any differentiations between Negroes and whites.[12]

Third, and related to the above, any argument that makes distinctions as to the possession of human rights in virtue of the truth of certain empirical generalizations invariably produces some unjust denials of those rights. That is to say, even if some of the generalizations about Negroes are correct, they are correct only in the sense that the distinguishing characteristics ascribed to Negroes are possessed by some or many Negroes but not by all Negroes. Yet, before any reason for differentiating among persons as to the possession of human rights can be a relevant reason, that reason must be relevant in respect to *each person* so affected or distinguished. To argue otherwise is to neglect the fact, among other things, that human rights are personal and of at least *prima facie* equal importance to each possessor of those rights.

A different reaction or argument of white Southerners in respect to recent events in the South is bewilderment. Rather than (or in addition to) arguing for the existence of principles of dif-

---

[11]See, Williams, op. cit., p. 113.

[12]This is to say nothing, of course, of the speciousness of any principle of differentiation that builds upon inequalities that are themselves produced by the unequal and unjust distribution of *opportunities.*

ferentiation, the white Southerner will say that he simply cannot understand the Negro's dissatisfaction with his lot. This is so because he, the white Southerner, has always treated his Negroes very well. With appreciable sincerity, he will assert that he has real affection for many Negroes. He would never needlessly inflict pain or suffering upon them. Indeed, he has often assumed special obligations to make certain that their lives were free from hunger, pain, and disease.

Now of course, this description of the facts is seldom accurate at all. Negroes have almost always been made to endure needless and extremely severe suffering in all too many obvious ways for all too many obviously wrong reasons. But I want to assume for my purposes the accuracy of the white Southerner's assertions. For these assertions are instructive just because they reveal some of the less obvious effects of a denial of human rights.

What is wholly missing from this description of the situation is the ability and inclination to conceptualize the Negro—any Negro—as the possible possessor of rights of any kind, and *a fortiori* of any human rights. And this has certain especially obnoxious consequences.

In the first place, the white Southerner's moral universe illustrates both the fact that it is possible to conceive of duties without conceiving of their correlative rights and the fact that the mistakes thereby committed are not chiefly mistakes of logic and definition. The mistakes matter morally. For what this way of conceiving most denies to any Negro is the opportunity to assert claims as a matter of right. It denies him the standing to protest against the way he is treated. If the white Southerner fails to do his duty, that is simply a matter between him and his conscience.

In the second place, it requires of any Negro that *he* make out his case for the enjoyment of any goods. It reduces all of *his* claims to the level of requests, privileges, and favors. But there are simply certain things, certain goods, that nobody ought to have to request of another. There are certain things that no one else ought to have the power to decide to refuse or to grant. To observe what happens to any person who is required to adopt habits of obsequious, deferential behavior in order to minimize the likelihood of physical abuse, arbitrary treatment, or economic destitution is to see most graphically how important human rights are and what their denial can mean. To witness what happens to a person's own attitudes, aspirations, and conceptions of himself[13] when he must

[13]Vlastos puts what I take to be the same point this way: "Any practice which tends to so weaken and confuse the personal esteem of a group of persons—slavery, serfdom or, in our own time racial segregation—may be morally condemned on this one ground, even if there were no other for indicting it" (Vlastos, op. cit., p. 71).

request or petition for the opportunity to voice an opinion, to consult with a public official, or to secure the protection of the law is to be given dramatic and convincing assurance of the moral necessity of a conception of human rights.

And there is one final point. In a real sense, a society that simply lacks any conception of human rights is less offensive than one which has such a conception but denies that some persons have these rights. This is so not just because of the inequality and unfairness involved in differentiating for the wrong reasons among persons. Rather, a society based on such denial is especially offensive because it implicitly, if not explicitly, entails that there are some persons who do not and would not desire or need or enjoy those minimal goods which all men do need and desire and enjoy. It is to read certain persons, all of whom are most certainly human beings, out of the human race. This is surely among the greatest of all moral wrongs.

I know of no better example of the magnitude of this evil than that provided by a lengthy account in a Southern newspaper about the high school band program in a certain city. The article described fully the magnificence of the program and emphasized especially the fact that it was a program in which *all high school students* in the city participated.

Negro children neither were nor could be participants in the program. The article, however, saw no need to point this out. I submit that it neglected to do so not because everyone knew the fact, but because in a real sense the writer and the newspaper do not regard Negro high school students as children—persons, human beings—at all.

What is the Negro parent who reads this article to say to his children? What are his children supposed to think? How does a Negro parent even begin to demonstrate to the world that his children are really children, too? These are burdens no civilized society ought ever to impose. These are among the burdens that an established and acknowledged system of human rights helps to eliminate.

women's liberation

betty roszak

Recent years have seen a resurgence of feminism that has taken mainstream America by surprise. It began with the discontent of lonely middle-class suburban housewives, whose malady was given a name by Betty Friedan in her immensely influential book, *The Feminine Mystique.* But it didn't become what we know as a "women's liberation movement" until the growth of the New Left from the civil rights and peace movements of the early 1960s. It wasn't until then that hundreds of young women, many of whom were seasoned veterans of antiwar and antisegregationist activities, began to realize the anomaly of their situation. Here they were, radical women involved in a struggle for human equality and an end to oppression, willing to dedicate years of effort to effecting political change, and what were they being allowed to do? Typing, mimeographing, addressing envelopes, sweeping, providing coffee and sexual diversion for the vigorous young men who were making all the decisions. Far from going forward together to change the world, men and women were once more stuck (and this time with a vengeance) with their time-honored roles: the men to think and act; the women to serve and drudge. The last equality—that between women and men—was never even mentioned. In fact, movement women found that they were even worse

From Betty Roszak, "The Human Continuum," in *Masculine/Feminine*, ed. Betty Roszak and Theodore Roszak (New York: Harper & Row, 1969), pp. 297–306. Copyright © 1969 by Betty Roszak and Theodore Roszak. Reprinted by permission of Harper & Row, Publishers, Inc.

off than apolitical women, because they were aware of and extremely sensitive to the hypocrisies of their male colleagues who talked idealistically of equality, but who acted scornful of women in their everyday lives. The rhetoric of equality was directed at black, brown, and Third World *men* only. The New Left of the late sixties had begun to take on a tough, aggressively male tone, born of the idolization of Ché Guevara, guerrilla warfare, and admiration for the exaggerated, overcompensating manliness of the Black Panthers. As nonviolence, exemplified by Martin Luther King, Jr., became discredited by revolutionary and black militancy, so the tough style became a political requirement. In deference to this new brutalism men found it easy to take the necessary traditional he-man attitude toward women, the attitude of dominance and power. This left women in a bewildering dilemma. Were they to remain in a movement which allowed them to exist only as lackeys and silently submissive bedmates, or would they refuse to accept a subordinate status?

As this dilemma is being resolved today, there sounds in the background the laughter of contemptuous radical men: "Crazy feminist bitches!" The words merely echo a shared male ridicule that knows no class lines. Women find themselves of necessity beginning to re-examine the traditions of misogyny that even radical men have unknowingly inherited.

In our cultural past "Woman" was the symbol of sex; and sex, though necessary, was at the same time known to be an abhorrent evil, a degrading passion. In the Middle Ages, the masculine world view of the church dared not make light of women. Church authorities of the fifteenth century, ever on the alert for the malevolence of the devil, used a popular handbook on the identification and treatment of witches, the *Malleus Maleficarum*, in searching out evil in the form of women. "What else is woman," says this medieval antisubversive activities manual, "but a foe to friendship, an unescapable punishment, a necessary evil, a natural temptation, a desirable calamity, a domestic danger, a delectable detriment, an evil of nature painted with fair colors?" By the eighteenth century, Rousseau, one of France's most prolific proponents of democratic equality, could write with impunity, "Women have in general no love of any art; they have no proper knowledge of any; and they have no genius," thus curtly dismissing half of humanity to a status of hopeless inferiority. By mid-nineteenth century, the "evil of nature" had turned into an object of scorn, and Schopenhauer's indictment of women as "that undersized, narrow-shouldered, broad-hipped, and short-legged race," denied women

Betty Roszak

even their beauty, their "fair colors," along with their intellectual capacity.

Today's predominantly male society no longer sees women as evil, at least on the surface. The ambivalent fear and attraction of the Middle Ages has changed along with the prevailing attitude toward sex. Now that sexuality has lost its mystery, the once dangerous and seductive female can be safely ignored and denied her power. The fear has turned to ridicule. One cannot ignore evil, but one can pretend that the ridiculous does not exist. Men irritably ask the rhetorical question (echoing Freud), "What do women want?" meaning, of course, that anything women want is absurd. The question is asked not of individual women but of the world, and in an exasperated tone, as if women were dumb and couldn't answer. The false barrier continues to be built: "We" cannot understand "Them." Why are "They" so restive? Further communication between the sexes seems useless. Always it is men talking to men about women.

The fact of ridicule is constantly with us. When it was proposed in 1969 in the British House of Commons that attention be paid to developing a contraceptive pill for men, "the idea provoked hearty laughter," according to Paul Vaughan in the London *Observer*. Moreover, he tells us, the British government has rejected outright any allocation of funds for research on a pill for men. When the question was under discussion in the House of Lords, one Labour peer advised the government to ignore "'these do-gooders who take all the fun out of life' (laughter)." Researchers explain their reluctance to tamper with the male germ cells. Yet the same researchers have not hesitated to tamper with the female germ cells in developing the pill for women. Nor have unpleasant side effects or hazards to women's health deterred them, while they quickly stopped research on a substance being tested on men because it was noted that when men drank alcohol while taking it, their eyes became reddened! Doctors have been known to laugh at the mention of labor pains during childbirth and in the not too distant past have been willing to stand by, calmly withholding anesthetics while women underwent great agonies in labor. So, too, male legislators have laughed at the idea of the legalization of abortion, hinting at unprecedented promiscuity (on the part of women, not men) if such a thing were allowed. Meanwhile, thousands of desperate women die each year as the direct result of male laws making abortion illegal.

Women are learning the meaning of this male laughter and indifference in the face of the most hazardous and serious bio-

125

logical enterprise women undertake, willingly or not. And in cultural enterprises, whenever women attempt to enter any of the male-dominated professions (who ever heard of a woman chairman of the board, a woman orchestra conductor, a woman Chief Justice, a woman President or a woman getting equal pay for equal work?), we again hear the familiar laughter of male ridicule. If we look at the image of woman men present to us in novels, drama, or advertising, we see a scatterbrained, helpless flunky, or a comical sex-pot, or a dumb beast of burden. Is this what they mean when they exhort us in popular song to "enjoy being a girl"? But women are beginning to relearn the old lesson: in this male-dominated world, it is a misfortune to be born female.

From the very moment of birth a higher value is placed by his society on the male infant, a value which accumulates and accelerates into his adult life. By the time the female infant has grown into adulthood, however, if she has learned society's lessons well, she will have come to acquiesce in her second-class status—to accept unconsciously the burden of her inferiority. No matter what honors she wins, what her exploits, what her achievements or talents, she will always be considered a woman first, and thus inferior to the least honored, talented and worthy male of that society—foremost a sexual being, still fair game for his aggressive sexual fantasies. As Albert Memmi puts it, ". . . every man, no matter how low he may be, holds women in contempt and judges masculinity to be an inestimable good."

Male society's disparagement of women has all the force of an unconscious conspiracy. It is even more subtle than the racist and colonial oppressions to which it is so closely allied, because it is softened and hidden by the silken padding of eroticism. We women grow to think that because we are wanted as lovers, wives, and mothers, it might be because we are wanted as human beings. But if by chance or natural inclination we attempt to move outside these male-defined and male-dependent roles, we find that they are, in reality, barriers.

For many women this is the first inkling of the fact of oppression. Pressed from birth into the mold of an exclusively sexual being, the growing girl soon develops what Sartre calls the "phantom personality"; she comes to feel that she is what "they" tell her she is. This other self envelops her like a second skin. When she begins to experience a natural sense of constriction (which is growth), her real feelings clash with what "they" say she should feel. The more forceful and vital she is, the more she will have to repress her real feelings, because girls are to be passive and manipulatable. She becomes frightened, suspicious, anxious about herself. A sense of malaise overcomes her. She must obey the social prohibitions which force her back into the mold of the sexual being. She is not to desire or act, but to *be* desired and acted upon. Many women give up the struggle right there and dully force themselves to remain stunted human beings. The butterfly must not be allowed to come forth from its chrysalis: her vitality is only allowed guilty expression in certain private moments or is turned into sullen resentment which smolders during all her unfulfilled life.

Family and home, which look like a refuge and a sanctuary, turn out to be the same kind of trap. Beyond the marriage ghetto there is outright rejection and exclusion. In the work world there are lower wages, union and employer discrimination, the prohibitive cost of child care. In the professions mere tokenism takes the place of acceptance and equality. The same is true in government and political activity. The single woman knows only too well the psychological exclusionism practiced by male society. She is suspect, or comic, if over a certain age. All men assume she would be married if she could—there must be something psychologically wrong with her if she isn't. And single women have the added burden of not being socially acceptable without an "escort"—a man, any man.

Further, women are the nonexistent people in the very life of the nation itself—now more so even than the blacks who have at last forced themselves into the nation's consciousness. The invisible man has become the invisible *woman*. William James called it a "fiendish punishment" that "one should be turned loose on society and remain absolutely unnoticed by all the members thereof." Yet that is the treatment male society metes out to those women who wish to escape from the male-defined erotic roles. Left out of the history books, not credited with a past worth mentioning in the masculine chronicles of state, women of today remain ignorant of women's movements of the past and the important role individual women have played in the history of the human race. Male historical scholarship sees the suffragists and feminists of the nineteenth century as figures of fun, worthy of only a paragraph here and there, as footnotes on the by-ways of social customs, far from the main roads of masculine endeavor: the wars, political intrigues, and diplomatic maneuverings which make up the history of power.

With the blacks and other oppressed minorities, women can say, "How can we hope to shape the future without some knowledge of our past?" If the historic heroines of feminism are ignored or treated trivially, today's women are hindered from dealing with their own repression. This undermining of self-confidence is

127

common to all oppressed peoples, along with the doubts of the reality of one's own perceptions. Women's self-rejection as worthwhile human beings thus becomes an inevitable extension of the cycle of oppression.

But radical women have begun to rebel against the false, exclusively sexual image men have created for them. And in rebelling, many women are seeing the need for bypassing the marriage ghetto altogether. They are recognizing the true nature of the institution of marriage as an economic bargain glossed over by misty sentimentalizing. Wash off the romantic love ideal, and underneath we see the true face of the marriage contract. It is grimly epitomized by the immortal slogan found chalked on innumerable honeymoon getaway cars: "She got him today; he'll get her tonight." Or, as put more sophisticatedly by Robert Briffault, "Whether she aims at freedom or a home a woman is thrown back on the defense of her own interests; she must defend herself against man's attempt to bind her, or sell herself to advantage. Woman is to man a sexual prey; man is to woman an economic prey." And this kind of oppression cuts across all economic class lines, even though there may be social differences between streetwalker Jane X, housewife Joan Y, and debutante Jacqueline Z. One may sell her body for a few dollars to the likeliest passerby; one for a four-bedroomed house in the suburbs; and one for rubies and yachts. But all must sell their bodies in order to participate in the bargain. Yet if women were to refuse to enter into the sexual bargain, they not only would refute the masculine idea of women as property, but they also would make it possible to free men from the equally self-destructive role of sole breadwinner. Thus there would be a chance to break the predatory cycle.

Beyond marriage and the old, outmoded roles, radical women are seeking new ways of dealing with the oppressive institutions of society. No longer will they acquiesce in the pattern of dominance and submission. They are beginning to take control of their own lives, building new relationships, developing new modes of work, political activity, child rearing and education. Rejection of male exploitation must start with psychic as well as economic independence. The new female consciousness is going to develop cooperative forms of child care; women's centers as sanctuaries for talk, planning, and action; all-female communes where women can escape for a while from the all-pervading male influence; the sharing of domestic drudgery with men in cooperative living arrangements; the building up of competence and self-confidence in such previously male-dependent endeavors as general mechanical repair work, carpentry, and construction.

By rejecting the false self for so long imposed upon us and in which we have participated unwittingly, we women can forge the self-respect necessary in order to discover our own true values. Only when we refuse to be made use of by those who despise and ridicule us, can we throw off our heavy burden of resentment. We must take our lives in our own hands. This is what liberation means. Out of a common oppression women can break the stereotypes of masculine-feminine and enter once more into the freedom of the human continuum.

Women's liberation will thus inevitably bring with it, as a concomitant, men's liberation. Men, no less than women, are imprisoned by the heavy carapace of their sexual stereotype. The fact that they gain more advantages and privileges from women's oppression has blinded them to their own bondage which is the bondage of an artificial duality. This is the male problem: the positing of a difference, the establishment of a dichotomy emphasizing oppositeness. Men are to behave in this way; women in that; women do this; men do the other. And it just so happens that the way men behave and act is important and valuable, while what women do is unimportant and trivial. Instead of identifying both the sexes as part of humanity, there is a false separation which is to the advantage of men. Masculine society has insisted on seeing in sexuality that same sense of conflict and competition that it has imposed upon its relation to the planet as a whole. From the bedroom to the board room to the international conference table, separateness, differentiation, opposition, exclusion, antithesis have been the cause and goal of the male politics of power. Human characteristics belonging to the entire species have been crystallized out of the living flow of human experience and made into either/or categories. This male habit of setting up boundary lines between imagined polarities has been the impetus for untold hatred and destruction. Masculine/feminine is just one of such polarities among many, including body/mind, organism/environment, plant/animal, good/evil, black/white, feeling/intellect, passive/active, sane/insane, living/dead. Such language hardens what is in reality a continuum and a unity into separate mental images always in opposition to one another.

If we think of ourselves as "a woman" or "a man," we are already participating in a fantasy of language. People become preoccupied with images of one another—surely the deepest and most desperate alienation there is. The very process of conceptualization warps our primary, unitary feelings of what we are. Mental images take the place of the primary stimuli of sex which involve the entire organism. Instead of a sense of identification, we have pornographic sex with its restrictive emphasis on genital stimulation. This "short circuiting between genitals and cortex" as William E. Galt calls it (in a brilliant article, "The Male–Female Dichotomy," in *Psychiatry*, 1943) is a peculiarly modern distortion of the original, instinctual nature of sex. We are suffering from D. H. Lawrence's "sex in the head." In childhood we know sexuality as a generalized body response; the body is an erotic organ of sensation. To this Freud gave the nasty name of polymorphous perversity. But it is actually the restriction to localized genitality of the so-called "normal" adult that is perverted, in the sense of a twisting away from the original and primary body eroticism. Biological evidence indicates that the sex response is a primitive, gross sensory stimulation—diffused and nonlocalizable. Phallic man, however, wishes to assert the primacy of his aggressive organ. The ego of phallic man divides him off from the rest of the world, and in this symbolic division he maintains the deep-seated tradition of man *against* woman, wresting his sexual pleasure *from* her, like the spoils of war. The total body response must be repressed in order to satisfy the sharpness of his genital cravings.

But in the primary sexual response of the body, there is no differentiation between man or woman; there is no "man," there is no "woman" (mental images), just a shared organism responding to touch, smell, taste, sound. The sexual response can then be seen as one part of the species' total response to and participation in, the environment. We sense the world with our sensitive bodies as an ever-changing flow of relationships in which we move and partake. Phallic man sees the world as a collection of things from which he is sharply differentiated. If we consider the phenomenon of the orgasm in this light, we can see that its basic qualities are the same for male and female. There can be no real distinction between the feminine and masculine *self*-abandonment in a sexual climax. The self, or controlling power, simply vanishes. All talk of masculine or feminine orgasm misses this point entirely, because this is a surrender which goes beyond masculine or feminine. Yet how many men are there who are willing to see their own sexual vitality as exactly this self-surrender?

When men want desperately to preserve that which they deem masculine—the controlling power—then they insist on the necessity of the feminine as that which must be controlled and mastered. Men force themselves into the role of phallic man and seek always to be hard, to be tough, to be competitive, to assert their "manhood." Alan Watts wisely sees this masculine striving for rigidity as "nothing more than an emotional paralysis" which causes men to misunderstand the bisexuality of their own nature, to force a necessarily unsatisfactory sexual response, and to be exploitative in their relations with women and the world.

According to Plato's myth, the ancients thought of men and women as originally a single being cut asunder into male and female by an angry god. There is a good biological basis to this myth; although the sexes are externally differentiated, they are still structurally homologous. Psychologically, too, the speculations of George Groddeck are apt:

> Personal sex cuts right across the fundamental qualities of human nature; the very word suggests the violent splitting asunder of humanity into male and female. *Sexus* is derived from *secare*, to cut, from which we also get *segmentum*, a part cut from a circle. It conveys the idea that man and woman once formed a unity, that together they make a complete whole, the perfect circle of the individuum and that both sections share the properties of this individuum. These suggestions are of course in harmony with the ancient Hebrew legend, which told how God first created a human being who was both male and female, Adam-Lilith, and later sawed this asunder.[1]

The dichotomizing of human qualities can thus be seen as a basic error in men's understanding of nature. Biologically, both sexes are always present in each. Perhaps with the overcoming of women's oppression, the woman in man will be allowed to emerge. If, as Coleridge said, great minds are androgynous, there can be no feminine or masculine ideal, but only as the poet realizes,

> . . . what is true is human,
> homosexuality, heterosexuality
> There is something more important:

> to be human
> in which kind
> is kind.[2]

[1] *The World of Man* (New York, Vision Press, 1951).
[2] Clayton Eshleman, from "Holding Duncan's Hand."

'because you are
a woman'

j. r. lucas

Plato was the first feminist. In the *Republic* he puts forward the
view that women are just the same as men, only not quite so good.
It is a view which has often been expressed in recent years, and
generates strong passions. Some of these have deep biological
origins, which a philosopher can only hope to recognize and not
to assuage. But much of the heat engendered is due to unnecessary
friction between views which are certainly compatible and probably correct. And here a philosopher can help. If we can divide the
issues neatly, at the joints, then we need not quarrel with one
another for saying something, probably true, because what is
being maintained is misconstrued and taken to mean something
else, probably false.

The feminist debate turns on the application of certain concepts of justice, equality and humanity. Should the fact—'the mere
fact'—of a person's being a woman disqualify her from being a
member of the Stock Exchange, the Bench of Bishops or the House
of Lords, or from obtaining a mortgage, owning property, having
a vote or going to heaven? Is it not, say the feminists, just as irrational and inequitable as disqualifying a man on the grounds of
the colour of his hair? Is it not, counter the anti-feminists, just as

From J. R. Lucas, "'Because You Are a Woman,'" *Philosophy*, 48 (1973) 161–171.
Reprinted by permission of the author and The Royal Institute of Philosophy.

rational as drawing a distinction between men on the one hand and children, animals, lunatics, Martians and computers on the other? Whereupon we come to enunciate the formal platitude that women are the same as men in some respects, different from them in others, just as men are the same in some respects as children, animals, lunatics, Martians and computers, and different in others. And then we have to embark on more substantial questions of the respects in which men and women are the same, and those in which they are different; and of whether any such differences could be relevant to the activity or institution in question, or could be comparable to the differences, generally acknowledged to exist, between *homo sapiens* and the rest of creation. Even if women are different from men, a feminist might argue, why should this be enough to debar them from the floor of the Stock Exchange, when, apparently, there is no objection to the presence of computers?

We are faced with two questions. We need to know first what exactly are the ways in which women differ from men, and this in turn raises issues of the methods whereby such questions may be answered. Only when these methodological issues have been discussed can we turn to the more substantial ones of morals and politics concerned with whether it can ever be right to treat a woman differently from a man on account of her sex, or whether that is a factor which must always be regarded as in itself irrelevant.

I

The facts of femininity are much in dispute. The development of genetic theory is some help, but not a decisive one. We know that men differ from women in having one Y-chromosome and only one X-chromosome whereas women have two X-chromosomes. Apart from the X- and Y-chromosomes, exactly the same sort of chromosomes turn up in men and women indifferently. The genetic make-up of each human being is constituted by his chromosomes, which occur in pairs, one of each pair coming from the father, the other from the mother. Men and women share the same gene pool. So far as chromosomes, other than the X- and Y-ones, are concerned, men and women of the same breeding community are far more alike than members of different species, or even men of different races. This constitutes a powerful argument against the doctrine, attributed by some to the Mahometans, that women have no souls; contrary to the view of many young males, they are not just birds; or, in more modern parlance, it gives empirical support to arguments based on the principle of Universal Humanity. Women are worthy of respect, for the same reasons as men

133

are. If it is wrong to hurt a man, to harm him, humiliate him or frustrate him, then it is wrong to hurt, harm, humiliate or frustrate a woman; for she is of the same stock as he, and they share the same inheritance and have almost all their chromosometypes in common.

Early genetic theory assumed a one–one correlation between pairs of hereditary genetic factors and their manifested effects in the individual. Whether I had brown eyes or blue eyes depended on whether I had the pair of factors BB, Bb or bB, in all of which cases I should have brown eyes, or whether I had bb, in which case I should have blue eyes. No other genetic factor was supposed to be relevant to the colour of my eyes, nor was the possession of a B or a b gene relevant to anything else about me. If this theory represented the whole truth, the feminist case would be simple. Sex is irrelevant to everything except sex. The fact of a man's being male or a woman's being female would be a 'mere fact' with no bearing on anything except sexual intercourse and the procreation of children. It would be rational to hold that only a male could be guilty of rape, and it might be permissible to have marriage laws which countenanced only heterosexual unions, and to look for proofs of paternity as well as of maternity. Perhaps we might go a very little further, and on the same grounds as we admit that negroes are not really eligible for the part of Iago, admit that males could not really expect to be employed as models for female fashions, and *vice versa*. Beyond these few and essentially unimportant exceptions, it would be as wrong for the law to discriminate between the sexes as it would be if it were to prefer blondes.

Simple genetic theory is, however, too simple. It needs to be complicated in two ways. First, although chromosomes occur in pairs, each single one being inherited more or less independently of every other one, each chromosome contains not just one, but many, many genetic factors, and these are not all independently inherited, and some, indeed, like the one responsible for haemophilia, are sex-linked. There are, so far as we know, relatively few effects—and those mostly bad—which are caused by factors contained in the Y-chromosome, and there is a slight *a priori* argument against many features being thus transmitted (because the Y-chromosome is much smaller than the others, and so, presumably, carries less genetic information): but there could well be more complicated effects due to a relatively rare recessive gene not being marked in the male as it probably would have been in the female. Mathematical talent might be like haemophilia or colour-blindness: it is consonant with what we know of genetic theory that only one in a thousand inherit the genetic factor, which if it is inherited by a boy then becomes manifest, but which if it is inherited by a girl, still in 999 cases out of a thousand is marked by a dominant unmathematicality. The second complication is more fundamental than the first. Genetic factors not only are not inherited independently of the others, but do not operate independently of the others. What is important is not simply whether I have BB, Bb, or bb, but whether I have one of these pairs in conjunction with some set of other pairs of factors. In particular, whether a person is male or female may affect whether or not some other hereditary factor manifests itself or not. Only men go bald. There are many physical features and physiological processes which are affected by whether a person is male or female. So far as our bodies are concerned, the fact of a person's being a man or a woman is not 'a mere fact' but a fundamental one. Although there are many similarities between men and women, the differences are pervasive, systematic and of great biological significance. Almost the first question a hospital needs to ask is 'M or F?'.

Many feminists are dualists, and while conceding certain bodily differences between men and women, deny that there is any inheritance of intellectual ability or traits of character at all. Genetic theory, as far as it goes, is against them. There is reasonable evidence for the inheritance of skills and patterns of behaviour in other animals, and in particular of those patterns of behaviour we should normally ascribe to the maternal instinct. Human beings are far too complicated to manifest many abilities or traits of character that are simple enough to be susceptible of scientific test; and although we often detect family resemblances in ways of walking and talking, as well as in temperament and emotion, it is not clear how far these are due to inherited factors and how far they have been acquired by imitation or learning. It is, however, a common experience to note resemblances between different members of the same family who have never seen each other and have had no opportunity of imitating one another. Such instances, when cited, are often dismissed as mere anecdotes, belonging to mythology rather than science, and unworthy of the attention of modern-minded thinkers in this day and age. It is difficult to stand one's ground in the face of the charge of being unscientific, for the word 'scientific' has strong evaluative overtones, and to be 'unscientific' smacks of quackery and prejudice. But it remains the case that all discussions about political and social issues must be 'unscientific' in that they are not exclusively based on the measurable results of repeatable experiments. For what we are concerned with is what people feel, decide, and ought to do about these things, and people are different, and feel differently and decide to do different things. If we refuse to admit to the argument any evidence other than the measurable results of reputable experiments, we may still be able to discuss questions of public health, but cannot even entertain those of justice or the political good. And if the feminist rejects all anecdotal evidence on principle, then she is making good her dualism by stipulation, because she is not prepared to recognize intellectual abilities or traits of character in the way in which they normally are recognized. This, of course, is not to urge that every story a boozy buffer cares to tell should be accepted as true or relevant; but only that the word 'scientific' needs to be handled with caution, and not used to rule out of court whole ranges of evidence and whole realms of experience. The canons of scientific evidence are, very properly, strictly drawn; and scientists accept the corollary that the topics amenable to scientific research are correspondingly limited. There are many discussions which cannot be evaluated within the canon of scientific argument upon the basis of scientific observations alone, among them discussions about what is right and good for individuals and societies. But they need not be any the worse for that, although they will be if the participants do not show the same fairness and reasonableness in their discussions as scientists do in their researches.

Another methodological issue is raised by those who acknowledge that there have been and are differences in the intellectual achievements and the typical behaviour of women as compared with men, but attribute all of them exclusively to the social pressures brought to bear upon women which have prevented them from exercising their talents to the full or giving rein to their natural inclinations. When the advocate of male supremacy marshals his masses of major poets against a solitary Sappho, the feminist explains that women have been so confined by domestic pressures and so inhibited by convention that those few with real poetic talent have never had opportunity to bring it to flower. Poets might be poor, but at least they could listen to the Muse undistracted by baby's cries: whereas potential poetesses, unless their lot were cast in Lesbos, were married off and made to think of clothes and nappies to the exclusion of all higher thoughts.

It is difficult to find hard evidence either for or against this thesis. In this it is like many rival explanations or interpretations in history or literature. What moves us to adopt one rather than another is that it seems to us more explanatory or more illuminating than the alternative; and what seems to us more explanatory or illuminating depends largely on our own experience and understanding—and our own prejudices. But although we are very liable to be swayed by prejudice, it does not follow that we inevitably are, and although we are often guided by subjective considerations in deciding between various hypotheses, it does not follow that there is nothing, really, to choose between them. We can envisage evidence, even if we cannot obtain it, which would decide between the two alternatives. The feminist claim would be established if totally unisex societies sprang up and flourished; or if there were as many societies in which the rôles of men and women were reversed as there were traditional ones. Indeed, the existence of any successful and stable society in which the rôles of the sexes are reversed is evidence in favour of the claim. Evidence against is more difficult to come by. Few people deny that social pressures have a very considerable bearing on our behaviour and capacities. Some people argue from the analogy with other animals, whose behaviour is indubitably determined genetically and differs according to their sex; or argue, as I have done, by extrapolation from purely physical features. Both arguments are respectable, neither conclusive. Man is an animal, but very unlike other animals, particularly in respect of the extreme plasticity of human behaviour, nearly all of which is learned. Very few of our responses are purely instinctive; and it is unsafe to claim confidently that maternal feelings must be. What would constitute evidence against the feminist claim would be some intellectual ability or character trait which seemed to be both relatively independent of social circumstance and distributed unevenly between the sexes. Mathematical talent might be a case in point. It seems to be much more randomly distributed in the population than other forms of intellectual ability. If Ramanujan could triumph over his circumstances, then surely numerate sisters to Sappho should abound. But this is far from being a conclusive argument.

There are no conclusive arguments about feminine abilities and attitudes. But the discoveries of the scientists, so far as they go, lend some support to traditional views. It could well be the case that intellectual and psychological characteristics are, like physical ones, influenced by genetic factors. If this is so, the way in which a particular pair of genes in an individual genotype will be manifested in the phenotype will depend on the other genes in the genotype, and may depend greatly on whether there are two X chromosomes or one X and one Y. It could be that the masculine mind is typically more vigorous and combative, and the feminine mind typically more intuitive and responsive, with correspondingly different ranges of interests and inclinations. It would make evolutionary sense if it were, and would fit in with what else we know about the nature of man: but it is still possible to maintain the contrary view; and even if there are in fact differences between men and women, it does not follow that their treatment should be different too.

II

If it could be established that there were no innate intellectual or emotional differences between men and women, the feminists' case would be pretty well made; but it does not follow that to admit that there are differences carries with it an adequate justification for every sort of discrimination, and it is useful to consider what sort of bearing various types of difference might have. Suppose, for example, that mathematical ability were distributed unevenly and according to the same pattern as haemophilia, so that only one in n males have it and only one in n^2 females. This would be a highly relevant factor in framing our educational policy. It would justify the provision of far more opportunities for boys to study higher mathematics than for girls. But it would not justify the total exclusion of girls. Most girls prefer nursing to numeracy, but those few who would rather solve differential equations ought not to be prevented from doing so on the grounds that they are female. Two principles underlie this judgment. First that the connexion between sex and mathematical ability is purely contingent; and secondly that we are in a position in which considerations of the individual's interests and deserts are paramount. Even if there are very few female mathematicians, there is no reason why any particular woman should not be a mathematician. And if any particular woman is, then her being a woman is irrelevant to her actual performance in mathematics. Her being a woman created a presumption, a purely contingent although usually reliable presumption, that she was no good at mathematics. It is like presumptive evidence in a court of law, which could be rebutted, and in this case was, and having been rebutted is of no more relevance in this individual situation, which is all we are concerned with.

Female mathematicians are rare. Few disciplines are so pure as mathematics. In most human activities—even in most academic pursuits—the whole personality is much more involved, and the irrelevance of a person's sex far more dubious. Differences between the sexes are likely to come into play most in ordinary human relations where one person tells another what to do, or persuades, or cajoles or encourages or warns or threatens or acquiesces. In so far as most positions in society are concerned with social relations, it cannot be argued that the differences between the sexes are, of necessity, irrelevant. Although it might be the case that working men would as readily take orders from a fore-woman as a foreman, or that customers would be as pleased to find a handsome boy receptionist as a pretty girl, there is no reason to suppose that it must be so. Moreover, life is not normally either an examination or a trial. It is one of the disadvantages of our meritocratic age that we too readily assume that all social transactions are exclusively concerned with the individual, who needs to be given every opportunity and whose rights must be zealously safeguarded. But examinations and trials are artificial and cumbersome exceptions to the general rule, in which no one individual is the centre of concern. To deny people the fruits of their examination success or to deprive them of their liberty on any grounds irrelevant to their own desert is wrong: but it is not so evidently wrong to frustrate Miss Amazon's hopes of a military career in the Grenadier Guards on the grounds not that she would make a bad soldier but that she would be a disturbing influence in the mess room. Laws and institutions are characteristically two-faced. They set norms for the behaviour of different parties, and need to take into consideration the interests and claims of more than one person. They also need to apply generally, and cannot be tailor-made to each particular situation: they define rôles rather than fit actual personalities, and rôles need to fit the typical rather than the special case. Even if Miss Amazon is sure not to attract sidelong glances from the licentious soldiery, her sisters may not be; and it may be easier to operate an absolute bar than leave it to the recruiting officer to decide whether a particular woman is sufficiently unattractive to be safe. This type of case turns up in many other laws and public regulations. We lay down rigid speed limits because they are easier to apply. There are many towns in which to drive at 30 mph would be dangerous, and many suburbs in which to drive at 45 mph would sometimes be safe. Some boys of ten are better informed about public affairs than other voters of thirty. But the advantage of having a fixed speed limit or a fixed voting age outweighs its admitted unfairness.

We can now see what sort of facts would bring what sort of principles to bear upon our individual decisions and the general structure of our laws and institutions. We need to know not only whether there are differences, but whether these differences are integrally or only contingently connected with a person's sex, and whether they apply in all cases or only as a rule. The more integrally and the more invariably a difference is connected with a person's sex, the more we are entitled to insist that the mere fact of being male or female can constitute a conclusive reason against being allowed to do something. The less integral a difference is, the more the arguments from Formal Equality (or Universalizability) and from Justice will come into play, requiring us to base our decisions only on the features relevant to the case in hand. The less invariable a difference is, the more the arguments from Humanity and again from Justice will come into play, requiring us to pay respect to the interests and inclinations of each individual person, and to weigh her actual interests, as against those of the community at large, on the basis of her actual situation and actual and reasonable desires.

However much I, a male, want to be a mother, a wife or a girlfriend, I am disqualified from those rôles on account of my sex, and I cannot reasonably complain. Not only can I not complain if individuals refuse to regard me as suitable in those rôles, but I have to acknowledge that it is reasonable for society generally to do so, and for the state to legislate accordingly. The state is justified in not countenancing homosexual 'marriages', because of our general understanding of what marriage really is, and the importance we attach to family life. For exactly the same reasons, women are debarred from being regarded in a fatherly or husbandly light; and hence also in those parts of the Christian Church that regard priests as being essentially fathers in God from being clergymen or bishops. How far rôles should be regarded as being integrally dependent on sex is a matter of dispute. In very intimate and personal relationships it is evident that the whole personality is involved, and that since a man—or at least many, non-Platonic men—responds to a woman in a different way from that in which he responds to a man or a woman to a woman, it is natural that these rôles should be essentially dependent on sex. But as the rôles become more limited, so the dependence becomes less. I could hardly complain if I was not given the part of Desdemona or a job as an *au pair* boy on account of my sex: but if I had very feminine features and had grown my hair long and golden, or if I were particularly deft at changing nappies, I might feel a little aggrieved, and certainly I could call in question any law that forbade a man to play the part of a woman or be a nursemaid. Some substantial public good would need to be shown to justify a legal decision enforceable by penal sanctions being uniformly based not on my actual inability to fill the rôle required but only my supposed unsuitability on account of my sex. We demand a higher standard of cogency in arguments justifying what laws there should be than in those concerned only with individual decisions; and although this standard can be satisfied, often by admitting considerations of the public good, yet the arguments need to be adduced, because, in framing laws, we need to be sensitive to individual rights and careful about our criteria of relevance. Although it may be the case that a nurse is a better nurse for having the feminine touch, we hesitate to deem it absolutely essential; and although many more women than men have been good nurses, we do not believe that it must invariably be so. There are male nurses. We reckon it reasonable to prefer a woman in individual cases, but do not insist upon it in all cases by law. We are reluctant to impose severe legal disqualifications, but equally would hesitate to impose upon employers an obligation not to prefer women to play female parts or to be nurses or to join a family in an *au pair* capacity. For we recognize that a person's sex can reasonably be regarded as relevant to his or her suitability for particular posts, and that many institutions will operate on this basis, and are entitled to. I am justified in refusing to employ a male *au pair* girl or a female foreman, although if there are many males anxious to be looking after young children or many women anxious to supervise the work of others, it may be desirable on grounds of Humanity to establish special institutions in which they can fulfil their vocations. If we will not let Miss Amazon join the Grenadier Guards, let there be an ATS or WRAC for her to join instead.

Although we are rightly reluctant to impose legal disqualifications on individuals on grounds extraneous to their individual circumstances, it is inherent in all political thinking that we may find considerations of the general case over-riding those of the individual one; and often we frame our laws with an eye to what men and women are generally like rather than what they invariably are. A man may not adopt an infant girl unless she is more than twenty-five years younger than he, for some men might otherwise use adoption to acquire not so much a daughter as a wife. In many societies women have less freedom in disposing of their property than men; for else, things being as they are, some women would be prevailed upon to divest themselves of it to their long-term disadvantage. Ardent feminists have chafed at the shackles of marriage, and demand freedom from this degrading institution for their sisters as well as themselves. But if this freedom were established it would be the libertine males who would enjoy the benefits of liberation, being then free to leave the women to bear the burdens of parenthood all on their own. If most mothers care more for their children and their homes than most fathers do, then in the absence of institutions that recognize the fact they will in fact be disadvantaged. Some discrimination is needed to redress the balance. But discrimination, even positive discrimination, can work to the disadvantage of individuals, however much it may benefit most people on the whole.

The would-be female Stakhanovite is penalized by the law forbidding firms to employ female labour for sixty hours a week, just as the youthful entrepreneur is handicapped by his legal incapacity, as a minor, to pledge his credit except for the necessities of life, and the skilled racing motorist by the law forbidding him to drive, however safely, at more than 70 miles per hour. In each case the justification is the same: the restriction imposed on the individual, although real and burdensome, is not so severe as to outweigh the benefits that are likely to accrue in the long run to women in general, or to minors, or to motorists. It is in the nature of political society that we forgo some freedoms in order that either we ourselves or other people can secure some good. All we can in general demand is that our sacrifices should not be fruitless, and that if we give up some liberty or immunity it is at least arguable that it will be on balance for the best.

Arguments in politics are nearly always mixed, and involve appeals to different principles, according to how the question is construed. We can elucidate some canons of relevance for some of the principles which may be invoked. Where the principle is that of Universal Humanity, the reason 'Because you are a woman' is always irrelevant to its general applicability, though it may affect the way it is specified: perhaps women feel more strongly about their homes than men do, so that although we ought not, on grounds of humanity, to hurt either men or women, deprivation of her home would constitute a greater hurt to a woman than to a man. The principle of Universal Humanity is pervasive in its applications, but is conclusive only over a much more limited range. It is always wrong to torture; but often we cannot help hurting people's feelings or harming their interests if other values —justice, liberty, the public good—are to be preserved. And therefore arguments based on the principle of universal humanity may be over-ridden by ones based on other principles, also valuable. When the principle invoked is that of Formal Equality (or Universalizability) the reason 'Because you are a woman' cannot be dismissed out of hand as necessarily irrelevant. A person's sex is not a 'mere fact', evidently and necessarily separate from all other facts, and such that it is immediately obvious that no serious argument can be founded upon it. Particularly with those rôles that involve relationships with other people, and especially where those relationships are fairly personal ones, it is likely to matter whether it is a man or a woman that is chosen. When some principle of Justice is at stake, the criteria of relevance become fairly stringent. We are concerned only with the individual's actions, attitudes and abilities, and the reason 'Because you are a woman' must either be integrally connected with matter in issue (as in 'Why cannot I marry the girl I love?) or be reliably, although only contingently, connected with it (as in 'Why cannot I get myself employed for 60 hours a week?'); and in the latter case we feel that Justice has been compromised, although perhaps acceptably so, if there is no way whereby an individual can prove she is an exception to the rule and be treated as such. As the interests of the individual become more peripheral, or can be satisfied in alternative ways that are available, the principle of justice recedes, and we are more ready to accept rules and institutions based on general principles of social utility or tradition, and designed only to fit the general case. It is legitimate to base public feeling on such differences as seem to be relevant, but the more a law or an institution is based on merely a contingent, and not an integral, concomitance, the more ready we should be to cater for exceptions.

With sufficient care we may be able to disentangle what is true in the feminists' contention from what is false. At least we should be able to avoid the dilemma, which seems to be taken for granted by most participants in the debate, that we must say that women either are in all respects exactly the same as men or else are in all respects different from, and inferior to, them, and not members of the same universe of discourse at all. I do not share Plato's feelings about sex. I think the sexes are different, and incomparable. No doubt, women are not quite as good as men, *in some respects:* but since men are not nearly as good as women in others, this carries with it no derogatory implication of uniform inferiority. Exactly what these differences are, and, indeed, what sort of differences they are, is a matter for further research; and exactly what bearing they should have in the application of the various principles we value in making up our mind about social matters is a matter for further philosophical thought. But without any further thought we can align our emotions with the proponents of Women's Lib on the most important issue of all. What angers them most is the depersonalization of women in the Admass society: and one cannot but sympathize with their protest against women being treated as mere objects of sexual gratification by men; but cannot avoid the conclusion that their arguments and activities in fact lead towards just that result which they deplore. If we are insensitive to the essential femininity of the female sex, we shall adopt an easy egalitarianism which, while denying that there are any genetic differences, allows us to conclude in most individual cases that women, judged by male standards of excellence, are less good than their male rivals. Egalitarianism ends by depersonalizing women and men alike.

preferential hiring

judith jarvis thomson

Many people are inclined to think preferential hiring an obvious injustice.[1] I should have said "feel" rather than "think": it seems to me the matter has not been carefully thought out, and that what is in question, really, is a gut reaction.

I am going to deal with only a very limited range of preferential hirings: that is, I am concerned with cases in which several candidates present themselves for a job, in which the hiring officer finds, on examination, that all are equally qualified to hold that job, and he then straightway declares for the black, or for the woman, because he or she *is* a black or a woman. And I shall talk only of hiring decisions in the universities, partly because I am most familiar with them, partly because it is in the universities that the most vocal and articulate opposition to preferential hiring is now heard—not surprisingly, perhaps, since no one is more vocal and articulate than a university professor who feels deprived of his rights.

From Judith Jarvis Thomson, "Preferential Hiring," *Philosophy and Public Affairs*, vol. 2, no. 4 (copyright © 1973 by Princeton University Press), pp. 364–384. Reprinted by permission of Princeton University Press.

[1]This essay is an expanded version of a talk given at the Conference on the Liberation of Female Persons, held at North Carolina State University at Raleigh, on March 26–28, 1973, under a grant from the S & H Foundation. I am indebted to James Thomson and the members of the Society for Ethical and Legal Philosophy for criticism of an earlier draft.

I suspect that some people may say, Oh well, in *that* kind of case it's all right, what we object to is preferring the less qualified to the better qualified. Or again, What we object to is refusing even to consider the qualifications of white males. I shall say nothing at all about these things. I think that the argument I shall give for saying that preferential hiring is not unjust in the cases I do concentrate on can also be appealed to to justify it outside that range of cases. But I won't draw any conclusions about cases outside it. Many people do have that gut reaction I mentioned against preferential hiring in *any* degree or form; and it seems to me worthwhile bringing out that there is good reason to think they are wrong to have it. Nothing I say will be in the slightest degree novel or original. It will, I hope, be enough to set the relevant issues out clearly.

I

But first, something should be said about qualifications.

I said I would consider only cases in which the several candidates who present themselves for the job are equally qualified to hold it; and there plainly are difficulties in the way of saying precisely how this is to be established, and even what is to be established. Strictly academic qualifications seem at a first glance to be relatively straight-forward: the hiring officer must see if the candidates have done equally well in courses (both courses they took, and any they taught), and if they are recommended equally strongly by their teachers, and if the work they submit for consideration is equally good. There is no denying that even these things are less easy to establish than first appears: for example, you may have a suspicion that Professor Smith is given to exaggeration, and that his "great student" is in fact less strong than Professor Jones's "good student"—but do you *know* that this is so? But there is a more serious difficulty still: as blacks and women have been saying, strictly academic indicators may themselves be skewed by prejudice. My impression is that women, white and black, may possibly suffer more from this than black males. A black male who is discouraged or down-graded for being black is discouraged or down-graded out of dislike, repulsion, a desire to avoid contact; and I suspect that there are very few teachers nowadays who allow themselves to feel such things, or, if they do feel them, to act on them. A woman who is discouraged or down-graded for being a woman is not discouraged or down-graded out of dislike, but out of a conviction she is not serious, and I suspect that while there are very few teachers nowadays who allow themselves to feel that women generally are not serious, there are many who allow themselves to feel of the particular individual women students they confront that Ah, this one isn't serious, and in fact that one isn't either, nor is that other one—women generally are, of course, one thing, but these particular women, really they're just girls in search of husbands, are quite another. And I suspect that this will be far harder to root out. A teacher could not face himself in the mirror of a morning if he had down-graded anyone out of dislike; but a teacher can well face himself in the mirror if he down-grades someone out of a conviction that that person is not serious: after all, life is serious, and jobs and work, and who can take the unserious seriously? who pays attention to the dilettante? So the hiring officer must read very very carefully between the lines in the candidates' dossiers even to assess their strictly academic qualifications.

And then of course there are other qualifications besides the strictly academic ones. Is one of the candidates exceedingly disagreeable? A department is not merely a collection of individuals, but a working unit; and if anyone is going to disrupt that unit, and to make its work more difficult, then this counts against him—he may be as well qualified in strictly academic terms, but he is not as well qualified. Again, is one of the candidates incurably sloppy? Is he going to mess up his records, is he going to have to be nagged to get his grades in, and worse, is he going to lose students' papers? This too would count against him: keeping track of students' work, records, and grades, after all, is part of the job.

What seems to me to be questionable, however, is that a candidate's race or sex is itself a qualification. Many people who favor preferential hiring in the universities seem to think it is; in their view, if a group of candidates is equally well qualified in respect of those measures I have already indicated, then if one is of the right race (black) or of the right sex (female), then that being itself a qualification, it tips the balance, and that one is the best qualified. If so, then of course no issue of injustice, or indeed of any other impropriety, is raised if the hiring officer declares for that one of the candidates straightway.

Why does race or sex seem to many to be, itself, a qualification? There seem to be two claims in back of the view that it is. First, there is the claim that blacks learn better from a black, women from a woman. One hears this less often in respect of women; blacks, however, are often said to mistrust the whites who teach them, with the result that they simply do not learn as well, or progress as far, as they would if taught by blacks. Secondly, and this one hears in respect of women as well as blacks, what is wanted is *role models.* The proportion of black and women faculty members in the larger universities (particularly as one moves up the ladder of rank) is very much smaller than the proportion of blacks and women in the society at large—even, in the case of women, than the proportion of them amongst recipients of Ph.D. degrees from those very same universities. Black and women students suffer a constricting of ambition because of this. They need to see members of their race or sex who are accepted, successful, professionals. They need concrete evidence that those of their race or sex *can* become accepted, successful professionals.

And perhaps it is thought that it is precisely by virtue of having a role model right in the classroom that blacks do learn better from a black, women from a woman.

Now it is obviously essential for a university to staff its classrooms with people who can teach, and so from whom its students can learn, and indeed learn as much and as well as possible—teaching, after all, is, if not the whole of the game, then anyway a very large part of it. So if the first claim is true, then race and sex *do* seem to be qualifications. It obviously would not follow that a university should continue to regard them as qualifications indefinitely; I suppose, however, that it would follow that it should regard them as qualifications at least until the proportion of blacks and women on the faculty matches the proportion of blacks and women among the students.

But in the first place, allowing this kind of consideration to have a bearing on a hiring decision might make for trouble of a kind that blacks and women would not be at all happy with. For suppose it could be made out that white males learn better from white males? (I once, years ago, had a student who said he really felt uncomfortable in a class taught by a woman, it was interfering with his work, and did I mind if he switched to another section?) I suppose we would feel that this was due to prejudice, and that it was precisely to be discouraged, certainly not encouraged by establishing hiring ratios. I don't suppose it is true of white males generally that they learn better from white males; I am concerned only with the way in which we should take the fact, if it were a fact, that they did—and if it would be improper to take it to be reason to think being a white male is a qualification in a teacher, then how shall we take its analogue to be reason to think being black, or being a woman, is a qualification in a teacher?

And in the second place, I must confess that, speaking personally, I do not find the claim we are looking at borne out in experience; I do not think that as a student I learned any better, or any more, from the women who taught me than from the men, and

I do not think that my own women students now learn any better or any more from me than they do from my male colleagues. Blacks, of course, may have, and may have had, very different experiences, and I don't presume to speak for them—or even for women generally. But my own experience being what it is, it seems to *me* that any defense of preferential hiring in the universities which takes this first claim as premise is so far not an entirely convincing one.

The second claim, however, does seem to me to be plainly true: black and women students do need role models, they do need concrete evidence that those of their race or sex can become accepted, successful, professionals—plainly, you won't try to become what you don't believe you can become.

But do they need these role models right there in the classroom? Of course it might be argued that they do: that a black learns better from a black teacher, a woman from a woman teacher. But we have already looked at this. And if they are, though needed, not needed in the classroom, then is it the university's job to provide them?

For it must surely be granted that a college, or university, has not the responsibility—or perhaps, if it is supported out of public funds, even the right—to provide just *any* service to its students which it might be good for them, or even which they may need, to be provided with. Sports seem to me plainly a case in point. No doubt it is very good for students to be offered, and perhaps even required to become involved in, a certain amount of physical exercise; but I can see no reason whatever to think that universities should be expected to provide facilities for it, or taxpayers to pay for those facilities. I suspect others may disagree, but my own feeling is that it is the same with medical and psychiatric services: I am sure that at least some students need medical and psychiatric help, but I cannot see why it should be provided for them in the universities, at public expense.

So the further question which would have to be answered is this: granting that black and female students need black and female role models, why should the universities be expected to provide them within their faculties? In the case of publicly supported universities, why should taxpayers be expected to provide them?

I don't say these questions can't be answered. But I do think we need to come at them from a quite different direction. So I shall simply sidestep this ground for preferential hiring in the universities. The defense I give will not turn on anyone's supposing that of two otherwise equally well qualified candidates, one may be better qualified for the job by virtue, simply, of being of the right race or sex.

II

I mentioned several times in the preceding section the obvious fact that it is the taxpayers who support public universities. Not that private universities are wholly private: the public contributes to the support of most of them, for example by allowing them tax-free use of land, and of the dividends and capital gains on investments. But it will be the public universities in which the problem appears most starkly: as I shall suggest, it is the fact of public support that makes preferential hiring in the universities problematic.

For it seems to me that—other things being equal—there is no problem about preferential hiring in the case of a wholly private college or university, that is, one which receives no measure of public support at all, and which lives simply on tuition and (non-tax-deductible) contributions.

The principle here seems to me to be this: no perfect stranger has a right to be given a benefit which is yours to dispose of; no perfect stranger even has a right to be given an equal chance at getting a benefit which is yours to dispose of. You not only needn't give the benefit to the first perfect stranger who walks in and asks for it; you needn't even give him a chance at it, as, e.g., by tossing a coin.

I should stress that I am here talking about *benefits*, that is, things which people would like to have, which would perhaps not merely please them, but improve their lives, but which they don't actually *need*. (I suspect the same holds true of things people do actually need, but many would disagree, and as it is unnecessary to speak here of needs, I shall not discuss them.) If I have extra apples (they're mine: I grew them, on my own land, from my own trees), or extra money, or extra tickets to a series of lectures I am giving on How to Improve Your Life Through Philosophy, and am prepared to give them away, word of this may get around, and people may present themselves as candidate recipients. I do not have to give to the first, or to proceed by letting them all draw straws; if I really do own the things, I can give to whom I like, on any ground I please, and in so doing, I violate no one's *rights*, I treat no one *unjustly*. None of the candidate recipients has a right to the benefit, or even to a chance at it.

There are four caveats. (1) Some grounds for giving or refraining from giving are less respectable than others. Thus, I might give the apples to the first who asks for them simply because he is the first who asks for them. Or again, I might give the apples to the first who asks for them because he is black, and because I am black and feel an interest in and concern for blacks which I do not feel in and for whites. In either case, not merely do I do what it is within my rights to do, but more, my ground for giving them to that person is a not immoral ground for giving them to him. But I might instead give the apples to the sixth who asks, and this because the first five were black and I hate blacks— or because the first five were white and I hate whites. Here I do what I have a right to do (for the apples are *mine*), and I violate no one's rights in doing it, but my ground for disposing of the apples as I did was a bad one; and it might even, more strongly, be said that I ought not have disposed of the apples in the way I did. But it is important to note that it is perfectly consistent, on the one hand, that a man's ground for acting as he did was a bad one, and even that he ought not have done what he did, and, on the other hand, that he had a right to do what he did, that he violated no one's rights in doing it, and that no one can complain he was unjustly treated.

The second caveat (2) is that although I have a right to dispose of my apples as I wish, I have no right to harm, or gratuitously hurt or offend. Thus I am within my rights to refuse to give the apples to the first five because they are black (or because they are white); but I am not within my rights to say to them "I refuse to give you apples because you are black (or white) and because those who are black (or white) are inferior."

And (3) if word of my extra apples, and of my willingness to give them away, got around because I advertised, saying or implying First Come First Served Till Supply Runs Out, then I cannot refuse the first five because they are black, or white. By so advertising I have *given* them a right to a chance at the apples. If they come in one at a time, I must give out apples in order, till the supply runs out; if they come in together, and I have only four apples, then I must either cut up the apples, or give them each an equal chance, as, e.g., by having them draw straws.

And lastly (4), there may be people who would say that I don't really, or don't fully own those apples, even though I grew them on my own land, from my own trees, and therefore that I don't have a right to give them away as I see fit. For after all, I don't own the police who protected my land while those apples were growing, or the sunlight because of which they grew. Or again, wasn't it just a matter of luck for me that I was born with a green thumb? —and why should I profit from a competence that I didn't deserve to have, that I didn't earn? Or perhaps some other reason might be put forward for saying that I don't own those apples. I don't want to take this up here. It seems to me wrong, but I want to let it pass. If anyone thinks that I don't own the apples, or, more generally, that no one really or fully owns anything, he will regard what I shall say in the remainder of this section, in which I talk about what may be done with what is privately owned, as an idle academic exercise. I'll simply ask that anyone who does think this be patient: we will come to what is publicly owned later.

Now what was in question was a job, not apples; and it may be insisted that to give a man a job is not to give him a benefit, but rather something he needs. Well, I am sure that people do need jobs, that it does not fully satisfy people's needs to supply them only with food, shelter, and medical care. Indeed, I am sure that people need, not merely jobs, but jobs that interest them, and that they can therefore get satisfaction from the doing of. But on the other hand, I am not at all sure that any candidate for a job in a university needs a job in a university. One would very much like it if all graduate students who wish it could find jobs teaching in universities; it is in some measure a tragedy that a person should spend three or four years preparing for a career, and then find there is no job available, and that he has in consequence to take work which is less interesting than he had hoped and prepared for. But one thing seems plain: no one *needs* that work which would interest him most in all the whole world of work. Plenty of people have to make do with work they like less than other work—no economy is rich enough to provide everyone with the work he likes best of all—and I should think that this does not mean they lack something they *need.* We are all of us prepared to tax ourselves so that no one shall be in need; but I should imagine that we are not prepared to tax ourselves (to tax barbers, truck drivers, sales-clerks, waitresses, and factory workers) in order that everyone who wants a university job, and is competent to fill it, shall have one made available to him.

All the same, if a university job is a benefit rather than some-thing needed, it is anyway not a "pure" benefit (like an apple), but an "impure" one. To give a man a university job is to give him an opportunity to do work which is interesting and satisfy-ing; but he will only *be* interested and satisfied if he actually does the work he is given an opportunity to do, and does it well.

What this should remind us of is that certain cases of prefer-ential hiring might well be utterly irrational. Suppose we have an eating club, and need a new chef; we have two applicants, a qual-ified French chef, and a Greek who happens to like to cook, though he doesn't do it very well. We are fools if we say to ourselves "We like the Greeks, and dislike the French, so let's hire the Greek." We simply won't eat as well as we could have, and eating, after all, was the point of the club. On the other hand, it's *our* club, and so *our* job. And who shall say it is not within a man's rights to dispose of what really is his in as foolish a way as he likes?

And there is no irrationality, of course, if one imagines that the two applicants are equally qualified French chefs, and one is a cousin of one of our members, the other a perfect stranger. Here if we declare directly for the cousin, we do not act irrationally, we violate no one's rights, and indeed do not have a morally bad ground for making the choice we make. It's not a morally splendid ground, but it isn't a morally bad one either.

Universities differ from eating clubs in one way which is important for present purposes: in an eating club, those who consume what the club serves are the members, and thus the owners of the club themselves—by contrast, if the university is wholly private, those who consume what it serves are not among the owners. This makes a difference: the owners of the university have a responsibility not merely to themselves (as the owners of an eating club do), but also to those who come to buy what if offers. It could, I suppose, make plain in its advertising that it is prepared to allow the owners' racial or religious or other preferences to outweigh academic qualifications in its teachers. But in the absence of that, it must, in light of what a university is normally expected to be and to aim at, provide the best teachers it can afford. It does not merely act irrationally, but indeed violates the rights of its student-customers if it does not.

On the other hand, this leaves it open to the university that in case of a choice between equally qualified candidates, it violates no one's rights if it declares for the black because he is black, or for the white because he is white. To the wholly *private* university, that is, for that is all I have so far been talking of. Other things being equal—that is, given it has not advertised the job in a manner which would entitle applicants to believe that all who are equally qualified will be given an equal chance at it, and given it does not gratuitously give offence to those whom it rejects—the university may choose as it pleases, and violates no one's rights in doing so. Though no doubt its grounds for choosing may be morally bad ones, and we may even wish to say, more strongly, that it ought not choose as it does.

What will have come out in the preceding is that the issue I am concerned with is a moral, and not a legal one. My understanding is that the law does prevent an employer wholly in the private sector from choosing a white rather than a black on ground of that difference alone—though not from choosing a black rather than a white on ground of that difference alone. Now if, as many people say, legal rights (or perhaps, legal rights in a relatively just society) create moral rights, then even a moral investigation should take the law into account; and indeed, if I am not mistaken as to the law, it would have to be concluded that blacks (but not whites) do have rights of the kind I have been denying. I want to sidestep all this. My question can be re-put: would a private employer's choosing a white (or black) rather than a black (or white) on ground of that difference alone be a violation of anyone's rights if there were no law making it illegal. And the answer seems to me to be: it would not.

III

But hardly any college or university in America is purely private. As I said, most enjoy some public support, and the moral issues may be affected by the extent of the burden carried by the public. I shall concentrate on universities which are entirely publicly funded, such as state or city universities, and ignore the complications which might arise in case of partial private funding.

The special problem which arises here, as I see it, is this: where a community pays the bills, the community owns the university.

I said earlier that the members, who are therefore the owners, of a private eating club may declare for whichever chef they wish, even if the man they declare for is not as well qualified for the job as some other; in choosing amongst applicants, they are *not* choosing amongst fellow members of the club who is to get some benefit from the club. But now suppose, by contrast, that two of us who are members arrive at the same time, and there is only one available table. And suppose also that this has never happened before, and that the club has not voted on any policy for handling it when it does happen. What seems to me to be plain is this: the headwaiter cannot indulge in preferential seating, he cannot simply declare for one or the other of us on just any ground he pleases. He must randomize: as it might be, by tossing a coin.

Or again, suppose someone arrives at the dining room with a gift for the club: a large and very splendid apple tart. And suppose that this, too, has never happened before, and that the club has not voted on any policy for handling it when it does happen. What seems to me plain is this: the headwaiter cannot distribute that tart in just any manner, and on any ground he pleases. If the tart won't keep till the next meeting, and it's impossible to convene one now, he must divide the tart amongst us equally.

Consideration of these cases might suggest the following principle: every owner of a jointly owned property has a right to either an equal chance at, or an equal share in, any benefit which that property generates, and which is available for distribution amongst the owners—equal chance rather than equal share if the benefit is indivisible, or for some reason is better left undivided.

Now I have all along been taking it that the members of a club jointly own the club, and therefore jointly own whatever the club owns. It seems to me possible to view a community in the same way: to suppose that its members jointly own it, and therefore jointly own whatever it owns. If a community is properly viewed in this way, and if the principle I set out above is true, then every member of the community is a joint owner of whatever the community owns, and so in particular, a joint owner of its university; and therefore every member of the community has a right to an equal chance at, or equal share in, any benefit which the university generates, which is available for distribution amongst the owners. And that includes university jobs, if, as I argued, a university job is a benefit.

Alternatively, one might view a community as an imaginary Person: one might say that the members of that community are in some sense participants in that Person, but that they do not jointly own what the Person owns. One might in fact say the same of a club: that its members do not jointly own the club or anything which the club owns, but only in some sense participate in the Person which owns the things. And then the cases I mentioned might suggest an analogous principle: every "participant" in a Person (Community-Person, Club-Person) has a right to either an equal chance at, or an equal share in, any benefit which is generated by a property which that Person owns, which is available for distribution amongst the "participants."

On the other hand, if we accept any of this, we have to remember that there are cases in which a member may, without the slightest impropriety, be deprived of this equal chance or equal share. For it is plainly not required that the university's hiring officer decide who gets the available job by randomizing amongst *all* the community members, however well- or ill-qualified, who want it. The university's student-customers, after all, have rights too; and their rights to good teaching are surely more stringent than each member's right (if each has such a right) to an equal chance at the job. I think we do best to reserve the term "violation of a right" for cases in which a man is unjustly deprived of something he has a right to, and speak rather of "overriding a right" in cases in which, though a man is deprived of something he has a right to, it is not unjust to deprive him of it. So here the

154

members' rights to an equal chance (if they have them) would be, not violated, but merely overridden.

It could of course be said that these principles hold only of benefits of a kind I pointed to earlier, and called "pure" benefits (such as apples and apple tarts), and that we should find some other, weaker, principle to cover "impure" benefits (such as jobs).

Or it could be said that a university job is not a benefit which is available for distribution amongst the community members— that although a university job is a benefit, it is, in light of the rights of the students, available for distribution only amongst those members of the community who are best qualified to hold it. And therefore that they alone have a right to an equal chance at it.

It is important to notice, however, that unless *some* such principle as I have set out is true of the publicly owned university, there is no real problem about preferential hiring in it. Unless the white male applicant who is turned away had a right that this should not be done, doing so is quite certainly not violating any of his rights. Perhaps being joint owner of the university (on the first model) or being joint participant in the Person which owns the university (on the second model), do not give him a right to an equal chance at the job; perhaps he is neither joint owner nor joint participant (some third model is preferable), and it is something else which gives him his right to an equal chance at the job. Or perhaps he hasn't a right to an equal chance at the job, but has instead some other right which is violated by declaring for the equally qualified black or woman straightway. It is here that it seems to me it emerges most clearly that opponents of preferential hiring are merely expressing a gut reaction against it: for they have not asked themselves precisely what right is in question, and what it issues from.

Perhaps there is lurking in the background some sense that everyone has a right to "equal treatment," and that it is this which is violated by preferential hiring. But what on earth right is this? Mary surely does not have to decide between Tom and Dick by toss of a coin, if what is in question is marrying. Nor even, as I said earlier, if what is in question is giving out apples, which she grew on her own land, on her own trees.

It could, of course, be argued that declaring for the black or woman straightway isn't a violation of the white male applicant's rights, but is all the same wrong, bad, something which ought not be done. As I said, it is perfectly consistent that one ought not do something which it is, nevertheless, no violation of anyone's rights to do. So perhaps opponents of preferential hiring might say that rights are not in question, and still argue against it on other grounds. I say they *might*, but I think they plainly do better not to. If the white male applicant has no rights which would be violated, and appointing the black or woman indirectly benefits other blacks or women (remember that need for role models), and thereby still more indirectly benefits us all (by widening the available pool of talent), then it is very hard to see how it could come out to be morally objectionable to declare for the black or woman straightway.

I think we should do the best we can for those who oppose preferential hiring: I think we should grant that the white male applicant has a right to an equal chance at the job, and see what happens for preferential hiring if we do. I shall simply leave open whether this right issues from considerations of the kind I drew attention to, and so also whether or not every member of the community, however well- or ill-qualified for the job, has the same right to an equal chance at it.

Now it is, I think, widely believed that we may, without injustice, refuse to grant a man what he has a right to only if *either* someone else has a conflicting and more stringent right, *or* there is some very great benefit to be obtained by doing so—perhaps that a disaster of some kind is thereby averted. If so, then there really is trouble for preferential hiring. For what more stringent right could be thought to override the right of the white male applicant for an equal chance? What great benefit obtained, what disaster averted, by declaring for the black or the woman straightway? I suggested that benefits are obtained, and they are not small ones. But are they large enough to override a right? If these questions cannot be satisfactorily answered, then it looks as if the hiring officer does act unjustly, and does violate the rights of the white males, if he declares for the black or woman straightway.

But in fact there are other ways in which a right may be overridden. Let's go back to that eating club again. Suppose that now it has happened that two of us arrive at the same time when there is only one available table, we think we had better decide on some policy for handling it when it happens. And suppose that we have of late had reason to be especially grateful to one of the members, whom I'll call Smith: Smith has done a series of very great favors for the club. It seems to me we might, out of gratitude to Smith, adopt the following policy: for the next six months, if two members arrive at the same time, and there is only one available table, then Smith gets in first, if he's one of the two; whereas if he's not, then the headwaiter shall toss a coin.

We might even vote that for the next year, if he wants apple tart, he gets more of it than the rest of us.

It seems to me that there would be no impropriety in our taking these actions—by which I mean to include that there would be no injustice in our taking them. Suppose another member, Jones, votes No. Suppose he says "Look. I admit we all benefited from what Smith did for us. But still, I'm a member, and a member in as good standing as Smith is. So I have a right to an equal chance (and equal share), and I demand what I have a right to." I think we may rightly feel that Jones merely shows insensitivity: he does not adequately appreciate what Smith did for us. Jones, like all of us, has a right to an equal chance at such benefits as the club has available for distribution to the members; but there is no injustice in a majority's refusing to grant the members this equal chance, in the name of a debt of gratitude to Smith.

It is worth noticing an important difference between a debt of gratitude and debts owed to a creditor. Suppose the club had borrowed $1000 from Dickenson, and then was left as a legacy, a painting appraised at $1000. If the club has no other saleable assets, and if no member is willing to buy the painting, then I take it that justice would precisely require *not* randomizing amongst the members who is to get that painting, but would instead require our offering it to Dickenson. Jones could not complain that to offer it to Dickenson is to treat him, Jones, unjustly: Dickenson has a right to be paid back, and that right is more stringent than any member's right to an equal chance at the painting. Now Smith, by contrast, did not have a right to be given anything, he did not have a right to our adopting a policy of preferential seating in his favor. If we fail to do anything for Dickenson, we do him an injustice; if we fail to do anything for Smith, we do *him* no injustice— our failing is, not injustice, but ingratitude. There is no harm in speaking of debts of gratitude and in saying that they are owed to a benefactor, by analogy with debts owed to a creditor; but it is important to remember that a creditor has, and a benefactor does not have, a right to repayment.

To move now from clubs to more serious matters, suppose two candidates for a civil service job have equally good test scores, but that there is only one job available. We could decide between them by coin-tossing. But in fact we do allow for declaring for A straightway, where A is a veteran, and B is not.[2] It may be that B is a nonveteran through no fault of his own: perhaps he was refused induction for flat feet, or a heart murmur. That is, those things in virtue of which B is a nonveteran may be things which

[2]To the best of my knowledge, the analogy between veterans' preference and the preferential hiring of blacks has been mentioned in print only by Edward T. Chase, in a Letter to the Editor, *Commentary*, February 1973.

it was no more in his power to control or change than it is in anyone's power to control or change the color of his skin. Yet the fact is that B is not a veteran and A is. On the assumption that the veteran has served his country,[3] the country owes him something. And it seems plain that giving him preference is a not unjust way in which part of that debt of gratitude can be paid.

And now, finally, we should turn to those debts which are incurred by one who wrongs another. It is here we find what seems to me the most powerful argument for the conclusion that the preferential hiring of blacks and women is not unjust.

I obviously cannot claim any novelty for this argument: it's a very familiar one. Indeed, not merely is it familiar, but so are a battery of objections to it. It may be granted that if we have wronged A, we owe him something: we should make amends, we should compensate him for the wrong done him. It may even be granted that if we have wronged A, we must make amends, that justice requires it, and that a failure to make amends is not merely callousness, but injustice. But (a) are the young blacks and women who are amongst the current applicants for university jobs amongst the blacks and women who were wronged? To turn to particular cases, it might happen that the black applicant is middle class, son of professionals, and has had the very best in private schooling; or that the woman applicant is plainly the product of feminist upbringing and encouragement. Is it proper, much less required, that the black or woman be given preference over a white male who grew up in poverty, and has to make his own way and earn his encouragements? Again, (b), did we, the current members of the community, wrong any blacks or women? Lots of people once did; but then isn't it for them to do the compensating? That is, if they're still alive. For presumably nobody now alive owned any slaves, and perhaps nobody now alive voted against women's suffrage. And (c) what if the white male applicant for the job has never in any degree wronged any blacks or women? If so, *he* doesn't owe any debts to them, so why should *he* make amends to them?

These objections seem to me quite wrong-headed.

Obviously the situation for blacks and women is better than it was a hundred and fifty, fifty, twenty-five years ago. But it is absurd to suppose that the young blacks and women now of an age to apply for jobs have not been wronged. Large-scale, blatant, overt wrongs have presumably disappeared; but it is only within

[3]Many people would reject this assumption, or perhaps accept it only selectively, for veterans of this or that particular war. I ignore this. What interests me is what follows if we make the assumption—as, of course, many other people do, more, it seems, than do not.

the last twenty-five years (perhaps the last ten years in the case of women) that it has become at all widely agreed in this country that blacks and women must be recognized as having, not merely this or that particular right normally recognized as belonging to white males, but all of the rights and respect which go with full membership in the community. Even young blacks and women have lived through down-grading for being black or female: they have not merely not been given that very equal chance at the benefits generated by what the community owns which is so firmly insisted on for white males, they have not until lately even been felt to have a right to it.

And even those who were not themselves down-graded for being black or female have suffered the consequences of the down-grading of other blacks and women: lack of self-confidence, and lack of self-respect. For where a community accepts that a person's being black, or being a woman, are right and proper grounds for denying that person full membership in the community, it can hardly be supposed that any but the most extraordinarily independent black or woman will escape self-doubt. All but the most extraordinarily independent of them have had to work harder— if only against self-doubt—than all but the most deprived white males, in the competition for a place amongst the best qualified.

If any black or woman has been unjustly deprived of what he or she has a right to, then of course justice does call for making amends. But what of the blacks and women who haven't actually been deprived of what they have a right to, but only made to suffer the consequences of injustice to other blacks and women? *Perhaps* justice doesn't require making amends to them as well; but common decency certainly does. To fail, at the very least, to make what counts as public apology to all, and to take positive steps to show that it is sincerely meant, is, if not injustice, then anyway a fault at least as serious as ingratitude.

Opting for a policy of preferential hiring may of course mean that some black or woman is preferred to some white male who as a matter of fact has had a harder life than the black or woman. But so may opting for a policy of veterans' preference mean that a healthy, unscarred, middle class veteran is preferred to a poor, struggling, scarred, nonveteran. Indeed, opting for a policy of settling who gets the job by having all equally qualified candidates draw straws may also mean that in a given case the candidate with the hardest life loses out. Opting for any policy other than hard-life preference may have this result.

I have no objection to anyone's arguing that it is precisely hard-life preference that we ought to opt for. If all, or anyway all of the equally qualified, have a right to an equal chance, then the argument would have to draw attention to something sufficiently powerful to override that right. But perhaps this could be done along the lines I followed in the case of blacks and women: perhaps it could be successfully argued that we have wronged those who have had hard lives, and therefore owe it to them to make amends. And then we should have in more extreme form a difficulty already present: how are these preferences to be ranked? shall we place the hard-lifers ahead of blacks? both ahead of women? and what about veterans? I leave these questions aside. My concern has been only to show that the white male applicant's right to an equal chance does not make it unjust to opt for a policy under which blacks and women are given preference. That a white male with a specially hard history may lose out under this policy cannot possibly be any objection to it, in the absence of a showing that hard-life preference is not unjust, and, more important, takes priority over preference for blacks and women.

Lastly, it should be stressed that to opt for such a policy is not to make the young white male applicants themselves make amends for any wrongs done to blacks and women. Under such a policy, no one is asked to give up a job which is already his; the job for which the white male competes isn't his, but is the community's, and it is the hiring officer who gives it to the black or woman in the community's name. Of course the white male is asked to give up his equal chance at the job. But that is not something he pays to the black or woman by way of making amends; it is something the community takes away from him in order that *it* may make amends.

Still, the community does impose a burden on him: it is able to make amends for its wrongs only by taking something away from him, something which, after all, we are supposing he has a right to. And why should *he* pay the cost of the community's amends-making?

If there were some appropriate way in which the community could make amends to its blacks and women, some way which did not require depriving anyone of anything he has a right to, then that would be the best course of action for it to take. Or if there were anyway some way in which the costs could be shared by everyone, and not imposed entirely on the young white male job applicants, then that would be, if not best, then anyway better than opting for a policy of preferential hiring. But in fact the nature of the wrongs done is such as to make jobs the best and most suitable form of compensation. What blacks and women were denied was full membership in the community; and nothing can more appropriately make amends for that wrong than precisely what will make them feel they now finally have it. And that means jobs. Financial compensation (the cost of which could be shared equally) slips through the fingers; having a job, and discovering you do it well, yield—perhaps better than anything else—that very self-respect which blacks and women have had to do without.

But of course choosing this way of making amends means that the costs are imposed on the young white male applicants who are turned away. And so it should be noticed that it is not entirely inappropriate that those applicants should pay the costs. No doubt few, if any, have themselves, individually, done any wrongs to blacks and women. But they have profited from the wrongs the community did. Many may actually have been direct beneficiaries of policies which excluded or down-graded blacks and women—perhaps in school admissions, perhaps in access to financial aid, perhaps elsewhere; and even those who did not directly benefit in this way had, at any rate, the advantage in the competition which comes of confidence in one's full membership, and of one's rights being recognized as a matter of course.

Of course it isn't only the young white male applicant for a university job who has benefited from the exclusion of blacks and women: the older white male, now comfortably tenured, also benefited, and many defenders of preferential hiring feel that he should be asked to share the costs. Well, presumably we can't demand that he give up his job, or share it. But it seems to me in place to expect the occupants of comfortable professorial chairs to contribute in some way, to make some form of return to the young white male who bears the cost, and is turned away. It will have been plain that I find the outcry now heard against preferential hiring in the universities objectionable; it would also be objectionable that those of us who are now securely situated should placidly defend it, with no more than a sigh of regret for the young white male who pays for it.

IV

One final word: "discrimination." I am inclined to think we so use it that if anyone is convicted of discriminating against blacks, women, white males, or what have you, then he is thereby convicted of acting unjustly. If so, and if I am right in thinking that preferential hiring in the restricted range of cases we have been looking at is *not* unjust, then we have two options: (a) we can simply reply that to opt for a policy of preferential hiring in those cases is not to opt for a policy of discriminating against white males, or

(b) we can hope to get usage changed—e.g., by trying to get people to allow that there is discriminating against and discriminating against, and that some is unjust, but some is not.

Best of all, however, would be for that phrase to be avoided altogether. It's at best a blunt tool: there are all sorts of nice moral discriminations [sic] which one is unable to make while occupied with it. And that bluntness itself fits it to do harm: blacks and women are hardly likely to see through to what precisely is owed them while they are being accused of welcoming what is unjust.

animal liberation

peter singer

I

We are familiar with Black Liberation, Gay Liberation, and a variety of other movements. With Women's Liberation some thought we had come to the end of the road. Discrimination on the basis of sex, it has been said, is the last form of discrimination that is universally accepted and practiced without pretense, even in those liberal circles which have long prided themselves on their freedom from racial discrimination. But one should always be wary of talking of "the last remaining form of discrimination." If we have learned anything from the liberation movements, we should have learned how difficult it is to be aware of the ways in which we discriminate until they are forcefully pointed out to us. A liberation movement demands an expansion of our moral horizons, so that practices that were previously regarded as natural and inevitable are now seen as intolerable.

Animals, Men and Morals is a manifesto for an Animal Liberation movement. The contributors to the book may not all see the issue this way. They are a varied group. Philosophers, ranging from professors to graduate students, make up the largest contin-

From *The New York Review of Books*, April 5, 1973. Reprinted by permission of the author. This article originally appeared as a review of a book edited by Stanley and Roslind Godlovitch and John Harris, *Animals, Men and Morals* (London: Taplinger, 1972). The "Postscript" has been added for this reprinting.

gent. There are five of them, including the three editors, and there is also an extract from the unjustly neglected German philosopher with an English name, Leonard Nelson, who died in 1927. There are essays by two novelist/critics, Brigid Brophy and Maureen Duffy, and another by Muriel the Lady Dowding, widow of Dowding of Battle of Britain fame and the founder of "Beauty Without Cruelty," a movement that campaigns against the use of animals for furs and cosmetics. The other pieces are by a psychologist, a botanist, a sociologist, and Ruth Harrison, who is probably best described as a professional campaigner for animal welfare.

Whether or not these people, as individuals, would all agree that they are launching a liberation movement for animals, the book as a whole amounts to no less. It is a demand for a complete change in our attitudes to nonhumans. It is a demand that we cease to regard the exploitation of other species as natural and inevitable, and that, instead, we see it as a continuing moral outrage. Patrick Corbett, Professor of Philosophy at Sussex University, captures the spirit of the book in his closing words:

> . . . We require now to extend the great principles of liberty, equality and fraternity over the lives of animals. Let animal slavery join human slavery in the graveyard of the past.

The reader is likely to be skeptical. "Animal Liberation" sounds more like a parody of liberation movements than a serious objective. The reader may think: We support the claims of blacks and women for equality because blacks and women really are equal to whites and males—equal in intelligence and in abilities, capacity for leadership, rationality, and so on. Humans and nonhumans obviously are not equal in these respects. Since justice demands only that we treat equals equally, unequal treatment of humans and nonhumans cannot be an injustice.

This is a tempting reply, but a dangerous one. It commits the non-racist and non-sexist to a dogmatic belief that blacks and women really are just as intelligent, able, etc., as whites and males—and no more. Quite possibly this happens to be the case. Certainly attempts to prove that racial or sexual differences in these respects have a genetic origin have not been conclusive. But do we really want to stake our demand for equality on the assumption that there are no genetic differences of this kind between the different races or sexes? Surely the appropriate response to those who claim to have found evidence for such genetic differences is not to stick to the belief that there are no differences, whatever the evidence to the contrary; rather one should be clear that the claim to equality does not depend on IQ. Moral equality is distinct from factual equality. Otherwise it would be nonsense to talk of the equality of human beings, since humans, as individuals, obviously differ in intelligence and almost any ability one cares to name. If possessing greater intelligence does not entitle one human to exploit another, why should it entitle humans to exploit nonhumans?

Jeremy Bentham expressed the essential basis of equality in his famous formula: "Each to count for one and none for more than one." In other words, the interests of every being that has interests are to be taken into account and treated equally with the like interests of any other being. Other moral philosophers, before and after Bentham, have made the same point in different ways. Our concern for others must not depend on whether they possess certain characteristics, though just what that concern involves may, of course, vary according to such characteristics.

Bentham, incidentally, was well aware that the logic of the demand for racial equality did not stop at the equality of humans. He wrote:

> The day *may* come when the rest of the animal creation may acquire those rights which never could have been withholden from them but by the hand of tyranny. The French have already discovered that the blackness of the skin is no reason why a human being should be abandoned without redress to the caprice of a tormentor. It may one day come to be recognized that the number of the legs, the villosity of the skin, or the termination of the *os sacrum*, are reasons equally insufficient for abandoning a sensitive being to the same fate. What else is it that should trace the insuperable line? Is it the faculty of reason, or perhaps the faculty of discourse? But a full-grown horse or dog is beyond comparison a more rational, as well as a more conversable animal, than an infant of a day, or a week, or even a month, old. But suppose they were otherwise, what would it avail? The question is not, Can they *reason?* nor Can they *talk?* but, Can they *suffer?*[1]

Surely Bentham was right. If a being suffers, there can be no moral justification for refusing to take that suffering into consideration, and, indeed, to count it equally with the like suffering (if rough comparisons can be made) of any other being.

So the only question is: Do animals other than man suffer? Most people agree unhesitatingly that animals like cats and dogs can and do suffer, and this seems also to be assumed by those

[1] *The Principles of Morals and Legislation*, ch. XVII, sec. 1, footnote to paragraph 4. (Italics in original.)

laws that prohibit wanton cruelty to such animals. Personally, I have no doubt at all about this and find it hard to take seriously the doubts that a few people apparently do have. The editors and contributors of *Animals, Men and Morals* seem to feel the same way, for although the question is raised more than once, doubts are quickly dismissed each time. Nevertheless, because this is such a fundamental point, it is worth asking what grounds we have for attributing suffering to other animals.

It is best to begin by asking what grounds any individual human has for supposing that other humans feel pain. Since pain is a state of consciousness, a "mental event," it can never be directly observed. No observations, whether behavioral signs such as writhing or screaming or physiological or neurological recordings, are observations of pain itself. Pain is something one feels, and one can only infer that others are feeling it from various external indications. The fact that only philosophers are ever skeptical about whether other humans feel pain shows that we regard such inference as justifiable in the case of humans.

Is there any reason why the same inference should be unjustifiable for other animals? Nearly all the external signs which lead us to infer pain in other humans can be seen in other species, especially "higher" animals such as mammals and birds. Behavioral signs—writhing, yelping, or other forms of calling, attempts to avoid the source of pain, and many others—are present. We know, too, that these animals are biologically similar in the relevant respects, having nervous systems like ours which can be observed to function as ours do.

So the grounds for inferring that these animals can feel pain are nearly as good as the grounds for inferring other humans do. Only nearly, for there is one behavioral sign that humans have but nonhumans, with the exception of one or two specially raised chimpanzees, do not have. This, of course, is a developed language. As the quotation from Bentham indicates, this has long been regarded as an important distinction between man and other animals. Other animals may communicate with each other, but not in the way we do. Following Chomsky, many people now mark this distinction by saying that only humans communicate in a form that is governed by rules of syntax. (For the purposes of this argument, linguists allow those chimpanzees who have learned a syntactic sign language to rank as honorary humans.) Nevertheless, as Bentham pointed out, this distinction is not relevant to the question of how animals ought to be treated, unless it can be linked to the issue of whether animals suffer.

This link may be attempted in two ways. First, there is a hazy

166

line of philosophical thought, stemming perhaps from some doctrines associated with Wittgenstein, which maintains that we cannot meaningfully attribute states of consciousness to beings without language. I have not seen this argument made explicit in print, though I have come across it in conversation. This position seems to me very implausible, and I doubt that it would be held at all if it were not thought to be a consequence of a broader view of the significance of language. It may be that the use of a public, rule-governed language is a precondition of conceptual thought. It may even be, although personally I doubt it, that we cannot meaningfully speak of a creature having an intention unless that creature can use a language. But states like pain, surely, are more primitive than either of these, and seem to have nothing to do with language.

Indeed, as Jane Goodall points out in her study of chimpanzees, when it comes to the expression of feelings and emotions, humans tend to fall back on non-linguistic modes of communication which are often found among apes, such as a cheering pat on the back, an exuberant embrace, a clasp of hands, and so on.[2] Michael Peters makes a similar point in his contribution to *Animals, Men and Morals* when he notes that the basic signals we use to convey pain, fear, sexual arousal, and so on are not specific to our species. So there seems to be no reason at all to believe that a creature without language cannot suffer.

The second, and more easily appreciated way of linking language and the existence of pain is to say that the best evidence that we can have that another creature is in pain is when he tells us that he is. This is a distinct line of argument, for it is not being denied that a non-language-user conceivably could suffer, but only that we could know that he is suffering. Still, this line of argument seems to me to fail, and for reasons similar to those just given. "I am in pain" is not the best possible evidence that the speaker is in pain (he might be lying) and it is certainly not the only possible evidence. Behavioral signs and knowledge of the animal's biological similarity to ourselves together provide adequate evidence that animals do suffer. After all, we would not accept linguistic evidence if it contradicted the rest of the evidence. If a man was severely burned, and behaved as if he were in pain, writhing, groaning, being very careful not to let his burned skin touch anything, and so on, but later said he had not been in pain at all, we would be more likely to conclude that he was lying or suffering from amnesia than that he had not been in pain.

[2] Jane van Lawick-Goodall, *In the Shadow of Man* (Houghton Mifflin, 1971), p. 225.

Even if there were stronger grounds for refusing to attribute pain to those who do not have a language, the consequences of this refusal might lead us to examine these grounds unusually critically. Human infants, as well as some adults, are unable to use language. Are we to deny that a year-old infant can suffer? If not, how can language be crucial? Of course, most parents can understand the responses of even very young infants better than they understand the responses of other animals, and sometimes infant responses can be understood in the light of later development.

This, however, is just a fact about the relative knowledge we have of our own species and other species, and most of this knowledge is simply derived from closer contact. Those who have studied the behavior of other animals soon learn to understand their responses at least as well as we understand those of an infant. (I am not just referring to Jane Goodall's and other well-known studies of apes. Consider, for example, the degree of understanding achieved by Tinbergen from watching herring gulls.)[3] Just as we can understand infant human behavior in the light of adult human behavior, so we can understand the behavior of other species in the light of our own behavior (and sometimes we can understand our own behavior better in the light of the behavior of other species).

The grounds we have for believing that other mammals and birds suffer are, then, closely analogous to the grounds we have for believing that other humans suffer. It remains to consider how far down the evolutionary scale this analogy holds. Obviously it becomes poorer when we get further away from man. To be more precise would require a detailed examination of all that we know about other forms of life. With fish, reptiles, and other vertebrates the analogy still seems strong, with molluscs like oysters it is much weaker. Insects are more difficult, and it may be that in our present state of knowledge we must be agnostic about whether they are capable of suffering.

If there is no moral justification for ignoring suffering when it occurs, and it does occur in other species, what are we to say of our attitudes toward these other species? Richard Ryder, one of the contributors to *Animals, Men and Morals*, uses the term "speciesism" to describe the belief that we are entitled to treat members of other species in a way in which it would be wrong to treat members of our own species. The term is not euphonious, but it neatly makes the analogy with racism. The non-racist would do well to bear the analogy in mind when he is inclined to defend

---

[3] N. Tinbergen, *The Herring Gull's World* (Basic Books, 1961).

human behavior toward nonhumans. "Shouldn't we worry about improving the lot of our own species before we concern ourselves with other species?" he may ask. If we substitute "race" for "species" we shall see that the question is better not asked. "Is a vegetarian diet nutritionally adequate?" resembles the slave-owner's claim that he and the whole economy of the South would be ruined without slave labor. There is even a parallel with skeptical doubts about whether animals suffer, for some defenders of slavery professed to doubt whether blacks really suffer in the way that whites do.

I do not want to give the impression, however, that the case for Animal Liberation is based on the analogy with racism and no more. On the contrary, *Animals, Men and Morals* describes the various ways in which humans exploit nonhumans, and several contributors consider the defenses that have been offered, including the defense of meat-eating mentioned in the last paragraph. Sometimes the rebuttals are scornfully dismissive, rather than carefully designed to convince the detached critic. This may be a fault, but it is a fault that is inevitable, given the kind of book this is. The issue is not one on which one can remain detached. As the editors state in their Introduction:

> Once the full force of moral assessment has been made explicit there can be no rational excuse left for killing animals, be they killed for food, science, or sheer personal indulgence. We have not assembled this book to provide the reader with yet another manual on how to make brutalities less brutal. Compromise, in the traditional sense of the term, is simple unthinking weakness when one considers the actual reasons for our crude relationships with the other animals.

The point is that on this issue there are few critics who are genuinely detached. People who eat pieces of slaughtered nonhumans every day find it hard to believe that they are doing wrong; and they also find it hard to imagine what else they could eat. So for those who do not place nonhumans beyond the pale of morality, there comes a stage when further argument seems pointless, a stage at which one can only accuse one's opponent of hypocrisy and reach for the sort of sociological account of our practices and the way we defend them that is attempted by David Wood in his contribution to this book. On the other hand, to those unconvinced by the arguments, and unable to accept that they are merely rationalizing their dietary preferences and their fear of being thought peculiar, such sociological explanations can only seem insultingly arrogant.

II

The logic of speciesism is most apparent in the practice of experimenting on nonhumans in order to benefit humans. This is because the issue is rarely obscured by allegations that nonhumans are so different from humans that we cannot know anything about whether they suffer. The defender of vivisection cannot use this argument because he needs to stress the similarities between man and other animals in order to justify the usefulness to the former of experiments on the latter. The researcher who makes rats choose between starvation and electric shocks to see if they develop ulcers (they do) does so because he knows that the rat has a nervous system very similar to man's, and presumably feels an electric shock in a similar way.

Richard Ryder's restrained account of experiments on animals made me angrier with my fellow men than anything else in this book. Ryder, a clinical psychologist by profession, himself experimented on animals before he came to hold the view he puts forward in his essay. Experimenting on animals is now a large industry, both academic and commercial. In 1969, more than 5 million experiments were performed in Britain, the vast majority without anesthetic (though how many of these involved pain is not known). There are no accurate U.S. figures, since there is no federal law on the subject, and in many cases no state law either. Estimates vary from 20 million to 200 million. Ryder suggests that 80 million may be the best guess. We tend to think that this is all for vital medical research, but of course it is not. Huge numbers of animals are used in university departments from Forestry to Psychology, and even more are used for commercial purposes, to test whether cosmetics can cause skin damage, or shampoos eye damage, or to test food additives or laxatives or sleeping pills or anything else.

A standard test for foodstuffs is the "LD50." The object of this test is to find the dosage level at which 50 percent of the test animals will die. This means that nearly all of them will become very sick before finally succumbing or surviving. When the substance is a harmless one, it may be necessary to force huge doses down the animals, until in some cases sheer volume or concentration causes death.

Ryder gives a selection of experiments, taken from recent scientific journals. I will quote two, not for the sake of indulging in gory details, but in order to give an idea of what normal researchers think they may legitimately do to other species. The point is not that the individual researchers are cruel men, but that they are behaving in a way that is allowed by our speciesist attitudes. As Ryder points out, even if only 1 percent of the experiments involve severe pain, that is 50,000 experiments in Britain each year, or nearly 150 every day (and about fifteen times as many in the United States, if Ryder's guess is right). Here then are two experiments:

> O. S. Ray and R. J. Barrett of Pittsburg gave electric shocks to the feet of 1,042 mice. They then caused convulsions by giving more intense shocks through cup-shaped electrodes applied to the animals' eyes or through pressure spring clips attached to their ears. Unfortunately some of the mice who "successfully completed Day One training were found sick or dead prior to testing on Day Two." [*Journal of Comparative and Physiological Psychology*, 1969, vol. 67, pp. 110–116]
>
> At the National Institute for Medical Research, Mill Hill, London, W. Feldberg and S. L. Sherwood injected chemicals into the brains of cats—"with a number of widely different substances, recurrent patterns of reaction were obtained. Retching, vomiting, defaecation, increased salivation and greatly accelerated respiration leading to panting were common features.". . .
>
> The injection into the brain of a large dose of Tubocuraine caused the cat to jump "from the table to the floor and then straight into its cage, where it started calling more and more noisily whilst moving about restlessly and jerkily . . . finally the cat fell with legs and neck flexed, jerking in rapid clonic movements, the condition being that of a major [epileptic] convulsion . . . within a few seconds the cat got up, ran for a few yards at high speed and fell in another fit. The whole process was repeated several times within the next ten minutes, during which the cat lost faeces and foamed at the mouth."
>
> This animal finally died thirty-five minutes after the brain injection. [*Journal of Physiology*, 1954, vol. 123, pp. 148–167]

There is nothing secret about these experiments. One has only to open any recent volume of a learned journal, such as the *Journal of Comparative and Physiological Psychology*, to find full descriptions of experiments of this sort, together with the results obtained—results that are frequently trivial and obvious. The experiments are often supported by public funds.

It is a significant indication of the level of acceptability of these practices that, although these experiments are taking place at this moment on university campuses throughout the country, there has, so far as I know, not been the slightest protest from the student movement. Students have been rightly concerned that their universities should not discriminate on grounds of race or sex, and that they should not serve the purposes of the military or big business. Speciesism continues undisturbed, and many students participate in it. There may be a few qualms at first, but since everyone regards it as normal, and it may even be a required part of a course, the student soon becomes hardened and, dismissing his earlier feelings as "mere sentiment," comes to regard animals as statistics rather than sentient beings with interests that warrant consideration.

Argument about vivisection has often missed the point because it has been put in absolutist terms: Would the abolitionist be prepared to let thousands die if they could be saved by experimenting on a single animal? The way to reply to this purely hypothetical question is to pose another: Would the experimenter be prepared to experiment on a human orphan under six months old, if it were the only way to save many lives? (I say "orphan" to avoid the complication of parental feelings, although in doing so I am being overfair to the experimenter, since the nonhuman subjects of experiments are not orphans.) A negative answer to this question indicates that the experimenter's readiness to use nonhumans is simple discrimination, for adult apes, cats, mice, and other mammals are more conscious of what is happening to them, more self-directing, and, so far as we can tell, just as sensitive to pain as a human infant. There is no characteristic that human infants possess that adult mammals do not have to the same or a higher degree.

(It might be possible to hold that what makes it wrong to experiment on a human infant is that the infant will in time develop into more than the nonhuman, but one would then, to be consistent, have to oppose abortion, and perhaps contraception, too, for the fetus and the egg and sperm have the same potential as the infant. Moreover, one would still have no reason for experimenting on a nonhuman rather than a human with brain damage severe enough to make it impossible for him to rise above infant level.)

The experimenter, then, shows a bias for his own species whenever he carries out an experiment on a nonhuman for a purpose that he would not think justified him in using a human being at an equal or lower level of sentience, awareness, ability to be self-directing, etc. No one familiar with the kind of results yielded by these experiments can have the slightest doubt that if this bias were eliminated the number of experiments performed would be zero or very close to it.

III

If it is vivisection that shows the logic of speciesism most clearly, it is the use of other species for food that is at the heart of our attitudes toward them. Most of *Animals, Men and Morals* is an attack on meat-eating—an attack which is based solely on concern for nonhumans, without reference to arguments derived from considerations of ecology, macrobiotics, health, or religion.

The idea that nonhumans are utilities, means to our ends, pervades our thought. Even conservationists who are concerned about the slaughter of wild fowl but not about the vastly greater slaughter of chickens for our tables are thinking in this way—they are worried about what we would lose if there were less wildlife. Stanley Godlovitch, pursuing the Marxist idea that our thinking is formed by the activities we undertake in satisfying our needs, suggests that man's first classification of his environment was into Edibles and Inedibles. Most animals came into the first category, and there they have remained.

Man may always have killed other species for food, but he has never exploited them so ruthlessly as he does today. Farming has succumbed to business methods, the objective being to get the highest possible ratio of output (meat, eggs, milk) to input (fodder, labor costs, etc.). Ruth Harrison's essay "On Factory Farming" gives an account of some aspects of modern methods, and of the unsuccessful British campaign for effective controls, a campaign which was sparked off by her *Animal Machines* (Stuart: London, 1964).

Her article is in no way a substitute for her earlier book. This is a pity since, as she says, "Farm produce is still associated with mental pictures of animals browsing in the fields, . . . of hens having a last forage before going to roost. . . ." Yet neither in her article nor elsewhere in *Animals, Men and Morals* is this false image replaced by a clear idea of the nature and extent of factory farming. We learn of this only indirectly, when we hear of the code of reform proposed by an advisory committee set up by the British government.

Among the proposals, which the government refused to implement on the grounds that they were too idealistic, were: *"Any animal should at least have room to turn around freely."*

Factory farm animals need liberation in the most literal sense. Veal calves are kept in stalls five feet by two feet. They are usually slaughtered when about four months old, and have been too big to turn in their stalls for at least a month. Intensive beef herds, kept in stalls only proportionately larger for much longer periods, account for a growing percentage of beef production. Sows are often similarly confined when pregnant, which, because of artificial methods of increasing fertility, can be most of the time. Animals confined in this way do not waste food by exercising, nor do they develop unpalatable muscle.

"*A dry bedded area should be provided for all stock.*" Intensively kept animals usually have to stand and sleep on slatted floors without straw, because this makes cleaning easier.

"*Palatable roughage must be readily available to all calves after one week of age.*" In order to produce the pale veal housewives are said to prefer, calves are fed on an all-liquid diet until slaughter, even though they are long past the age at which they would normally eat grass. They develop a craving for roughage, evidenced by attempts to gnaw wood from their stalls. (For the same reason, their diet is deficient in iron.)

"*Battery cages for poultry should be large enough for a bird to be able to stretch one wing at a time.*" Under current British practice, a cage for four or five laying hens has a floor area of twenty inches by eighteen inches, scarcely larger than a double page of the *New York Review of Books*. In this space, on a sloping wire floor (sloping so the eggs roll down, wire so the dung drops through) the birds live for a year or eighteen months while artificial lighting and temperature conditions combine with drugs in their food to squeeze the maximum number of eggs out of them. Table birds are also sometimes kept in cages. More often they are reared in sheds, no less crowded. Under these conditions all the birds' natural activities are frustrated, and they develop "vices" such as pecking each other to death. To prevent this, beaks are often cut off, and the sheds kept dark.

How many of those who support factory farming by buying its produce know anything about the way it is produced? How many have heard something about it, but are reluctant to check up for fear that it will make them uncomfortable? To non-speciesists, the typical consumer's mixture of ignorance, reluctance to find out the truth, and vague belief that nothing really bad could be allowed seems analogous to the attitudes of "decent Germans" to the death camps.

There are, of course, some defenders of factory farming. Their arguments are considered, though again rather sketchily, by John Harris. Among the most common: "Since they have never known anything else, they don't suffer." This argument will not be put by anyone who knows anything about animal behavior, since he will know that not all behavior has to be learned. Chickens attempt to stretch wings, walk around, scratch, and even dustbathe or build a nest, even though they have never lived under conditions that allowed these activities. Calves can suffer from maternal deprivation no matter at what age they were taken from their mothers. "We need these intensive methods to provide protein for a growing population." As ecologists and famine relief organizations know, we can produce far more protein per acre if we grow the right vegetable crop, soy beans for instance, than if we use the land to grow crops to be converted into protein by animals who use nearly 90 percent of the protein themselves, even when unable to exercise.

There will be many readers of this book who will agree that factory farming involves an unjustifiable degree of exploitation of sentient creatures, and yet will want to say that there is nothing wrong with rearing animals for food, provided it is done "humanely." These people are saying, in effect, that although we should not cause animals to suffer, there is nothing wrong with killing them.

There are two possible replies to this view. One is to attempt to show that this combination of attitudes is absurd. Roslind Godlovitch takes this course in her essay, which is an examination of some common attitudes to animals. She argues that from the combination of "animal suffering is to be avoided" and "there is nothing wrong with killing animals" it follows that all animal life ought to be exterminated (since all sentient creatures will suffer to some degree at some point in their lives). Euthanasia is a contentious issue only because we place some value on living. If we did not, the least amount of suffering would justify it. Accordingly, if we deny that we have a duty to exterminate all animal life, we must concede that we are placing some value on animal life.

This argument seems to me valid, although one could still reply that the value of animal life is to be derived from the pleasures that life can have for them, so that, provided their lives have a balance of pleasure over pain, we are justified in rearing them. But this would imply that we ought to produce animals and let them live as pleasantly as possible, without suffering.

At this point, one can make the second of the two possible replies to the view that rearing and killing animals for food is all right so long as it is done humanely. This second reply is that so long as we think that a nonhuman may be killed simply so that a human can satisfy his taste for meat, we are still thinking of nonhumans as means rather than as ends in themselves. The factory farm is nothing more than the application of technology to this concept. Even traditional methods involve castration, the separation of mothers and their young, the breaking up of herds, branding or ear-punching, and of course transportation to the abattoirs and the final moments of terror when the animal smells blood and senses danger. If we were to try rearing animals so that they lived and died without suffering, we should find that to do so on anything like the scale of today's meat industry would be a sheer impossibility. Meat would become the prerogative of the rich.

I have been able to discuss only some of the contributions to this book, saying nothing about, for instance, the essays on killing for furs and for sport. Nor have I considered all the detailed questions that need to be asked once we start thinking about other species in the radically different way presented by this book. What, for instance, are we to do about genuine conflicts of interest like rats biting slum children? I am not sure of the answer, but the essential point is just that we *do* see this as a conflict of interests, that we recognize that rats have interests too. Then we may begin to think about other ways of resolving the conflict—perhaps by leaving out rat baits that sterilize the rats instead of killing them.

I have not discussed such problems because they are side issues compared with the exploitation of other species for food and for experimental purposes. On these central matters, I hope that I have said enough to show that this book, despite its flaws, is a challenge to every human to recognize his attitudes to non-humans as a form of prejudice no less objectionable than racism or sexism. It is a challenge that demands not just a change of attitudes, but a change in our way of life, for it requires us to become vegetarians.

Can a purely moral demand of this kind succeed? The odds are certainly against it. The book holds out no inducements. It does not tell us that we will become healthier, or enjoy life more, if we cease exploiting animals. Animal Liberation will require greater altruism on the part of mankind than any other liberation movement, since animals are incapable of demanding it for themselves, or of protesting against their exploitation by votes, demonstrations, or bombs. Is man capable of such genuine altruism? Who knows? If this book does have a significant effect, however, it will be a vindication of all those who have believed that man has within himself the potential for more than cruelty and selfishness.

POSTSCRIPT

Since this review is now appearing alongside philosophical discussions of rights and equality, it is worth noting that we can find indications of speciesism even amongst philosophers.

Richard Wasserstom's "Rights, Human Rights, and Racial Discrimination" [reprinted in this volume, pp. 109–122], serves as an example. Wasserstrom defines "human rights" as those that humans have, and nonhumans do not have. He then argues that there are human rights, in this sense, to well-being and freedom. In defending the idea of a human right to well-being, Wasserstrom says that although we have no means of assessing the comparative worth of different people's enjoyment of, for instance, relief from acute physical pain, we know that denial of the opportunity to experience a good such as this makes it impossible to live a full or satisfying life. Wasserstrom then goes on to say: "In a real sense, the enjoyment of these goods differentiates human from nonhuman entities" [p. 119]. But this statement is incredible— for when we look back to find what the expression "these goods" is supposed to refer to, we find that the *only* example we have been given is relief from acute physical pain—and this, surely, is something that nonhumans may appreciate as well as humans.

Later, too, Wasserstrom points out that the grounds for discrimination between blacks and whites that racists sometimes offer are not relevant to the question of capacity for bearing acute pain, and therefore should be disregarded. So again Wasserstrom is taking capacity for perceiving acute pain as crucial. I would want to say that if Wasserstrom's argument is valid against discrimination on the basis of race—and I think it is—then an exactly parallel argument applies against the grounds usually offered for discrimination on the basis of species, since these grounds are also not relevant to the question of ability to bear acute pain. When Ray and Barrett, in the experiment I described in the review, gave electric shocks to over a thousand mice, they must have assumed that the mice *do* feel acute physical pain, since the aim of the experiment was to find out where the mice were most sensitive; and nothing else, surely, is relevant to the question of whether it is legitimate to use mice for this purpose.

I should make it quite clear, of course, that I do not believe Richard Wasserstrom is deliberately endorsing a speciesist position, or in any way condoning the infliction of acute physical pain on nonhumans. I draw attention to the point only in order to show how easy it is, even for a philosopher, to accept unthinkingly a prevailing ideology that places other animals outside the sphere of equal consideration. I would guess that most of Wasserstrom's readers, with similar predispositions, will not have noticed on a first reading that the only basis he offers for "human rights" applies to nonhumans too.

4
CIVIL DISOBEDIENCE

the justification
of civil disobedience

john rawls

1. INTRODUCTION

I should like to discuss briefly, and in an informal way, the grounds of civil disobedience in a constitutional democracy. Thus, I shall limit my remarks to the conditions under which we may, by civil disobedience, properly oppose legally established democratic authority; I am not concerned with the situation under other kinds of government nor, except incidentally, with other forms of resistance. My thought is that in a reasonably just (though of course not perfectly just) democratic regime, civil disobedience, when it is justified, is normally to be understood as a political action which addresses the sense of justice of the majority in order to urge reconsideration of the measures protested and to warn that in the firm opinion of the dissenters the conditions of social cooperation are not being honored. This characterization of civil disobedience is intended to apply to dissent on fundamental questions of internal policy, a limitation which I shall follow to simplify our questions.

Originally presented at the meetings of the American Political Science Association, September, 1966. Some revisions have been made and two paragraphs have been added to the last section. Copyright © 1968 by John Rawls. By permission of the author.

2. THE SOCIAL CONTRACT DOCTRINE

It is obvious that the justification of civil disobedience depends upon the theory of political obligation in general, and so we may appropriately begin with a few comments on this question. The two chief virtues of social institutions are justice and efficiency, where by the efficiency of institutions I understand their effectiveness for certain social conditions and ends the fulfillment of which is to everyone's advantage. We should comply with and do our part in just and efficient social arrangements for at least two reasons: first of all, we have a natural duty not to oppose the establishment of just and efficient institutions (when they do not yet exist) and to uphold and comply with them (when they do exist); and second, assuming that we have knowingly accepted the benefits of these institutions and plan to continue to do so, and that we have encouraged and expected others to do their part, we also have an obligation to do our share when, as the arrangement requires, it comes our turn. Thus, we often have both a natural duty as well as an obligation to support just and efficient institutions, the obligation arising from our voluntary acts while the duty does not.

Now all this is perhaps obvious enough, but it does not take us very far. Any more particular conclusions depend upon the conception of justice which is the basis of a theory of political obligation. I believe that the appropriate conception, at least for an account of political obligation in a constitutional democracy, is that of the social contract theory from which so much of our political thought derives. If we are careful to interpret it in a suitably general way, I hold that this doctrine provides a satisfactory basis for political theory, indeed even for ethical theory itself, but this is beyond our present concern.[1] The interpretation I suggest is the following: that the principles to which social arrangements must conform, and in particular the principles of justice, are those which free and rational men would agree to in an original position of equal liberty; and similarly, the principles which govern men's relations to institutions and define their natural duties and obligations are the principles to which they would consent when so situated. It should be noted straightway that in this interpretation of the contract theory the principles of justice are understood as the outcome of a hypothetical agreement. They are principles which would be agreed to if the situation of the original position

[1] By the social contract theory I have in mind the doctrine found in Locke, Rousseau, and Kant. I have attempted to give an interpretation of this view in: "Justice as Fairness," *Philosophical Review* (April, 1958); "Justice and Constitutional Liberty," *Nomos*, VI (1963); "The Sense of Justice," *Philosophical Review* (July 1963).

were to arise. There is no mention of an actual agreement nor need such an agreement ever be made. Social arrangements are just or unjust according to whether they accord with the principles for assigning and securing fundamental rights and liberties which would be chosen in the original position. This position is, to be sure, the analytic analogue of the traditional notion of the state of nature, but it must not be mistaken for a historical occasion. Rather it is a hypothetical situation which embodies the basic ideas of the contract doctrine; the description of this situation enables us to work out which principles would be adopted. I must now say something about these matters.

The contract doctrine has always supposed that the persons in the original position have equal powers and rights, that is, that they are symmetrically situated with respect to any arrangements for reaching agreement, and that coalitions and the like are excluded. But it is an essential element (which has not been sufficiently observed although it is implicit in Kant's version of the theory) that there are very strong restrictions on what the contracting parties are presumed to know. In particular, I interpret the theory to hold that the parties do not know their position in society, past, present, or future; nor do they know which institutions exist. Again, they do not know their own place in the distribution of natural talents and abilities, whether they are intelligent or strong, man or woman, and so on. Finally, they do not know their own particular interests and preferences or the system of ends which they wish to advance: they do not know their conception of the good. In all these respects the parties are confronted with a veil of ignorance which prevents any one from being able to take advantage of his good fortune or particular interests or from being disadvantaged by them. What the parties do know (or assume) is that Hume's circumstances of justice obtain: namely, that the bounty of nature is not so generous as to render cooperative schemes superfluous nor so harsh as to make them impossible. Moreover, they assume that the extent of their altruism is limited and that, in general, they do not take an interest in one another's interests. Thus, given the special features of the original position, each man tries to do the best he can for himself by insisting on principles calculated to protect and advance his system of ends whatever it turns out to be.

I believe that as a consequence of the peculiar nature of the original position there would be an agreement on the following two principles for assigning rights and duties and for regulating distributive shares as these are determined by the fundamental institutions of society: first, each person is to have an equal right to the most extensive liberty compatible with a like liberty for all; second, social and economic inequalities (as defined by the institutional structure or fostered by it) are to be arranged so that they are both to everyone's advantage and attached to positions and offices open to all. In view of the content of these two principles and their application to the main institutions of society, and therefore to the social system as a whole, we may regard them as the two principles of justice. Basic social arrangements are just insofar as they conform to these principles, and we can, if we like, discuss questions of justice directly by reference to them. But a deeper understanding of the justification of civil disobedience requires, I think, an account of the derivation of these principles provided by the doctrine of the social contract. Part of our task is to show why this is so.

3. THE GROUNDS OF COMPLIANCE WITH AN UNJUST LAW

If we assume that in the original position men would agree both to the principle of doing their part when they have accepted and plan to continue to accept the benefits of just institutions (the principle of fairness), and also to the principle of not preventing the establishment of just institutions and of upholding and complying with them when they do exist, then the contract doctrine easily accounts for our having to conform to just institutions. But how does it account for the fact that we are normally required to comply with unjust laws as well? The injustice of a law is not a sufficient ground for not complying with it any more than the legal validity of legislation is always sufficient to require obedience to it. Sometimes one hears these extremes asserted, but I think that we need not take them seriously.

An answer to our question can be given by elaborating the social contract theory in the following way. I interpret it to hold that one is to envisage a series of agreements as follows: first, men are to agree upon the principles of justice in the original position. Then they are to move to a constitutional convention in which they choose a constitution that satisfies the principles of justice already chosen. Finally they assume the role of a legislative body and guided by the principles of justice enact laws subject to the constraints and procedures of the just constitution. The decisions reached in any stage are binding in all subsequent stages. Now whereas in the original position the contracting parties have no knowledge of their society or of their own position in it, in both a constitutional convention and a legislature, they do know certain general facts about their institutions, for example, the statistics regarding employment and output required for fiscal and economic policy. But no one knows particular facts about his own social class or his place in the distribution of natural assets. On each occasion the contracting parties have the knowledge required to make their agreement rational from the appropriate point of view, but not so much as to make them prejudiced. They are unable to tailor principles and legislation to take advantage of their social or natural position; a veil of ignorance prevents their knowing what this position is. With this series of agreements in mind, we can characterize just laws and policies as those which would be enacted were this whole process correctly carried out.

In choosing a constitution the aim is to find among the just constitutions the one which is most likely, given the general facts about the society in question, to lead to just and effective legislation. The principles of justice provide a criterion for the laws desired; the problem is to find a set of political procedures that will give this outcome. I shall assume that, at least under the normal conditions of a modern state, the best constitution is some form of democratic regime affirming equal political liberty and using some sort of majority (or other plurality) rule. Thus it follows that on the contract theory a constitutional democracy of some sort is required by the principles of justice. At the same time it is essential to observe that the constitutional process is always a case of what we may call imperfect procedural justice: that is, there is no feasible political procedure which guarantees that the enacted legislation is just even though we have (let us suppose) a standard for just legislation. In simple cases, such as games of fair division, there are procedures which always lead to the right outcome (assume that equal shares is fair and let the man who cuts the cake take the last piece). These situations are those of perfect procedural justice. In other cases it does not matter what the outcome is as long as the fair procedure is followed: fairness of the process is transferred to the result (fair gambling is an instance of this). These situations are those of pure procedural justice. The constitutional process, like a criminal trial, resembles neither of these; the result matters and we have a standard for it. The difficulty is that we cannot frame a procedure which guarantees that only just and effective legislation is enacted. Thus even under a just constitution unjust laws may be passed and unjust policies enforced. Some form of the majority principle is necessary but the majority may be mistaken, more or less willfully, in what it legislates. In agreeing to a democratic constitution (as an instance of imperfect procedural justice) one accepts at the same time the principle of majority rule. Assuming that the constitution is just and that

185

we have accepted and plan to continue to accept its benefits, we then have both an obligation and a natural duty (and in any case the duty) to comply with what the majority enacts even though it may be unjust. In this way we become bound to follow unjust laws, not always, of course, but provided the injustice does not exceed certain limits. We recognize that we must run the risk of suffering from the defects of one another's sense of justice; this burden we are prepared to carry as long as it is more or less evenly distributed or does not weigh too heavily. Justice binds us to a just constitution and to the unjust laws which may be enacted under it in precisely the same way that it binds us to any other social arrangement. Once we take the sequence of stages into account, there is nothing unusual in our being required to comply with unjust laws.

It should be observed that the majority principle has a secondary place as a rule of procedure which is perhaps the most efficient one under usual circumstances for working a democratic constitution. The basis for it rests essentially upon the principles of justice and therefore we may, when conditions allow, appeal to these principles against unjust legislation. The justice of the constitution does not insure the justice of laws enacted under it; and while we often have both an obligation and a duty to comply with what the majority legislates (as long as it does not exceed certain limits), there is, of course, no corresponding obligation or duty to regard what the majority enacts as itself just. The right to make law does not guarantee that the decision is rightly made; and while the citizen submits in his conduct to the judgment of democratic authority, he does not submit his judgment to it.[2] And if in his judgment the enactments of the majority exceed certain bounds of injustice, the citizen may consider civil disobedience. For we are not required to accept the majority's acts unconditionally and to acquiesce in the denial of our and others' liberties; rather we submit our conduct to democratic authority to the extent necessary to share the burden of working a constitutional regime, distorted as it must inevitably be by men's lack of wisdom and the defects of their sense of justice.

4. THE PLACE OF CIVIL DISOBEDIENCE IN A CONSTITUTIONAL DEMOCRACY

We are now in a position to say a few things about civil disobedience. I shall understand it to be a public, nonviolent, and

[2]On this point see A. E. Murphy's review of Yves Simon's *The Philosophy of Democratic Government* (1951) in the *Philosophical Review* (April, 1952).

conscientious act contrary to law usually done with the intent to bring about a change in the policies or laws of the government.[3] Civil disobedience is a political act in the sense that it is an act justified by moral principles which define a conception of civil society and the public good. It rests, then, on political conviction as opposed to a search for self or group interest; and in the case of a constitutional democracy, we may assume that this conviction involves the conception of justice (say that expressed by the contract doctrine) which underlies the constitution itself. That is, in a viable democratic regime there is a common conception of justice by reference to which its citizens regulate their political affairs and interpret the constitution. Civil disobedience is a public act which the dissenter believes to be justified by this conception of justice and for this reason it may be understood as addressing the sense of justice of the majority in order to urge reconsideration of the measures protested and to warn that, in the sincere opinion of the dissenters, the conditions of social cooperation are not being honored. For the principles of justice express precisely such conditions, and their persistent and deliberate violation in regard to basic liberties over any extended period of time cuts the ties of community and invites either submission or forceful resistance. By engaging in civil disobedience a minority leads the majority to consider whether it wants to have its acts taken in this way, or whether, in view of the common sense of justice, it wishes to acknowledge the claims of the minority.

Civil disobedience is also civil in another sense. Not only is it the outcome of a sincere conviction based on principles which regulate civic life, but it is public and nonviolent, that is, it is done in a situation where arrest and punishment are expected and accepted without resistance. In this way it manifests a respect for legal procedures. Civil disobedience expresses disobedience to law within the limits of fidelity to law, and this feature of it helps to establish in the eyes of the majority that it is indeed conscientious and sincere, that it really is meant to address their sense of justice.[4] Being completely open about one's acts and being willing to accept the legal consequences of one's conduct is a bond given to make good one's sincerity, for that one's deeds are conscientious is not easy to demonstrate to another or even before oneself. No doubt it is possible to imagine a legal system in which conscientious belief that the law is unjust is accepted as a defense for

---

[3]Here I follow H. A. Bedau's definition of civil disobedience. See his "On Civil Disobedience," *Journal of Philosophy* (October, 1961).
[4]For a fuller discussion of this point to which I am indebted, see Charles Fried, "Moral Causation," *Harvard Law Review* (1964).

THE JUSTIFICATION OF CIVIL DISOBEDIENCE

noncompliance, and men of great honesty who are confident in one another might make such a system work. But as things are such a scheme would be unstable; we must pay a price in order to establish that we believe our actions have a moral basis in the convictions of the community.

The nonviolent nature of civil disobedience refers to the fact that it is intended to address the sense of justice of the majority and as such it is a form of speech, an expression of conviction. To engage in violent acts likely to injure and to hurt is incompatible with civil disobedience as a mode of address. Indeed, an interference with the basic rights of others tends to obscure the civilly disobedient quality of one's act. Civil disobedience is nonviolent in the further sense that the legal penalty for one's action is accepted and that resistance is not (at least for the moment) contemplated. Nonviolence in this sense is to be distinguished from nonviolence as a religious or pacifist principle. While those engaging in civil disobedience have often held some such principle, there is no necessary connection between it and civil disobedience. For on the interpretation suggested, civil disobedience in a democratic society is best understood as an appeal to the principles of justice, the fundamental conditions of willing social cooperation among free men, which in the view of the community as a whole are expressed in the constitution and guide its interpretation. Being an appeal to the moral basis of public life, civil disobedience is a political and not primarily a religious act. It addresses itself to the common principles of justice which men can require one another to follow and not to the aspirations of love which they cannot. Moreover by taking part in civilly disobedient acts one does not foreswear indefinitely the idea of forceful resistance; for if the appeal against injustice is repeatedly denied, then the majority has declared its intention to invite submission or resistance and the latter may conceivably be justified even in a democratic regime. We are not required to acquiesce in the crushing of fundamental liberties by democratic majorities which have shown themselves blind to the principles of justice upon which justification of the constitution depends.

5. THE JUSTIFICATION OF CIVIL DISOBEDIENCE

So far we have said nothing about the justification of civil disobedience, that is, the conditions under which civil disobedience may be engaged in consistent with the principles of justice that support a democratic regime. Our task is to see how the characterization of civil disobedience as addressed to the sense of justice of the majority (or to the citizens as a body) determines when such action is justified.

First of all, we may suppose that the normal political appeals to the majority have already been made in good faith and have been rejected, and that the standard means of redress have been tried. Thus, for example, existing political parties are indifferent to the claims of the minority and attempts to repeal the laws protested have been met with further repression since legal institutions are in the control of the majority. While civil disobedience should be recognized, I think, as a form of political action within the limits of fidelity to the rule of law, at the same time it is a rather desperate act just within these limits, and therefore it should, in general, be undertaken as a last resort when standard democratic processes have failed. In this sense it is not a normal political action. When it is justified there has been a serious breakdown; not only is there grave injustice in the law but a refusal more or less deliberate to correct it.

Second, since civil disobedience is a political act addressed to the sense of justice of the majority, it should usually be limited to substantial and clear violations of justice and preferably to those which, if rectified, will establish a basis for doing away with remaining injustices. For this reason there is a presumption in favor of restricting civil disobedience to violations of the first principle of justice, the principle of equal liberty, and to barriers which contravene the second principle, the principle of open offices which protects equality of opportunity. It is not, of course, always easy to tell whether these principles are satisfied. But if we think of them as guaranteeing the fundamental equal political and civil liberties (including freedom of conscience and liberty of thought) and equality of opportunity, then it is often relatively clear whether their principles are being honored. After all, the equal liberties are defined by the visible structure of social institutions; they are to be incorporated into the recognized practice, if not the letter, of social arrangements. When minorities are denied the right to vote or to hold certain political offices, when certain religious groups are repressed and others denied equality of opportunity in the economy, this is often obvious and there is no doubt that justice is not being given. However, the first part of the second principle which requires that inequalities be to everyone's advantage is a much more imprecise and controversial matter. Not only is there a problem of assigning it a determinate and precise sense, but even if we do so and agree on what it should be, there is often a wide variety of reasonable opinion as to whether the principle is satisfied. The reason for this is that the principle applies primarily to fundamental economic and social policies. The choice of these depends upon theoretical and speculative beliefs as well as upon a wealth of concrete information, and all of this mixed with judgment and plain hunch, not to mention in actual cases prejudice and self-interest. Thus unless the laws of taxation are clearly designed to attack a basic equal liberty, they should not be protested by civil disobedience; the appeal to justice is not sufficiently clear and its resolution is best left to the political process. But violations of the equal liberties that define the common status of citizenship are another matter. The deliberate denial of these more or less over any extended period of time in the face of normal political protest is, in general, an appropriate object of civil disobedience. We may think of the social system as divided roughly into two parts, one which incorporates the fundamental equal liberties (including equality of opportunity) and another which embodies social and economic policies properly aimed at promoting the advantage of everyone. As a rule civil disobedience is best limited to the former where the appeal to justice is not only more definite and precise, but where, if it is effective, it tends to correct the injustices in the latter.

Third, civil disobedience should be restricted to those cases where the dissenter is willing to affirm that everyone else similarly subjected to the same degree of injustice has the right to protest in a similar way. That is, we must be prepared to authorize others to dissent in similar situations and in the same way, and to accept the consequences of their doing so. Thus, we may hold, for example, that the widespread disposition to disobey civilly clear violations of fundamental liberties more or less deliberate over an extended period of time would raise the degree of justice throughout society and would insure men's self-esteem as well as their respect for one another. Indeed, I believe this to be true, though certainly it is partly a matter of conjecture. As the contract doctrine emphasizes, since the principles of justice are principles which we would agree to in an original position of equality when we do not know our social position and the like, the refusal to grant justice is either the denial of the other as an equal (as one in regard to whom we are prepared to constrain our actions by principles which we would consent to) or the manifestation of a willingness to take advantage of natural contingencies and social fortune at his expense. In either case, injustice invites submission or resistance; but submission arouses the contempt of the oppressor and confirms him in his intention. If straightway, after a decent period of time to make reasonable political appeals in the normal way, men were in general to dissent by civil disobedience from infractions of the fundamental equal liberties, these liberties would, I believe, be more rather than less secure. Legitimate civil disobedience properly exercised is a stabilizing device in a constitutional regime, tending to make it more firmly just.

Sometimes, however, there may be a complication in connection with this third condition. It is possible, although perhaps unlikely, that there are so many persons or groups with a sound case for resorting to civil disobedience (as judged by the foregoing criteria) that disorder would follow if they all did so. There might be serious injury to the just constitution. Or again, a group might be so large that some extra precaution is necessary in the extent to which its members organize and engage in civil disobedience. Theoretically the case is one in which a number of persons or groups are equally entitled to and all want to resort to civil disobedience, yet if they all do this, grave consequences for everyone may result. The question, then, is who among them may exercise their right, and it falls under the general problem of fairness. I cannot discuss the complexities of the matter here. Often a lottery or a rationing system can be set up to handle the case; but unfortunately the circumstances of civil disobedience rule out this solution. It suffices to note that a problem of fairness may arise and that those who contemplate civil disobedience should take into account. They may have to reach an understanding as to who can exercise their right in the immediate situation and to recognize the need for special constraint.

The final condition, of a different nature, is the following. We have been considering when one has a right to engage in civil disobedience, and our conclusion is that one has this right should three conditions hold: when one is subject to injustice more or less deliberate over an extended period of time in the face of normal political protests; where the injustice is a clear violation of the liberties of equal citizenship; and provided that the general disposition to protest similarly in similar cases would have acceptable consequences. These conditions are not, I think, exhaustive but they seem to cover the more obvious points; yet even when they are satisfied and one has the right to engage in civil disobedience, there is still the different question of whether one should exercise this right, that is, whether by doing so one is likely to further one's ends. Having established one's right to protest one is then free to consider these tactical questions. We may be acting within our rights but still foolishly if our action only serves to provoke the harsh retaliation of the majority; and it is likely to do so if the majority lacks a sense of justice, or if the action is poorly timed or not well designed to make the appeal to the sense of justice effective. It is easy to think of instances of this sort, and in each case these practical questions have to be faced. From the standpoint of the theory of political obligation we can only say that the exercise of the right should be rational and reasonably designed to advance the protester's aims, and that weighing tactical questions presupposes that one has already established one's right, since tactical advantages in themselves do not support it.

6. CONCLUSION: SEVERAL OBJECTIONS CONSIDERED

In a reasonably affluent democratic society justice becomes the first virtue of institutions. Social arrangements irrespective of their efficiency must be reformed if they are significantly unjust. No increase in efficiency in the form of greater advantages for many justifies the loss of liberty of a few. That we believe this is shown by the fact that in a democracy the fundamental liberties of citizenship are not understood as the outcome of political bargaining nor are they subject to the calculus of social interests. Rather these liberties are fixed points which serve to limit political transactions and which determine the scope of calculations of social advantage. It is this fundamental place of the equal liberties which makes their systematic violation over any extended period of time a proper object of civil disobedience. For to deny men these rights is to infringe the conditions of social cooperation among free and rational persons, a fact which is evident to the citizens of a constitutional regime since it follows from the principles of justice which underlie their institutions. The justification of civil disobedience rests on the priority of justice and the equal liberties which it guarantees.

It is natural to object to this view of civil disobedience that it relies too heavily upon the existence of a sense of justice. Some may hold that the feeling for justice is not a vital political force, and that what moves men are various other interests, the desire for wealth, power, prestige, and so on. Now this is a large question the answer to which is highly conjectural and each tends to have his own opinion. But there are two remarks which may clarify what I have said: first, I have assumed that there is in a constitutional regime a common sense of justice the principles of which are recognized to support the constitution and to guide its interpretation. In any given situation particular men may be tempted to violate these principles, but the collective force in their behalf is usually effective since they are seen as the necessary terms of cooperation among free men; and presumably the citizens of a democracy (or sufficiently many of them) want to see justice done. Where these assumptions fail, the justifying conditions for civil disobedience (the first three) are not affected, but the rationality of engaging in it certainly is. In this case, unless the costs of repressing civil dissent injure the economic self-interest (or whatever) of the majority, protest may simply make the position of the minority worse. No doubt as a tactical matter civil disobedience is more effective when its appeal coincides with other interests, but a constitutional regime is not viable in the long run without an attachment to the principles of justice of the sort which we have assumed.

Then, further, there may be a misapprehension about the manner in which a sense of justice manifests itself. There is a tendency to think that it is shown by professions of the relevant principles together with action of an altruistic nature requiring a considerable degree of self-sacrifice. But these conditions are obviously too strong, for the majority's sense of justice may show itself simply in its being unable to undertake the measures required to suppress the minority and to punish as the law requires the various acts of civil disobedience. The sense of justice undermines the will to uphold unjust institutions and so a majority despite its superior power may give way. It is unprepared to force the minority to be subject to injustice. Thus, although the majority's action is reluctant and grudging, the role of the sense of justice is nevertheless essential, for without it the majority would have been willing to enforce the law and to defend its position. Once we see the sense of justice as working in this negative way to make established injustices indefensible, then it is recognized as a central element of democratic politics.

Finally, it may be objected against this account that it does not settle the question of who is to say when the situation is such as to justify civil disobedience. And because it does not answer this question, it invites anarchy by encouraging every man to decide the matter for himself. Now the reply to this is that each man must indeed settle this question for himself, although he may, of course, decide wrongly. This is true on any theory of political duty and obligation, at least on any theory compatible with the principles of a democratic constitution. The citizen is responsible for what he does. If we usually think that we should comply with the law, this is because our political principles normally lead to this conclusion. There is a presumption in favor of compliance in the absence of good reasons to the contrary. But because each man is responsible and must decide for himself as best he can whether the circumstances justify civil disobedience, it does not follow that he may decide as he pleases. It is not by looking to our personal interests or to political allegiances narrowly construed, that we should make up our mind. The citizen must decide on the basis of the principles of justice that underlie and guide the interpretation of the constitution and in the light of his sincere conviction as to how these principles should be applied in the circumstances. If he concludes that conditions obtain which justify civil disobedience and conducts himself accordingly, he has acted conscientiously and perhaps mistakenly, but not in any case at his convenience.

In a democratic society each man must act as he thinks the principles of political right require him to. We are to follow our understanding of these principles, and we cannot do otherwise. There can be no morally binding legal interpretation of these principles, not even by a supreme court or legislature. Nor is there any infallible procedure for determining what or who is right. In our system the Supreme Court, Congress, and the President often put forward rival interpretations of the Constitution. Although the Court has the final say in settling any particular case, it is not immune from powerful political influence that may change its reading of the law of the land. The Court presents its point of view by reason and argument; its conception of the Constitution must, if it is to endure, persuade men of its soundness. The final court of appeal is not the Court, or Congress, or the President, but the electorate as a whole.[5] The civilly disobedient appeal in effect to this body. There is no danger of anarchy as long as there is a sufficient working agreement in men's conceptions of political justice and what it requires. That men can achieve such an understanding when the essential political liberties are maintained is the assumption implicit in democratic institutions. There is no way to avoid entirely the risk of devisive strife. But if legitimate civil disobedience seems to threaten civil peace, the responsibility falls not so much on those who protest as upon those whose abuse of authority and power justifies such opposition.

[5]For a presentation of this view to which I am indebted, see A. M. Bickel, *The Least Dangerous Branch* (Indianapolis, 1962), especially chapters 5 and 6.

rawls on
civil disobedience

peter singer

This is an appropriate point at which to consider the theory of civil disobedience proposed by John Rawls in his much-discussed book, *A Theory of Justice*,[1] for Rawls's conception of the proper role of disobedience in a constitutional democracy has much in common with the kind of disobedience we have just been discussing. According to Rawls, civil disobedience is an act which 'addresses the sense of justice of the community and declares that in one's considered opinion the principles of social co-operation among free and equal men are not being respected'.[2] Civil disobedience is here regarded as a form of address, or an appeal. Accordingly Rawls comes to conclusions similar to those I have reached about the form which such disobedience should take. It should, he says, be non-violent and refrain from hurting or interfering with others because violence or interference tends to obscure the fact that what is being done is a form of address. While civil disobedience may 'warn and admonish, it is not itself a threat'. Similarly, to show sincerity and general fidelity to law, one should

From Peter Singer, *Democracy and Disobedience*, © 1973 Oxford University Press. By permission of The Clarendon Press, Oxford.

[1] Clarendon Press, Oxford, 1972. The theory of civil disobedience is to be found in ch. 6, mostly in sects. 55, 57, and 59.
[2] Ibid., p. 364.

be completely open about what one is doing, willing to accept the legal consequences of one's act.

I am therefore in agreement with Rawls on the main point: limited disobedience, far from being incompatible with a genuinely democratic form of government, can have an important part to play as a justifiable form of protest. There are, however, some features of Rawls's position which I cannot accept. These features derive from the theory of justice which is the core of the book. The reader may have noticed that the sentence I quoted above contains a reference to 'the sense of justice of the community' and to the 'principles of social cooperation among free and equal men'. Rawls's justification of civil disobedience depends heavily on the idea that a community has a sense of justice which is a single sense of justice on which all can agree, at least in practice if not in all theoretical details. It is the violation of this accepted basis of society which legitimates disobedience. To be fair to Rawls, it must be said that he is not maintaining that men ever do or did get together and agree on a sense of justice, and on the principles of social co-operation. Rather the idea is that a basically just society will have a sense of justice that corresponds to the principles that free and equal men would have chosen, had they met together to agree, under conditions designed to ensure impartiality, to abide by the basic principles necessary for social co-operation. It should also be said that Rawls does not maintain that every society in fact has such a sense of justice, but he intends his theory of disobedience to apply only to those that do. (As an aside, he suggests that the wisdom of civil disobedience will be problematic when there is no common conception of justice, since disobedience may serve only to rouse the majority to more repressive measures.)[3]

This is not the place to discuss Rawls's theory of justice as a whole. I want to discuss only its application to our topic. From his view that civil disobedience is justified by 'the principles of justice which regulate the constitution and social institutions generally', Rawls draws the consequence that 'in justifying civil disobedience one does not appeal to principles of personal morality or to religious doctrines. . . . Instead one invokes the commonly shared conception of justice which underlies the political order.'[4]

Even bearing in mind that this is intended to apply only to societies in which there is a common conception of justice, one can see that this is a serious limitation on the grounds on which

[3]Ibid., pp. 386–387.
[4]Ibid., p. 365.

disobedience can be justified. I shall suggest two ways in which this limitation could be unreasonable.

Firstly, if disobedience is an appeal to the community, why can it only be an appeal which invokes principles which the community already accepts? Why could one not be justified in disobeying in order to ask the majority to alter or extend the shared conception of justice? Rawls might think that it could never be necessary to go beyond this shared conception, for the shared conception is broad enough to contain all the principles necessary for a just society. Disobedience, he would say, can be useful to ensure that society does not depart too seriously from this shared conception, but the conception itself is unimpeachable. The just society, on this view, may be likened to a good piece of machinery: there may occasionally be a little friction, and some lubrication will then be necessary but the basic design needs no alteration.

Now Rawls can, of course, make this true by definition. We have already seen that he intends his theory of disobedience to apply only to societies which have a common conception of justice. If Rawls means by this that his theory applies only when the shared conception of justice encompasses all the legitimate claims that anyone in the society can possibly make then it follows that no disobedience which seeks to extend or go beyond the shared conception of justice can be legitimate. Since this would follow simply in virtue of how Rawls had chosen to use the notion of a shared conception of justice, however, it would be true in a trivial way, and would be utterly unhelpful for anyone wondering whether he would be justified in disobeying in an actual society.

If Rawls is to avoid this trivializing of his position it would seem that he must be able to point to at least some societies which he thinks have an adequate sense of justice. This course would invite our original question: why will disobedience be justified only if it invokes this particular conception of justice? This version of the theory elevates the conception of justice at present held by some society or societies into a standard valid for all time. Does any existing society have a shared conception of justice which cannot conceivably be improved? Maybe we cannot ourselves see improvements in a particular society's conception of justice, but we surely cannot rule out the possibility that in time it may appear defective, not only in its application, but in the fundamentals of the conception itself. In this case, disobedience designed to induce the majority to rethink its conception of justice might be justified.

I cannot see any way in which Rawls can avoid one or other of these difficulties. Either his conception of justice is a pure ideal, in which case it does not assist our real problems, or it unjustifiably excludes the use of disobedience as a way of making a radical objection to the conception of justice shared by some actual society.

Rawls's theory of civil disobedience contains a second and distinct restriction on the grounds of legitimate disobedience. As we have seen, he says that the justification of disobedience must be in terms of justice, and not in terms of 'principles of personal morality or religious doctrine'. It is not clear exactly what this phrase means, but since Rawls opposes it to 'the commonly shared conception of justice which underlies the political order' we may take it to include all views that are not part of this shared conception. This makes it a substantial restriction, since according to Rawls there are important areas of morality which are outside the scope of justice. The theory of justice is, he says, 'but one part of a moral view'.[5] As an example of an area of morality to which justice in inapplicable, Rawls instances our relations with animals. It is, he says, wrong to be cruel to animals, although we do not owe them justice. If we combine this view with the idea that the justification of civil disobedience must be in terms of justice, we can see that Rawls is committed to holding that no amount of cruelty to animals can justify disobedience. Rawls would no doubt admit that severe and widespread cruelty to animals would be a great moral evil, but his position requires him to say that the licensing, or even the promotion of such cruelty by a government (perhaps to amuse the public, or as is more likely nowadays, for experimental purposes) could not possibly justify civil disobedience, whereas something less serious would justify disobedience if it were contrary to the shared conception of justice. This is a surprising and I think implausible conclusion. A similar objection could be made in respect of any other area of morality which is not included under the conception of justice. Rawls does not give any other examples, although he suggests (and it is implied by his theory of justice) that our dealings with permanent mental defectives do not come under the ambit of justice.[6]

So far I have criticized Rawls's theory of disobedience because of certain restrictions it places on the kind of reason which can justify disobedience. My final comment is different. Rawls frequently writes as if it were a relatively simple matter to determine whether a majority decision is just or unjust. This, coupled with his view that the community has a common conception of justice, leads him to underestimate the importance of a settled, peaceful method of resolving disputes. It could also lead one to the view

[5]Ibid., p. 512.
[6]Ibid., p. 510.

that there are cases in which the majority is clearly acting beyond its powers, that is, that there are areas of life in which the decision-procedure is entirely without weight, for instance, if it tries to restrict certain freedoms. (This view is similar to that discussed earlier in connection with rights.) Consider the following passage:

> It is assumed that in a reasonably just democratic regime there is a public conception of justice by reference to which citizens regulate their political affairs and interpret the constitution. The persistent and deliberate violation of the basic principles of this conception over any extended period of time, especially the infringement of the fundamental equal liberties, invites either submission or resistance. By engaging in civil disobedience a minority forces the majority to consider whether it wishes to have its actions construed in this way, or whether, in view of the common sense of justice, it wishes to acknowledge the legitimate claims of the minority.[7]

There will, of course, be some instances in a society when the actions of the majority can only be seen as a deliberate violation for selfish ends of basic principles of justice. Such actions do invite submission or resistance'. It is a mistake, though, to see these cases as in any way typical of those disputes which lead people to ask whether disobedience would be justified. Even when a society shares a common conception of justice, it is not likely to agree on the application of this conception to particular cases. Rawls admits that it is not always clear when the principles of justice have been violated, but he thinks it is often clear, especially when the principle of equal liberty (for Rawls the first principle of justice) is involved. As examples, he suggests that a violation of this principle can clearly be seen when 'certain religious groups are repressed' and when 'certain minorities are denied the right to vote or to hold office. . . .'[8] These cases appear straightforward, but are they? Timothy Leary's League for Spiritual Discovery claimed to be a religious group using the drug LSD as a means of exploring the ultimate spiritual reality. At least three other groups —the Neo-American Church, the Church of the Awakening, and the Native American Church—have used hallucinogenic drugs as part of religious ceremonies. Of these groups, only the last has legal permission to do so. Is freedom of worship being denied to the others? When is a group a religious group? There are similar problems about denying minorities the vote. Is the denial of the vote to children a violation of equal liberty? Or to convicted prisoners? It may seem obvious to us that these are legitimate excep-

[7]Ibid., pp. 365–366.
[8]Ibid., p. 372.

tions, but then it seemed obvious to many respectable citizens a hundred years ago that blacks and women should not have the vote, and it seemed obvious to Locke that the suppression of atheism and Roman Catholicism were quite compatible with the principle of religious toleration.

When we go beyond religious persecution and the denial of voting rights, it is even easier to find complex disputes on which sincere disagreement over the justice of an action is likely to occur. Many of the issues which have led to civil disobedience in recent years have been of this more complex kind. This is why I do not think it helpful to assume that most issues arise from deliberate disregard of some common principles, or to try to specify limits, whether in the form of rights or of principles of justice, on what the majority can legitimately do.

law and civil disobedience

r. m. dworkin

1. INTRODUCTION

The literature on civil disobedience seems to me deficient in two respects. The first represents a conceptual block. Lawyers and philosophers have been careful to separate the legal issue of whether the law is valid from the moral issues of whether it should be obeyed. They argue in the alternative: If the law is invalid, then no problem of civil disobedience arises. It the law is valid, then the moral problem is presented of whether it is ever proper to disobey a valid law. The structure of this argument hides the fact that the validity of a law may be in doubt. The dissenters may believe that the law they break is invalid, the officials who judge them may disagree, and both sides may have plausible or colorable arguments for their positions. If so, then the issues are different from what they would be if the law were clearly valid or clearly invalid, and theories designed for these alternatives are irrelevant.

The case of doubtful law is by no means a special or exotic case. On the contrary. In the United States, at least, almost any law that would tempt a significant number of people to dissent

Reprinted from *Ethics and Social Justice*, vol. 4 of *Contemporary Philosophic Thought: The International Philosophy Year at Brockport*, edited by Howard E. Kiefer and Milton K. Munitz, © 1968 by Ronald Dworkin, by permission of State University of New York Press.

would be doubtful—if not clearly invalid—on constitutional grounds. The Constitution makes the essentials of our conventional political morality relevant to the question of validity; any statute that appears to compromise that morality raises constitutional questions, and if the compromise is serious, the constitutional doubts are serious also.

Certainly the constitutional standing of the present draft laws is doubtful. Congress did not declare war in Vietnam, the national interest there may not be great enough to justify risk of life under the due process clause, the draft as administered discriminates amongst citizens in a way that might be condemned by the due process and equal protection clauses, taken together, and the law that forbids counselling draft resistance hampers speech on a vital political issue, contrary to the policy behind the First Amendment. These doubts are strong enough so that dissenters might reasonably believe that the laws are invalid, though I think a majority of lawyers would hold, on balance, that they are not. We need a theory of civil disobedience (if that is the right phrase) that covers this sort of case.

The second deficiency in the literature is a matter of standpoint. Almost all of it speaks to the issue of what a man should do who thinks that a law is immoral. It does not speak to the decision the government must make if someone does break the law out of conscience. When should the government stay its hand, and tolerate rather than punish dissent?

The theorists have said little about this, I suppose, because they think there is little to say. They believe that a government can do nothing but enforce its laws once these have been enacted and until they have been repealed. They assume that a citizen who disobeys out of conscience is necessarily pitted against the rest of society. Even when he is justified in breaking the law, the majority is justified, at least according to its own standards, in prosecuting him. Indeed, some of the dissenters themselves assume that punishment is appropriate; they feel almost cheated if they are not prosecuted, because this implies that they have been evasive or clandestine, or that the community has not taken note of their act.

These two gaps in the literature are connected. The case that the government should stay its hand is obviously stronger when it is arguable that the law is invalid, and the failure to make that case may be traced to the traditional structure of argument that focuses on the rare occasion on when it is not. I shall therefore attempt to answer this question: If it is unclear whether a criminal law is constitutional, in the sense that a reasonable lawyer might think it is not, and someone breaks that law out of conscience, how should the state respond? In Section 2 I shall argue that the state has a general responsibility of leniency in these circumstances, because our practices encourage men to follow their own judgment when the law is unclear, even though we do not guarantee immunity from punishment if they do. In Section 3 I shall consider how the state might acquit this responsibility in the case of draft offenses, consistently with other policies it thinks it ought to pursue. I do not mean to suggest that a man should never disobey when the law is clear, or that the state should always punish him when he does. But those are the special cases, and I am anxious to avoid the limitations that preoccupation with these cases has imposed.

2. THE RESPONSIBILITY OF LENIENCY

There are practical reasons for not prosecuting conscientious dissenters. These men are rarely enemies of the state; they are often among its most loyal and dedicated citizens. Jailing them solidifies their alienation, and the alienation of many who are thereby deterred.

What objection could there be to tolerating rather than prosecuting dissent? The most powerful objection, many people think, is that a policy of tolerance would be unfair to the majority of citizens. It would be unfair, so the argument goes, because the bulk of our citizens "play the game," by obeying even those laws which they themselves disapprove or find disadvantageous. If those who will not play the game go unpunished, then they are allowed to secure the benefits of deference to law, without shouldering the burdens. It is no answer to this argument that the system might change so that everyone has the privilege of disobeying laws he believed immoral. The majority wants no such change; the present system will continue and those who do not want to keep its rules should quit the community.

This argument is limited, however, by the hidden assumption I mentioned, the assumption that the law is clear. We cannot apply the argument to cases like the present draft until we confront this further question: What should a citizen do when the law is unclear, and he thinks it allows what others think it does not? I do not mean to ask, of course, what it is *legally* proper for him to do, or what his *legal* rights are—that would be begging the question, because that depends upon whether he is right or they are right. I mean to ask what his proper course is as a citizen, what we would consider to be "playing the game."

There is no consensus on this question—no obvious answer on which most citizens would readily agree—and that fact is itself significant. If we examine our legal institutions and practices, however, we may find support for one or another position. I shall proceed by setting out three possible answers, and then attempting to show which of these best fits our practices and expectations. The three possibilities I want to consider are these:

(1) If the law is doubtful and it is therefore unclear whether it permits someone to do what he wants, he should assume the worst, and act on the assumption that it does not.

(2) If the law is doubtful, he may follow his own judgment— that is, he may do what he wants if he believes that the case that the law permits this is stronger than the case that it does not. But he may follow his own judgment only until an authoritative institution, like a court, decides the other way, in a case involving him or someone else. Once an institutional decision has been reached, he must abide by that decision, even though he thinks that it was wrong. (There are, in theory, many subdivisions of this second possibility. We might say that the individual's choice is foreclosed by the contrary decision of any court, including the lowest court in the system if the case is not appealed. Or we may require a decision of some particular court or institution. I shall discuss this second possibility in its most liberal form, namely that the individual is free to follow his own judgment until a contrary decision of the highest court competent to pass on the issue, which in the case of constitutional issues involved in draft refusal is the United States Supreme Court.)

(3) If the law is doubtful, he may follow his own judgment even after a contrary decision by the highest competent court. Of course, he must take the contrary decision of any court into account in making his judgment of what the law requires. Otherwise the judgment would not be an honest or reasonable one, because the doctrine of precedent, which is an established part of our legal system, has the effect of allowing the decisions of courts, and particularly high appellate courts, to *change* the law. Suppose, for example, that a taxpayer believes that he is not required to pay tax on certain forms of income. If the Supreme Court decides to the contrary, he might, taking into account the practice of according great weight to the decision of the Supreme Court on tax matters, decide that the Court's decision has itself tipped the balance, and that the law now requires him to pay the tax.

Someone might think that this qualification erases the difference between the third and the second models, but it does not. The doctrine of precedent gives varying weights to the decisions of different courts, and especially great weight to the decisions of the Supreme Court, but it does not make the decision of any court

204

conclusive. It is distinctly possible that even after a contrary decision an individual may still reasonably believe that the law is on his side. This is especially likely in the fields of constitutional law that are relevant to civil disobedience. The Supreme Court has shown itself more likely, in this area than in any other, to overrule its past decisions if it is persuaded that these have unduly limited personal or political rights.

We do not follow the doctrine, in other words, that the Constitution is always what the Supreme Court says it is. Oliver Wendell Holmes followed no such rule in his famous dissent in the *Gitlow* case. A few years before, in *Abrams*, he had lost his battle to persuade the court that the First Amendment protected an anarchist who had been urging general strikes against the government. A similar issue was presented in *Gitlow*, and Holmes once again went into dissent. "It is true," he said, "that in my opinion this criterion was departed from in [*Abrams*] but the convictions that I expressed in that case are too deep for it to be possible for me as yet to believe that it . . . settled the law." Holmes voted to acquit Gitlow, on the ground that what Gitlow had done was no crime even though the Court had recently held that it was.

Here, then, are three models we might choose in attempting to specify how a dissenter should behave. Other models are possible, of course, but these three may serve as paradigms.

I think it plain that we do not follow the first of these paradigms, that is, that we do not expect citizens to assume the worst. If no court has decided the issue, and a man thinks that the case that the law allows him to do what he wants is better than the case that it does not, we think it perfectly proper for him to follow his own judgment. It is worth pausing a moment to consider what society would lose if it did follow the first paradigm or, to put the matter the other way, what society gains from the fact that people follow their own judgment in cases like this.

When the law is uncertain, in the sense that the lawyers can reasonably disagree on what a court ought to decide, this is generally because different legal principles and policies collide and it is unclear what the best accommodation of these conflicting legal principles and policies would be. Our practice, in which different parties are encouraged to pursue their own understanding, provides a means for testing hypotheses relevant to this issue. If the question is whether a particular rule would have certain undesirable consequences, or whether these consequences would have limited or broad ramifications, then it is useful, before the issue is decided, to have the experience that is provided if some people proceed on that rule. If the question is whether a particular solution would offend principles of justice or fair play deeply respected by the community, or how grave the offense to these principles would be, it is useful, again, to test the community's response on an experimental basis.

If the first paradigm were followed, we would lose the advantages of these tests. The law would suffer, particularly if this paradigm were applied to constitutional issues. When it is doubtful whether a statute, particularly a criminal statute, is constitutional, the doubt can often be traced to the fact that the statute strikes some people as being unfair or unjust, because it infringes some principle of liberty or justice or fairness which they take to be built into the Constitution. If our practice were that whenever a law is doubtful on these grounds, one must act as if it is valid, then the chief vehicle we have for challenging the law on moral grounds would be lost, and over time the law we obeyed would certainly become less fair and just, and the liberty of our citizens would certainly be diminished.

We would lose almost as much if we used a variation of the first paradigm, that a citizen must assume the worst unless he can anticipate that the courts will agree with his view of the law. If everyone deferred to his guess of what the courts would do, society and its law would be poorer. Our assumption, in rejecting the first paradigm, was that the record a citizen makes in following his own judgment, together with the arguments he makes supporting that judgment when he has the chance, are helpful in forging the best judicial decision. This remains true even when, at the time the citizen acts, the odds are against his success in court. We must remember, too, that the value of the citizen's example is not exhausted once the decision has been made. Our practices require that the decision be criticized, by the profession and the schools, and the record of dissent may be invaluable here.

Of course a man must consider what the courts will do when he decides whether it would be *prudent* to follow his own judgment. But it is essential that we separate the calculation of prudence from the question of what, as a good citizen, he is entitled to do. We are investigating how society ought to treat him when its courts believed that he judged wrong, and for that reason we are asking what he is entitled to do when his judgment differs from others. We will beg the question if we assume that what he may properly do depends on his guess as to how society will treat him.

We must also reject the second paradigm, that if the law is unclear a citizen may properly follow his own judgment until the highest court has ruled that he is wrong. It fails to take into account the fact that any court, including the Supreme Court, may overrule itself. In almost every case, when a court does reverse its prior decision, it applies its new decision retroactively. If the Court should hold a particular criminal law unconstitutional, for example, it would almost certainly extend its decision backwards and hold that citizens who had infringed that law before the new decision were not guilty of any crime.

In 1940 the Supreme Court decided that a West Virginia law requiring students to salute the Flag was constitutional. In 1943, it reversed itself, and decided that such a statute was unconstitutional after all. What was the duty, as citizens, of those people who in 1941 and 1942 objected to saluting the Flag on grounds of conscience, and thought that the Supreme Court's 1940 decision was wrong? We can hardly say that their duty was to follow the first decision. They believed that saluting the Flag was unconscionable, and they believed, reasonably, that no law required them to do so. The Supreme Court later decided that in this way they were right. Some will say that they should have obeyed the Court's first decision, meanwhile working in the legislatures to have the law repealed, and in the courts to find some way to challenge the law again without actually violating it.

That would be, perhaps, a plausible recommendation if conscience were not involved, because it would then be arguable that the gain in orderly procedure was worth the personal sacrifice of patience. But conscience was involved, and if the dissenters had obeyed the law while biding their time, they would have suffered the irreparable injury of having done what their conscience forbade them to do. It is one thing to say that an individual must sometimes violate his conscience when he knows that the law commands him to do it. It is quite another to say that he must violate his conscience even when he believes that the law does not require it, because it would inconvenience his fellow citizens if he took the most direct, and perhaps the only, method of attempting to show that he is right and they are wrong.

Since a court may overrule itself, then those same reasons we listed for rejecting the first paradigm count against the second as well. If we do not have the pressure of dissent from those who think that the law has been misunderstood, we will not get the most effective presentation of the view that it has been. We will not have a dramatic statement of the degree to which the earlier decision coerces conscience, a demonstration that is surely pertinent to the question of whether the first decision was right. We will increase the chance of being governed by rules that offend the principles we claim to serve.

These considerations force us, I think, from the second paradigm, but some will want to substitute a variation of it. They will argue that once the Supreme Court has decided that a criminal law is valid, then citizens have a duty to abide by that decision until they have a reasonable belief, not merely that the decision is bad law, but that the Supreme Court is likely to overrule it. Under this view the West Virginia dissenters who refused to salute the Flag in 1942 were acting properly, because they might reasonably anticipate that the Supreme Court would change its mind. But if the Supreme Court were to hold the draft laws constitutional, it would be improper to continue to challenge these laws, because there would be no great likelihood that the Court would soon change its mind.

The same objections apply to this suggestion as applied to the comparable variation of the first paradigm. Once we say that a citizen may properly follow his own judgment of the law, in spite of his judgment that the courts will probably find against him, there is no reason why he should act differently because a contrary decision is already on the books.

I conclude that the third paradigm, or something close to it, is the fairest statement of a man's social duty in our community. A citizen's allegiance is to the law, not to any particular person's view of what the law is, and he does not behave improperly or unfairly so long as he proceeds on his own considered and reasonable view of what the law requires.

Let me repeat that this is not the same as saying that an individual may disregard what the courts have said in deciding what to do. The doctrine of precedent lies near the core of our legal system, and no one is making a reasonable effort to follow the law unless he grants courts the general power to alter it by their decisions. But this aspect of the doctrine of precedent varies in its force, as I said, and someone who believes that a Supreme Court decision wrongly infringed fundamental personal rights need not regard that decision as conclusive.

One large question remains before we can apply these observations to the problems of civil disobedience. I have been talking about the case of a man who believes that the law is not what other people think, or what the courts have held. This description may fit some of those who disobey statutes out of conscience, but it does not fit most of them. The bulk of dissenters are not lawyers or political philosophers; they believe the law contradicts our legal ideals, but they may not have considered whether it is invalid for that reason. Of what relevance to their situation, then, is the proposition that one may properly follow one's own view of the law?

To answer this, I shall have to return to a theme I mentioned at

208

the outset. Our Constitution injects an extraordinary, and increasing, portion of our political morality into the issue of whether a law is valid. Anyone who believes that a law is profoundly immoral, on the ground that it is grossly unfair or unjust to some of our citizens, would be almost certain to think it unconstitutional if he understood the present reach of the due process and equal protection clauses. (I use this strong language— "profoundly immoral" and "grossly unfair"— because these clauses are complex, and someone who thought a law mildly unfair might hold this outweighed by other considerations and therefore believe the law valid.)

Let me list some of the grounds on which the dissenters believe that the present draft is immoral. They believe that the United States has no legitimate interest at stake in Vietnam, certainly no interest large enough to justify forcing immense personal sacrifice upon a selected segment of our population. They believe that if an army is to be raised to fight that war, it is immoral to raise it by a draft that defers or exempts college students, and thus discriminates against the economically underprivileged. They believe that there is no morally relevant difference between objection to all wars on religious grounds, and objection to a particular war on moral grounds, and that the draft, by making this distinction, implies that those who hold the second view are less worthy of the government's respect than those who hold the first. They believe that the law that makes it a crime to counsel draft resistance stifles those who oppose the war, because it is morally impossible to argue, with sincerity and passion, that the war is profoundly immoral, and stop short of encouraging and assisting those who refuse to fight it. Not everyone who holds the draft laws immoral believes all of this, but most of them believe at least some of it.

Lawyers will recognize, in these moral positions, arguments that the laws in question are violations of due process, of equal protection, and of freedom of speech. The statement that the majority of draft dissenters believe they are breaking the law therefore needs qualification. They hold beliefs that, if true, very strongly support the view that the law is on their side; the fact that they have not reached that further conclusion is traceable, in at least most cases, to their lack of legal sophistication. If we believe that people who follow their own judgment of the law are acting properly, it would seem wrong not to extend that view to those dissenters whose judgments come to the same thing. No part of the case that I made for the third paradigm would entitle us to distinguish them from their more knowledgable colleagues.

We might draw these tentative conclusions from the argument

so far: When the law is uncertain, in the sense that a plausible case can be made on both sides, then a citizen who follows his own judgment is not behaving unfairly. That privilege extends to those who believe that the law is clear, but also believe that it is deeply immoral because grossly unfair to some citizens. The argument we began by considering—that it would be unfair to tolerate draft dissenters because they are not "playing the game" of American society—is therefore invalid. On the contrary, this feature of our practices places on our government an affirmative responsibility of leniency, because if we believe that those who follow their own views are behaving properly, we ought to protect them.

It does not follow that we are never justified in prosecuting and punishing dissenters. Obviously we could not follow the simple practice of acquitting everyone who thinks the law is on his side. But we can follow the more complex practice of attempting to accommodate those whose views of the law are plausible, even though our officials think they are wrong, so long as we can do this without great damage to other policies.

In Section 3, I shall describe the techniques available for accommodating dissent, and the limits of these techniques. Before turning to these practical questions, however, I want to consider a philosophical objection to my argument so far.

Someone will say that I think that law is a "brooding omnipresence in the sky." I spoke of people making judgments about what the law requires even in cases in which the law is unclear and undemonstrable. I spoke of cases in which a man might think that the law requires one thing even though the Supreme Court has said that it requires another, and even when it was not likely that the Supreme Court would soon change its mind. I will therefore be charged with the view that there is always a "right answer" to a legal problem, to be found in natural law, or locked up in some transcendental strongbox.

Of course the strongbox of law is nonsense. When I say that people hold views on the law when the law is doubtful, and that these views are not merely predictions of what the courts will hold, I intend no such metaphysics. I mean only to summarize as accurately as I can a host of the practices that are part of our legal process.

We make claims of legal right and duty, even when we know these are not demonstrable, and we support these with arguments even when we know that these arguments will not appeal to everyone. We make these arguments to each other, in the professional journals and the classroom, and we make them to courts. We respond to these arguments, when others make them, by judging them good or bad or mediocre. In so doing we assume that some arguments for a given doubtful position are better than others, and that the case on one side of a doubtful proposition may be stronger than the case on the other, which is what I take a claim of law in a doubtful case to mean. We distinguish, without too much difficulty, between these arguments and predictions of what the courts will decide.

These practices are poorly represented by the theory that judgments of law on doubtful issues are nonsense, or are merely predictions of what the courts will do. Those who hold these theories cannot mean to deny the fact of these practices; perhaps they mean that these practices are not sensible, because they are based on suppositions that do not hold, or for some other reason. But this makes their objection mysterious, because they never specify what they take the purposes underlying the practices to be, and unless they are specified, one cannot decide whether the practices are sensible. I understand the policies behind the practices to be those I described earlier, having to do with the development and testing of the law through experimentation and through the adversary process. We pursue these policies by inviting our citizens to make determinations about the strengths and weaknesses of legal arguments for themselves, or through their own counsel, and to act on these judgments, though we qualify that permission by the limited threat that they may suffer if the courts do not agree. Our success depends on whether there is sufficient agreement within the community on what counts as a good or bad argument so that, although different people will reach different judgments, these differences will be neither so profound nor so frequent as to make the system unworkable, or overly dangerous for those who do act on their own lights. I believe there is sufficient agreement on criteria of argument to avoid these traps, although it remains one of the outstanding tasks of legal philosophy to exhibit and clarify these criteria. In any event, the practices I have described have not yet been shown to be misguided, and we may therefore properly take them into account in determining whether it is just and fair to be lenient to those who break what others think is the law.

3. HOW SHOULD THE STATE RESPOND?

In the remaining section of this paper I want to consider the large practical question I mentioned a moment ago. Granted that the government has what I called a responsibility of leniency to those who break the law out of conscience, what steps should it take to acquit that responsibility? I shall make some suggestions, using the draft cases as examples. I cannot explore any of these in detail; my purpose is rather to indicate the variety of techniques available.

The legislature can repeal or amend the statute that purports to make the dissenter's act a crime. Every program our legislature adopts is a medley of policies and restraining principles. We accept loss of efficiency in crime detection and urban renewal, for example, so that we can respect the rights of accused criminals and compensate property owners for their damages. A legislature may properly defer to its responsibility of leniency, therefore, by adjusting or compromising its other policies. The relevant questions are these: What means can be found for maximizing tolerance while minimizing impact on policy? How strong is the responsibility of leniency in this case—how deeply is the conscience of the minority involved, and how strong the case that the law is invalid after all? How important is the policy in question—is the interference that a compromise would cause too great a price to pay? These questions are no doubt too simple, but they suggest the nerve of the choices that must be made.

They argue, I think, for repeal of the law that makes it a crime to counsel draft resistance or aid draft resisters. If those who want to counsel draft resistance are given free reign, the number who will resist induction may increase, but not, I think, significantly beyond the number who would resist in any event. If I am wrong, then the fact of this residual discontent is of importance to policy makers, and it ought not to be hidden under a ban on speech. Conscience is deeply involved—it is hard to believe that many who counsel resistance do so on any other grounds. The case is strong that the laws that make counseling a crime are unconstitutional; even those who do not find the case persuasive will admit that its arguments are substantial.

If we turn to draft resistance itself, however, the state's response becomes more problematical. Those who believe that the war in Vietnam is itself a grotesque blunder will favor any change in the law that makes peace more likely. But if we stick to the standpoint of those who favor the war, then we must admit that a policy that continues the draft but wholly exempts dissenters would be unwise. The responsibility of leniency supports two alternatives that have been mentioned, however: the volunteer army, and an expanded conscientious objector category that includes those who find this war immoral. There is something to be said against both of these proposals, but once we recognize the principle that requires respect for dissent, that may tip the balance in their favor.

If Congress does not amend its laws to accommodate dissenters, the executive branch of government may respond by exercising its discretion not to prosecute. Many non-lawyers are unaware of the practice that lawyers call prosecutorial discretion. Under that practice, it falls to certain public officials (the Justice Department or the District Attorney, for example) to decide whether to prosecute someone believed guilty of a crime. Practice varies from jurisdiction to jurisdiction; some prosecutors pay more and others less attention to such factors as whether the accused is young, inexperienced or ignorant, what damage he caused, the likelihood of his reforming without correction, and so forth.

I do not suggest that prosecutors ought to exercise this discretion in favor of anyone who acts out of conscience. If failing to prosecute would jeopardize what the law recognizes as the moral rights of other citizens, that is a strong argument for prosecution. The law may be wrong but the government must act on the assumption that it is not, and the force of this assumption can be shown by an example. There are many sincere and ardent segregationists: their view is that the civil rights laws and decisions are unconstitutional, because they compromise principles of local government and of freedom of association, and this is a colorable, though not a persuasive, view. But if we tolerate the man who blocks the schoolhouse door, then we violate the rights of the schoolgirl he blocks. The nation has decided that she has the right to enter and it must act consistently upon this confrontation.

The draft laws do not rest on a presumption of underlying moral rights, however. There is a great deal of flexibility and discretion built into the draft—no one is entitled to have his draft board classify others in particular ways, or to have the army use any particular system for assigning men to dangerous posts once drafted.

If there is no question of jeopardizing legal rights, then the decision whether to prosecute a dissenter must rest on practical considerations similar to those that the legislator had to face. The prosecutor has much less flexibility, of course. His is a yes-or-no decision; he cannot accommodate conflicting policies through devices like a volunteer army or alternative service. Still, he is able to weigh these conflicting policies, and he must make the limited choices he has in the light of his judgments. He must weigh the long-term impact of rending the society, and the strength of the responsibility for leniency, against the damage to the policies represented by the law.

These factors suggest that those who counsel resistance should not be prosecuted, provided, of course, that the means they use do not encourage violence or otherwise trespass on the rights of others. The calculation is more complicated in the case of those who refuse induction when drafted. The crucial question is whether a failure to prosecute will lead to wholesale refusals to serve. It may not—there are social pressures, including the threat of career disadvantages, that would operate to force many young Americans to serve if drafted, even if they knew they would not go to jail if they refused. If the number would not much increase, then the state should leave the dissenters alone, and I see no great harm in delaying any prosecution until the effect of that policy becomes clearer. If the number of those who refuse induction turns out to be large, this would argue for prosecution. But it would also make the problem academic, because if there is sufficient dissent to bring us to that pass, we will not be able to pursue our policy in any event.

Perhaps these recommendations of prosecutorial discretion are surprising. It goes against our traditions to leave crime unpunished. But if discretion not to prosecute is ever proper, and if I am right that we owe leniency to those who break doubtful laws on grounds of conscience, I cannot see why that discretion is not appropriate here.

There is a trace of paradox in the suggestion, however. I argued earlier that when the law is unclear citizens have the right to follow their own judgment, partly on the ground that this practice helps shape issues for adjudication; now I propose a course that eliminates or postpones adjudication. But the contradiction is only apparent. It does not follow from the fact that a practice facilitates adjudication, and renders it more useful in developing the law, that a trial should follow whenever citizens appeal to that practice. It remains an open question whether, in the particular case, the issues are ripe for adjudication, and whether adjudication would settle these issues in a manner that would decrease the chance, or remove the grounds, for further dissent.

In the draft cases the answer to these questions is negative. There is considerable ambivalence about the war, and considerable uncertainty and ignorance about the scope of the moral issues involved in the draft. It is far from the best time for a court to pass on these issues, and tolerating dissent for a time is one way of allowing the debate to continue until it has produced something clearer. It is plain, moreover, that an adjudication of the constitutional issues now will not settle the law. Those who have doubts that the draft is constitutional will have the same doubts even if the Supreme Court says that it is, and our practices of precedent, as Holmes said, will encourage them to hold these doubts. Certainly this is so if the Supreme Court appeals to the "political question" doctrine, and refuses to pass on the constitutional issues at all. Under this waning but still powerful doctrine the Court denies its jurisdiction to consider matters seriously affecting, for example, foreign and defense policy, and it seems likely that the Court would appeal to that doctrine in the draft cases.

Suppose, finally, that Congress refuses to amend its statutes to accommodate dissenters, and that the prosecutor refuses his discretion in their behalf. This, after all, is what has and probably will happen. What ought the Court to do?

This is a complex question, and I shall deal with it too shortly. If the acts of dissent occur before the Supreme Court has held the laws valid, or before it has ruled that the political question doctrine applies, then the courts should acquit. The Supreme Court has often reversed convictions on the ground that the criminal law in question is too vague, and there seems little difference in principle between a criminal law whose terms are vague and a criminal law whose terms are precise, but whose constitutionality is in doubt.

If the acts of dissent occur after the Supreme Court has ruled, then acquittal on the ground of vagueness is no longer appropriate. The Court's decision will not have settled the law, but the Court will have done all that it believes can be done to settle it. The courts may still, however, exercise their sentencing discretion, and use light or minimal sentences as a mark of respect for the dissenters' position.

5

PUNISHMENT

the justification of punishment

r. s. downie

Traditionally two very general sorts of justification have been offered for the practice of punishment: retributivist and utilitarian. According to the theory of retribution, punishment is justified insofar as it is a morally fitting response to the violation of a law. Sometimes the theory is expressed in the ambiguous form: punishment is justified by guilt. This form of words is ambiguous because it may mean that guilt is a necessary condition of punishment, or it may mean that guilt is a necessary and a sufficient condition of punishment. The first of these claims is entirely innocuous—it is indeed part of the definition of punishment that it is for an offence (real or supposed)—and can be conceded by all without further ado. But insofar as the first claim simply states part of the definition of punishment it cannot constitute any part of its justification. Hence, insofar as the retributive theory sets out to be justificatory it logically must involve the more radical of the two claims—that guilt is a necessary and a sufficient condition of the infliction of punishment on an offender. Is the theory plausible?

It might be said against it that it does not reflect actual practice either in the law or in more informal normative orders such as schools or the family. In these institutions we find such prac-

From R. S. Downie, *Roles and Values* (London: Methuen & Co., Ltd., 1971). Reprinted by permission of Methuen & Co., Ltd.

THE JUSTIFICATION OF PUNISHMENT

tices as the relaxation of punishment for first offenders, warnings, pardons, and so on. Hence, it may seem that actual penal practice is at variance with the retributive theory if it is saying that guilt is a necessary and a sufficient condition of punishment. Only in games, it may be said, do we find a sphere where the infringement of rules is a necessary and a sufficient condition of the infliction of a penalty, and even in games there may be a 'playing the advantage' rule.

It is not clear, however, that the retributivist need be disturbed by this objection. He might take a high-handed line with the objection and say that if it is the case that actual penal practice does not reflect his theory then so much the (morally) worse for actual practice. Whatever people in fact do, he might argue, it is morally fitting that guilt be a necessary and a sufficient condition of the infliction of punishment.

A less high-handed line, and one more likely to conciliate the opponents of the retributivist theory, is to say that the statement of the theory so far provided is to be taken as a very general one. When it is said that guilt is a necessary and a sufficient condition of punishment it is not intended that punishment should in every case follow inexorably. There are cases where extenuating circumstances may be discovered and in such cases it would be legitimate to recommend mercy or even to issue a pardon. It is unfair to the retributivist to depict his theory as the inflexible application of rules. There is nothing in the theory which forbids it the use of all the devices in the law and in less formal institutions whereby punishment may in certain circumstances be mitigated. Even the sternest of retributivists can allow for the concept of mercy. Perhaps the objection may be avoided completely if the theory is stated more carefully as: guilt and nothing other than guilt may justify the infliction of punishment. To state the theory in this way is to enable it to accommodate the complex operation of extenuating factors which modify the execution of actual systems of law. But to say this is not yet to explain why guilt and nothing other than guilt may justify the infliction of punishment. Indeed, we might ask the retributivist to tell us why we should punish anyone at all.

Retributivists give a variety of answers to this question. One is that punishment annuls the evil which the offender has created. It is not easy to make sense of this claim. No amount of punishment can undo an offence that has been committed: what has been has been. Sometimes metaphors of punishment washing away sin are used to explain how punishment can annul evil. But such ideas can mislead. Certainly, the infliction of punishment may, as

220

a matter of psychological fact, remove some people's *feelings* of guilt. But we may query whether this is necessarily a good thing. Whether or not it is, however, it is not the same as annulling the evil committed.

A second retributivist idea is that the offender has had some sort of illicit pleasure and that the infliction of pain will redress the moral balance. People speak of the criminal as 'paying for what he has done' or as 'reaping a harvest of bitterness'; the infliction of suffering is regarded as a fitting response to crime. But this view may be based on a confusion of the idea that 'the punishment must fit the crime', which is acceptable if it means only that punishment ought to be proportionate, with the idea that punishment is a fitting response to crime, which is not so obviously acceptable. It may be that the traditional *lex talionis* is based on a confusion of the two ideas. At any rate, it is the idea of punishment as the 'fitting response' which is essential to the retributivist position.

A third claim sometimes made by the retributivists is that an offender has a right to punishment. This claim is often mocked by the critics of retributivism on the grounds that it is an odd right that would gladly be waived by the holder! It might be thought that the view can be defended on the grounds that the criminal's right to punishment is merely the right correlative to the authority's duty to punish him. Such a defence is not plausible, however, for, even supposing there is a right correlative to a legal authority's duty to punish criminals, it is much more plausible to attribute this right to the society which is protected by the deterrent effect of punishment.

There are two arguments, more convincing than the first, which can be put forward in defence of the view that the offender has a right to punishment. One of these requires us to take the view in conjunction with the premise that punishment annuls evil. If punishment can somehow wash away the guilt of the offender then it is plausible to say that the offender has a right to be punished. The difficulty with this argument, however, is that it simply transfers the problems. It is now intelligible to say that the offender has a right to punishment, but, as we have already seen, it is not at all clear what it means to say that punishment annuls evil.

The other argument invites us to consider what the alternative is to punishing the criminal. The alternative, as we shall shortly see, may be to 'treat' him and attempt a 'cure' by means of various psychological techniques. Now this would be rejected as morally repugnant by many retributivists, on the grounds that an offender has freely decided to break the law and should be regarded as a self-determining rational being who knew what he was doing. An offender, so described, may be said to have a right to *punishment* (as distinct from psychological treatment, moral indoctrination, or brain-washing in the interests of the State). Such an argument produces a favourable response from many criminals who, when they have served their time in prison, feel that the matter is then over and that they ought to be protected from the attentions of moral doctors and the like. So stated, there may be some truth in the 'right to punishment' doctrine, however easy it is for the sophisticated to mock it.

So far we have been concerned to suggest detailed criticism of the retributivist theory. But there are two general criticisms which are commonly made of it at the moment (for it is a most unfashionable theory in philosophical and other circles). The first is that insofar as its claims are intelligible and prima facie acceptable, they are disguised utilitarian claims.

This criticism is valid against certain ways in which retributivists sometimes state their claims. For example, they have sometimes regarded the infliction of punishment as the 'emphatic denunciation by the community of a crime'. But we might well ask why society should bother to denounce crime unless it hopes by that means to do some good and diminish it. A second example of a retributivist claim which easily lends itself to utilitarian interpretation is that the infliction of punishment reforms the criminal by shocking him into a full awareness of his moral turpitude. The question here is not whether this claim is in fact plausible (criminologists do not find it so) but whether the justification of punishment it offers is essentially retributivist. It seems rather to be utilitarian, and in this respect like the more familiar version of the reform theory we shall shortly examine.

It seems, then, that this criticism does have some force against certain retributivist claims, or against certain ways of stating retributivist claims. But the criticism does not do radical damage to retributivism. Provided the theory is stated in such a way that it is clear that the justification of punishment is necessarily only that it is a fitting response to an offender, then the fact that punishment may sometimes also do good need not count against retributivism. It is, however, an implication of retributivism that it must sometimes be obligatory to punish when punishment is not expected to do any good beyond itself.

It is precisely this implication which is used as the basis for the second criticism of retributivism. This criticism is a straightforward moral judgement, that the theory is morally objectionable in that it requires us to inflict punishment, which is by definition unpleasant and therefore as such evil, for no compensating greater good. The critics therefore invite us to reject the theory as a barbarous residue of old moral ideas.

In the context of philosophical analysis it is important to avoid taking sides in moral argument, as far as this can be done. But it may be worth pointing out that perhaps the great majority of ordinary people have sympathy with some form of retributivism. Contemporary philosophers often appeal to what the 'ordinary moral agent' would do or say in certain circumstances, or what the morality of 'common sense' would hold on certain topics, but if they make this appeal in settling questions of the justification of punishment they may find that the ordinary person adheres to some form of retributivism. Since there is generally something to be said for an appeal in moral matters to what people ordinarily think, let us consider whether the implication of retributivism is really so morally repugnant.

The implication is that on some occasions it will be obligatory to punish an offender even though this will do no good beyond itself, and that even when some further good is in fact accomplished by the punishment this is irrelevant to its justification. Now it may be that this implication is thought to be morally objectionable because the clause 'no good beyond itself' is equated with 'no good at all'. But a retributivist will claim that the mere fact of inflicting punishment on an offender is good in itself. It is not that a *further* good will result (although it may do so) but that the very fact of the punishment is fitting and to that extent good.

This argument may be made more convincing by an example. Let us suppose that a Nazi war criminal responsible for the cruel torture and deaths of many innocent people has taken refuge in South America where he is living *incognito*. Let us suppose that he has become a useful and prosperous member of the community in which he is living. Let us suppose that the whereabouts of this criminal are discovered and it becomes possible to bring him to justice and punish him. It is very doubtful whether such punishment will have any utilitarian value at all; the criminal will not in any way be 'reformed' by treatment, and the deterrence of other war criminals seems an unrealistic aim. We can at least imagine that the punishment of such a criminal will have minimal utilitarian value and may even have disvalue in utilitarian terms. Nevertheless, many people might still feel that the criminal ought to be brought to justice and punished, that irrespective of any further good which may or may not result from the punishment, it is in itself good that such a man should be punished for his crimes. To see some force in this special pleading is to see that retributivism is not completely without moral justification although it can never on its own constitute a complete theory of the justification of punishment.

I have tried to find merits in the retributivist theory because it is frequently dismissed with contempt by philosophers and others at the present time, but we shall now consider theories of the justification of punishment with more obvious appeal. These are all different forms of utilitarianism and they therefore have in common the claim that the justification of punishment necessarily rests in the value of its consequences. There are two common forms of utilitarian justification: in terms of deterrence and in terms of reform.

According to the deterrence form of the utilitarian theory the justification of punishment lies in the fact that the threats of the criminal law will deter potential wrong-doers. But since threats are not efficacious unless they are carried out, proved wrong-doers must in fact have unpleasant consequences visited on them. The increase in the pain of the criminal, however, is balanced by the increase in the happiness of society, where crime has been checked. The theory is modified to account for two classes of people for whom the threats of the law cannot operate: the cases of infants and madmen on the one hand, and on the other hand cases in which accident, coercion and other 'excusing conditions' affected the action. In such cases the threats of the law would clearly have little effect and punishment would therefore do no social good.

A deterrent theory of this general sort has often been accepted by utilitarian philosophers from the time of Bentham, but it is frequently criticized. The most common criticism is that it does not rule out the infliction of 'punishment' or suffering on the innocent. Utilitarians, that is, argue that where excusing conditions exist punishment would be wasted or would be socially useless. But their argument shows only that the threat of punishment would not be effective in particular cases where there are excusing conditions; the infliction of 'punishment' in such cases would still have deterrent values on *others* who might be tempted to break the law. Moreover, people who have committed a crime may hope to escape by pleading excusing conditions and hence there would be social efficacy in punishing those with excuses. Presumably this is the point of 'strict liability' in the civil law. But if the deterrent theory commits us to such implications it is at variance with our ordinary views, for we do not accept that the punishment of the lunatic (say) is permissible whatever its social utility.

Utilitarians have sometimes tried to meet this objection by arguing that a system of laws which did not provide for excusing conditions might cause great misery to society. There would be widespread alarm in any society in which no excusing conditions were allowed to affect judicial decisions in criminal cases, and indeed (a utilitarian might argue) such a system might not receive the co-operation of society at large, without which no judicial system can long operate. The utilitarian reply, then, is that while punishment is justified by its deterrent value we must allow excusing conditions since they also have social utility.

It is doubtful, however, whether this reply is adequate. For if excusing conditions are allowed only insofar as they have social utility there remains the possibility that some unusual cases may crop up in which the infliction of suffering or 'punishment' on an innocent person would have social utility which would far outweigh the social utility of excusing him. This is not only a logical possibility on the deterrent theory but a very real possibility in communities in which the 'framing' of an innocent person might prevent rioting of a racial or religious kind. But this implication of the deterrent theory is at odds with widely accepted moral views. Rather it would be held that the rights of the individual must come before the good of society. This does not mean that the rights of the individual must never be sacrificed to the general good but only that there are certain basic rights, the rights of man, or rights which belong to persons as such, which must never be violated no matter what social good will accrue. It is the weakness of the deterrent version of the utilitarian justification of punishment that it cannot accommodate this truth. Here the deterrent theory contrasts adversely with the retributive theory which does stress the rights of the individual against those of society.

Despite this criticism, however, the deterrent theory cannot be entirely dismissed for it does have relevance at the level of legislation. Whereas it is a failure if it is regarded as an attempt to provide a complete justification of punishment it does succeed in bringing out one of the functions of punishment — that of acting as a deterrent to the potential criminal.

The second conception in terms of which utilitarians try to justify the infliction of punishment is that of 'reform'. They argue that when a criminal is in prison or in some other detention centre a unique opportunity is created for equipping him with a socially desirable set of skills and attitudes. The claim is that such a procedure will have a social utility which outweighs that of conventional punishment.[1] The theory is often based on a psychological or sociological study of the effects of certain kinds of deprivation, cultural starvation, and general lack of education on the individual's outlook, and the hope is that these may be put right by re-education or psychological treatment in the period when there would otherwise be conventional punishment.

There are certain oddities about the reform theory if it is intended to be a justification for punishment. The first is that the processes of reform need not involve anything which is painful or unpleasant in the conventional sense. Some critics of the theory would rule it out on that ground alone. In reply, the advocates of the theory might say that insofar as the criminal is *compelled* to undergo reform the process can count as 'punishment' in the conventional sense; at least the criminal is deprived of his liberty and that is in itself unpleasant whatever else may happen to him during his period of enforced confinement. A different line of defence might be to concede that reform is not punishment in the conventional sense and to go on to point out that the reform theory is an attempt to replace punishment with a practice which has greater utilitarian justification. According to this line, punishment cannot be justified on utilitarian grounds and the utilitarian must therefore replace punishment with a practice which is justifiable.

There is a second respect in which the reform theory has consequences which are at variance with traditional ideas on punishment. The processes of reform may involve what might be called 'treatment'. It happens to be true that many advocates of the theory are influenced by psychological doctrines to the effect that the criminal is suffering from a disease of social maladjustment from which he should be cured. Hence, the processes of reform may include more than re-education in the conventional sense; they may involve what is nearer to brainwashing (and from a strictly utilitarian point of view there is everything to be said in favour of this if it is in fact effective). A merit of the retributive theory is to insist that persons as ends in themselves should be protected against undue exposure to the influence of moral 'doctors' no matter how socially effective their treatment may be.

The third respect in which the theory departs from traditional ideas is that it gives countenance to the suggestion that the criminal may legitimately be detained until he is reformed. But in some

[1]This theory must be distinguished from that mentioned in the discussion of retributivism—that conventional punishment reforms by 'shocking' the criminal into an awareness of what he has done. Apart from the question of its consistency with the tenets of retributivism this claim does not seem to be supported by the facts; conventional punishment is said by criminologists in fact to increase the criminal's resentment against society.

advanced cases of social disease the cure may take some time. And what of the incurables? Here again the retributive theory reminds us of the inhumanity of treating people simply as social units to be moulded into desirable patterns.

So far we have considered three oddities of the reform theory, but none of these, of course, invalidates it. The first point simply brings out the nature of the reform theory, and the second and third are hardly implications in the strict sense but merely probable consequences if the practice which the theory reflects is developed in a certain direction. The fatal defect of the theory is rather that it is inadequate as an account of the very many complex ways in which the sanctions of the criminal law are intended to affect society. The reform theory concentrates on only one kind of case, that of the person who has committed an offence or a number of offences and who might do so again. Moreover, it is plausible only for a certain range of cases in this class; those requiring treatment rather than conventional punishment. But it must be remembered that the criminal law is also intended for those, such as murderers, traitors, and embezzlers, for whom the possibility of a second offence is limited. Moreover, the criminal law serves also to deter ordinary citizens who might occasionally be tempted to commit offences. The inadequacy of the reform theory lies in its irrelevance to such important types of cases.

It is clear, then, that no one of the accounts of punishment provides on its own an adequate justification of punishment. The retributive theory, which is often taken to be an expression of barbarism, in fact provides a safeguard against the inhumane sacrifice of the individual for the social good, which is the moral danger in the utilitarian theory. Bearing in mind this moral doctrine about the rights of the individual we can then incorporate elements from both the deterrent and the reform versions of utilitarian justification. Only by drawing from all three doctrines can we hope to reflect the wide range of cases to which the criminal law applies.

the responsibility
of criminals

william kneale

1

Under the common law of England the defence of insanity is a complete answer to any criminal charge. But according to the rule laid down in McNaghten's case of 1843 the defence is established only if it is proved that the accused at the time of the offence was labouring under such a defect of reason from disease of the mind that he did not know the nature and quality of the act he was doing or, if he did know this, did not know that what he was doing was wrong. At the time the rule was formulated it was the last clause which attracted most attention. Peel, the Prime Minister of the day, when reporting McNaghten's acquittal to Queen Victoria, wrote: "It is a lamentable reflection that a man may be at the same time so insane as to be reckless of his own life and the lives of others, and to be pronounced free from moral responsibility, and yet capable of preparing for the commission of murder with the utmost caution and deliberation and of taking every step which will enable him to commit it with certainty." And Victoria in her reply protested with underlinings and exclamation marks against the absurdity of bringing in a verdict of "not guilty on ac-

From *The Responsibility of Criminals* by William Kneale (Marett Memorial Lecture, 1967). © 1967 Oxford University Press. By permission of The Clarendon Press, Oxford.

count of insanity" for a malefactor who was perfectly conscious and aware of what he did.[1] During the present century, however, many psychologists have argued that the relevant notion of insanity should be defined still more widely; and although this has not yet been done in England, the law has recently been altered to allow for a plea of diminished responsibility in murder trials. Since the phrase "diminished responsibility" does not occur elsewhere in our law and has not received any special definition, it must be assumed that the word "responsibility," as it occurs in this phrase, was intended by the legislature to bear an ordinary, non-legal sense appropriate to the context. Unfortunately no one has been able to explain satisfactorily what the phrase as a whole can mean; and when we try to think it out, we come on some very curious problems.

If, as the dictionary tells us, "responsibility" means "liability to be called to answer or account for one's acts," how can it possibly have degrees? Either one is to be called to account for a particular deed or one is not: there is no middle course. It might, no doubt, be said that a man in a certain mental condition was responsible for some things he did but not for others, and that in this way the range of occasions of responsibility was diminished for him. He might, for example, be responsible in certain circumstances for killing X but not for killing Y, because his constitution or his upbringing or both made him likely to have an overmastering passion against Y in those circumstances, though not against X. But this cannot be the way in which the phrase "diminished responsibility" is to be understood here, since the plea is not treated as a complete defence on any occasion but always as a partial excuse on the strength of which a jury may classify a killing as something less than murder. Does it then mean that a man who has killed someone may be responsible in the sense that he can be called to account and yet have diminished responsibility because he cannot be made to pay so big a penalty as others might whose responsibility was not diminished? This seems to be the most plausible interpretation of the phrase used by the legislature, but it is not at all easy to see how it should be applied in practice. If a man's responsibility can be diminished at all by his condition and circumstances, may it not perhaps be diminished in various degrees? And if so, what degree is to be required for acceptance of the plea of diminished responsibility? Is even the slightest emotional or volitional abnormality enough?

In a lecture to the Cambridge Institute of Criminology in 1960

[1] *Queen Victoria's Early Letters*, ed. J. Raymond (1963) p. 85.

Lady Wootton of Abinger described the recent change as an attempt to modify a system that was essentially punitive (I think she meant "retributive") by smuggling into it humane ideas and aims which were totally incompatible with it. In her view the new ideas could never be expressed clearly in the language of responsibility, and it was therefore to be expected that lawyers and jurymen, who have to wrestle with them, would always be plagued with contradictions and unanswerable questions until the concept of responsibility was allowed to wither away. "Forget responsibility," she said, "and we can ask, not whether an offender ought to be punished, but whether he is likely to benefit from punishment."[2] I do not remember any declaration by another writer against responsibility which is as outspoken and uncompromising as this, but there are undoubtedly many persons of intelligence who share Lady Wootton's dislike for talk of responsibility and think, as she does, that it is fated to disappear with the progress of scientific enlightenment. What attitude should we adopt towards their revolutionary suggestions?

If they are right, resistance to the change they want is not only stupid but inhumane. On the other hand, total abandonment of the concept of responsibility would involve such enormous changes in the pattern of human life that we cannot contemplate it seriously until the case for it has been stated much more carefully. It is certainly not impossible that words which have been used freely by millions of people for thousands of years should presently be found worthless for any but historical purposes: "witchcraft" is an obvious example. But if there is a scientific mistake or a hopeless muddle in all ordinary talk of moral responsibility, it seems we must not only reform our penal system in the way Lady Wootton wishes but refrain from all moral praise or blame of our fellow men, since to say that a man is morally praiseworthy or blameworthy for an act is ordinarily held to imply that he is morally responsible for it. Indeed, the connexion is so close that the word "responsible" and the phrase "to blame" have come to be treated as interchangeable in that metaphorical usage in which we say that the bad weather was responsible, or to blame, for the poor harvest. Nor will it be enough to abstain from moral judgement on acts already performed, a course that might perhaps have something to be said in its favour. For on the supposition that men are never to be held responsible it will be both senseless and useless to remind men of their responsibilities, that is to say, futile to tell them that they will be blameworthy if they fail to do certain

[2]The Times, 13 Feb 1960. Other expressions of the same view are to be found in her Social Science and Social Pathology (1959), ch. viii.

acts in the future. But can we imagine a characteristically human form of life in which all this is lacking?

In what follows I am going to suggest that we have various uses of the word "responsible," and that, although these are closely connected, they are not inseparable. A few moments ago I gave an example of the use of the word to indicate a causal connexion. Clearly this is derivative from talk about the responsibility of men for their deeds, but I do not suppose that Lady Wootton wants to ban it, any more than she would wish to ban metaphorical uses of the word "witchcraft." If this is so, may it not be possible for us to make important distinctions even between the uses in which men are said to be responsible for their deeds? I shall argue that we can distinguish at least three such cases, and that, while Lady Wootton is right in urging us to reject a certain kind of talk about responsibility, she is wrong in supposing that what she wants can only come about through the withering away of a single un-differentiated concept of responsibility hitherto used in all contexts by all plain men and legislators. In order to carry out this programme I must evidently deal first with the historical connexion between responsibility and retribution, since that is where Lady Wootton starts.

2

As the dictionary says, "responsible" meant originally "liable to be called to answer"[3] or, more shortly, "accountable." The corresponding word in ancient Greek is ὑπεύθυνος, which means literally "subject to an audit or rectification (εὔθυνα)," and it was applied first to officers of state who had to render accounts and face a scrutiny at the end of their term of office. In modern times the most primitive of the surviving uses of "responsible" is that in which we say that the Cabinet is constitutionally responsible to the House of Commons for its conduct of the national affairs or that the Domestic Bursar is statutorily responsible to the Governing Body for the management of the college catering. When we say shortly that the Bursar is responsible for the catering, we mean more generally that he is expected to look after it, and that if any-one has any criticism to make he should address it to the Bursar. If, however, some outsider who has no title to interfere sends a complaint to the Bursar, the latter, while admitting that he is responsible, may go back in irritation to the old sense and say "That does not mean that I am answerable to you, Sir." For the basic no-

---

[3]It is interesting to note that "answer," *respondere*, and ἀποκρινεσθαι were all used first in the legal sense of "answer a charge." I owe this and a number of other valuable comments to Professor Herbert Hart.

tion of responsibility is clearly that of being accountable under some rule to a determinate authority for a determinate sphere of action; and from this, it seems, all special uses are derived by analogy or metaphor or shift of emphasis. When, for example, we say that the bad weather was responsible for the poor harvest, we talk metaphorically of the non-human cause of a disaster in terms originally introduced for talking of certain causes. And when a business man says that an applicant for credit must be supported by a responsible backer, he does not mean that the backer must be one who may justly be called to account if the debtor defaults (though that, no doubt, is true), but rather that the backer must be a person who can in practice be called to account because he is not a fly-by-night but a solid citizen with a stake in the country. What, then, is the special point of talking about *moral* responsibility? How is this usage related to the original notion of responsibility?

I think it began with a belief that the moral law, or, as older writers would say, the natural law, requires an audit of all human behaviour and a settlement of moral accounts in which the wicked are made to pay for their misdeeds. And this belief in turn seems to be connected with an attempt to assimilate all moral obligations to the obligations undertaken by borrowers. If I am right, the development of our language for talking about these matters has had very important effects on human thought, and it is therefore proper to spend a little time in trying to establish the facts.

Consider first the word "ought" and words of similar meaning in other languages. "Ought" began life as a past tense of "owe" but has come to be used exclusively in an extended sense to suggest that something can properly be claimed from a man. "Should" has a similar relation to "shall," which in old English had the sense of "owe." In German *sollen* can still be used in certain contexts with that sense, though it is most commonly used now with the general sense of "ought." In French *devoir* and in Italian *dovere* retain the two senses of "owe" and "ought" which they inherit from the Latin *debere*. Our English "debt" is a derivative from *debitum*, the past participle of *debere*, but so too are our words "due" and "duty," which can still move back and forth between the special and the general. *Debere* itself seems to be a contraction of *dehibere* which meant originally "keep" or "retain" but came at a very early date to have the sense of "keep what should be returned." In Greek οψειλειν may mean either "owe" or "ought": and a little work with dictionaries will show that there are many similar words in other languages. There are, of course, other idioms for talking about what we ought to do, but some which at first

232

sight seem independent of the notion of debt prove on closer examination to be connected with it. Thus the metaphor of being bound, which occurs in the moral vocabulary of many languages, seems to have been applied first in connexion with those obligations which arise, like debts, from promises. It came to be a maxim of Roman law that *obligationes* might arise also from *delicta*, or wrongful acts, but those arising from contracts were commonly treated as primary; and it is therefore no accident that in languages subject to the influence of Roman law derivatives of the word *obligatio* are still used, as "bond" is used in English, with the special sense of "instrument of debt."

So far we have considered talk of duty in general as it might occur before the time for performance of the act or abstention which had been likened to discharge of a debt. But suppose a man has failed in performance. According to the way of thinking to which I have drawn attention he is still in debt, though it may be impossible now for him to pay in the way intended by the person who originally said that he had a debt. He must therefore pay in some other way, i.e., give compensation. There are lots of usages which bear witness to this way of thinking. In German the word for guilt, namely *Schuld*, is also the word for debt; and although "guilt" in English seems to have a different origin, the phrase "guilty of death" was at one time used in the sense of "subject to the death penalty." Furthermore, in all languages of which I have any knowledge the notion of punishment is closely connected with that of payments. In English we have the standard phrase "pay the penalty" and the colloquial threat "He shall pay for this." In Latin we have *poenas solvere* and in Greek τινειν. Sometimes, however, by a further extension of the commercial analogy punishment is considered as a negative wage earned by wrongdoing. This was the original point of the use of the word "deserve"; and the metaphor is still very much alive in St. Paul's *Epistle to the Romans* vi: 23, where he says "The wages of sin is death." When we talk of punishment as retribution we have a similar conception in mind. In this case payment is supposed to be made by the punishing authority, but it is payment of something undesirable, i.e., what I have called a negative wage, and the purpose of the payment is to settle the wrongdoer's moral account. So strong indeed is the association of account-keeping with punishment in our thought that the word "atonement," which originally meant "union" or "reconciliation," has come to have the sense of "expiation" or "paying the penalty." Presumably this happened because it was taken for granted that there could be no reconciliation until the moral account had been made to balance. Sometimes it is allowed that

THE RESPONSIBILITY OF CRIMINALS

an aggrieved party can set the account straight by writing off what is due to him. That was the original sense of the English "forgive" and of the low Latin *perdonare*, from which "pardon" is derived. The idea is expressed very clearly in the Lord's Prayer: "Forgive us our debts as we forgive our debtors." Here the Greek words translated by "debts" is οϕειληματα, derived from the verb οϕειλειν which I mentioned earlier as capable of meaning either "owe" or "ought." But in many religious systems it is thought there can be no remission, i.e., that it is impossible that the account should be squared except by actual payment of some kind. That is the doctrine of *karma* in Hinduism, and it seems to be assumed also in Anselm's version of the Christian doctrine of redemption, according to which even God could not save us without paying the price of our sins, though the debt was due to himself. Incidentally, the word "redemption" was originally a commercial term which meant in general "buying back" but could have the special sense of "buying back what has been pledged as security for a loan." Such terminology was more appropriate to the older theory, expounded by Origen and accepted by many Fathers of the Church, according to which Christ's salvation of man was payment of ransom to the devil in respect of rights which the latter had gained over man at the fall. It is a curious piece of evidence for the wide acceptance of an analogy between guilt and debt that the language of redemption has been used by Christians in the presentation of theological views which are so very different; and it is an extremely curious historical fact that there has never been an authoritative decision of the Church between those views.

In the earliest legal system of which we have record, that of Hammurabi, there is a lot about penalties, but these are considered as damages which a malefactor must pay to an aggrieved party, either human or divine. Thus there is a price to be paid to a man for the killing of a member of his household, just as for the killing of one of his animals, and the price varies according to the social status of the aggrieved party and the relationship which the dead man bore to him. The same was true in the earliest Roman law, in customary Norse law, and in primitive English law. It has been maintained, indeed, that there was at first no special criminal law, since all cases of wrongdoing were treated in the same way as those special cases which are called in modern legal parlance torts or civil wrongs, that is to say, cases where damages are payable. According to this account of the development of law, the only motive for active intervention in disputed cases by kings or other public officers was a wish to prevent the indefinite continuation of feuds that might disturb the peace of society. Their aim, it is said, was to get a settlement, and for this purpose it was important that they should be able to point to a set tariff of penalties such as that in the famous passage of *Exodus* xxi about an eye for an eye and a tooth for a tooth. I think it is a mistake to suggest that all primitive law is concerned with reparation for injuries. There are quite early codes which reveal a conviction that some kinds of wrongdoing, in particular homicide and certain sexual offences, should be punished apart from the demands of any plaintiffs. An example is the *Exodus* code to which I have just referred. But it is interesting to notice that penalties which cannot be regarded as damages to an injured man are often represented as satisfaction to an affronted god. In St. Anselm's version of the atonement doctrine all human sin, being disobedience by a creature to its creator, is an offence for which divine honour requires infinite satisfaction.

At first sight it appears that believers in the doctrine of moral accounting have often applied their theory without any regard for the requirement of *mens rea*, or guilty intent, which is now regarded as fundamental in criminal law, unless expressly excluded in favour of so-called strict liability. In ancient Greek legend Oedipus had to pay a penalty for killing his father, although it was fated that he should do so and his act was unintentional in the sense that he did not know he was killing his father. Similarly many Christians have held that unbaptised children who die without having done anything intentionally will properly be made to pay infinitely in respect of a debt inherited from their ancestor Adam. At various periods men have been held liable to pay for things done accidentally, and sometimes even dumb animals or inanimate objects such as axes have been solemnly tried and found guilty of homicide. It is said, for example, that such trials took place in civilised Athens. If one started from consideration of these cases, one might be led to think that primitive men began with a notion of guilt which did not involve intention on the part of the agent and that the modern refinement of *mens rea* were introduced later. But I think that this would be a mistake, and that anyone who tried to develop such an hypothesis would find himself unable to give a plausible explanation of the course of history. It seems much wiser to start from the consideration that in the overwhelming majority of cases at all times guilt has been imputed to human beings who did what they did intentionally. Having assumed this, we can then try to explain the other cases by supposing that our ancestors sometimes misinterpreted their own traditional formulae. Let us suppose, for example, that there is a law like that of *Exodus* xxi: 15 saying "He that smiteth his father or his mother shall be surely put to death," and that a man has in fact smitten his father, though unintentionally. To us it seems clear that, even if the law were just, the man should not be made to pay the penalty, because it is appropriate only for disobedience to a generally accepted commandment "Smite not thy father or thy mother," in which "smite" must be understood to have the sense of "smite intentionally." But a judge who thinks himself bound to maintain the utmost rigour in his judgements may conceivably insist on taking the word in its widest sense and justify his interpretation by saying that, if the legislator had intended to exclude cases like this, he could have done so explicitly. Such misplaced rigorism is most likely to occur when the legislator is supposed to be divine. For it is not safe to assume that gods, whose ways are notoriously mysterious, share the commonsensical views of men, and so a judge who by lax interpretation fails to secure the satisfaction they demand may bring disaster on himself and his community. In any case, if I am right, the legal maxim which makes guilt depend on intention is primarily a principle of interpretation designed to preserve the ordinary standards of human legislation against perversely rigorous misunderstanding of penal laws.

When the doctrine of moral accounting is combined with a belief in divine creation of the world and God is supposed to be the creditor of all men, a special difficulty arises. How can it be just that a man who is dependent in everything on God should be required to pay a penalty to God in respect of anything he has done? He seems to be in a situation like that of a slave whose owner exacts extra labour from him because of a slip that is due to the slave's poor condition and so ultimately to the master's treatment of him. Such reflections were not unknown in pagan antiquity, but they were not so worrying then as they became later, because the pagan gods were not in general regarded as creators or supposed to be universally just. To Christian theologians these thoughts have always been disturbing, and even theologians who believe, like St. Augustine, in the hereditary corruption of human nature have commonly insisted that Adam at least had freedom of choice, because they hope to justify the ways of God by speaking of human will as the first cause of sin and the root of evil. Those who, like Bradwardine and Jonathan Edwards, have declared openly that God's act in creation was the first cause of all our acts, including our sins, are exceptional, and what they have said has usually been met by strong opposition because it seems to clash with the doctrine of divine justice.

In recent times problems of this sort, which once bulked very large in the long and intricate debate about freedom of the will,

236

have ceased to worry people as much as they used to do. Perhaps one reason is a general decline of religious belief. But another is certainly a loss of faith in the principle of moral accounting which underlay most of the older talk about moral responsibility, and this reason has influenced the religious no less than the irreligious. For many people of both groups now reject the retributivist theory of punishment, which is a form of the theory of moral accounting. Sometimes such rejection is based on an assumption that retribution is identical with revenge. This seems to me to be a mistake. For although people who seek revenge often use phrases of moral accounting, such as "He shall pay for this," the hatred and anger that they show are not essential to the retributivist theory, and it is wrong to reject retribution merely because one dislikes hatred. There are versions of the doctrine in which retribution is simply a natural necessity independent of human passions. There is, however, a much better reason for rejecting the retributivist theory, namely, dissatisfaction with the whole web of metaphor to which it belongs.

3

When I began to present evidence for the existence of a widespread theory of moral accounting, you may perhaps have been inclined to say that I was confusing etymology with philosophical analysis. Although the word "ought" started life as a variant of "owe," that fact is of no philosophical interest if people in our time do not think that "ought" has many of the same implications as "owe." And it must be admitted that some intelligent persons are surprised when they first hear of the historical connexion between these words. On the other hand, when I went on to speak of the use of accounting terms in connexion with punishment, you were probably inclined to allow that what I said had some relevance to modern practice. It seems, therefore, that the language of moral accounting, which began with an extended use of debt words to cover the whole range of duty, still has an influence on penal theory that it could scarcely retain if we understood our situation aright.

When applying a system of criminal law, we must, of course, consider very carefully what punishment it allows for each wrongdoing, and we may perhaps find the language of accounting useful for expression of some of the judgements we make in this connexion. We may speak, for example, of the different penalties that criminals of various kinds may be made to *pay* for their offences, and we may talk sensibly of the possibility of a prisoner's *earning* remission by good conduct. But it is a mistake to suppose that we can use the same language profitably when the question under discussion is the moral justice of the criminal law itself. For there are no penal provisions in the moral law, and it is not true that a wrong act gives rise to a moral debt, except in the important special case where it imposes on the agent an obligation to make such reparation as he can for a hurt to another person. In many cases of hurt it is already very difficult to decide what is appropriate reparation, because there can be no restoration of the situation as it was before the wrongdoing; but at least we know what considerations are relevant, namely the nature and amount of the suffering to be alleviated. When, however, we pass from compensation in a strict sense to the notion of expiating a sin or nullifying it by suffering, we have no standard by which to determine what suffering is appropriate to each sinner. For the old maxim of an eye for an eye is obviously inapplicable except in a very small range of cases. How, for example, can a childless youth who curses his mother have precisely the same done to him? In short, the whole theory of retribution seems to arise from a muddle-headed attempt to extend the notion of reparation beyond the limits within which it makes good sense. Such an attempt is sometimes favoured by the thought that all wrongdoing is an offence against God. But that is certainly not the only source of the belief in moral accounting, since the doctrine has been held by atheists.

If, as I have suggested, dropping of the doctrine of moral accounting has helped to free men from old theological perplexities about the responsibilities of creatures in relation to their creator, may it not perhaps also help to free them from more modern perplexities about the responsibility of persons who are psychologically abnormal? This is no doubt part of what Lady Wootton wants to maintain, and I for my part am prepared to accept it as correct. For if no one is responsible in the sense that he can justly be called to balance his moral account by expiation of his wrongdoings, as distinct from paying his debts in a properly limited interpretation of that phrase, it is useless to ask what difference mental abnormality makes to that kind of responsibility.

So much is clear, and yet some philosophers are inclined to say that we must retain the notion of moral desert as a limitation of what may be done to prisoners for the public good. That is what F. H. Bradley had in mind when he wrote:

> Punishment is punishment only when it is deserved. We pay the penalty because we owe it and for no other reason: and if punishment is inflicted for any other reason whatever than because it is

merited by wrong, it is a gross immorality, a crying injustice, an abominable crime, and not what it pretends to be. We may have regard for whatever considerations we please—our own convenience, the good of society, the benefit of the offender; we are fools and worse if we fail to do so. Having once the right to punish, we may modify the punishment according to the useful and the pleasant, but these are external to the matter, they cannot give us the right to punish, and nothing can do that but criminal desert.[4]

I think Bradley has overstated his case by saying that punishment should not be inflicted for any other reason than because it is deserved. This formula suggests that punishment is to be inflicted for its own sake. But one may hold the opposite view, according to which punishment is a necessary evil, to be inflicted only for the public good, and still avoid the gross immorality of which Bradley speaks if one adopts the limiting principle that no one is to be punished beyond his deserts. For my own part I am prepared to agree that punishment can never be justified in the wide sense of being shown to be morally desirable unless it can be justified in the narrow sense of being shown to be just to the person punished. But I do not now believe, as I once did, that acceptance of this thesis commits us to some form of the retributivist theory. In order for the punishment of a criminal to be just it is not necessary, or even possible, that it should be something deserved by him under a natural penal law. All penal law is positive law, and if we say, as no doubt we shall continue to do, that punishment is not in general just unless deserved, we should not read into the word "deserved" anything inconsistent with this. Although the word started life as part of a vocabulary for expressing a theory of moral accounting which we now reject, it can still be retained, provided the statement that a criminal deserves his punishment is now taken to mean that he has brought it upon himself by an offence done of his own free will against a positive law that is itself just.

You will notice that in this explanation of a reasonable use of the word "deserve" I have spoken of a law that is itself just. This is essential, because we certainly do not want to argue that whenever anyone is punished in accordance with some positive law he deserves what he gets. One point of continuing to talk about desert is precisely to allow for criticism of positive law, and this we can do if we recognise that words which were first introduced in connexion with a simple undifferentiated notion of law may take on new subtleties of meaning after the distinction of positive from natural or moral law. To suppose that because penal law is all

[4] "The Vulgar Notion of Responsibility," in Ethical Studies (1927), pp. 26–27.

positive there can be no sense in talking of the moral justice or injustice of any particular punishment would be as foolish as to suppose that because property law is all positive there can be no sense in talking of the moral justice or injustice of any particular distribution of property. What is needed is only the possibility of passing a moral judgement on the legislation as a whole. In the case of penal legislation such a judgement will involve a balancing of the evil of the suffering to be inflicted under the law against the evil that promulgation and enforcement of the law may be expected to prevent within a system which includes also suitably related provision against other types of crime.

All this is relevant to our problem about responsibility. When we decide that no one is to be held responsible in the sense of accountable for his wrongdoings under a natural law requiring expiation, we need not forswear all uses of the word "responsible" if we can find a good sense for it in relation to our man-made penal system. And it seems that we can find such a sense. For when we say that an accused person is morally responsible in respect of an act with which he is charged, we may mean only that it is morally proper to hold him accountable in respect of that act under a penal law of the land, or in other words that he can rightly be made to pay the prescribed penalty if in fact he did the deed. Perhaps Lady Wootton would have us reject this use also, on the ground that it can only lead to the posing of unanswerable questions about the limits of responsibility. But it is important to notice that this use is quite independent of the retributivist theory of punishment to which she chiefly objects. Whether or not it is a profitable use, that is to say, a use free from confusion, must depend on the clarity or unclarity of the criterion for determining when it is morally proper to hold a man accountable for anything under a law of the land. That is the question to which we must now turn.

4

When the notion of responsibility is connected with a scheme of moral accounting, it is commonly said that men are responsible only for what they do of their own free will, i.e., that they should not be called to account for what they do unintentionally or during insanity or under certain forms of duress. Since the development of meaning we have just considered is apparently no more than the substitution of accountability under just positive law for accountability under natural law, it may perhaps be supposed that it cannot involve any development of the criterion for responsibility. Whether we retain or reject the retributivist principle, we wish to say that no punishment is just unless the criminal has brought it on himself by an offence done of his own free will, and this formula seems to bring back again many of the difficulties of the old doctrine. I do not want to suggest that we can evade the problem of free will by abandoning the retributivist theory of punishment, but I think it worth noticing that the shift to a utilitarian or forward-looking theory does in fact enable us to find a new ground for using the phrase "X may properly be called to account for Y."

The point is made very clearly by Bentham in ch. xiii of his *Principles of Morals and Legislation,* which has the title "Cases Unmeet for Punishment." According to his general theory the chief purpose of the legislator in making a code of criminal law should be to produce an artificial reconciliation of human interests by attaching to the various anti-social acts called crimes such unpleasant consequences for the agent as will be just sufficient to make them unattractive to potential criminals. He recognises that infliction of punishment may give satisfaction to aggrieved persons, and perhaps also to disinterested onlookers, and he is even prepared to allow that such satisfaction is unobjectionable if it comes as a free bonus from the operation of a rationally designed system of deterrents. But unlike some modern English judges, he is not prepared to allow that it should have any place in determining what penalties are to be imposed, and in the chapter to which I have referred he is especially concerned to show that utilitarianism imposes strict limits on the scope of criminal justice. In particular he argues that it provides a good explanation for the various defences recognised as valid in the criminal courts of civilised nations. According to his argument punishment is unfitting in four kinds of cases:

1. where it is groundless, because there is really no mischief to prevent,
2. where it must be inefficacious,
3. where it is unprofitable, because it involves greater loss to the community than the mischief it is designed to prevent,
4. where it is needless, because the mischief it is designed to prevent can be prevented in some other way, e.g., by simple instruction of the ignorant.

The second of these is the heading that interests us now. For it is said by Bentham to cover not only cases where the punishment serves no useful purpose (because it is under a penal law that has been made too late to be of any use, or because it is under no penal law at all, or because it is insufficiently publicised) but also all cases of infancy, insanity, intoxication, unintentionality, unconsciousness, missupposal, opposite superior force, physical danger, threatened mischief, duress, necessity, physical compulsion, restraint. What these latter cases are supposed by Bentham to have in common is that the persons concerned are all at the time of action in conditions that make them not susceptible to influence by threats. Thus, for example, a person who may in future be subject to physical compulsion cannot be deterred by fear of punishment from doing what he will then be compelled to do, and so infliction of punishment now on a person who has done something regrettable under physical compulsion is useless, even though it may be in accordance with a duly promulgated general provision of penal law.

Professor Hart has objected that Bentham's analysis proves at most the ineffectiveness of threats of punishment to persons who are themselves in any of the specified conditions. It is still conceivable, he thinks, that infliction of punishment on them might have the result of producing more conformity in others. For in a system of strict liability anyone who is at all susceptible to influence by threats knows that, if he is caught, he can have no hope of evading punishment by any excuse, and this consideration may perhaps make him more careful than he would be otherwise.[5] This criticism does not involve any attack on the fundamental assumption of utilitarianism, and I think Bentham could reply by saying, as Professor Hart himself has done on other occasions, that there is a strong moral presumption against a general system of strict liability because it deprives citizens of security against being made to suffer for what they do without *mens rea*. But behind Professor Hart's objection there may perhaps be the thought that Bentham's rationale of our customary limitation of responsibility by the requirement of *mens rea* cannot be on the right lines if it allows even the possibility of justifying strict liability by the collection of suitable evidence about its effect on human behaviour. I sympathise strongly with those who dislike strict liability, but I do not think we can assert a *priori* that it is wrong in all conceivable circumstances. If there is a mistake at this point in the Benthamite theory, it is not that the theory may perhaps allow a place for strict liability in exceptional circumstances, but rather that it takes no account of any evil except suffering as such and may for that reason admit strict liability too easily. There is, I believe, a special evil in

[5]"Prolegomenon to the Principles of Punishment," *Aristotelian Society Proceedings,* 1959–1960. I understand that there was in fact no strict liability in the English law of Bentham's day.

the deliberate infliction of suffering on other human beings who cannot help themselves, and therefore a good reason why we should not ordinarily punish persons who have done all that is humanly possible to avoid breaking the law. Most often strict liability has been introduced because some offence whose consequences are thought to be very serious has been found to be also one in respect of which there may be great difficulty in proving guilty intent. But to my mind it is least objectionable when the offence for which it is imposed is possible only for persons engaged in a special activity (e.g., sale of intoxicating drink) that may be avoided without hardship by anyone who is unwilling to face the special risks attached to it by the legislature.

Putting aside these special difficulties, we may say that according to Bentham's account of the requirement of *mens rea*, a man may be held responsible for an offence and so a fitting subject for punishment, as distinct from medical treatment or educational therapy of some kind, if he is a person who broke the law because of a character defect such as laziness or greed which is corrigible in general by threats of punishment under a morally admissible penal code. I put in the last phrase because we do not want to find ourselves driven to the conclusion that a man is responsible merely because he might be made law-abiding by some monstrous threat we are not prepared to use. And I have used the phrase "corrigible in general" to allow for the obvious fact that convicted criminals have not been deterred from the particular offences of which they are found guilty. But it must be admitted there is a serious difficulty here. If Bentham is right, the mere fact that a man has committed a crime is some evidence to show that he is not responsible for unless he is mentally defective in such a degree that he is obviously unfit to plead, he must be presumed to have known of the existence of penalties for acts of the kind he did, and yet it is clear he was not influenced by that knowledge when he acted.

It may perhaps be answered that we cannot decide whether or not a man is responsible until we have brought the legal penalties to his attention in a really vivid way by punishing him once or twice. But if we take this line, we shall be driven to say that any criminals who persist in repeating their offences are not responsible. That is to say, in many cases in which there is no obvious presumption against responsibility, we shall have to punish up to a certain point in an experimental way, hoping we may teach the criminals to take our threats seriously and govern themselves accordingly; but if after a certain number of punishments we find any of them reverting quickly to their crimes, we must conclude that we were mistaken in their case and treat them henceforth as persons who are not responsible. At first hearing this may sound strange and perhaps even shocking. For when we say that no one should be punished unless he deserves it, we ordinarily assume that the question of responsibility can be settled before the punishment is inflicted. From the point of view of the retributive theory there is indeed a monstrous paradox in the contention that criminals may be punished experimentally, and the paradox is not diminished by the suggestion that criminals are to be presumed responsible until the contrary is proved. For if responsibility is understood in the way required by Bentham's theory of punishment, it must be admitted that what we know of a convicted criminal before his punishment suggests already that he may perhaps be non-responsible, since he has broken the law in spite of his knowledge that there are penalties attached to the act.

Whatever the theoretical difficulties, it cannot be denied we often reason and act in this way when we are at our most humane. If, for example, a child breaks a family rule, we first warn him and then, if he repeats his offence, we punish him mildly. But if we find that he continues to break the rule in spite of punishment, we become worried and think that he ought perhaps to have different treatment. Perhaps this way of thinking is new, but it is certainly not confined to parents who have made themselves nervous by reading too much child psychology. For even in the criminal courts it is now recognised that persistent offenders may by the very fact of their persistence prove that they are not fit subjects for further punishment in the ordinary sense of that word. Unfortunately no one has yet found a dependable method of curing or reforming such persons. Those who are a serious danger to the public must obviously be kept in some form of preventive detention; but many persistent offenders are no more than a nuisance, and we cannot bring ourselves to imprison these for life nor yet to certify them as lunatics. We must hope that psychological advances will help us to cope with such problem criminals better than we have done so far; but I think it unlikely that we shall ever be able to detect them all before they start on careers of crime; and if we cannot do so, we shall have to punish them at the beginning in what I have called an experimental way, that is to say, on the hopeful assumption that they are responsible in the sense allowed by Bentham's theory.

These considerations go to show that we can make good use of the word "responsible" within a utilitarian theory of punishment if we take it to mean "suitable for punishment under a just law." But I think that in practice we all expect more than this minimum from persons we call morally responsible, even though we are well aware of the defects of the retributivist theory and have no intention of returning to it. A paranoiac madman who believes he is the victim of a dastardly conspiracy may nevertheless hesitate to use violence against those whom he hates as persecutors, if he thinks that doing so will bring him straight into their hands and so lead to greater immediate suffering for himself. Genuine kleptomaniacs are not, as many persons think, unaffected by the fear of being found out and punished. What is peculiar about them is that they do not steal from ordinary motives of greed but rather to get the triumph of secret success in handling what is forbidden; and the answer to a question sometimes asked by magistrates is that they will not take things under the nose of a policeman unless they think that even in this situation they can escape detection. Again dogs and various other animals can be trained by threats, though not of course by threats attached to rules expressed in verbal form. In each of these cases the use of threats, made credible by occasional punishments, might perhaps be justified if there were great need for conformity and this could not be obtained by gentler methods; but most of us would refuse to agree that in these cases liability to punishment under a just law entailed full moral responsibility. And the reason is plain. Often when we say that a man is morally responsible for doing something wrong, we wish to convey nothing at all about punishment (which may perhaps be inappropriate for his particular wrongdoing, say verbal cruelty to a member of his family), but only that he is blameworthy. If therefore anyone asserts without qualification that we should get rid of the notion of responsibility, he commits himself to the view that no one should ever be blamed for anything. Perhaps Lady Wootton intends this, thinking of blame as a kind of penalty within the untenable theory of moral accounting. If so, I believe she is mistaken. In order to see why, let us consider what we mean by "blame" and "blameworthy."

5

We often use the word "blame" to mean the same as "fix responsibility on." But if we take "responsibility" here in a moral sense, it looks as though we were going round in circles. For in this sense we say that to hold a man responsible is to consider him blameworthy and then that to blame him is to fix responsibility on him. It is easy, however, to escape from the circle. In its basic use "blame" does not mean "fix responsibility on," but rather "speak ill of," "censure," "find fault with." If the blame is expressed to the person blamed, it may also be called reproach, reproof, reprimand, chiding, or scolding according to the relation of the speaker to the person addressed and the manner he adopts. In all cases it is assumed that the person blamed could have chosen to act otherwise, but it is not essential that blame should be expressed to the person blamed for the purpose of influencing his behaviour in future, or indeed that it should be made known to anyone. We can blame dead men in our hearts.

At first sight the statement that a man is blameworthy, being equivalent to the statement that he deserves blame, may seem to presuppose acceptance of the theory of moral accounting; for clearly the desert of which we speak here is not desert under a positive law. But in practice an assertion of this kind is understood to mean primarily that it would be correct to say that the man did wrong in circumstances where he could have chosen to act otherwise. No doubt a man who has been blamed publicly for something he did not do or for something he could not avoid doing may say that he has been treated unfairly, since publication of incorrect blame is a kind of hurt. Similarly blame that is correct may be described as just. All this is suggested in a very natural way by talk of desert in connexion with blame. But justice in our judgements of the acts and characters of men depends simply on truth, not on satisfaction of an independent requirement for the squaring of moral accounts, and we may therefore hold a man blameworthy without holding that publication of our blame would be a good act. Even when we have decided that a man is blameworthy in the strict sense, we have still to decide whether it would be morally right to publish our blame, either to the man himself or to others, since the over-all rightness, or moral expediency, of a social act of censure is not to be identified with its justice in that special usage in which justice is here equated with truth. In certain cases, for example, we may consider that censure will inflict useless suffering, or even that it may lead to some undesirable development in the character of the person censured.

Why, indeed, should we ever blame a man to his face? Is publication of blame simply expression of resentment? It has often been remarked that when we are hurt or threatened by supposedly free agents we may feel resentment which we should not feel against automata or madmen who behaved in a superficially similar way. Perhaps verbal expression or such resentment sometimes serves a useful purpose by producing in a quicker and more economical way the results that might have been produced by a good hiding. That is the sort of explanation that is suggested by biological consideration of the place of resentment in animal life. But it is wrong to think of blame as essentially the expression of resentment, whether personal or impersonal. For it is possible to blame a man without being in any way resentful towards him, and it is also possible to be influenced by blame from another in a way quite different from that in which one would be influenced by his expression of resentment. When they are rational, that is to say, in good working order as beings with minds, men have a peculiar ability of being moved in their choices by a desire to rectify their shortcomings and in particular their defects of character. But to blame a man to his face is to tell him he has some such defect, and so, if the blame is based on a convincing analysis, it *may* sometimes be effective in producing a change for the better. Human nature is so complex, however, that it is by no means certain that blame will always have this effect, even on a generally rational hearer; and the prospects are least favourable when the blame is accompanied by marks of resentment, since hostility breeds hostility. But there is at least the possibility that censure may lead to reform, and we cannot conceive a characteristically human form of life in which no account is taken of this.

Now I want to suggest that one basic element in our modern concept of moral responsibility is that of susceptibility to influence by moral considerations, in particular by thought of the need to rectify one's own shortcomings, and that the non-responsibility of psychopaths consists precisely in their unresponsiveness to these considerations. I have spoken especially of the need to rectify our shortcomings, which is a second-order moral consideration, because we talk of responsibility most often in connexion with faults. If, as is very unlikely, there were a man who responded without fail to all first-order moral considerations and so was entirely free from moral faults, we should certainly not say that he was lacking in moral responsibility; but it is also difficult to conceive any circumstances in which we should want to speak of him as responsible. Throughout its history the word "responsible" has retained its original meaning of "subject to audit," but in the usage which now interests us the audit is one imposed neither by nature, as in the retributivist theory, nor by political society, as in the utilitarian theory, but by conscience, and the adjustment which it is intended to achieve is not a squaring of accounts by payment of any kind but the correction of character faults.

If a man is of such a sort that he cannot be altered by self-censure, he is not morally responsible, i.e., not a fit person to be called to an audit of conscience. I think Aristotle was thinking of such persons when he said in his *Nicomachean Ethics* that some men are incorrigible and gave it as a mark of their peculiar defect that they are not subject to remorse. But he seems to have believed

247

that all persons in this condition could have been reformed by suitable censure at an earlier age, whereas we have recently come to recognise that men may be non-responsible in my third sense without having gone through a stage of being responsible. Indeed we are now inclined to think that the condition is always pathological. The difference is interesting and important. Aristotle's teaching corresponds to the ordinary untutored assumptions we make in dealing with each other. We always treat men as morally responsible until the contrary is proved, and we find it difficult to know what to think of an otherwise normal man who does evil deeds deliberately and shows no sign of remorse. If we can convince ourselves that he came to this condition through a gradual blunting of his susceptibility to moral considerations, we may perhaps say, as Aristotle did, that he is very wicked indeed and think of him as incorrigible only because he requires a stiffer dose of censure than we have ever been able to give him. But a close study of unusual cases, which is not possible for judges and jurymen, seems to show that there is a sort of moral deafness which can never be penetrated by any amount of moral shouting; and when it appears that we have to do with a man who suffers from this, the sensible course is not to work ourselves up to still greater heights of indignation, but rather to try other means of producing a change for the better, if we can think of any which are morally permissible.

You will notice that this third account of moral responsibility is like that I have attributed to Bentham, except that it refers to blame where he spoke of punishment. The difference is important, but it may easily be overlooked because punishment is commonly accompanied by blame and the two may be confused together under such phrases as "expression of disapproval." What is essential to the new account is that a morally responsible person can be moved by recognition of his own moral defects; and censure by others is relevant only as a method by which a man's moral defects may be brought to his notice. Conceivably the desirable effect might be produced in a man in some other way, e.g., by his discovery, either in real life or in fiction, of persons who criticised themselves by higher standards than those he applied to himself. But our new definition, like Bentham's, implies that we must in general deal with our fellow men, including those who are criminals, in an experimental fashion, starting with the assumption that they can be moved by considerations of the kind we call moral, provided these are presented in a way which does not arouse an unfavourable attitude such as resentment. Similarly we must be prepared to face the possibility of total failure.

6

What practical conclusions may we draw from all this? I think there are two.

First, it is quite unrealistic to suggest that we should dispense entirely with the notion of responsibility, since the attempt to do so would involve rejection of much more than an outworn metaphor. In the context of penal justice, which especially interests Lady Wootton, it would mean abandonment of the requirement of *mens rea* and introduction of a general system of strict liability. For we have seen that one important use of the word "responsible" is to distinguish persons who may properly be punished, or at any rate detained against their will, from those who should be left in full liberty. It is true that Lady Wootton's main concern is to withdraw from the courts all questions about the sanity of prisoners, except perhaps the preliminary question whether they are fit to plead, and it may be that if she were asked to produce a new code she would be content with an alteration of practice whereby the word "guilty" would not be taken to exclude psychopathic abnormality but would be understood always in an extended sense like that it had in the now obsolete verdict of "Guilty but insane," which is said to have been introduced on the suggestion of Queen Victoria. Sometimes, however, her pronouncements are so sweeping that it seems she would abolish all the ordinary defences of accident, mistake, etc., by which an accused person may at present disclaim responsibility and would require a criminal court in every case to consider only whether the person brought before it had done the action alleged against him in the broadest possible interpretation of the charge, i.e., without any requirement of intentionality, before handing him over to reform commissioners for treatment in whatever way they thought best. If this is indeed her proposal, it seems to me extraordinary and by no means progressive. Possibly she thinks that in practice her reform commissioners would separate out cases of accident, mistake, and the rest for treatment similar to that they get now under the principle of *mens rea*, namely, immediate release. But if so, why not provide for this in advance, as we do at present by use of the legal concept of responsibility? What men need in society before all else is security from arbitrary interference, and it seems to me that it is the first task of the courts to provide this.

Secondly, Lady Wootton is right in thinking that courts of criminal justice should not be asked to decide whether an accused person has *full* moral responsibility. The reason, however, is not, as she suggests, that it is impossible to make any good sense of the question, but rather that judges and juries have neither the evidence nor the training required for answering it. If, as I have said, full moral responsibility involves ability to respond to moral considerations, the question whether an offender has such responsibility must be left to be settled, if at all, after conviction, when he can be studied with much greater care and treated, as Lady Wootton wishes, in the way most likely to improve him. In the past, when hanging was the penalty for murder, it seemed necessary to find an answer in the court room, because it was thought that no one should be executed who was not fully responsible. But since the abolition of the death penalty the situation has changed radically, and for the better. If a person is found to be of a pathologically selfish character and not easily to be restrained, either by moral considerations or by fear of punishment, it is unlikely he will now get treatment which seems to him less disagreeable than that given to offenders who are thought fully responsible. On the contrary, since he is a greater danger to society, he may well be detained for a longer period. In practice the defence of insanity as defined by the McNaghten rules has rarely been offered in any but murder cases, because the prospect of detention in a criminal lunatic asylum for an indefinite period is more disagreeable to most people than the prospect of any legal punishment except death; and for similar reasons it seems that no criminal now has any incentive to pretend that he suffers from a serious mental disorder of the volitional kind. Why then should we continue to think of the defects of this kind as excuses of the same order as accident or mistake which must obviously be investigated before conviction and sentence? And if there is to be detention in either case, why should we try to settle the nature of the appropriate treatment once and for all at the time of sentence before any persons with real experience of criminals have had any opportunity to collect evidence by patient examination? No doubt distinctions must be made among convicted persons, but this can be done much better at a later stage.

The change in legal procedure which I think desirable might conceivably be achieved, as I suggested a moment ago, by withdrawing from criminal courts all debatable questions about the sanity of accused persons and using the word "guilty" in the wide sense advocated by Queen Victoria. But in view of the associations which that word has gathered it would be much better if magistrates and juries were no longer asked to decide on the guilt of the persons brought before them but only to say whether they convicted those persons of wilfully (i.e., intentionally) doing acts that are forbidden by law.

To make such a system work satisfactorily there must, of

course, be a greatly improved service for the individual care of convicted persons and a new code of continuing legal safeguards to prevent any injustice to them, in particular by unnecessarily long detention. I have not attempted to work out the details, and I realise that what I have said is no more than a bare beginning. But I am sure that the first step towards reform of the penal law must be an effort to get rid of confused thinking. So long as we are muddled and uncertain about our aims it is always possible that we may fall into injustice or inefficiency——or, what is more likely, both at once.

murder
and the principles
of punishment:
england and the
united states [1]

h. l. a. hart

I

English people have probably been more disturbed and more divided by the use of the death penalty for murder than any people who still retain it as a form of punishment for that offence. Since Bentham ceased writing in 1832, the question of the death penalty has always been the subject of anxious scrutiny in England. The issue is considered to be one which deeply concerns a man's conscience, and it is recognized that views on this matter may cut across political loyalties. Accordingly, when the matter is debated in the House of Commons it has usually been thought right to relax the strict party discipline which normally governs debate and

Reprinted by special permission of the *Northwestern University Law Review*, © 1958, volume 52, number 4.

[1] [This article was written in 1957. Certain later changes in English and American law are described on pp. 245–251 of Professor Hart's book *Punishment and Responsibility* (Oxford: Clarendon Press, 1968). — Ed.]

to allow members to vote free from claims of party loyalty. This has resulted in members of different parties voting on the same side when the issue of capital punishment has arisen. Outside the legislature, however, advocacy of abolition has seldom been left to the unorganized efforts of individuals. Associations for the abolition of the death penalty have for many years been a familiar feature of English life; some of these have commanded the services of distinguished writers and speakers, and received some financial support, and conducted studies into statistical and other relevant facts.[2]

In the last 100 years there have been successive Parliamentary assaults on the death penalty, but only in the last ten years have these had the support of an actual majority. As far back as 1866, only four years after the abolition of the death penalty for a wide range of offences, a Select Committee of twelve considered its abolition for the offence of murder and five members of this body voted for abolition. In 1930 a Select Committee of the House of Commons reported in favour of a suspension of the death penalty for murder in cases tried by civil courts for an experimental period of five years.[3] Since the war, concern about the use of the death penalty for murder has been much intensified and three times in the last ten years Parliament came very near to suspending it for all forms of murder. In 1948 the House of Commons voted for a five-year suspension, but this provision was deleted by the House of Lords from the great Criminal Justice Bill of that year. In 1955 a similar motion was defeated in the House of Commons by a vote of 245 to 214, a majority of only thirty-one. In February 1956 the House of Commons on a free vote passed a resolution calling for the abolition or suspension of the death penalty by a vote of 292 to 246, a majority of forty-six.

This resolution marks the crossing of a great divide in the English treatment of murder and its words bear repetition here:

> That this house believes that the death penalty for murder no longer
> accords with the needs or the true interests of a civilised society and

---

[2]The Howard League for Penal Reform for twenty-five years prior to 1950 worked for the abolition of capital punishment and made the first collection of statistics from abolition countries in Scandinavia. This inquiry led to the formation of the National Council for the Abolition of the Death Penalty which represented a number of national societies opposed to capital punishment and published a study made by its secretary of homicide rates in abolition countries. *Calvert, Capital Punishment in the Twentieth Century* (1927).

[3]See *Select Committee on Capital Punishment, Report* (1930). Six Conservative members of this committee of fifteen withdrew from the commission; the recommendations are those of the remaining majority of nine (seven Labour, two Liberal). This report was never debated in Parliament. See *Calvert, The Death Penalty Enquiry* (1931).

calls upon Her Majesty's Government to introduce forthwith legislation for its abolition or for its suspension for an experimental period.[4]

In due course the House of Lords rejected the legislation which was passed by the House of Commons in the spirit of this resolution.[5] There are ways in our curious Constitution of circumventing the opposition of our Upper Chamber, but in practice these are not available unless the Government of the day is in favour of the measures which the House of Commons passes. In this case the Government was opposed to suspension or abolition of the death penalty for all forms of murder and refused to lend its aid. It is perhaps worth noting that it was by no means clear that the majority of the electorate concurred with the majority of the House of Commons. The Government was convinced that public opinion was opposed to the abolition of the death penalty, and certainly many members of Parliament must have voted for abolition even though they believed that a majority of their own constituents were opposed to it.[6] This illustrates the survival of the theory that the English Member of Parliament is not a delegate but a representative of his constituents. His duty even in a democracy is not to act on some real or supposed mandate from his constituents to vote in a given manner, but, at least when freed from party discipline, to consider each measure as it comes up before the House of Commons and to vote in accordance with his judgement.

Though no legislation was passed to give effect to the resolution of February 1956, two things of major importance resulted from it. First, all executions were suspended. The method by which this suspension was secured was the granting of reprieves in exercise of the Royal Prerogative on the "advice" of the Home

[4]548 *H.C. Deb.* 2652, 2655 (1956).

[5]This was the bill introduced before the House of Commons resolution by a private member, Mr. Silverman, on 15 Nov. 1955, providing for the suspension of the death penalty for ten years to continue indefinitely after that period if no action was taken to restore it.

[6]See 548 *H.C. Deb.* 2575 (1956). "I shall not argue that there is yet a majority of public opinion in favour of abolition." (Mr. Herbert Morrison.) See also 198 *H.L. Deb.* 790, 804 (1956), for criticism of members of the Commons disregarding their constituents' known views. The issue was never put before the electorate at any general election and no member of the House of Commons who voted in favour of it referred to it in his election address; (ibid., at 824). In the House of Lords debate of the Silverman Bill in July 1956, eight bishops voted for the suspension of the death penalty and two against; two peers holding judicial office voted for suspension and eight against; (ibid., at 840–842). Opposition to abolition or suspension was particularly strong among the police and prison services. See *Royal Commission on Capital Punishment, Report,* Cmd. No. 8932, para. 61 (1953) (hereinafter cited as *Royal Commission Report*). A Gallup Poll in 1953 showed 73 per cent in favour of the death penalty and a poll in 1955 showed 50 per cent in favour and 37 per cent against. These fluctuations, however, were said to be influenced by two recent cases. 198 *H.L. Deb.* 689 (1956).

Secretary. Until the new legislation mentioned below such a reprieve was granted in every case, though prior to February 1956 in more than half the number of cases where a prisoner was convicted of murder and sentenced to death the sentence was carried out.[7]

The second result of the vote in the House of Commons was that the Government itself introduced a compromise measure which became law under the title of the Homicide Act of 21 March 1957. This act eliminates the death penalty except for five categories of murder, the most important of which are murders done in the course of theft, murders by shooting or by causing an explosion, and murder of a police officer acting in the execution of his duty.[8]

In the intervals between these Parliamentary debates, public discussion of the death penalty was conducted vigorously in the press, on the radio, and at public meetings organized by various bodies, including the Howard League. Since 1953, this discussion has been of a markedly higher quality than before. This was due to the publication, in 1953, and the subsequent wide dissemination of the *Report of the Royal Commission on Capital Punishment*,[9] summing up the results of four years' study of the facts, the figures, the law, and the moral principles which stand behind the law, in relation to murder and its punishment. This Commission visited many parts of Europe and the United States and addressed questionnaires to many countries in search of information; it was aided by evidence given to it by many celebrated experts and jurists. Among those in the United States were Justice Felix Frankfurter, Professor Herbert Wechsler of Columbia University and Professor Thorsten Sellin. Within the confines of this report there is a far more comprehensive, dispassionate, and lucid evaluation of the arguments both as to questions of fact and to questions of law and principle relevant to murder and its punishment, than in any of the many books published in either of our countries on this subject. Certainly the publication of this report in England introduced altogether new standards of clarity and relevance into dis-

[7]Executions were resumed in July 1957.
[8]Ibid., s. 5. The other cases of capital murder under the act are: murder done in the course of or for the purpose of preventing lawful arrest or of effecting or assisting an escape from legal custody, murder of a prison officer by a prisoner, and repeated murders. The act also abolishes constructive malice and introduces into the law of murder the doctrine of diminished responsibility, which provides that a person who kills shall not be convicted of murder if he was suffering from such abnormality of mind as "substantially impaired his mental responsibility," but only of manslaughter carrying a maximum penalty of imprisonment for life. Ibid., s. 2. For criticism, see Elliott, "The Homicide Act, 1957," C. L. R. (1957), p. 282; Prevezer, "The English Homicide Act: A New Attempt to Revise the Law of Murder," 57 C. L. R. (1957), p. 624.
[9]Cmd. 8932.

cussions of a subject which had too often been obscured by ignorance and prejudice. The value of this most remarkable document
was not diminished by the fact that the Commission's terms of
reference postulated the retention of the death penalty and extended only to the consideration of the *limitations* on its use; nor
was it diminished by the fact that the recent Homicide Act of
1957 proceeded on principles in two respects opposed to the
conclusions of the Royal Commission.

2

It is profitable, I think, to consider some major contrasts between
the way in which murder and its punishment is regarded in
England and this country. Of course I am very conscious of the
fallacy of speaking of the United States as if it were a single
country; and there is certainly a great diversity in the statutory
definition of murder and in its treatment in the different state of
the Union.[10] We share indeed the common-law concept of murder,
malice aforethought, and the distinction between murder and
manslaughter, but against this common background five major
differences stand out.

First, until the Homicide Act of 1957 English law had never
admitted the notion of different degrees of murder, but had adhered obstinately to the simple division of criminal homicide into
murders for which the death sentence is mandatory and manslaughter for which only a maximum sentence of imprisonment
for life is prescribed. Efforts for many years had been made to
introduce the gradations of murder so familiar in American law.
In 1866 a Select Commission reported in favour of dividing murder
into two degrees, for one of which capital punishment was reserved, and two successive Governments and several private
members introduced bills to give effect to this recommendation,
but without success.[11] In 1948, after the House of Lords had deleted
the suspension of the death penalty from the Criminal Justice
Bill, the House of Commons voted for a compromise clause introduced by the Government, which reserved the death penalty for

[10]Ten states employ the common-law definition without grading into degrees.
Capital punishment has been abolished in Maine, Michigan, Wisconsin, and
Minnesota, and, except for murders committed by those already under sentence
of life imprisonment, in Rhode Island and North Dakota.

Where the death penalty exists, a discretion is usually given to the court or
jury to substitute life imprisonment, but the death penalty is mandatory for first-
degree murder in Connecticut, Massachusetts, North Carolina, and Vermont, and
except for most felony murder, New York.

[11]The government introduced bills in 1866 and 1867. See *Royal Commission Report*,
pp. 467–470, App. 12.

five categories of murder committed with express malice, but this was rejected by the House of Lords and dropped from the bill.[12]

Finally the Royal Commission, in its report of 1953, gave more careful consideration to the introduction of degrees of murder in English law than this subject had ever received before; yet, after a most exhaustive consideration of the practice in the United States and elsewhere, the conclusion was reached that the quest for a satisfactory definition of degrees of murder was "chimerical" and must be abandoned.[13] Only in 1957 was a breach made in this tradition by the Homicide Act, which reserves the death penalty for five classes of murder. The particular classes chosen may appear somewhat curious to American lawyers, but it is to be remembered that they do not represent an attempt to distinguish between murders according to heinousness or moral gravity, but to select for capital punishment those types of murder in which the deterrent effect is likely to be most powerful.

Of greater importance than the English refusal to contemplate degrees of murder is the even greater reluctance of English lawyers to confer a discretion upon the court as to the penalty in murder cases and, above all, the solid conviction that such a discretion should not be imparted to a jury. Although, as Justice Frankfurter has stated, the various American states present a crazy quilt pattern defeating any generalization, the *normal* method by which American justice seeks to determine the appropriate penalty in murder cases is a combination of degrees of murder and the device of entrusting a discretion as to the penalty of the court, except for certain cases where the death penalty is mandatory for first-degree murder. English legal and public opinion has, of course, always been disturbed by the fact that the rigid English law of murder makes the death penalty mandatory for offences of widely different moral character; and indeed the death penalty would not have been tolerated at all had it been carried out in all cases where it was imposed. But until very recently the method of mitigating the rigidity of the law has been the clumsy device of leaving the ultimate disposition of each case to the Executive. Accordingly, it is the Home Secretary, exercising the Royal Prerogative of mercy, who in the end draws the distinction so universally felt between, e.g., the cold-blooded murderer out for gain and the woman who kills an imbecile child to whom she can no longer attend. Over the last fifty years, reprieves have been granted in nearly half of the cases where the courts have sentenced the prisoner to death.

Thus it has been said with some truth that the English courts

[12] Sea ibid., pp. 170–172, 471.
[13] bid., p. 189 (para. 534).

merely determine which murderers *may* be executed.[14] Perhaps English lawyers have never thought out in detail their reasons for entrusting to a single man, in the person of the Home Secretary, a discretion which they would withhold from the court and above all from the jury. However, the unwillingness to entrust this discretion to the court, where it is more than mere conservatism, springs from the knowledge that the Home Secretary, in reviewing a case and considering a reprieve, has access to a wide range of information which could not come to light in court and goes far beyond the facts required to show guilt at trial. He may consider the whole background of a prisoner's life, including information which has come to light only since the trial, and, odious as his responsibility is felt to be, it is the conviction of most English lawyers that he does something which the courts cannot do.

On the other hand, the disadvantages of this system have been felt acutely in recent years. The Royal Commission felt that the main evil of the existing law was that a grotesque combination of a solemn sentence of death passed after a trial in court, followed, in nearly half the cases, by a reprieve made by the Executive, was needed to achieve a morally tolerable result. This clumsy expedient, whatever its advantages, could scarcely fail to create the impression that the law which the courts administer lags behind the best informed, enlightened, standards of the day, and almost as often as not the decision reached by the court had to be set right by the Executive.[15] The Royal Commission reached the conclusion that if the death penalty were not to be abolished for murder the only satisfactory solution was to entrust a discretion to the jury to enable it to give effect to considerations which at present lead the Home Secretary to recommend a reprieve.[16] In England this conclusion has not been adopted; "jury discretion" is too generally distrusted as an expedient for determining punishment.[17]

The third major difference between the law in England and in the United States is in relation to felony murder, or, as we call it, "constructive murder." This has finally been eliminated from English law by the Homicide Act 1957 in deference to the conviction that it is unjust or in some way inconsistent with enlightened

[14]Michael and Wechsler, "A Rationale of the Law of Homicide," *C. L. R.* (1937), p. 701, at 706 no. 19.
[15]See *Royal Commission Report*, paras. 17–22, 606–608, 790 ss.2 and 42.
[16]Ibid., paras. 594–611, 790 ss.6–43.
[17]See especially the debate in the House of Lords on the scheme for "jury discretion" 185 *H.L. Deb* 137–188 (1953). All the legal members present except Lord Chorley (ibid., 170) condemned it as completely unworkable and the Lord Chief Justice said "Rather than take part in such a performance as that I would resign the office I hold, for *I think it would be destructive of everything in British law*"; ibid., 177 (my italics).

principles of punishment that a person should be convicted of murder if he killed a person while engaged upon some felonious act not in itself likely to result in the death of, or grievous injury to, another person.[18] Gradually the scope of felony murder had been reduced, first by the insistence that it should be used only in cases where actual violence had in fact been the cause of death, and then by the insistence that the death should have been the natural or probable outcome of the felony upon which the prisoner was engaged. Though there had been a few cases in recent years where a broader interpretation of felony murder was given by an English court,[19] on the whole the conviction was widespread that it had ceased to be defensible.

This, of course, is in clear contrast with the United States where it is not deemed extraordinary to insist that a man who embarks on violent crime and sets a chain of events in motion must "take the consequences." This attitude, which conflicts with the importance attached to the principle that a "subjective test" of criminal liability should be adhered to as far as possible,[20] no doubt reflects the wide prevalence of crimes of violence and the common fear of rape in some parts of America. In England, even judges regarded as generally conservative in their attitudes toward the law of murder, such as the Lord Chief Justice and Mr. Justice Humphreys, concurred in the view that constructive malice should be abolished and that murder should be confined in terms or in effect to cases of intentional killing or infliction of grievous bodily harm.

The fourth difference which requires attention is the attitude, common in English penological thought, that a sentence of imprisonment longer than ten years should not be served except under the most extreme circumstances. Under the practice prior to the Homicide Act 1957, a murderer whose death sentence had been commuted for one of life imprisonment very rarely served a period of more than fifteen years, and the usual period served was very much less.[21] By contrast, in some states in America sentences of twenty-eight years are not uncommonly served for first-degree murder and seventeen years for second-degree murder.[22] It is of

---

[18]See *Royal Commission Report,* pp. 34–41.
[19]E.g., *R. v. Jarmain (1946)* K.B. 74.
[20]Still "objective standards" creep in by the back door. See *R. v. Ward* (1956) 1 Q.B. 351 (C.C.A.), criticized by Prevezer, "Murder by Mistake," C. L. R. (1956), p. 375.
[21]*Royal Commission Report*, paras. 644–656.
[22]Ibid., app. 16, table B:

Massachusetts 1900–1950

1st. degree murder	*Average 28 yrs.*	*Longest 41 yrs.*
2nd. degree murder	*Average 17 yrs.*	*Longest 40 yrs.*

course obvious that, since murderers who would have previously been executed will now be sentenced to imprisonment as a result of the Homicide Act, a new consideration will have to be given to the question of the length of imprisonment which can be imposed consistently with our general penological notions. Much experience in abolition countries on the continent is available; it is thought by many to demonstrate that even where there is no death penalty, extended sentences of imprisonment are not in fact necessary for the public safety. Only one of the murderers whose sentence of death had been commuted to imprisonment and had been released is known to have committed a murder in England in this century.

Last, we should note the attitude of English law in regard to the notion of double jeopardy in criminal cases. If some substantial error is made by the trial court, whether it be a misdirection to the jury or the admission of inadmissible evidence, the result in England is that the conviction is quashed by the court of appeal and the prisoner acquitted. In such circumstances the prisoner does not run the risk of a second trial, and in very many cases where a prisoner in the United States would be subjected to a second trial he would, in England, be acquitted on appeal.[23] There is indeed a power given to our court of criminal appeal to maintain the decision of the trial court in spite of misdirection or other error, but only if such error is not a "substantial miscarriage of justice."[24] It might be thought that the result of the English system is that the appellate courts are less quick to detect error in the trial than is true in the United States, but I can only say, after consideration of many cases, that I think that this is not so. The result of our system is that we never have any instances of considerable delay between the actual conviction and sentence and its execution. A period of more than three months would be considered indecent and an intolerable cruelty to the prisoner and his family. This, of course, contrasts with the occasional case in the United States where years may intervene between sentence of death and its execution.

---

[23]See *Woolmington* v. *Director of Public Prosecution* (1935) A.C. 462. The trial judge wrongly directed the jury that if the fact of killing by the accused was established by the prosecution, it was then for the accused to show that he had not killed with malice aforethought. On appeal the conviction was quashed because of this misdirection, and the prisoner acquitted and discharged.

[24]Criminal Appeal Act, 1907, 7 Edw. VII, c. 23, s. 4(1). Only where "if the jury had been properly directed they would inevitably come to the same conclusion" can misdirection be treated as other than a substantial miscarriage of justice for the purpose of this section. See *Woolmington* v. *Director of Public Prosecution, supra,* at p. 482.

3

So far we have considered the chief differences in the law and penological ideas concerning murder in our two countries. Let us now turn to the question of the rate and types of murder prevalent in England and in the United States. Here we do indeed tread upon ground which is full of pitfalls. We must remember how blunt are our sociological tools for assessing the quantity of crime of any type, and in particular the crime of homicide. Of course, it is easy to find out how many are charged and convicted of specific crimes; but, if we are to begin the possibly hopeless task of assessing the value of any particular punishment, what is needed is some rational estimate of the underlying figures of the crimes actually perpetrated.

In England, for more than seventy years, figures showing the number of "murders known to the police" have, along with similar figures for other crimes, been collected by the Government from all of the various police forces in the country. These are annually presented to Parliament by the Home Office and published as the *Criminal Statistics for England and Wales.* The authorities are well aware of the difficulties of classifying particular cases and have often emphasized that, while every effort is made to secure uniformity as between different police forces, and scrupulous attention is paid to the need to distinguish cases where a reported death might be due to suicide, self-defence, accident, and felonious attack, it is impossible to guarantee that any figures so collected are immune from error.

Figures compiled in this way must necessarily be imperfect as a guide to the amount of murder, if only because there must be a certain number of cases which are never reported to the police. Yet they are considered to be the best index; they are much better, for example, than figures from registration offices[25] showing the number of deaths officially recorded as due to murder. Hence it is regrettable that until recently only Great Britain, the Commonwealth Countries, Denmark, and a few states in the United States kept full figures on this basis. Since 1930, however, the *Uniform Crime Reports,* issued biannually by the F.B.I., show figures obtained from police authorities in most of the urban and rural areas of the country for cases of "murder and non-negligent manslaughter" known to the police. These figures now cover 90 per cent of the urban population, 68 per cent of the rural population, and 81 per cent of the total population.[26] They have been fiercely criticized

[25] For a criticism of such figures see *Royal Commission Report,* app. 6, para. 27.
[26] See, e.g., 26 *U.S. Dept of Justice, Uniform Crime Report* (1955), p. 72 (hereinafter cited as *Uniform Crime Reports*).

at times[27] and, with respect to certain crimes at any rate, it is clear that the basis of classification may have varied from district to district and perhaps was influenced by the wish to make things look better than they are. A warning is now contained in these reports to the effect that, in publishing the data sent in by the chiefs of police of different cities, the F.B.I. does not vouch for their accuracy. Nevertheless it seems that the general standards for reporting crimes have risen considerably,[28] and, though they must be open to question at many points, it is now reasonable to regard these figures as a rough minimum estimate of the homicides that they report. Of course, if there is a need for caution in comparing the figures reported by the police for one district with the figures reported by the police for another even in the same country, obviously there is an even greater need for caution in comparing the figures reported by the police of different countries. Yet, with all these qualifications, it is still illuminating to draw attention to some contrasts between the figures for Great Britain and those for the United States.

The relevant figures for England and Wales most worth attention are, I think, the following. In the fifty years from 1900 to 1949 inclusive, a total of 7,454 murders were known to the police; this included 2,001 babies under the age of one year.[29] If we break down these fifty years into five decades of ten years the rate per million of population of murder (including babies under one year) is an average rate of 4.6, 4.1, 3.9, 3.3, 4.0 for each of these five decades.[30] The annual average figure of murder known to the police for these fifty years is 149 to the nearest unit; and the actual figure for each of these fifty years is quite frequently very near this average.

In this same period of fifty years in England and Wales, 1,210 persons were sentenced to death for murder but only 632 were executed. This is an annual average of twenty-four death sentences and thirteen executions.[31] Slightly more than half the number of those sentenced to death were executed and the remainder are accounted for almost wholly by the intervention of the Executive.

[27]See Warner, "Crimes Known to the Police—An Index of Crimes?" 45 *Harv. L. Rev.* (1932), p. 307.
[28]Sec. 25 *Uniform Crimes Reports* 72–73 (1954) where the claim is made that the "reliability of major crime estimates is considered excellent." A short account is also given of the methods now used to correct deviations from "acceptable standards" in record keeping and reporting and of several methods used for test checking of reported figures.
[29]*Royal Commission Report*, app. 3, table 1.
[30]Ibid., app. 6, table 46, and para. 89.
[31]Ibid., paras. 37–43. In 23 cases the conviction was quashed by the Court of Appeal.

H. L. A. Hart

In rough figures, therefore, in England and Wales during this period one person was executed for every twelve murders known to the police, and one person was convicted for every six murders known to the police.[32]

The scale of criminal homicide in the United States is very different from the humble English figures. According to the note on the classification of offences included in all issues of the *Uniform Crime Reports*, "murder and non-negligent manslaughter" is said to comprise all wilful felonious homicides as distinguished from deaths caused by negligence. Accordingly, when faced with a corpse the police must, before classifying the case under this head, exclude the possibilities of negligent homicide, suicide, accidental death, and justifiable homicide (defined in the *Reports* as the killing of a felon by a police officer in line of duty or the killing of a hold-up man by a private citizen). Each year the *Uniform Crime Reports* then purport to *estimate* the total number of murders and non-negligent manslaughters in the whole country on the basis of figures actually reported from police authorities now covering approximately four-fifths of the total population. The *Reports* claim that these estimates are "conservative" indications of the "nationwide major crime problem."[33]

To make some comparisons with England and Wales I have chosen the ten-year period from 1945 to 1954, during which the estimated total of offences under the head of murder and non-negligent manslaughter in the United States was 72,679: this gives a yearly average (to the nearest unit) of 7,268.[34] These figures, expressed (as the English figures are) as rates per *million* of population, vary during these ten years between 60 and 40 per million. This is between fifteen and ten times the rate in England and Wales for the fifty-year period of 1900–1949. It should be remembered, however, that certain types of homicide included under the American classification of "murder and non-negligent

[32]In the years 1900–1949, while there were 7,454 murders known to the police, the total number of convictions was 1,246; of these thirty-four youths under eighteen and two pregnant women were not sentenced to death. Of the 1,210 death sentences passed, 23 were quashed by the Court of Appeal. The number of convictions, 1,246, looks small in comparison with the total numbers of murders known to the police, 7,454 of which 2,001 were babies under one year. But during these same 50 years 1,674 suspects committed suicide and 1,226 persons were found either guilty but insane and acquitted or unfit to plead. Ibid., app. 3, table 1. In terms of annual average, for every 149 murders known to the police (or 109, if babies under one year are excluded) there are 25 convictions, 33 suicides by suspects and 25 persons are found guilty but insane or unfit to plead. During the entire period 1900–1949 3,130 persons were charged with murder, an annual average of 63.
[33]See, e.g., 26 *Uniform Crime Reports*, 72 (1956).
[34]The annual estimated total appears each year as the first table in the second semi-annual bulletin of the *Uniform Crime Reports*. The separate figures for these

manslaughter" are excluded from the British figures, which are for murder alone.[35] The chief, if not the only, cases of non-negligent manslaughter are those where a plea of provocation might be successfully maintained, but unfortunately it is not possible to estimate separate figures for "murders" and "non-negligent manslaughters." Perhaps, especially in the southern states, the number of instances of provoked homicides which would be treated as manslaughter by the courts might be considerable.

In many parts of the country, particularly in the southern states, the rates of murder and non-negligent homicide are very much higher than the average for the whole country quoted above and amount to as much as fifty times the English murder rates; in other parts of the country the rates are much lower than the national average. Thus if we take the urban centres in Georgia for the three years 1950–1952, the respective rates per million of population are 177.9, 182.3, and 206.7, while the rate in New Hampshire urban centres is 7.4, 4.1, and 19.5 per million. For the same three years the rates for urban centres, covering a population of about nineteen million, in the five states of Illinois, Michigan, Indiana, Missouri, and Wisconsin were respectively 42.1, 48.3, and 45.8 per million. These figures show how different the magnitude of the murder problem in the United States is from the

years together with the estimated population for the United States taken from *Bureau of Census, Dept. of Commerce, Statistical Abstract of the United States* (1955), p. 13, table 8, are as follows:

Year	Murder and Non-Negligent Manslaughter	Total Population Residing in U.S.A. (in thousands)
1945	6,847	132,481
1946	8,442	140,054
1947	7,760	143,446
1948	7,620	146,093
1949	6,990	148,665
1950	7,020	151,234
1951	6,820	153,384
1952	7,210	155,755
1953	7,120	158,306
1954	6,850	161,195

According to 25 *Uniform Crime Reports*, 69 (1954), in the 20 years from 1935–1954, 146,869 persons (an annual average of 7,344) were wilfully and unlawfully slain in the United States. The highest year in these twenty was 1946 with 8,442 wilful killings. For each one million persons there were 61 murders in 1935 and 42 in 1954.

[35]The English criminal statistics give separate figures for murders known to the police, but do not distinguish between negligent and non-negligent manslaughter. The combined annual figures for both murder and manslaughter (negligent as well as non-negligent) in England and in Wales during 1900–1949 were about 8 per million inhabitants, while in the same period in about 2,200 cities in the United States the number of murders and non-negligent manslaughters was about 56 per million. See *Royal Commission Report*, app. 6, paras. 12, 24, 88.

problem in England, and it would be possible to present this difference in many dramatic ways. In Chicago alone, for example, the *number* of murders and non-negligent homicides in each of the three years 1950–1952 (257, 249, and 289) was nearly double the number of murders in the whole of England and Wales (139, 132, and 146).[36]

During the ten-year period between 1945 and 1954, 775 persons were executed for murder by the civil authorities, an average of seventy-seven per year. This, compared with the average annual estimated number of murders and non-negligent manslaughters for those years (7,268), gives a ratio of less than 1:100;[37] in England the ratio of executions to murders known to the police for the fifty years 1900–1949 was about 1:12.

Though we lack satisfactory figures, most authorities share the view that the number of murders committed by professional criminals is far greater in the United States than it is in England; a far greater proportion of murder in England is due to jealousy, drink, quarrel, lust, and even irritation than in the United States. The Royal Commission estimated that for the period of 1900–1949, 20 percent of convicted murderers in England, at the most, were professional criminals.[38] In England insanity, defined even by the stringent legal criteria used (until 1957) for assessing criminal responsibility, plays a very great part: of the total of 3,129 persons committed to trial for murder during the fifty years 1900–1949, 428 were held unfit to plead and 798 adjudged guilty but insane under the M'Naghten rules. The combined figures for these two categories of insanity (1,226) were slightly greater than the total of those convicted and sentenced to death for murder (1,210) during this period.[39] The relevant figures for the United States are apparently not available.

4

Let us now turn to the principles to which men appeal when they argue for or against the death penalty. In any public discussion of

[36]All American figures in this paragraph are from 21 *Uniform Crime Reports*, 90, 92, 95 (1950); 22 ibid., at 87, 89, 93 (1951); 23 ibid., at 93, 95, 99 (1952). For England and Wales see *Royal Commission Report*, app. 3, table 1.
[37]See *Bureau of Census, Dept. of Commerce, Statistical Abstract of the United States* (1955), p. 154, table 188.
[38]See *Royal Commission Report*, app. 6, table 2 and paras. 12, 13. In 1930 Judge Marcus Kavanagh told the Select Committee on Capital Punishment that "the larger number of people who are killed in the United States are killed by criminals." Ibid., para. 12.
[39]*Royal Commission Report*, app. 3, table 1. Respite was granted an additional forty-seven persons, after sentence of death, by the Home Secretary on grounds of insanity. Ibid., at p. 301.

this subject the question that is likely to be the central one is "What is the character and weight of the evidence that the death penalty is required for the protection of society? What is the evidence that it has a uniquely deterrent force compared with the alternative of imprisonment?"[40] Later we shall examine what evidence there is to answer this question, but first we should consider what is implied if this question is treated—as undoubtedly most ordinary men now do treat it—as the root of the matter, as the fundamental question in considering whether the death penalty should be abolished or retained.

To treat this question as the root of the matter is implicitly to adopt what is called, I think unhappily, a theory of punishment. I say "unhappily" because theories of punishment are not theories in any normal sense. They are not, as scientific theories are, assertions or contentions as to what is or what is not the case; the atomic theory or the kinetic theory of gases is a theory of this sort. On the contrary, those major positions concerning punishment which are called deterrent or retributive or reformative "theories" of punishment are moral *claims* as to what justifies the practice of punishment—claims as to why, morally, it *should* or *may* be used. Accordingly, if it is held that the central question concerning the death penalty is whether or not it is needed to protect society from harm, then, although *this* question is itself a question of fact, the moral claim (or "theory" of punishment) implied is the "utilitarian" position that what justifies the practice of punishment is its propensity to protect society from harm. Let us call this implicit moral claim "the utilitarian position."

There are indeed ways of defending and criticizing the death penalty which are quite independent of the utilitarian position and of the questions of fact which the utilitarian will consider as crucial. These are perhaps more commonly expressed in England than in America. For some people the death penalty is ruled out en-

[40]A careful examination of the English Parliamentary debates confirms this, although it is certainly not apparent at first sight. Thus the Archbishop of York, in the Lords debate in July 1956, insisted "on the moral necessity of retribution within our penal code." The Lord Chancellor agreed with the view elsewhere expressed by Lord Justice Denning that "the ultimate justification of any punishment is not that it is a deterrent, but that it is the emphatic denunciation by the community of a crime." 198 *H.L. Deb.* 576 (1956). But the Lord Chancellor also said that "the real crux" of the question at issue is whether capital punishment is a uniquely effective deterrent; ibid., at 577. The Archbishop stated that "the question of deterrence comes to the head as a vitally important matter," ibid., at 597. See also Lord Salisbury (a retentionist): "For me, as for many others, it is on the deterrent value of capital punishment that the whole balance of the argument must turn"; Ibid., at 820. For an illuminating philosophical analysis of the arguments in this debate see Gallie, "The Lords Debate on Hanging, July 1956: Interpretation and Comment," *Philosophy*, vol. 32 (Apr. 1957), p. 132.

tirely as something absolutely evil which, like torture, should never be used however many lives it might save. Those who take this view find that they are sometimes met by the counter-assertion that the death penalty is something which morality actually demands, a uniquely appropriate means of retribution or "reprobation" for the worst of crimes, even if its use adds nothing to the protection of human life. Here we have two sharply opposed yet similar attitudes: for the one the death penalty is morally excluded; for the other it is a moral necessity: but both alike are independent of any question of fact or evidence as to what the use of the death penalty does by way of furthering the protection of society. Argument in support of views as absolute as these can consist only of an invitation, on the one hand, to consider in detail the execution of a human being, and on the other hand, to consider in detail some awful murder, and then to await the emergence either of a conviction that the death penalty must never be used or, alternatively, that it must never be completely abandoned.

It is important to realize that what differentiates the utilitarian position from these absolute attitudes is not that the latter adopt a specific moral attitude while the utilitarian position confines itself to "the facts." The utilitarian position, which treats the welfare of society as the justification of punishment, is also a moral claim just as these absolute positions are; what differentiates them is that the utilitarian position commits one, as the absolute positions do not, to a factual inquiry as to the effects upon society of the use of the death penalty.

Is the utilitarian position coherent? Is it possible to hold it without paradox or without commitment to consequences against which most ordinary people's moral sense would rebel? Or when the consequences of the utilitarian position are exposed do men feel compelled by other moral principles which they hold at least as firmly to abandon or qualify the utilitarian position? What are these other moral principles? Do they imply the tacit admission that something going under the ambiguous name of "retribution" or "reprobation" required attention in any acceptable "theory" of punishment? If so, to what specific aspect of punishment are these notions relevant? I think that most of the puzzles about the principles of punishment which trouble ordinary men can be reduced to these questions.

Let us consider some of the claims that are urged against the utilitarian position. They are often obscurely presented and I shall try to put them clearly.

The first is this. It is often said that men punish and always have punished for a vast number of different reasons. They have punished to secure obedience to laws, to gratify feelings of revenge, to satisfy a public demand for severe reprisals for outrageous crimes, because they believed a deity demands punishment, to match with suffering the moral evil inherent in the perpetration of a crime, or simply out of respect for tradition. If there are these many reasons, why should we select the protection of society from harm and give this primacy as the "basis" of punishment? Surely it is only one reason among many which stand on an equal level insofar as a claim upon our attention is concerned.

Here plainly we must distinguish two questions commonly confused. They are, first "Why do men in fact punish?" This is a question of fact to which there may be many different answers such as those exemplified above. The second question, to be carefully distinguished from the first, is "What justifies men in punishing? Why is it morally good or morally permissible for them to punish?" It is clear that no demonstration that in fact men have punished or do punish for certain reasons can amount *per se* to a justification for this practice unless we subscribe to what is itself a most implausible moral position, namely, that whatever is generally done is justified or morally right. Short of this, if we think that punishment is *justified* because, for example, it satisfies a public demand or because it meets the evil of misconduct with suffering, we must add to our statement of fact that men in fact do punish for such reasons, the further *moral* claim that it is good or at least morally permissible to punish for such reasons.

When this simple point is made clear and the two questions "Why do men punish?" and "What justifies punishment?" are forced apart, very often the objector to the utilitarian position will turn out to be a utilitarian of a wider and perhaps more imaginative sort. He will perhaps say that what justifies punishment is that it satisfies a popular demand (perhaps even for revenge) and explain that it is good that it satisfies this demand because if it did not there would be disorder in society, disrespect for the law, or even lynching. Such a point of view, of course, raises disputable questions of fact as to the extent to which satisfaction of popular demand is important in the ways indicated. None the less, this objection itself turns out to be a utilitarian position, emphasizing that the good to be secured by punishment must not be narrowly conceived as simply protecting society from the harm represented by the particular type of crime punished, but also as a protection from a wider set of injuries to society.

Very often, however, because the question of fact and the question of justification are not thus distinguished, the fact, or the alleged fact, of a public demand for punishment (or a particular kind of punishment) is cited as if it were *per se* a justification; or, at least, the precise moral principle which treats such a demand (or some element of it) as a justification for punishment is never clearly stated or exposed for criticism.

But the objector who criticizes the utilitarian position by reminding us of the diversity of reasons for which men punish may not always turn out to be a wider utilitarian in the way I have suggested. Sometimes the objector will take his stand on absolutes and claim that meeting the moral evil of misconduct with suffering is, as Kant urged, good *per se*, so that, even on the last day of society, the murderer not only may but must be executed. But before we say that no argument is possible between the utilitarian and objectors of this sort, it is necessary to inquire whether the objector would hold his position unless he also believed that punishment was necessary to protect society from harm. Would he really rely on his absolutist position to justify going *beyond* the limits of what the utilitarian would admit by way of punishment, and inflict a punishment more severe than one required on utilitarian principles?[41] Sometimes the answer is "yes" and then we are left to a clash of fundamental moral claims in which the absolutist must simply expose for inspection and acceptance his claim that there is somehow some intrinsic total good in meeting the moral evil of misconduct with suffering; this, he must say, is something morally "called for" independently of its place in a social mechanism designed for the protection of society or other beneficial effects.

Consider now a more fundamental objection, to the utilitarian position which is implied in holding the central question in relation to the death penalty to be the question "What is the evidence that it is needed to protect society?" "Surely," says the objector, "the protection of society cannot be your justification, for if it were, why should you stop where you not only do stop, but think you ought to stop, in using punishment as an instrument for the protection of society? Why not employ torture if that would effectively stop, e.g., parking offences; or at any rate why not employ a punishment immeasurably more severe than we normally contemplate for this type of offence? Why not, if in a particular case it were necessary and possible in order to protect society, put up an innocent man, fake his guilt and execute him? What moral, as distinguished from practical, objection could there be on utilitarian grounds to the staged trials or to the shooting of the inno-

[41]It seems that the Archbishop of York and the Lord Chancellor, while insisting that the primary purpose of punishment is retribution (see *supra*, p. 71, n. 40), would have said "no" at this point.

cent *pour encourager les autres?* Does not the common insistence that punishment be applied only to one who has in fact broken the law and, in the case of serious crime, done so with *mens rea* show that you are guided by considerations quite different from utilitarian principles?"

Here we must go carefully; for in this type of objection, which certainly troubles the plain man's utilitarianism, many different issues are involved. Clearly it is part of a *sane* utilitarianism that no punishment must cause more misery than the offence unchecked; and it might well be that the misery caused to the victim and his friends by torture or other very severe punishments would be worse than any misery caused by a minor offence for which it was used as a punishment. No doubt also a consistent utilitarian answer could be given to the other objections. The state of general alarm and terror which might arise in society if it were known that the innocent were likely to be seized and subjected to the pains of punishment in order to serve the needs of society might be worse than any advance in security or social welfare brought about by these means could outweigh. Furthermore, administrative and judicial officers might refuse to give effect to the use of "punishment" in such circumstances and would hence "nullify" it.

Yet though such answers *can* be made they do not seem to account for the character of the normal unwillingness to "punish" those who have not broken the law at all, nor for the moral objection to strict liability which permits the punishment of those who act without *mens rea*. We cannot be so easily rid of the argument that some elements other than those which even the broadest utilitarian admits are involved. Bentham himself confronted the doctrine of *mens rea* and asked why we do and should excuse from criminal responsibility persons who have committed a crime owing to their mental condition, either temporary (mistake, accident, duress, etc.) or relatively enduring (insanity, infancy). He thought that it was enough to say that the *threat* of punishment would here be socially useless. It could not deter such persons or other people like them and hence on plain utilitarian grounds, which enjoin us not to cause useless suffering, they should be excused from punishment. He even went so far as to say that this is all that could be *meant* by the restriction of punishment to those who have a "vitious will" (as Blackstone had termed *mens rea*).[42] But there is a *non sequitur* in Bentham's argument. He claims to show that *punishment* of such persons as we excuse on such grounds would be wrong because it would be socially useless ("in-

[42]See Bentham, *An Introduction to The Principles of Morals and Legislation*, chap. XIII, "Cases Unmeet for Punishment."

efficacious"), whereas he only shows that the *threat* of punishment would be ineffective so far as such persons are concerned. Their *actual* punishment might well be "useful" in Benthamite terms because, if we admit such excuses, crime may be committed in the hope (surely sometimes realized) that a false plea of mistake, accident, or mental aberration would succeed.

Apart from this inconclusive argument, this unqualified utilitarianism does not reproduce the real moral objection that most thinking people have to the application of the pains of punishment to the innocent or to those who, by reason of their mental condition, are thought unable to comply with the law's demands. This moral objection normally would be couched as the insistence that it is *unjust*, or *unfair*, to take someone who has not broken the law, or who was unable to comply with it, and use him as a mere instrument to protect society and increase its welfare. Such an objection in the name of *fairness* or *justice* to individuals would still remain even if we were certain that in the case of the "punishment" of one who had not broken the law the fact of his innocence would not get out or would not cause great alarm if it did. Similarly, even if it were shown that the admission as an excuse of types of insanity or other defences in fact led, owing to successful fake pleas, to utilitarian "losses," i.e., to a greater prevalence of crime than would be the case if the system allowed for no such excuse, we would still be morally reluctant to allow punishment in such cases. To our tolerance of such a system there would indeed be some limit; but even if we were convinced that the social danger of the evasion of punishment through false pleas were overwhelming, and were forced to extend the area of strict liability, we would *wittingly* be choosing between two distinct principles: the utilitarian principle which justifies punishment by its propensity to protect society from harm, and a principle of justice which requires us to confine punishment to those who have broken the law and had at least some minimum capacity to comply with it.[43] Hence it still remains for the utilitarian to give some coherent

[43]The distinction between the efficacy of (1) the *threat* of punishment and (2) the *actual* punishment should be remembered when modern restatements of the Benthamite rationale of punishment are considered. This is true of the best of such modern restatements such as Michael and Wechsler's well known "A Rationale of the Law of Homicide," 37 *C. L. R.* (1937), pp. 701, 1261, and *Criminal Law and its Administration* (1940). See also Wechsler, Book Review, 37 *C. L. R.* (1937), p. 687.

On the whole these authors consistently identify the criminally "responsible" with those whom the threat of punishment *could* deter or as they sometimes phrase it are "capable of choosing to avoid the act in order to avoid punishment." This class, of course, is not necessarily the same as those whose *punishment* might benefit society (whether by deterring them, or others by example or both) and may (for the reasons stated above) well be a narrower class. But certainly to confine punishment to those who *could* be deterred by the threat (though *in fact* they were

reason why he should object to the use of punishment in the way suggested, and the question for him is whether he can do this without adopting the theory that the fundamental justification of punishment is not the protection of society but the return of suffering for the moral evil done. Must he, in order to make sense of his refusal to punish those who have not broken the law, adopt the notions of retribution, reprobation, expiation, or atonement? Is it true, as his opponent claims, that the only reason we can have for restricting the use of punishment in the way suggested is the moral conviction that what justifies punishment is a return of suffering for moral guilt.

There is a coherent answer which a cautious utilitarian can make to this objection without admitting notions of retribution, unless "retribution" means merely that punishment must be confined to those who have broken the law and could have helped

---

not deterred) accords with the common conviction that it would be unjust or unfair to punish those who could not be influenced by the threat of punishment; whereas a policy of punishing all those whose *actual* punishment might be socially useful would not accord with *this* conviction. On the other hand, it is by no means clear that a theory of punishment which thus restricts punishment to those who could not be but actually were not deterred by the threat of punishment evades all the difficulties of "free will" as these authors suggest (e.g., 37 C. L. R., at p. 690). For *prima facie* at any rate the statement that some one "could have been" deterred from a crime which he in fact committed means that in *the actual circumstances* in which he committed the crime he could have acted otherwise; and surely the classical "problem" of free will is just whether we ever have a right to make any such statement. But as these authors claim, and as I argue above, the restriction of punishment to those who have committed crimes voluntarily (i.e., not under the usual excusing conditions of mistake, accident, insanity, or the like) can be explained perfectly well without resort to retributive "theories" of punishment.

The authors carefully consider the possibility that loyalty to the principle that only the deterrable be punished might lead to the admission of certain excuses, e.g., the "irresistible impulse" test of insanity, and this might weaken the deterrent effect of the law upon those who could be deterred but hope successfully to evade punishment by simulating this excuse. They urge that the danger of this weakening the "net deterrent efficacy" of the law is not "decisive" in favour of rejecting this excuse, since its *rejection* might also lead to socially undesirable results in the form of, e.g., nullification of the system and "public excitement" which the execution of clearly undeterrable persons might produce. See ibid., at 752–757.

But it is important here to emphasize (as these authors do not) that there are moral objections (at least as firm as any utilitarian principles) to punishing persons who are clearly undeterrable (incapable of effective choice) and these objections are *not* merely subordinate aspects of the social desirability of avoiding public excitement and nullification of the system, etc. Indeed the reason why we should expect "public excitement" or the nullification of a system which permitted "the undeterrables" to be executed is precisely because it is widely considered (independently of social welfare) *unfair* or *unjust* to punish them. A theory of punishment which disregarded these moral convictions or viewed them simply as factors, frustration of which made for socially undesirable excitement is a different kind of theory from one which *out of deference to those convictions themselves* restricts punishment to those who are deterrable or capable of acting so as to avoid punishment.

this; but like all objections which are recurrent in the history of an idea this one shows something important. It shows that the utilitarian position, to be plausible, must be regarded as a claim to the *outer* limits of punishment; as fixing a *maximum* beyond which punishment is not justified. The utilitarian position, in however sophisticated a version, cannot plausibly be regarded as something which we can use in an unqualified fashion. There are many different ways in which we think it morally incumbent on us to *qualify* or *limit* the pursuit of the utilitarian goal by the methods of punishment. Some punishments are ruled out as too barbarous or horrible to be used whatever their social utility; we also limit punishments in order to maintain a scale for different offences which reflects, albeit very roughly, the distinction felt between the moral gravity of these offences. Thus we make some approximation to the ideal of justice of treating morally like cases alike and morally different ones differently.

Much more important than these is the qualification which civilized moral thought places on the pursuit of the utilitarian goal by the demand that punishment should not be applied to the innocent; indeed, so insistent is this demand that no system of rules which generally provided for the application of punishment to the innocent would normally be called a system of punishment. But the moral basis of this claim that such a limit must be imposed on the pursuit of the utilitarian goal need not be, and in most ordinary persons' minds is not, a recognition that the fundamental justification of punishment is other than the pursuit of the utilitarian goal. To see this point clearly we again must distinguish two very different types of questions. The first is "What justifies the general practice of punishment?," and the utilitarian answer that the justification lies in the need to protect society from harm is, by itself, an adequate answer to this question. There is, however, a further question: "What justifies us in applying the system of punishment to a particular individual?" Something more is involved in this question, for a necessary condition of the just *application* of punishment to a particular individual includes the requirement that he has broken the law. There are many ways of presenting this distinction: it is the distinction between the justification of punishment as a practice and the liability to punishment, or the distinction between the general question "What justifies us in maintaining laws by the practice of punishment?" and the particular question "Who may be punished?" It is important to see that, while the conviction that something more is required when we come to the particular question than sufficed for the general question is sound, it is not a recognition of an alternative basis or justification for the general practice of punishment. For the stipulation that punishment should not be applied except to an individual who has broken the law, may be made not to secure that moral evil should meet its return in punishment, but to protect the individual from society. It may be the recognition of the claim of the individual that he should not be sacrificed for the welfare of society unless he has broken its law; his breach of the law is, as it were, a condition or a licence showing us when there is liability to punishment. It is not an alternative basis for the system and could not (as a retributive or reprobative theory could) justify our using penalties more severe than would be required on utilitarian grounds. No doubt this recognition of the individual's claim not to be sacrificed to society except where he has broken laws is not itself absolute. Given enough misery to be avoided by the sacrifice of an innocent person, there may be situations in which it might be thought morally permissible to take this step. But, again, if we took the step, we would have to face a clash between two principles. We would then sacrifice the principle of fairness designed to protect the individual from society to the principle that an overwhelming advantage to society should be secured at any cost; but a clash between two principles is different from the simple application of a single utilitarian principle that anything which benefits society is permissible.

Of course, the distinction just emphasized between (1) a utilitarian justification of punishment qualified by recognition of the innocent individual's claim not to be sacrificed to society, and (2) a frankly retributive "theory" in which punishment is justified simply as a return for moral evil, must become meaningless if crime is regarded (as it is in some contemporary thought) always and only as a disease, with the corollary that it should be treated always and only with preventatives and cures. From this point of view a utilitarianism qualified by the principle that it is just only to inflict punishment on those who have voluntarily broken the law is as absurd as a theory that says, as an extreme retributivist theory does, that the justification for punishment is simply to match the past evil of misconduct with the pain of suffering. Indeed, the notion of fairness or justice would be almost senseless in the context of this outlook, for the contention that it is fair or just to punish those who have broken the law must be absurd if the crime is merely a manifestation of a disease. This point of view, which in effect would replace the notion of punishment with the idea of social hygiene, may rest either on philosophical determinism, or on the conviction that in no case where a crime has been committed are there any adequate empirical grounds for the belief that the criminal could have done other than he did. These viewpoints are not, of course, to be dismissed lightly, but they can be discussed only if we are prepared to drop the whole range of concepts involved in the institution of punishment. Necessarily these considerations are outside the confines of this discussion of a specific form of punishment.

If we look back on this discussion it appears that the utilitarianism of the plain man, if it is to be tenable, must be qualified in the face of the question: "Why not punish the innocent if in a given case it promotes the welfare of society?" The qualification to be made is the admission that the individual has a valid claim not to be made the instrument of society's welfare unless he has broken its laws; but to recognize this qualification of utilitarianism is not to recognize a different basis or justification for the practice of punishment.

There has emerged from this consideration of punishment, therefore, a need to distinguish between two pairs of distinct questions. The first set brings out the difference between asking "Why do men punish in fact?" and "What justifies them in doing so?" The second brings out the difference between asking "What justifies in general the practice of punishment?" and "What more is required, given that there is this general justification for the practice, in order to justify its use in any particular case?"

5

Let us now return to the central question: "What is the weight and character of the evidence that the death penalty is required for the protection of society?" Here there are two main approaches and both of them are strewn with pitfalls. One of them is through statistics, the other through what has been termed a "common-sense" conception of the strength of the fear of death as a motive in human conduct.

Statistics have now been collected and surveyed in a more thorough fashion than ever before. Yet the *Report of the Royal Commission,* after considering the expert scrutiny of the figures available in Europe, the Commonwealth, and the United States, reached only a negative, though still an important, conclusion. This was the finding that there is no clear evidence in any of the figures that the abolition of the death penalty has ever led to an increase in the rate of homicide or that its restoration has ever led to a fall.[44] Important as this is, it is of equal importance to appreciate that this investigation also showed how little we know, and per-

[44] *Royal Commission Report,* para. 65.

haps can ever know, about the effect of the penalty on social life. There are three cardinal points.

(i) Comparisons between countries which retain the death penalty and countries which have abolished it are practically useless. The rate in death penalty England is lower than the rate in the abolition Scandinavian countries;[45] the rate in abolition Wisconsin is higher than death penalty England but lower than many death penalty states in the United States. Obviously differences in population, in social, economic, and psychological conditions may render fallible any inference from the experiences of one country as to what may be expected from the death penalty or its abolition in any other.

(ii) The only rational use of the figures is to compare the statistical history of one country before and after abolition, or before and after the introduction or reintroduction of the death penalty, and to ask whether there are any changes in the murder rate correlated with these changes in the penalty. But there are many pitfalls here which reduce the utility of the available statistics. The foremost of them in importance are these: (a) In many countries formal abolition came only after a long period of gradual desuetude. In Norway, for example, the last execution was in 1876 but formal abolition came only in 1905, and such has been the pattern of many abolition countries in Europe and the Commonwealth. Where this "gradualness" obtains it is difficult to estimate when the death penalty ceased in practice to be a serious threat. (b) In any case, even if the point at which the death penalty either ceased to be or became a serious threat could be precisely marked, its operation on the murder rate is likely to be a long term effect: "There is unlikely to be in any civilised country a string of would-be murderers straining at the leash waiting only for the death penalty to be removed to commit murder: or vice versa. The effect is likely to be cumulative."[46]

(iii) The best and most impressive types of evidence come from cases where one of a bloc of several neighbouring states of

---

[45]The rates per million of population of murders in England and Wales and "intentional homicide" in Norway for three decades in 1910–1940 were as follows:

England and Wales	4.1	3.9	3.3
	(1910–1919)	(1920–1929)	(1930–1939)
Norway	5.4	4.9	5.0
	(1911–1920)	(1921–1930)	(1931–1940)

The Norwegian figures do not include babies, which constitute 28.5 per cent of the English figures. See *Royal Commission Report*, app. 3, table 1, app. 6 s. 89, table 46.
[46]Gold, "Should the Death Penalty Be Abolished?" Letter in *Listener* (9 Feb. 1956), p. 217.

similar population and similar social and economic conditions has abolished or introduced the death penalty for murder while the others have not changed it. Nebraska and North and South Dakota are examples of such a bloc, and the rise and fall of the murder rate in these three states was much the same during the period 1930–1948, although South Dakota reintroduced the death penalty in 1939 after previous abolition, Nebraska retained capital punishment (but made use of it only twice in this period), and North Dakota was an abolition state. Such comparisons between fairly homogeneous states suggest that the murder rates in such states are conditioned by factors operating independently of the death penalty.[47] There is, however, too little of such evidence to justify a positive inference.

In fact, perhaps the most important lesson from a dispassionate survey of the statistics is the need to distinguish between the two following propositions. (1) There is no evidence from the statistics that the death penalty is a superior deterrent to imprisonment. (2) There is evidence that the death penalty is not a superior deterrent to imprisonment. The Commission's conclusion is strictly confined to the first of these propositions, though many advocates of abolition speak as if the second were a warranted conclusion from the figures. That this is not so may be dramatically illustrated from the following facts. In the thirty years from 1910 to 1939 the ten-year average murder rate in England fell from 4 1 to 3.3 per million. Yet if the death penalty had been abolished at the beginning of this period (1910), and if this had resulted in 100 more murders than there actually were during this period, there would still have been a substantial decrease (from 4.1 to 3.5 per million) in the murder rate following this abolition.[48] We would have said "in this case abolition was not followed by an increase but by a decrease in the murder rate" and have been tempted to treat this as evidence that there was no connexion between the rate of crime and the form of penalty. This serves to show the importance of presenting our conclusion in the negative form that there is no evidence from the figures in favour of capital punishment.

If we turn from the statistical evidence to the other "evidence," the latter really amounts simply to the alleged truism that men fear death more than any other penalty, and that therefore it *must* be a stronger deterrent than imprisonment. No one has proclaimed his faith in this proposition more strongly than the great Victorian judge and historian of the Criminal Law, James Fitzjames Stephen. He said:

[47] *Royal Commission Report*, para. 64, app. paras. 51–54, tables 24–28.
[48] Gold, *supra*, n. 46, at p. 217.

No other punishment deters men so effectually from committing crimes as the punishment of death. This is one of those propositions which it is difficult to prove, simply because they are in themselves more obvious than any proof can make them. It is possible to display ingenuity in arguing against it, but that is all. The whole experience of mankind is in the other direction. The threat of *instant* death is the one to which resort has always been made when there was an absolute necessity for producing some result. . . . No one goes to *certain inevitable* death except by compulsion. Put the matter the other way. Was there ever yet a criminal who, when sentenced to death and *brought out to die,* would refuse the offer of a commutation of his sentence for the severest secondary punishment? Surely not. Why is this? It can only be because "All that a man has will he give for his life." In any secondary punishment, however terrible, there is hope; but death is death; its terror cannot be described more forcibly.[49]

This estimate of the paramount place in human motivation of the fear of death reads impressively, but surely it contains a *suggestio falsi* and once this is detected its cogency as an argument in favour of the death penalty for murder vanishes. For there is really no parallel between the situation of a convicted murderer offered the alternative of life imprisonment in the shadow of the gallows, and the situation of the murderer contemplating his crime. The certainty of death is one thing; perhaps for normal people nothing can be compared with it. But the existence of the death penalty does not mean for the murderer *certainty* of death *now;* it means a not very high probability of death in the future. And futurity and uncertainty, the hope of an escape, rational or irrational, vastly diminishes the difference between death and imprisonment as deterrents, and may diminish it to vanishing point. And the hope of escape is not so very irrational even in America or in the best policed states. In England, if we compare the number of murders known to the police with the number of convictions and executions, the chance of conviction appears to be one in six, and the chance of execution one in twelve. If, however, we assume that the very large number of suspects who commit suicide would have been caught anyway, the chance of conviction increases to one in three, and of execution to one in six. It would, of course, be ridiculous to think that these figures are appreciated by potential murderers, but they do serve to show that the way in which a convicted murderer may view the immediate prospect of the gallows

[49]Stephen, "Capital Punishments," *Fraser's Magazine,* vol. 69 (1864), p. 753 (my italics), quoted in the *Royal Commission Report,* para. 57.

after he has been caught must be a poor guide to the effect of this prospect upon him when he is contemplating committing his crime.

But there is a more important reason why this insistence on the unique status of the fear of death as a motive helps us very little here. In all countries murder is committed to a very large extent either by persons who, though sane, do not in fact count the cost, or are so mentally deranged that they cannot count it. In all countries the proportion of "insane" murderers is very high, and in England and Wales in the fifty years from 1900 to 1949 the numbers of those who were charged with murder and found insane, by very stringent tests, exceeded the number of persons who were sentenced to death. In England, moreover, for every four murders known to the police approximately one suspect commits suicide, and it is likely that many of these suicides had made up their mind to die before they committed the crime.

For these reasons, many would not attach even as much weight as did the Royal Commission to what they term the common-sense argument from human nature. The Commission said:

> . . . Prima facie the penalty of death is likely to have a stronger effect as a deterrent to normal human beings than any other form of punishment, and there is some evidence (though no convincing statistical evidence) that this is in fact so. But this effect does not operate universally or uniformly, and there are many offenders on whom it is limited and may often be negligible. It is accordingly important to view this question in just perspective and not to base a penal policy in relation to murder on exaggerated estimates of the uniquely deterrent force of the death penalty.[50]

Certainly if as much weight as this is attached to the "common-sense" argument it is necessary to remember other aspects of the death penalty. One day, indeed, the still young sciences of psychology and sociology may confirm the speculation that the fear of death has the potency thus claimed for it, or perhaps that the death penalty has had some unique influence in building up and maintaining our moral attitude to murder. But we certainly cannot take this to be established, and those who base their advocacy of the death penalty on this rough "common-sense" psychology must seriously consider psychological theories that run in the other direction. For at present, theories that the death penalty may operate as a stimulant to murder, consciously or unconsciously, have some evidence behind them. The use of the death penalty by the state may lower, not sustain, the respect for life. Very large

[50] Royal Commission Report, para. 68.

279

numbers of murderers are mentally unstable, and in them at least the bare thought of execution, the drama and the notoriety of a trial, the gladiatorial element of the murderer fighting for his life, may operate as an attractive force, not as a repulsive one. There are actual cases of murder so motivated, and the psychological theories which draw upon them must be weighed against the theory that the use of the death penalty creates or sustains our inhibition against murder.

6

What, then, is the final upshot? My purpose has been to lay bare the known facts and relevant principles and not, of course, to press upon the reader the inferences which I would draw in considering the question of abolition or retention in England. I shall, however, add this very simple final consideration. If we adopt the kind of qualified utilitarian attitude toward punishment which appears to me to accord (as an unqualified utilitarianism does not) with the moral convictions which most of us share, then it is vital to consider where the onus of proof lies in this matter of the death penalty. Is it upon those who object to the death penalty to show positive evidence that it is socially useless, if not harmful? Or is it upon those who would retain it to show that it is socially beneficial? Three main factors made the death penalty and the mode of its use in England appear a *prima facie* evil and therefore only to be retained if there was some positive evidence that it was required in order to minimize murder, or because it served some other valuable purpose which other punishments could not serve. These factors were: (1) *prima facie* the taking of a life, even by the State, with its attendant suffering not only for the criminal but for many others, is an evil to be endured only for the sake of some good; (2) the death penalty is irrevocable and the risk of an innocent person being executed is never negligible;[51] and (3) the use of the death penalty in England was possible only at the cost of constant intervention by the Executive after the courts had tried

[51] For Parliamentary discussion of the possibility of mistake see 548 *H.C. Deb.* 2540–3, 2557–9, 2583, 2597–8 (1956). Mr. Chuter Ede who, as Home Secretary, had himself refused a reprieve in the well-known case of Timothy Evans, stated subsequently that he no longer thought that Evans was guilty. In arguing in the debate in February 1956, in favour of abolition, he claimed that if before Evans's execution evidence had been available which came to light after the execution, public opinion would not have allowed the execution to have taken place. This case and Mr. Ede's statement (since he had in 1948 as Home Secretary urged retention of the death penalty) must have weighed with many who voted for suspension. 548 *H.C. Deb.* 2558–9, 2583 (1956).

and sentenced the prisoner to death. Of course, it is possible that sincere and thoughtful men may differ in their moral estimation of these three factors. But the first two of these factors are as applicable in the United States as in England, and there is some analogy to the third factor in the possibility, inescapable in the United States, and sometimes realized, of long periods intervening between the sentence of death and its execution.

6

WAR

war and murder

g. e. m. anscombe

1. THE USE OF VIOLENCE BY RULERS

Since there are always thieves and frauds and men who commit violent attacks on their neighbours and murderers, and since without law backed by adequate force there are usually gangs of bandits; and since there are in most places laws administered by people who command violence to enforce the laws against lawbreakers; the question arises: what is a just attitude to this exercise of violent coercive power on the part of rulers and their subordinate officers?

Two attitudes are possible: one, that the world is an absolute jungle and that the exercise of coercive power by rulers is only a manifestation of this; and the other, that it is both necessary and right that there should be this exercise of power, that through it the world is much less of a jungle than it could possibly be without it, so that one should in principle be glad of the existence of such power, and only take exception to its unjust exercise.

It is so clear that the world is less of a jungle because of rulers and laws, and that the exercise of coercive power is essential to these institutions as they are now——all this is so obvious, that probably only Tennysonian conceptions of progress enable people who do not wish to separate themselves from the world to think that nevertheless such violence is objectionable, that some day, in this present dispensation, we shall do without it, and that the

From *Nuclear Weapons: A Catholic Response*, edited by Walter Stein, Copyright © 1961 by the Merlin Press Ltd., published by Sheed & Ward, Inc., New York.

pacifist is the man who sees and tries to follow the ideal course, which future civilization must one day pursue. It is an illusion, which would be fantastic if it were not so familiar.

In a peaceful and law abiding country such as England, it may not be immediately obvious that the rulers need to command violence to the point of fighting to the death those that would oppose it; but brief reflection shows that this is so. For those who oppose the force that backs law will not always stop short of fighting to the death and cannot always be put down short of fighting to the death.

Then only if it is in itself evil violently to coerce resistant wills, can the exercise of coercive power by rulers be bad as such. Against such a conception, if it were true, the necessity and advantage of the exercise of such power would indeed be a useless plea. But that conception is one that makes no sense unless it is accompanied by a theory of withdrawal from the world as man's only salvation; and it is in any case a false one. We are taught that God retains the evil will of the devil within limits by violence: we are not given a picture of God permitting to the devil all that he is capable of. There is current a conception of Christianity as having revealed that the defeat of evil must always be by pure love without coercion; this at least is shown to be false by the foregoing consideration. And without the alleged revelation there could be no reason to believe such a thing.

To think that society's coercive authority is evil is akin to thinking the flesh evil and family life evil. These things belong to the present constitution of mankind; and if the exercise of coercive power is a manifestation of evil, and not the just means of restraining it, then human nature is totally depraved in a manner never taught by Christianity. For society is essential to human good; and society without coercive power is generally impossible.

The same authority which puts down internal dissension, which promulgates laws and restrains those who break them if it can, must equally oppose external enemies. These do not merely comprise those who attack the borders of the people ruled by the authority; but also, for example, pirates and desert bandits, and, generally, those beyond the confines of the country ruled whose activities are viciously harmful to it. The Romans, once their rule in Gaul was established, were eminently justified in attacking Britain, where were nurtured the Druids whose pupils infested northern Gaul and whose practices struck the Romans themselves as "dira immanitas." Further, there being such a thing as the common good of mankind, and visible criminality against it, how can we doubt the excellence of such a proceeding as that violent suppression of the man-stealing business[1] which the British government took it into its head to engage in under Palmerston? The present-day conception of "aggression," like so many strongly influential conceptions, is a bad one. Why *must* it be wrong to strike the first blow in a struggle? The only question is, who is in the right.

Here, however, human pride, malice and cruelty are so usual that it is true to say that wars have mostly been mere wickedness on both sides. Just as an individual will constantly think himself in the right, whatever he does, and yet there is still such a thing as being in the right, so nations will constantly wrongly think themselves to be in the right—and yet there is still such a thing as their being in the right. Palmerston doubtless had no doubts in prosecuting the opium war against China, which was diabolical; just as he exulted in putting down the slavers. But there is no question but that he was a monster in the one thing, and a just man in the other.

The probability is that warfare is injustice, that a life of military service is a bad life "militia or rather malitia," as St. Anselm called it. This probability is greater than the probability (which also exists) that membership of a police force will involve malice, because of the character of warfare: the extraordinary occasions it offers for viciously unjust proceedings on the part of military commanders and warring governments, which at the time attract praise and not blame from their people. It is equally the case that the life of a ruler is usually a vicious life: but that does not show that ruling is as such a vicious activity.

The principal wickedness which is a temptation to those engaged in warfare is the killing of the innocent, which may often be done with impunity and even to the glory of those who do it. In many places and times it has been taken for granted as a natural part of waging war: the commander, and especially the conqueror, massacres people by the thousand, either because this is part of his glory, or as a terrorizing measure, or as part of his tactics.

2. INNOCENCE AND THE RIGHT TO KILL INTENTIONALLY

It is necessary to dwell on the notion of non-innocence here employed. Innocence is a legal notion; but here, the accused is not pronounced guilty under an existing code of law, under which he has been tried by an impartial judge, and therefore made the tar-

[1] It is ignorance to suppose that it takes modern liberalism to hate and condemn this. It is cursed and subject to the death penalty in the Mosaic law. Under that code, too, runaway slaves of all nations had asylum in Israel.

get of attack. There is hardly a possibility of this; for the administration of justice is something that takes place under the aegis of
a sovereign authority; but in warfare—or the putting down by
violence of civil disturbance—the sovereign authority is itself
engaged as a party to the dispute and is not subject to a further
earthly and temporal authority which can judge the issue and pro-
nounce against the accused. The stabler the society, the rarer it
will be for the sovereign authority to have to do anything but apprehend its internal enemy and have him tried; but even in the
stablest society there are occasions when the authority has to fight
its internal enemy to the point of killing, as happens in the struggle
with external belligerent forces in international warfare; and then
the characterization of its enemy as non-innocent has not been
ratified by legal process.

This, however, does not mean that the notion of innocence
fails in this situation. What is required, for the people attacked to
be non-innocent in the relevant sense, is that they should themselves be engaged in an objectively unjust proceeding which the
attacker has the right to make his concern; or—the commonest
case—should be unjustly attacking him. Then he can attack them
with a view to stopping them; and also their supply lines and armament factories. But people whose mere existence and activity
supporting existence by growing crops, making clothes, etc. constitute an impediment to him—such people are innocent and it is
murderous to attack them, or make them a target for an attack
which he judges will help him towards victory. For murder is the
deliberate killing of the innocent, whether for its own sake or as a
means to some further end.

The right to attack with a view to killing is something that belongs only to rulers and those whom they command to do it. I
have argued that it does belong to rulers precisely because of that
threat of violent coercion exercised by those in authority which is
essential to the existence of human societies. It ought not to be
pretended that rulers and their subordinates do not choose[2] the
killing of their enemies as a means, when it has come to fighting
in which they are determined to win and their enemies resist to
the point of killing: this holds even in internal disturbances.

When a private man struggles with an enemy he has no right
to aim to kill him, unless in the circumstances of the attack on him
he can be considered as endowed with the authority of the law

[2]The idea that they may lawfully do what they do, but should not *intend* the death
of those they attack, has been put forward and, when suitably expressed, may seem
high-minded. But someone who can fool himself into this twist of thought will
fool himself into justifying anything, however atrocious, by means of it.

and the struggle comes to that point. By a "private" man, I mean a man in a society; I am not speaking of men on their own, without government, in remote places; for such men are neither public servants nor "private." The plea of self-defence (or the defence of someone else) made by a private man who has killed someone else must in conscience—even if not in law—be a plea that the death of the other was not intended, but was a side effect of the measures taken to ward off the attack. To shoot to kill, to set lethal man-traps, or, say, to lay poison for someone from whom one's life is in danger, are forbidden. The deliberate choice of inflicting death in a struggle is the right only of ruling authorities and their subordinates.

In saying that a private man may not choose to kill, we are touching on the principle of "double effect." The denial of this has been the corruption of non-Catholic thought, and its abuse the corruption of Catholic thought. Both have disastrous consequences which we shall see. This principle is not accepted in English law: the law is said to allow no distinction between the foreseen and the intended consequences of an action. Thus, if I push a man over a cliff when he is menacing my life, his death is considered as intended by me, but the intention to be justifiable for the sake of self-defence. Yet the lawyers would hardly find the laying of poison tolerable as an act of self-defence, but only killing by a violent action in a moment of violence. Christian moral theologians have taught that even here one may not seek the death of the assailant, but may in default of other ways of self-defence use such violence as will in fact result in his death. The distinction is evidently a fine one in some cases: what, it may be asked, can the intention be, if it can be said to be absent in this case, except a mere wish or desire?

And yet in other cases the distinction is very clear. If I go to prison rather than perform some action, no reasonable person will call the incidental consequences of my refusal—the loss of my job, for example—intentional just because I knew they must happen. And in the case of the administration of a pain-relieving drug in mortal illness, where the doctor knows the drug may very well kill the patient if the illness does not do so first, the distinction is evident; the lack of it has led an English judge to talk nonsense about the administration of the drug's not having *really* been the cause of death in such a case, even though a post mortem shows it was. For everyone understands that it is a very different thing so to administer a drug, and to administer it with the intention of killing. However, the principle of double effect has more important applications in warfare, and I shall return to it later.

3. THE INFLUENCE OF PACIFISM

Pacifism has existed as a considerable movement in English speaking countries ever since the first world war. I take the doctrine of pacifism to be that it is *eo ipso* wrong to fight in wars, not the doctrine that it is wrong to be compelled to, or that any man, or some men, may refuse; and I think it false for the reasons that I have given. But I now want to consider the very remarkable effects it has had: for I believe its influence to have been enormous, far exceeding its influence on its own adherents.

We should note first that pacifism has as its background conscription and enforced military service for all men. Without conscription, pacifism is a private opinion that will keep those who hold it out of armies, which they are in any case not obliged to join. Now universal conscription, except for the most extraordinary reasons, i.e., as a regular habit among most nations, is such a horrid evil that the refusal of it automatically commands a certain amount of respect and sympathy.

We are not here concerned with the pacifism of some peculiar sect which in any case draws apart from the world to a certain extent, but with a pacifism of people in the world, who do not want to be withdrawn from it. For some of these, pacifism is prevented from being a merely theoretical attitude because they are liable to, and so are prepared to resist conscription; or are able directly to effect the attitude of some who are so liable.

A powerful ingredient in this pacifism is the prevailing image of Christianity. This image commands a sentimental respect among people who have no belief in Christianity, that is to say, in Christian dogmas; yet do have a certain belief in an ideal which they conceive to be part of "true Christianity." It is therefore important to understand this image of Christianity and to know how false it is. Such understanding is relevant, not merely to those who wish to believe Christianity, but to all who, without the least wish to believe, are yet profoundly influenced by this image of it.

According to this image, Christianity is an ideal and beautiful religion, impracticable except for a few rare characters. It preaches a God of love whom there is no reason to fear; it marks an escape from the conception presented in the Old Testament, of a vindictive and jealous God who will terribly punish his enemies. The "Christian" God is a *roi fainéant,* whose only triumph is in the Cross; his appeal is a goodness and unselfishness, and to follow him is to act according to the Sermon on the Mount — to turn the other cheek and to offer no resistance to evil. In this account some of the evangelical counsels are chosen as containing the whole of

Christian ethics: that is, they are made into precepts. (Only some of them; it is not likely that someone who deduces the *duty* of pacifism from the Sermon on the Mount and the rebuke to Peter, will agree to take "Give to him that asks of you" equally as a universally binding precept.)

The turning of counsels into precepts results in high-sounding principles. Principles that are mistakenly high and strict are a trap; they may easily lead in the end directly or indirectly to the justification of monstrous things. Thus if the evangelical counsel about poverty were turned into a precept forbidding property owning, people would pay lip service to it as the ideal, while in practice they went in for swindling. "Absolute honesty!" it would be said: "I can respect that—but of course that means having no property; and while I respect those who follow that course, I have to compromise with the sordid world myself." If then one must "compromise with evil" by owning property and engaging in trade, then the amount of swindling one does will depend on convenience. This imaginary case is paralleled by what is so commonly said: absolute pacifism is an ideal; unable to follow that, and committed to "compromise with evil," one must go the whole hog and wage war *à outrance.*

The truth about Christianity is that it is a severe and practicable religion, not a beautifully ideal but impracticable one. Its moral precepts (except for the stricter laws about marriage that Christ enacted, abrogating some of the permissions of the Old Law) are those of the Old Testament; and its God is the God of Israel.

It is ignorance of the New Testament that hides this from people. It is characteristic of pacifism to denigrate the Old Testament and exalt the New: something quite contrary to the teaching of the New Testament itself, which always looks back to and leans upon the Old. How typical it is that the words of Christ "You have heard it said, an eye for an eye and a tooth for a tooth, but I say to you . . ." are taken as a repudiation of the ethic of the Old Testament! People seldom look up the occurrence of this phrase in the juridical code of the Old Testament, where it belongs, and is the admirable principle of law for the punishment of certain crimes, such as procuring the wrongful punishment of another by perjury. People often enough *now* cite the phrase to justify private revenge; no doubt this was as often "heard said" when Christ spoke of it. But no justification for this exists in the personal ethic taught by the Old Testament. On the contrary. What do we find? "Seek no revenge," (Leviticus xix, 18), and "If you find your enemy's ox or ass going astray, take it back to him; if you see the ass of someone who hates you lying under his burden, and would forbear to help him: you must help him" (Exodus xxiii, 4–5). And "If your enemy is hungry, give him food, if thirsty, give him drink" (Proverbs xxv, 21).

This is only one example; given space, it would be easy to show how false is the conception of Christ's teaching as *correcting* the religion of the ancient Israelites, and substituting a higher and more "spiritual" religion for theirs. Now the false picture I have described plays an important part in the pacifist ethic and in the ethic of the many people who are not pacifists but are influenced by pacifism.

To extract a pacifist doctrine—i.e., a condemnation of the use of force by the ruling authorities, and of soldiering as a profession —from the evangelical counsels and the rebuke to Peter, is to disregard what else is in the New Testament. It is to forget St. John's direction to soldiers: "do not blackmail people; be content with your pay"; and Christ's commendation of the centurion, who compared his authority over his men to Christ's. On a pacifist view, this must be much as if a madam in a brothel had said: "I know what authority is, I tell this girl to do this, and she does it . . ." and Christ had commended her faith. A centurion was the first Gentile to be baptized; there is no suggestion in the New Testament that soldiering was regarded as incompatible with Christianity. The martyrology contains many names of soldiers whose occasion of martyrdom was not any objection to soldiering, but a refusal to perform idolatrous acts.

Now, it is one of the most vehement and repeated teachings of the Judaeo-Christian tradition that the shedding of innocent blood is forbidden by the divine law. No man may be punished except for his own crime, and those "whose feet are swift to shed innocent blood" are always represented as God's enemies.

For a long time the main outlines of this teaching have seemed to be merely obvious morality: hence, for example, I have read a passage by Ronald Knox complaining of the "endless moralizing," interspersed in records of meaness, cowardice, spite, cruelty, treachery and murder, which forms so much of the Old Testament. And indeed, that it is terrible to kill the innocent is very obvious; the morality that so stringently forbids it must make a great appeal to mankind, especially to the poor threatened victims. Why should it need the thunder of Sinai and the suffering and preaching of the prophets to promulgate such a law? But human pride and malice are everywhere so strong that now, with the fading of Christianity from the mind of the West, this morality once more stands out as a demand which strikes pride- and fear-ridden people as too intransigent. For Knox, it seemed so obvious as to be dull; and he failed to recognize the bloody and beastly records that it accompanies for the dry truthfulness about human beings that so characterizes the Old Testament.[3]

Now pacifism teaches people to make no distinction between the shedding of innocent blood and the shedding of any human blood. And in this way pacifism has corrupted enormous numbers of people who will not act according to its tenets. They become convinced that a number of things are wicked which are not; hence, seeing no way of avoiding "wickedness," they set no limits to it. How endlessly pacifists argue that all war must be *à outrance!* that those who wage war must go as far as technological advance permits in the destruction of the enemy's people. As if the Napoleonic wars were perforce fuller of massacres than the French war of Henry V of England. It is not true: the reverse took place. Nor is technological advance particularly relevant; it is mere squeamishness that deters people who would consent to area bombing from the enormous massacres *by hand* that used once to be committed.

The policy of obliterating cities was adopted by the Allies in the last war; they need not have taken that step, and it was taken largely out of a villainous hatred, and as corollary to the policy, now universally denigrated, of seeking "unconditional surrender." (That policy itself was visibly wicked, and could be and was judged so at the time; it is not surprising that it led to disastrous consequences, even if no one was clever and detached enough to foresee this at the time.)

Pacifism and the respect for pacifism is not the only thing that has led to a universal forgetfulness of the law against killing the innocent; but it has had a great share in it.

4. THE PRINCIPLE OF DOUBLE EFFECT

Catholics, however, can hardly avoid paying at least lip-service to that law. So we must ask: how is it that there has been so comparatively little conscience exercised on the subject among them? The answer is: double-think about double effect.

The distinction between the intended, and the merely foreseen, effects of a voluntary action is indeed absolutely essential to Christian ethics. For Christianity forbids a number of things as being bad in themselves. But if I am answerable for the foreseen consequences of an action or refusal, as much as for the action itself, then these prohibitions will break down. If someone inno-

[3]It is perhaps necessary to remark that I am not here adverting to the total extermination of certain named tribes of Canaan that is said by the Old Testament to have been commanded by God. That is something quite outside the provisions of the Mosaic Law for dealings in war.

cent will die unless I do a wicked thing, then on this view I am his murderer in refusing: so all that is left to me is to weigh up evils. Here the theologian steps in with the principle of double effect and says: "No, you are no murderer, if the man's death was neither your aim nor your chosen means, and if you had to act in the way that led to it or else do something absolutely forbidden." Without understanding of this principle, anything can be—and is wont to be—justified, and the Christian teaching that in no circumstances may one commit murder, adultery, apostasy (to give a few examples) goes by the board. These absolute prohibitions of Christianity by no means exhaust its ethic; there is a large area where what is just is determined partly by a prudent weighing up of consequences. But the prohibitions are bedrock, and without them the Christian ethic goes to pieces. Hence the necessity of the notion of double effect.

At the same time, the principle has been repeatedly abused from the seventeenth century up till now. The causes lie in the history of philosophy. From the seventeenth century till now what may be called Cartesian psychology has dominated the thought of philosophers and theologians. According to this psychology, an intention was an interior act of the mind which could be produced at will. Now if intention is all important—as it is—in determining the goodness or badness of an action, then, on this theory of what intention is, a marvellous way offered itself of making any action lawful. You only had to "direct your intention" in a suitable way. In practice, this means making a little speech to yourself: "What I mean to be doing is. . . ."

This perverse doctrine has occasioned repeated condemnations by the Holy See from the seventeenth century to the present day. Some examples will suffice to show how the thing goes. Typical doctrines from the seventeenth century were that it is all right for a servant to hold the ladder for his criminous master so long as he is merely avoiding the sack by doing so; or that a man might wish for and rejoice at his parent's death so long as what he had in mind was the gain to himself; or that it is not simony to offer money, not *as a price* for the spiritual benefit, but only *as an inducement* to give it. A condemned doctrine from the present day is that the practice of *coitus reservatus* is permissible; such a doctrine could only arise in connexion with that "direction of intention" which sets everything right no matter what one does. A man makes a practice of withdrawing, telling himself that he *intends* not to ejaculate; of course (if that is his practice) he usually does so, but then the event is "accidental" and *praeter intentionem:* it is, in short, a case of "double effect."

294

This same doctrine is used to prevent any doubts about the obliteration bombing of a city. The devout Catholic bomber secures by a "direction of intention" that any shedding of innocent blood that occurs is "accidental." I know a Catholic boy who was puzzled at being told by his schoolmaster that it was an *accident* that the people of Hiroshima and Nagasaki were there to be killed; in fact, however absurd it seems, such thoughts are common among priests who know that they are forbidden by the divine law to justify the direct killing of the innocent.

It is nonsense to pretend that you do not intend to do what is the means you take to your chosen end. Otherwise there is absolutely no substance to the Pauline teaching that we may not do evil that good may come.

5. SOME COMMONLY HEARD ARGUMENTS

There are a number of sophistical arguments, often or sometimes used on these topics, which need answering.

Where do you draw the line? As Dr. Johnson said, the fact of twilight does not mean you cannot tell day from night. There are borderline cases, where it is difficult to distinguish, in what is done, between means and what is incidental to, yet in the circumstances inseparable from, those means. The obliteration bombing of a city is not a borderline case.

The old "conditions for a just war" are irrelevant to the conditions of modern warfare, so that must be condemned out of hand. People who say this always envisage only major wars between the Great Powers, which Powers are indeed now "in blood stepp'd insofar" that it is unimaginable for there to be a war between them which is not a set of enormous massacres of civil populations. But these are not the only wars. Why is Finland so far free? At least partly because of the "posture of military preparedness" which, considering the character of the country, would have made subjugating the Finns a difficult and unrewarding task. The offensive of the Israelis against the Egyptians in 1956 involved no plan of making civil populations the target of military attack.

In a modern war the distinction between combatants and noncombatants is meaningless, so an attack on anyone on the enemy side is justified. This is pure nonsense, even in war, a very large number of the enemy population are just engaged in maintaining the life of the country, or the sick, or aged, or children.

It must be legitimate to maintain an opinion—viz. that the destruction of cities by bombing is lawful—if this is argued by competent theologians and the Holy See has not pronounced. The argument

295

from the silence of the Holy See has itself been condemned by the Holy See (Denzinger, 28th Edition, 1127). How could this be a sane doctrine in view of the endless twistiness of the human mind?

Whether a war is just or not is not for the private man to judge: he must obey his government. Sometimes, this may be, especially as far as concerns causes of war. But the individual who joins in destroying a city, like a Nazi massacring the inhabitants of a village, is too obviously marked out as an enemy of the human race, to shelter behind such a plea.

Finally, horrible as it is to have to notice this, we must notice that even the arguments about double effect—which at least show that a man is not willing openly to justify the killing of the innocent—are now beginning to look old-fashioned. Some Catholics are not scrupling to say that *anything* is justified in defence of the continued existence and liberty of the Church in the West. A terrible fear of communism drives people to say this sort of thing. "Our Lord told us to fear those who can destroy body and soul, not to fear the destruction of the body" was blasphemously said to a friend of mine; meaning: "so, we must fear Russian domination more than the destruction of people's bodies by obliteration bombing."

But whom did Our Lord tell us to fear, when he said: "I will tell you whom you shall fear" and "Fear not them that can destroy the body, but fear him who can destroy body and soul in hell"? He told us to fear God the Father, who can and will destroy the unrepentant disobedient, body and soul, in hell.

A Catholic who is tempted to think on the lines I have described should remember that the Church is the spiritual Israel: that is, that Catholics are what the ancient Jews were, salt for the earth and the people of God—and that what was true of some devout Jews of ancient times can equally well be true of us now: "You compass land and sea to make a convert, and when you have done so, you make him twice as much a child of hell as yourselves." Do Catholics sometimes think that they are immune from such a possibility? That the Pharisees—who sat in the seat of Moses and who were so zealous for the true religion—were bad in ways in which we cannot be bad if we are zealous? I believe they do. But our faith teaches no such immunity, it teaches the opposite. "We are in danger all our lives long." So we have to fear God and keep his commandments, and calculate what is for the best only within the limits of that obedience, knowing that the future is in God's power and that no one can snatch away those whom the Father has given to Christ.

It is not a vague faith in the triumph of "the spirit" over force (there is little enough warrant for that), but a definite faith in the divine promises, that makes us believe that the Church cannot fail. Those, therefore, who think they must be prepared to wage war with Russia involving the deliberate massacre of cities, must be prepared to say to God: "We had to break your law, lest your Church fail. We could not obey your commandments, for we did not believe your promises."

on the morality of war: a preliminary inquiry

richard wasserstrom

Americans—at least those who are not pacifists—have had the good fortune of not having had to worry very much until recently about the subject of the morality of war. Although the United States was involved in several major wars in this century, and although these wars were not by any means free of problems of morality, still the morality of the cause and the immorality of the opponents encouraged Americans to accept quite complacently the rightness of American behavior. Two things changed all of this. Atomic and hydrogen bombs increased the stakes of war enormously; the destruction of mankind is a consequence different in kind, not degree. And the Vietnam war, although commendable for little else, did succeed in making relevant and meaningful to all reflective persons the question of by what criteria wars are *really* to be assessed. For myself, at least, it is the present war

From Richard Wasserstrom, "On the Morality of War: A Preliminary Inquiry," *Stanford Law Review*, vol. 21 (1969), pp. 1627–1656 (the entire article unabridged). Copyright 1969 by the Board of Trustees of the Leland Stanford Junior University. By permission of the author and the publisher.

*An earlier version of one portion of this article was read at the Eastern Division meeting of the American Philosophical Association in December 1968 and was published under the title "Three Arguments Concerning the Morality of War," in 65 *Journal of Philosophy* 578 (1968). The commentators were Professors Gideon Gottlieb and Jerome Schneewind. The comments of both were helpful, Professor Schneewind's especially so in respect to several of the themes discussed in the first section of this article.

that has led me to consider and to attempt to unravel what I have found to be extraordinarily difficult issues relating to the morality of war.

Yet, while the war in Vietnam is the occasion for this inquiry, it is not the subject of the inquiry. I have purposely, to the extent to which it is possible to do so, tried to exclude that war and my views about it from consideration. I have instead endeavored to identify a number of the issues that are raised by a discussion of any war, and to analyze and assess a number of the problems that intrude upon any rational consideration of the topic. The major focus is upon several arguments concerning the morality of war, chiefly the argument that any war is immoral if it involves the intentional killing of innocent persons, and the argument that any war is immoral because it involves the use of deadly force. But this Article is also concerned, in a quite general way, with elucidating and evaluating several of the different perspectives from which war can be morally assessed. In preparation for those discussions it deals with some preliminary but significant problems of definition and analysis.

A number of problems have been omitted, including some that are particularly acute today in the United States: those that relate to the obligations and rights of a citizen when his country is at war. Thus, this inquiry is not directed to a consideration of the duty, if any, to resist an immoral war or to the right to be free of certain obligations to one's country, even in time of war. Nor, to take a related issue, is it addressed directly to the liabilities and duties of those engaged in war—the duty, if any, to refrain from committing certain acts, even in time of war and even if ordered to do them. These are large and important issues. They are not taken up only because the matters that are discussed require considerable analysis and are in some respects at least preliminary to them.

1

The issues dealt with are numerous, complicated, and, most significantly, relatively unattended to by philosophers. The subject of war has, in fact, quite clearly been slighted in two respects— war has not been the subject of extensive, serious, and critical inquiry within the academy, and such inquiry as has been undertaken has not benefited from the kinds of clarifying and critical examination—the narrowing of issues and the defining of terms —that are the peculiar province of the philosopher. There are at least two important areas in which the consequences of philosophical abstention are readily observable.

Consider first the discussions and arguments that typically take place today concerning the morality of war. Someone will insist that all war is immoral; another that it is immoral or unjust for us to be fighting in Vietnam; still a third that there is nothing immoral about the war, as long as it is not a war of aggression. It is not clear, however, that these claims are sufficiently unambiguous to be dealt with sensibly. They may even be consistent. They must be broken down into several more specific claims before truly informed discussion can proceed.

There are, I think, at least three sets of questions that deserve to be distinguished and kept straight in discussions of the morality of war, even though they often are not. The first relates to the behavior of countries as opposed to persons. When we talk about the morality of war we sometimes appear to be assessing the intentions and behavior of persons and sometimes the intentions and conduct of countries. But are countries assessable on moral grounds in the same way and for the same reasons that persons are? The second concerns the rightness or wrongness of an action when contrasted with the praise or blame attendant upon it. Someone can do the wrong thing, and nonetheless be free of blame. When we talk about the morality of war, are the relevant categories those of rightness–wrongness or those of praiseworthiness–blameworthiness, or both? The third involves the difference between particular acts, particular wars, and war as an institution. We can evaluate the morality of individual actions leading up to or taking place within a war;[1] we can evaluate the morality of a particular war; and we can assess the morality of war as a human phenomenon. Although the symmetry is, perhaps, imperfect, the differences seem no less significant than those between an individual law, a particular legal system, and the idea of a legal system.

A more serious omission relates to the most typical of all philosophical issues—that of definition. There is a lot of talk about war, but what do we mean when we say of something that it is a war? It is neither idle philosophical curiosity nor ingrained philosophical habit that requires that some attention be given at the beginning to analytical considerations. Rather, it is important

[1]Actually, the issues are a good deal more complex than this. Consider, for example, the different things that might count as individual actions: (a) the action of an individual occurring at a particular time and place (for instance, an ordinary foot soldier shooting and killing an unarmed prisoner although he has not been ordered to do so); (b) the action of an individual who orders others to do something (for instance, a battalion commander orders his men to shoot and kill the prisoners they have taken); (c) the action of a group of persons acting collectively (for instance, a bomber squadron dropping incendiary bombs in a particular raid on a particular city); and (d) various kinds of continuing actions by persons or groups (such as commanding a particular campaign or fighting a particular campaign).

that analysis be undertaken here, as elsewhere, because a great deal can turn on what the subject under investigation is taken to be. It is not simply that we need common agreement as to the nature of the subject under investigation—although that is an important enough goal. It is, instead, that we must make certain that we do not surreptitiously, and hence uncritically, resolve important substantive issues via the definitional route.

The danger of defining away important problems is illustrated first with one example not connected with war, and then with several taken from the literature on war. The non–war-related example comes from a quite well-known article by the philosopher Anthony Quinton entitled, "On Punishment."[2] In his piece Quinton deals with one of the issues that has floated through the philosophical literature on punishment for quite some time: the so-called problem of the punishment of the innocent. Without going into any unnecessary details, the problem is this. It is thought by some to count as a decisive objection to utilitarianism that it would permit, if not require, the punishment of persons known to be innocent if the consequences of punishing them proved to be more desirable than those of any alternative course of conduct.

For my purposes it is not important to try to assess the merits of this particular philosophical claim. What is of interest is the way Quinton deals with it. He says this:

> For the necessity of not punishing the innocent is not moral but logical. It is not, as some retributivists think, that we *may* not punish the innocent and *ought* only to punish the guilty, but that we *cannot* punish the innocent and *must* only punish the guilty. Of course, the suffering or harm in which punishment consists can be and is inflicted on innocent people, but this is not punishment; it is judicial error or terrorism or, in Bradley's characteristically repellent phrase, "social surgery." The infliction of suffering on a person is only properly described as punishment if that person is guilty.[3]

Now, there are at least two criticisms that might be made of this account. First, it might be said that Quinton has simply erred in describing the nature of punishment. The guilt or innocence of the person punished — or even the believed guilt or innocence of the person punished — is not an important or central feature of all typical cases of punishment.[4]

[2]Quinton, "On Punishment," *Philosophy, Politics and Society* 83 (1st series P. Laslett ed. 1956).
[3]Id. at 86.
[4]It is not an easy question how we would or should decide this matter. Up to a point, though, there surely are arguments that can be given and evidence that can be offered in support of the truth or falsity of Quinton's claim. Beyond a certain point, or in certain contexts, there is nothing to be said other than to understand

Second, and more importantly, even if it were to be concluded that, within limits, Quinton is entitled to define "punishment" as he pleases, it would still be necessary to see whether major and problematic substantive issues had thereby been covertly resolved. Even if Quinton is right that punishing the innocent is not punishment, he has not at all succeeded in answering the question whether it is right intentionally to do to innocent persons the sorts of things that utilitarianism appears to permit and perhaps require. Yet his argument can be read as an invitation to regard the substantive moral issues as now resolved.[5]

Similar possibilities for this kind of confusion abound in the literature dealing with war. In particular, when the topic is the assessment of the morality of war, or participation in a particular war, it is easy to see how what is taken to be the typical or standard example of war may have a very great impact on the moral evaluation that is to follow. Thus, when a seventeenth-century writer says of war that it is "a just contest carried on by the state's armed forces"[6] he has already gone a long way toward judging the rightness of war. Indeed, it is not surprising that within the tradition that does assert the morality of some wars and some participation in wars, one approach that is adopted is to exclude from the very meaning of war precisely those cases that are hardest to justify.

So, John Ruskin in his essay "War" makes what appears at first glance to be a truly startling claim.[7] "War," he asserts, "is the foundation of all great art."[8] The history of western civilization, Ruskin says, is unambiguous on this score. Art reached its highest point with the Gothic period because of that era's "passionate delight in war itself, for the sake of war."[9] Then, the decline set in.

[A]s peace is established or extended in Europe, the arts decline. They reach an unparalleled pitch of costliness, but lose their life, enlist themselves at last on the side of luxury and various corruption, and among wholly tranquil nations, wither utterly away; remaining

---

what is meant by Quinton when he uses the term "punishment." See H. L. A. Hart, "Prolegomenon to the Principles of Punishment," in *Punishment and Responsibility* (1968). On the general question of resolving substantive issues via the definitional process see Morris, "Verbal Disputes and the Philosophy of John Austin," 7 *U.C.L.A.L.* Rev. 27 (1960).

[5] For criticisms of Quinton on just this point see Kaufman, "Anthony Quinton on Punishment," 20 *Analysis* 10 (1959).

[6] A. Gentili, *On the Law of War*, quoted in D. Wells, *The War Myth*, 25 (1967).

[7] Ruskin, "War," *The Crown of Wild Olive* (1866), reprinted in *Man and Warfare*, 35, 36–61 (W. Irmscher ed. 1964).

[8] Id. at 37.

[9] Id. at 39.

only in partial practice among races who, like the French and us, have still the minds, though we cannot all live the lives, of soldiers.[10]

This is surely a provocative thesis. However, Ruskin renders it substantially less unsettling than it first appears to be, by acknowledging the troublesome cases and admitting that for these particular kinds of war his generalization does not apply. So, immediately after he reports that all great nations are "nourished in war, and wasted by peace,"[11] he goes on to note that

It is not *all* war of which this can be said. . . . It is not the rage of a barbarian wolf-flock, . . . nor the habitual restlessness and rapine of mountaineers, . . . nor the occasional struggle of a strong peaceful nation for its life, as in the wars of the Swiss with Austria; nor the contest of merely ambitious nations for extent of power. . . . None of these forms of war build anything but tombs.[12]

An interesting example of this definitional problem and a more contemporary one is the argument advanced by Paul Ramsey, the Protestant theologian, in his book, *War and the Christian Conscience*.[13] Ramsey's general thesis is that war can be moral, that it is sometimes right to wage war, and that all arguments to the contrary are unconvincing. The most difficult argument for Ramsey, because it is one of the strongest against his position, is that the development of atomic and hydrogen bombs has made the stakes too high. The risks of total annihilation are so great, the argument goes, that no war can today be morally justified. Although this is an important thesis, for present purposes what is of interest is not its persuasiveness but rather one of the ways Ramsey selects to deal with it. What he says is this:

It seems to me that an answer to this question is to be found in the fact that megaton weapons are no longer weapons *of war*, and that their all-out use would not be war. . . . It is right that the enemy be made to realize that he will have to exceed the limits of warfare to gain his ends, that he will have to destroy utterly where he thought to conquer and to bend. Then only will he be deterred from using a weapon that is not a weapon of war.[14]

Were substantial quantities of nuclear weapons used against each other by the opponents in an international conflict today, that

[10]Id.
[11]Id. at 40.
[12]Id.
[13]P. Ramsey, *War and the Christian Conscience* (1961).
[14]Id. at 167–168.

303

would not, Ramsey insists, be war at all. It would instead be "mutual devastation."[15]

This approach is, I believe, strikingly similar to Quinton's, and the risks are equally great. In part the problem is once again that the analysis just seems incorrect. Our sense of what it is that makes something a war does not readily rule anything out on the grounds that the weaponry employed is *too destructive*. But here, just as in the case of Quinton, there will be a point at which continued disagreement and argument concerning the correct analysis of *war* will be neither particularly productive nor important.

The danger of Ramsey's approach is not so much that he has got the nature of war wrong, as that he will lead us to neglect what may be the central concern of many of those who are most worried about the possibility of war today. What Ramsey has not resolved, of course, is the problem of the morality of nuclear conflict and of the widespread use of nuclear devices. And yet he gives the appearance of having done so by tacitly if not expressly assuring us that in considering the morality of war we need not worry about mutual thermonuclear destruction. To be completely fair to Ramsey, though, it may be that he means to argue that all nuclear conflict must be immoral. If so, he makes the point somewhat elliptically.

It is important, therefore, for reasons that transcend mere philosophical curiosity, that we do say something more precise about the nature of war. Typically, if not necessarily, war is an international phenomenon involving the use of a certain amount of deadly force under a claim of right. Typically, too, the analysis of what constitutes a war may rest on the analyst's choice between war as a highly refined and rule-encompassed, game-like activity and war as an all-out attempt by one country to dominate another. The manner in which these abstract features manifest themselves in any particular war will play a significant role in the moral assessment made of that war.

In the first place, war is something that takes place between countries, nation-states, rather than lesser groups or individuals. Private wars, if there still are any, are anomalies, and wars against poverty or disease are such only in a secondary or metaphorical sense. Civil wars and some private wars that have taken place (as, for example, in China) are neither metaphors nor anomalies. Rather, they are enough like the standard case of war to make it appropriate so to describe them.

Thus, in most if not all civil wars what is at issue is a claim that what has hitherto been one country is more properly two. If this

[15]Id.

is correct, then civil wars are different in just this respect from other kinds of internal strife, which are seldom even called wars, such as insurrections (where there is opposition to the enforcement of laws but no strong demand for rival nationhood) or revolutions (where it is assumed that there is one country and the fight is over who shall govern it and how it shall be organized).

The second significant characteristic, and perhaps the most essential and distinctive one of all, is that wars almost surely involve the use of a variety of forms of violence under a claim of right. The same actions would in almost any other context be regarded as the most reprehensible and immoral of acts. More specifically it is, I think, a minimal, necessary attribute of war that it involve a specialized group of persons—an army of some kind —and that persons making up this group must be *prepared to kill* the soldiers of the opposing army. They may perhaps be prepared to kill others besides soldiers of the opposing army, but for the moment, we are speaking of a minimal condition. If these persons were not prepared both to use deadly force and to regard its use as appropriate in a variety of contexts, we would certainly be in doubt as to whether what was going on was a war.[16]

This, it should be noted, is certainly not Ramsey's view, alluded to earlier, that if certain forms of mass destruction are used against everyone, what is happening is no longer a war. Nor is it identical with the view that war implies being prepared to do anything and everything that may be deemed helpful to achieve victory.[17] It is instead a necessary feature of war.

The third and final characteristic is not really one feature but rather a choice between two different ones. For it is clear, I think, that in any discussion of the nature of war reference must at some time be made to two distinct conceptions of war. Under one conception war is a circumscribed, clearly definable instrument of foreign policy; under the other conception, war is some indeterminate, indefinable, and unlimited fight or struggle between countries. In a real sense the concept of war is systematically

[16]This is very different from a general preparedness to use deadly force in defense of oneself; for what is distinctive about preparedness in war is that the use of deadly force is deemed appropriate in any number of contexts in which classical self-defense doctrines would not obtain. Thus, once a war is under way, it is perfectly justifiable, at a minimum, to kill any and all enemy combatants (although only with certain weapons, up to the moment they offer to surrender and even though they pose no direct or even serious threat to the lives of the soldiers on the other side. This surely distinguishes war from every other human practice and institution except possibly human slavery.

[17]As a practical matter, of course, in most wars the accepted norms in respect to justifiable violence are at least this permissive, and the criterion of *helpfulness* is often given such an extended meaning that almost no conduct is clearly impermissible if it succeeds.

ambiguous since it can and does simultaneously involve these two very different notions. Quite often both of these conceptions are invoked by the same author at the same time, without any awareness of what is happening. One example of this can be found in the work of the famous German writer on war, Clausewitz.

The first thing that we must do, Clausewitz tells us, is to define war:

> We shall not begin with a pedantic definition, but confine ourselves to war's essence: the duel. War is nothing but a duel on a larger scale. . . . Each [side] seeks by physical force to overthrow the other, render him incapable of further resistance, and compel his opponent to do his will. . . . War is an act of force, and there is no limit to the application of that force. . . . Thus there can be wars of all degrees of importance and energy, from a war of extermination down to a mere state of armed observation.[18]

On the surface, at least, this is surely a muddled view. It is hard to imagine a more fully rule-governed, rule-defined, stylized way of fighting than a duel. If war is a duel writ large, then war is a sort of game. *War* is one means—that of combat between competing armies—to decide which of two or more contesting countries shall win a particular dispute. When one side wins, this settles the dispute in the winner's favor and the war is over.

Three things are important about this concept of war. First, it is an encounter that directly involves only armies. Second, it is conducted in accordance with reasonably well-defined and generally accepted rules that determine *how* the "game" of war is to be played. And third, it is conducted in accordance with less well-articulated but nonetheless identifiable rules or standards concerning *when* it is appropriate to engage in war.

Illustrations of the formal rules relating to how a war is to be fought are plentiful. Two of the most famous are the Hague Convention Number 4 of 1907[19] and the Geneva Convention of 1929.[20] These prohibit such things as the inhumane treatment of prisoners of war, the employment of poisoned weapons, and the improper use of flags of truce.[21]

---

[18]Von Clausewitz, *On War*, in *War, Politics, and Power*, 63–72 (E. Collins ed. 1962).
[19]Convention Respecting the Laws and Customs of War on Land, Feb. 23, 1909, 36 Stat. 2277, reprinted in 2 W. Malloy, *Treaties, Conventions, International Acts, Protocol and Agreements Between the United States and Other Powers 1776–1909*, at 2269 (1910).
[20]Prisoners of War, Convention with Other Powers, Jan. 16, 1932, 47 Stat. 2021, T.S. No. 846; Amelioration of the Condition of the Wounded and the Sick of Armies in the Field (Red Cross Convention), Convention with Other Powers, Jan. 16, 1932, 47 Stat. 2021, T.S. No. 847.
[21]See sources cited in note 20 *supra;* Annex to the Convention Respecting the Laws

Illustrations of rules that relate to the conditions under which war can be undertaken can also be found. One example is found in article I of the Hague Convention Number 3 of 1907. It provides: "The Contracting Powers recognize that hostilities between them must not commence without a previous and explicit warning, in the form of either a reasoned declaration of war or of an ultimatum with a conditional declaration of war."[22]

An extreme example of this kind of rule is found in the Kellogg-Briand Peace Pact of 1928,[23] which appears to rule out resort to war at all, at least for the settlement of disputes or as an instrument of national policy. The language of the Pact is:

Article I
The High Contracting Parties solemnly declare in the names of their respective peoples that they condemn recourse to war for the solution of international controversies, and renounce it as an instrument of national policy in their relations with one another.

Article II
The High Contracting Parties agree that the settlement or solution of all disputes or conflicts of whatever nature or whatever origin they may be, which may arise among them, shall never be sought except by pacific means.[24]

On this view, then, war is a reasonably carefully defined and circumscribed kind of combative activity that one country can carry on in respect to one or more other countries. The circumstances under which war can properly be engaged in and the ways in which it may be carried on are both subject to identifiable rules, standards, and agreements of various sorts.

It is not as easy to describe the other concept of war found both in Clausewitz and in history. One example is, no doubt, Nazi Germany. The Nazi leaders expressly repudiated the notion of "chivalrous warfare," and, in the words of the Nuremberg Tribunal, embraced in full that "conception of 'total war' with which aggressive wars were waged."

[I]n this conception of "total war" the moral ideas underlying the conventions which seek to make war more humane are no longer regarded as having force or validity. Everything is made subordi-

---

and Customs of War on Land, Feb. 23, 1909, art. XXIII, 36 Stat. 2277, reprinted in 2 W. Malloy, *supra*, note 19, at 2269, 2285; 2 W. Malloy, *supra* note 19, at 2282–2287.
[22]Convention Relative to the Opening of Hostilities, Feb. 23, 1909, 36 Stat. 2259, reprinted in 2 W. Malloy, *supra*, note 19, at 2259.
[23]Treaty with Other Powers Providing for the Renunciation of War as an Instrument of National Policy, Aug. 27, 1928, 46 Stat. 2343, T.S. No. 796.
[24]Id.

nate to the overmastering dictates of war. Rules, regulations, assurances, and treaties, all alike, are of no moment; and so, freed from the restraining influence of international law, the aggressive war is conducted by the Nazi leaders in the most barbaric way. Accordingly, war crimes were committed when and wherever the Fuehrer and his close associates thought them to be advantageous.[25]

If Nazi Germany constitutes a kind of paradigm case, the behavior of all of the countries involved in the Second World War appears to have come very close to embracing this concept of war. Even the United States apparently chose to ignore many if not all of the laws of war that it seemed imprudent to follow, on the grounds that being involved in a fight to the finish with the Axis powers, there was no behavior that could properly be ruled out except on strategic grounds.[26]

Even if the moral difference that separates these two notions of war and the attitudes, conceptions, and the like that accompany them is by no means certain, it is clear that if a war were actually to be fought according to all of the rules and standards of the "game" of war, the task of moral assessment would necessarily be different from that presented by a relatively ruleless war like World War II. It is important, therefore, that, whenever relevant, we keep these two conceptions distinct.

2

Before we examine the moral criteria for assessing war, we must examine the claim that it is not possible to assess war in moral terms. Proponents of this position assert that moral predicates either cannot meaningfully or should not be applied to wars. For want of a better name for this general view, I shall call it moral nihilism in respect to war. If it is correct, there is, of course, no point in going further.

It is apparent that anyone who believes that all moral predicates are meaningless, or that all morality (and not just conventional morality) is a sham and a fraud, will regard the case of the morality of war as an a fortiori case. This is not the position I am

[25]Opinion and Judgment of the Nuremberg Tribunal 56–57 (1947), reprinted in 41 *Am. J. Int. L.* 172 (1947).
[26]The clearest examples are the saturation bombings of the cities of Europe and the dropping of the two atomic bombs on Japan.
    Given the fact that atomic and hydrogen bombing is not clearly proscribed by these "laws," it is certainly questionable whether they really do preclude any very significant behavior at all. For a general discussion of this point see Lewy, "Superior Orders, Nuclear Warfare, and the Dictates of Conscience: The Dilemma of Military Obedience in the Atomic Age," 55 *Am. Pol. Sci. Rev.* 3 (1961).

interested in considering. Rather the view I call moral nihilism in respect to war is, I think, more interesting in the sense that it is restricted to the case of war. What I have in mind is this: During the controversy over the rightness of the Vietnam War there have been any number of persons, including a large number in the university, who have claimed that in matters of war (but not in other matters) morality has no place. The war in Vietnam may, they readily concede, be stupid, unwise, or against the best interests of the United States, but it is neither immoral nor unjust—not because it is moral or right, but because these descriptions are *in this context* either naive or meaningless or inapplicable.

Nor is this view limited to the Vietnam war. Consider, for instance, the following passage from a speech given only a few years ago by Dean Acheson:

> [T]hose involved in the Cuban crisis of October, 1962, will remember the irrelevance of the supposed moral considerations brought out in the discussions. Judgment centered about the appraisal of dangers and risks, the weighing of the need for decisive and effective action against considerations of prudence; the need to do enough, against the consequences of doing too much. Moral talk did not bear on the problem. Nor did it bear upon the decision of those called upon to advise the President in 1949 whether and with what degree of urgency to press the attempt to produce a thermonuclear weapon. A respected colleague advised me that it would be better that our nation and people should perish rather than be party to a course so evil as producing that weapon. I told him that on the Day of Judgment his view might be confirmed and that he was free to go forth and preach the necessity for salvation. It was not, however, a view which I could entertain as a public servant.[27]

Admittedly, the passage just reproduced is susceptible of different interpretations. Acheson may be putting forward the view that even if moral evaluation is relevant to the "ends" pursued by any country (including our own) it is not relevant to the policies adopted in furtherance of these ends. But at times, at least, he appears to expound a quite different view, namely, that in the realm of foreign affairs moral judgments, as opposed to strategic or prudential ones, are simply misplaced and any attempts at moral assessment misdirected.

Whatever may be the correct exegesis of this text, I want to treat it as illustrative of the position that morality has no place in

[27]Acheson, "Ethics in International Relations Today," in *The Vietnam Reader*, 13 (M. Raskin and B. Fall eds., 1965).

the assessment of war.[28] There are several things worth considering in respect to such a view. In the first place, the claim that in matters of war morality has no place is ambiguous. To put it somewhat loosely, the claim may be descriptive, or it may be analytic, or it may be prescriptive. Thus, it would be descriptive if it were merely the factual claim that matters relating to war uniformly turn out to be decided on grounds of national interest or expediency rather than by appeal to what is moral.[29] This claim I will not consider further; it is an empirical one better answered by students of American (and foreign) diplomatic relations.

It would be a prescriptive claim were it taken to assert that matters relating to war ought always be decided by appeal to (say) national interest rather than an appeal to the moral point of view. For reasons which have yet to be elucidated, on this view the moral criteria are capable of being employed but it is undesirable to do so. I shall say something more about this view in a moment.[30]

The analytic point is not that morality ought not be used, but rather that it cannot. On this view the statement "The United States is behaving immorally in the way it is waging war in Vietnam" (or, "in waging war in Vietnam") is not wrong but meaningless.

What are we to make of the analytic view? As I have indicated, it could, of course, be advanced simply as an instance of a more sweeping position concerning the general meaninglessness of the moral point of view. What I find particularly interesting, though, is the degree to which this thesis is advanced as a special view about war and not as a part of a more general claim that all morality is meaningless.[31]

I think that there are at least four reasons why this special view may be held. First, the accusation that one's own country is involved in an immoral war is personally very threatening. For one thing, if the accusation is well-founded it may be thought to imply that certain types of socially cooperative behavior are forbidden to the citizen and that other kinds of socially deviant behavior are obligatory upon him. Yet, in a time of war it is following just this sort of dictate that will be treated most harshly by the actor's own government. Hence the morally responsible citizen is put in a most troublesome moral dilemma. If his country is engaged in an im-

[28]Acheson's view is admittedly somewhat broader than this since it appears to encompass all foreign relations.
[29]Such a view could also hold, although it need not, that it would be desirable for matters relating to war to be determined on moral grounds, even though they are not.
[30]See notes 36–38 *infra* and accompanying text.
[31]Much of this analysis applies with equal force to what I call the prescriptive view, which is discussed more fully at notes 36–38 *infra* and accompanying text. Although I refer only to the analytic view, I mean to include them both where appropriate.

Richard Wasserstrom

moral war then he may have a duty to oppose and resist; yet opposition and resistance will typically carry extraordinarily severe penalties.

The pressure is, I suspect, simply too great for many of us. We are unwilling to pay the fantastically high personal price that goes with the moral point of view, and we are equally unwilling to plead guilty to this most serious charge of immorality. So we solve the problem by denying the possibility that war can be immoral. The relief is immediate; the moral "heat" is off. If war cannot be immoral, then one's country cannot be engaged in an immoral war, but only a stupid or unwise one. And whatever one's obligations to keep one's country from behaving stupidly or improvidently, they are vastly less stringent and troublesome than obligations imposed by the specter of complicity in an immoral war. We may, however, pay a price for such relief since we obliterate the moral distinctions between the Axis and the Allies in World War II at the same time as the distinctions between the conduct of the United States in 1941–1945 and the conduct of the United States in 1967–1968 in Vietnam.

Second, I think the view that moral judgments are meaningless sometimes seems plausible because of the differences between personal behavior and the behavior of states. There are not laws governing the behavior of states in the same way in which there are positive laws governing the behavior of citizens. International law is a troublesome notion just because it is both like and unlike our concept of positive law.

Now, how does skepticism about the law-like quality of international law lead to the claim that it is impossible for war to be either moral or immoral? It is far from obvious. Perhaps it is because there is at least one sense of justice that is intimately bound up with the notion of rule-violation; namely, that which relates justice to the following of rules and to the condemnation and punishment of those who break rules. In the absence of positive laws governing the behavior of states, it may be inferred (although I think mistakenly) that it is impossible for states to behave either justly or unjustly.[32] But even if justice can be said to be analyzable solely in terms of following rules, morality certainly cannot. Hence the absence of international laws cannot serve to make the moral appraisal of war impossible.

[32]It is a mistake just because justice is not analyzable solely in terms of rule-following and rule-violating behavior.

One of the genuine puzzles in this whole area is why there is so much talk about *just* and *unjust* wars. Except in this very limited context of the relationship of justice to rules, it appears that the predicates "just" and "unjust" when applied to wars are synonymous with "moral" and "immoral."

311

Third, there is the substantially more plausible view that, in absence of positive laws *and* in the absence of any machinery by which to punish even the grossest kinds of immorality, an adequate excuse will always exist for behaving immorally. This is one way to take Hobbes' assertion that in the state of nature the natural laws bind in conscience but not in action. Even this view, however, would not render the moral assessment of the behavior of states meaningless; it would only excuse immorality in the absence of effective international law. More importantly, though, it, too, misstates the general understanding of morality in its insistence that morality depends for its *meaning* on the existence of guarantees of moral conformity by others.

Fourth, and still more plausible, is the view that says there can be no moral assessment of war just because there is, by definition, no morality in war. If war is an activity in which anything goes, moral judgments on war are just not possible.

To this there are two responses. To begin with, it is not, as our definitional discussion indicates, a necessary feature of war that it be an activity in which everything is morally permissible. There is a difference between the view that war is unique because killing and violence are morally permissible in contexts and circumstances where they otherwise would not be and the view that war is unique because everything is morally permissible.[33]

A less absolutist argument for the absurdity of discussing the morality of war might be that at least today the prevailing (although not necessary) conception of war is one that as a practical matter rules out no behavior on moral grounds. After all, if flamethrowers are deemed perfectly permissible, if the bombing of cities is applauded and not condemned, and if thermonuclear weapons are part of the arsenal of each of the major powers, then the remaining moral prohibitions on the conduct of war are sufficiently insignificant to be ignored.

The answer to this kind of an argument requires, I believe, that we distinguish the question of what is moral in war from that of the morality of war or of war generally. I return to this distinction later,[34] but for the present it is sufficient to observe that the argument presented only goes to the question of whether moral judgment can meaningfully be made concerning the *way* in which war is conducted. Paradoxically, the more convincing the argument from war's conduct, the stronger is the moral argument *against* engaging in war at all. For the more it can be shown that engaging in war will inevitably lead to despicable behavior to which no

[33]See notes 16–17 *supra* and accompanying text.
[34]See notes 39–46 *infra* and accompanying text.

moral predicates are deemed applicable, the more this also constitutes an argument against bringing such a state of affairs into
being.[35]

There is still another way to take the claim that in matters of
war morality has no place. That is what I have called the prescriptive view: that national interest ought to determine policies in respect to war, not morality. This is surely one way to interpret the
remarks of Dean Acheson reproduced earlier. It is also, perhaps,
involved in President Truman's defense of the dropping of the
atomic bomb on Hiroshima. What he said was this:

> Having found the bomb, we have to use it. We have used it against
> those who attacked us without warning at Pearl Harbor, against
> those who have starved and beaten and executed American prison-
> ers of war, against those who have abandoned all pretense of obeying
> international laws of warfare. We have used it in order to shorten
> the agony of war, in order to save the lives of thousands and thou-
> sands of young Americans.[36]

Although this passage has many interesting features, I am concerned only with President Truman's insistence that the dropping
of the bomb was justified because it saved the lives "of thousands
and thousands of young Americans."

Conceivably, this is merely an elliptical way of saying that on
balance fewer lives were lost through the dropping of the bomb
and the accelerated cessation of hostilities than through any alternative course of conduct. Suppose, though, that this were not the
argument. Suppose, instead, that the justification were regarded
as adequate provided only that it was reasonably clear that fewer
American lives would be lost than through any alternative course
of conduct. Thus, to quantify the example, we can imagine someone maintaining that Hiroshima was justified because 20,000 fewer
Americans died in the Pacific theater than would have died if the
bomb had not been dropped. And this is justified even though
30,000 more Japanese died than would have been killed had the
war been fought to an end with conventional means. Thus, even
though 10,000 more people died than would otherwise have been
the case, the bombing was justified because of the greater number
of American lives saved.

[35]But suppose someone should argue that the same argument applies to the question of *when* and *under what circumstances* to wage war, and that here, too, the only
relevant criteria of assessment are prudential or strategic ones. Again, my answer
would be that this also constitutes a perfectly defensible and relevant reason for
making moral judgment about the desirability of war as a social phenomenon.
[36]Address to the Nation by President Harry S. Truman, Aug. 9, 1945, quoted in R.
Tucker, *The Just War*, 21–22 n. 14 (1960).

On this interpretation the argument depends upon valuing the lives of Americans higher than the lives of persons from other countries. As such, is there anything to be said for the argument? Its strongest statement, and the only one that I shall consider, might go like this: Truman was the President of the United States and as such had an obligation always to choose that course of conduct that appeared to offer the greatest chance of maximizing the interests of the United States.[37] As President, he was obligated to prefer the lives of American soldiers over those from any other country, and he was obligated to prefer them just because they were Americans and he was their President.

Some might prove such a point by drawing an analogy to the situation of a lawyer, a parent, or a corporation executive. A lawyer has a duty to present his client's case in the fashion most calculated to ensure his client's victory; and he has this obligation irrespective of the objective merits of his client's case. Similarly, we are neither surprised nor dismayed when a parent prefers the interests of *his* child over those of other children. A parent *qua* parent is certainly not behaving immorally when he acts so as to secure satisfactions for his child, again irrespective of the objective merits of the child's needs or wants. And, *mutatis mutandis*, a corporate executive has a duty to maximize profits for his company. Thus, as public servants, Dean Acheson and Harry Truman had no moral choice but to pursue those policies that appeared to them to be in the best interest of the United States. And to a lesser degree, all persons *qua* citizens of the United States have a similar, if slightly more attenuated, obligation. Therefore morality has no real place in war.

The analogy, however, must not stop halfway. It is certainly both correct and important to observe that public officials, like parents, lawyers, and corporate executives, do have special moral obligations that are imposed by virtue of the position or role they fill. A lawyer does have a duty to prefer his client's interests in a way that would be improper were the person anyone other than a client. And the same sort of duty, I think, holds for a parent, an executive, a President, and a citizen in their respective roles. The point becomes distorted, however, when it is supposed that such an obligation always, under all circumstances, overrides any and all other obligations that the person might have. The case of the lawyer is instructive. While he has an obligation to attend to his

---

[37]Other arguments that might be offered — such as that the President was justified because Japan was the aggressor, or that he was justified because this was essentially an attack on combatants — are discussed at notes 39–46 *infra* and accompanying text.

314

client's interests in very special ways, there are many other things that it is impermissible for the lawyer to do in furtherance of his client's interests—irrespective, this time, of how significantly they might advance that interest.

The case for the President, or for public servants generally, is similar. While the President may indeed have an obligation to prefer and pursue the national interests, this obligation could only be justified—could only be a moral obligation—if it were enmeshed in a comparable range of limiting and competing obligations. If we concede that the President has certain obligations to prefer the national interest that no one else has, we must be equally sensitive to the fact that the President also has some of the same obligations to other persons that all other men have—if for no other reason than that all persons have the right to be treated or not treated in certain ways. So, whatever special obligations the President may have cannot by themselves support the view that in war morality ought have no place.

In addition, the idea that one can separate a man's personality from the duties of his office is theoretically questionable and practically unbelievable. Experience teaches that a man cannot personally be guided by moral dictates while abjuring them in public life even if he wants to.

It is also unlikely that a man on becoming President will try to adopt such an approach unless there is something about the office that compels a dual personality. Common sense indicates there is not. If there were, it would mean that the electorate could not purposely choose someone to follow a course not dictated by the "national interest" since, whatever his pre-election promises, the office would reform him.

But the major problem with the national-interest argument is its assumption that the national interest not only is something immutable and knowable but also that it limits national interest to narrowly national concerns. It is parochial to suppose that the American national interest really rules out solicitude for other states in order to encourage international stability.

Finally, national interest as a goal must itself be justified. The United States' position of international importance may have imposed on it a duty of more than national concern. The fact that such a statement has become hackneyed by constant use to justify American interference abroad should not blind us to the fact that it may be viable as an argument for a less aggressive international responsibility.[38]

[38]It is probably a reaction to the parochial view of national interest that makes plausible movements that seek to develop a single world government and a notion of *world* rather than *national* citizenship.

3

If we turn now to confront more directly the question of the morality of war, it is evident that there is a variety of different perspectives from which, or criteria in terms of which, particular wars may be assessed. First, to the extent to which the model of war as a game continues to have a place, wars can be evaluated in terms of the degree to which the laws of war—the rules for initiating and conducting war—are adhered to by the opposing countries. Second, the rightness or wrongness of wars is often thought to depend very much upon the *cause* for which a war is fought. And third, there is the independent justification for a war that is founded upon an appeal of some kind to a principle of self-defense.

In discussing the degree to which the laws of war are followed or disregarded there are two points that should be stressed. First, a skepticism as to the meaningfulness of any morality *within* war is extremely common. The gnomic statement is Sherman's: "War is hell." The fuller argument depends upon a rejection of the notion of war as a game. It goes something like this. War is the antithesis of law or rules. It is violence, killing and all of the horror they imply. Even if moral distinctions can be made in respect to such things as the initiation and purposes of a war, it is absurd to suppose that moral distinctions can be drawn once a war has begun. All killing is bad, all destruction equally wanton.[39]

Now, there does seem to me to be a fairly simple argument of sorts that can be made in response. Given the awfulness of war, it nonetheless appears plausible to discriminate among degrees of awfulness. A war in which a large number of innocent persons are killed is, all other things being equal, worse than one in which only a few die. A war in which few combatants are killed is, *ceteris paribus*, less immoral than one in which many are killed. And more to the point, perhaps, any unnecessary harm to others is surely unjustifiable. To some degree, at least, the "laws of war" can be construed as attempts to formalize these general notions and to define instances of unnecessary harm to others.[40]

[39]This may be what Paul Henri Spaak had in mind when he said: "I must . . . say that the proposal to humanize war has always struck me as hypocrisy. I have difficulty in seeing the difference from a moral and humane point of view between the use of a guided missile of great power which can kill tens and even hundreds of people without regard for age or sex, and which if used repeatedly will kill millions, and the use of an atomic bomb which achieves the same result at the first stroke. Does crime against humanity begin only at the moment when a certain number of innocent people are killed or at the moment when the first one is killed?" Quoted in R. Tucker, *supra* note 36, at 78–79 n.71.

[40]This is the view put forward by Michael Walzer in his piece "Moral Judgment in Time of War," *Dissent*, May–June 1967, at 284.

I purposely say "to some degree" because there are powerful objections to

The second criterion, the notion of the cause that can be invoked to justify a war, may involve two quite different inquiries. On the one hand, we may intend the sense in which cause refers to the *consequences* of waging war, to the forward-looking criteria of assessment. Thus, when a war is justified as a means by which to make the world safe for democracy, or on the grounds that a failure to fight now will lead to a loss of confidence on the part of one's allies, or as necessary to avoid fighting a larger, more destructive war later, when these sorts of appeals are made, the justification is primarily consequential or forward-looking in character. Here the distinction between morality and prudence — never a very easy one to maintain in international relations — is always on the verge of collapse. On the other hand, a war may be evaluated through recourse to what may be termed backward-looking criteria. Just as in the case of punishment or blame where what happened in the past is relevant to the justice of punishing or blaming someone, so in the case of war, what has already happened is, on this view, relevant to the justice or rightness of the war that is subsequently waged. The two backward-looking criteria that are most frequently invoked in respect to war are the question of whether the war was an instance of aggression and the question of whether the war involved a violation of some prior promise, typically expressed in the form of a treaty or concord.

Two sorts of assertions are often made concerning the role of the treaty in justifying resort to war. First, if a country has entered into a treaty not to go to war and if it violates that treaty, it is to be condemned for, in effect, having broken its promise. And second, if a country has entered into a treaty in which it has agreed to go to war under certain circumstances and if those circumstances come to pass, then the country is at least justified in going to war — although it is not in fact obligated to do so.

Once again, even if we pass over the difficult analytic questions that might be asked about whether countries can promise to do anything and, if they can, what the nature and duration of such promises are, it is clear that treaties can be relevant but not deci-

---

taking the "laws of war" too seriously, particularly if they are to be construed as laws or even binding rules. I have alluded to some of the problems already. Note 26 *supra*. More generally, there are at least four respects in which their character as laws seems suspect: (1) There is no authoritative body to make or declare them. (2) The distinctions made by the rules are specious and unconvincing (for example, the use of irregular-shaped bullets and projectiles filled with glass violates our standards of land warfare, *see* U.S. Dept. of the Army, The Law of Land Warfare, art. 34 (Basic Field Manual 27–10, 1956), but the use of an atomic bomb does not). (3) The sanctions are typically applied only to the losing side. (4) The countries involved tend to regard their own behavior as lawful because falling under some exception or other.

sive factors. This is so just because it is sometimes right to break our promises and sometimes wrong to keep them. The fact that a treaty is violated at best tends to make a war unjust or immoral in some degree, but it does not necessarily render the war unjustified.[41]

The other backward-looking question, that of aggression, is often resolved by concluding that under no circumstances is the initiation of a war of aggression justified. This is a view that Americans and America have often embraced. Such a view was expounded at Nuremberg by Mr. Justice Jackson when he said:

> [T]he wrong for which their [the German] fallen leaders are on trial is not that they lost the war, but that they started it. And we must not allow ourselves to be drawn into a trial of the causes of war, for our position is that no grievances or policies will justify resort to aggressive war. . . . Our position is that whatever grievances a nation may have, however objectionable it finds that *status quo*, aggressive warfare is an illegal means for settling those grievances or for altering those conditions.[42]

A position such as this is typically thought to imply two things: (1) The initiation of war is never justifiable; (2) the warlike response to aggressive war is justifiable. Both views are troublesome.

To begin with, it is hard to see how the two propositions go together very comfortably. Conceivably, there are powerful arguments against the waging of aggressive war. Almost surely, though, the more persuasive of these will depend, at least in part, on the character of war itself—on such things as the supreme importance of human life, or the inevitable injustices committed in every war. If so, then the justifiability of meeting war with war will to that degree be called into question.

To take the first proposition alone, absent general arguments about the unjustifiability of all war, it is hard to see how aggressive war can be ruled out in a wholly a priori fashion. Even if we assume that no problems are presented in determining what is and is not aggression, it is doubtful that the quality of aggression could always be morally decisive in condemning the war. Would a war undertaken to free innocent persons from concentration camps or from slavery always be unjustifiable just because *it was aggressive?*

[41]I discuss this distinction between injustice and unjustifiability at notes 50–55 *infra* and accompanying text.
[42]Quoted in R. Tucker, *supra* note 36, at 12.

Richard Wasserstrom

Surely this is to rest too much upon only one of a number of relevant considerations.[43]

From a backward-looking point of view, the claim that a warring response to aggressive war is always justified is even more perplexing. One way to take this claim is to regard it as plain retributivism. A country is justified in fighting back because the aggressor hit first. Since aggression is wrong, it deserves to be thwarted and punished. The difficulty with this position is, in part, that retributivism generally is more plausible as a statement of necessary rather than of sufficient conditions. Thus, it would be one thing to claim that a war was *only* justified if undertaken in response to aggression, but it is quite another thing to assert that a war is justified *provided* it is undertaken in response to aggression. For reasons already stated, I think even this would be unsatisfactory, but it would surely come closer to being right than a view that finds aggression to be a sufficient justification for making war. A number of these issues reappear in the related problem of self-defense as a justification.

In order to understand the force of the doctrine of self-defense when invoked in respect to war, and to assess its degree of legitimate applicability, it is necessary that we look briefly at self-defense as it functions as a doctrine of municipal criminal law. The first thing to notice is that the doctrine of self-defense does not depend upon either typically retributive or typically consequential considerations. Instead, it rests upon the prevention by the intended victim of quite immediate future harm to himself. To be sure, the doctrine is backward-looking in its insistence that an "attack" of some sort be already under way. But the fact that it is not retributive can be seen most clearly from the fact that self-defense cannot be invoked in response to an attack that is over. In the same fashion, the doctrine is forward-looking in its insistence upon the prevention of future harm.

Second, it is by no means clear whether the doctrine can be understood better as a justification or as an excuse. It can be understood to rest upon the notion that one is *entitled* to defend oneself from a serious and imminent attack upon life and limb. Concomitantly, the doctrine can be interpreted to depend upon the proposition that it is a natural, almost unavoidable—and hence excusable—reaction to defend oneself when attacked.

[43]G. E. M. Anscombe makes the same point in her article "War and Murder," in *Nuclear Weapons—A Catholic Response*, 45, 47 (1961): "The present-day conception of 'aggression,' like so many strongly influential conceptions, is a bad one. Why *must* it be wrong to strike the first blow in a struggle? The only question is, who is in the right." [Reprinted in this volume, pp. 285–297.]

In either case what is important is that we keep in mind two of the respects in which the law qualifies resort to the claim of self-defense. On one hand, the doctrine cannot be invoked successfully if the intended victim could have avoided the encounter through a reasonable escape or retreat unless the attack takes place on one's own property. And on the other hand, the doctrine requires that no more force be employed than is reasonably necessary to prevent the infliction of comparable harm.

Now how does all of this apply to self-defense as a justification for engaging in war? In the first place, to the extent to which the basic doctrine serves as an excuse, the applicability to war seems doubtful. While it may make sense to regard self-defense of one's person as a natural, instinctive response to an attack, it is only a very anthropomorphic view of countries that would lead us to elaborate a comparable explanation here.[44]

In the second place, it is not even clear that self-defense can function very persuasively as a justification. For it to do so it might be necessary, for example, to be able to make out a case that countries die in the same way in which persons do, or that a country can be harmed in the same way in which a person can be. Of course, persons in the country can be harmed and killed by war, and I shall return to this point in a moment, but we can also imagine an attack in which none of the inhabitants of the country will be killed or even physically harmed unless they fight back. But the country, as a separate political entity, might nonetheless disappear. Would we say that this should be regarded as the equivalent of human death? That it is less harmful? More harmful? These are issues to which those who readily invoke the doctrine of self-defense seldom address themselves.

Even if we were to decide, however, that there is no question but that a country is justified in relying upon a doctrine of self-defense that is essentially similar to that which obtains in the criminal law, it would be essential to observe the constraints that follow. Given even the unprovoked aggressive waging of war by one country against another, the doctrine of self-defense could not be invoked by the country so attacked to justify waging unlimited defensive war or insisting upon unconditional surrender. Each or both of these responses might be justifiable, but not simply because a country was wrongly attacked. It would, instead, have to

---

[44]Such a view certainly exists, however; we talk, for instance, about national pride and honor; insults to a country, etc. One real question is whether this way of thinking ought to be exorcised. In any event, however, countries do not respond "instinctively" in the way in which persons sometimes do, and, hence, the excuse rationale is just not appropriate.

be made out that something analogous to retreat was neither possible nor appropriate, and, even more, that no more force was used than was reasonably necessary to terminate the attack.

There is, to be sure, an answer to this. The restrictions that the criminal law puts upon self-defense are defensible, it could be maintained, chiefly because we have a municipal police force, municipal laws, and courts. If we use no more than reasonable force to repel attacks, we can at least be confident that the attacker will be apprehended and punished and, further, that we live in a society in which this sort of aggressive behavior is deterred by a variety of means. It is the absence of such a context that renders restrictions on an international doctrine of self-defense inappropriate.

I do not think this answer is convincing. It is relevant to the question of what sorts of constraints will be operative on the behavior of persons and countries, but it is not persuasive as to the invocation of *self*-defense as a justification of war. To use more force than is reasonably necessary to defend oneself is, in short, to do more than defend oneself. If such non–self-defensive behavior is to be justified, it must appeal to some different principle or set of principles.

There are, therefore, clearly cases in which a principle of self-defense does appear to justify engaging in a war: at a minimum, those cases in which one's country is attacked in such a way that the inhabitants are threatened with deadly force and in which no more force than is reasonably necessary is employed to terminate the attack.

One might argue, of course, for some of the reasons discussed above, that this is too restrictive a range for the legitimate application of the principle. More specifically, it might be observed that I have provided an unduly restricted account of the cases in which the use of deadly force is permissible in our legal system; namely, to defend certain classes of third parties from attacks threatening serious bodily harm or death, and to prevent the commission of certain felonies. These, clearly, would also have ostensibly important applications to the justifiable use of deadly force in the international setting. I shall return to this point when I discuss the problem of war and the death of innocent persons in part 4. At present, however, I want to consider an argument for refusing to accord any legitimacy whatsoever to an appeal to self-defense. The argument is a version of what can appropriately be called the pacifist position. The formulation I have in mind is found in the writings of the nineteenth-century pacifist, Adin Ballou, and it merits reproduction at some length. What Ballou says is this:

321

If it [self-defense] be the true method, it must on the whole work well. It must preserve human life and secure mankind against injury, more certainly and effectually than any other possible method. Has it done this? I do not admit it. How happens it that, according to the lowest probable estimate, some fourteen thousand millions of human beings have been slain by human means, in war and otherwise? Here are enough to people eighteen planets like the earth with its present population. What inconceivable miseries must have been endured by these worlds of people and their friends, in the process of those murderous conflicts which extinguished their earthly existence! . . . If this long-trusted method of self-preservation be indeed the best which nature affords to her children, their lot is most deplorable. To preserve what life has been preserved at such a cost, renders life itself a thing of doubtful value. If only a few thousands, or even a few millions, had perished by the two edged sword; if innocence and justice and right had uniformly triumphed; if aggression, injustice, violence, injury and insult, after a few dreadful experiences, had been overawed; if gradually the world had come into wholesome order—a state of truthfulness, justice and peace; if the sword of self-defense had frightened the sword of aggression into its scabbard, there to consume in its rust; then might we admit that the common method of self-preservation was the true one. But now we have ample demonstration that *they who take the sword, perish with the sword.* Is it supposable that if no injured person or party, since the days of Abel, had lifted up a deadly weapon, or threatened an injury against an offending party, there would have been a thousandth part of the murders and miseries which have actually taken place on our earth? Take the worst possible view; resolve all the assailed and injured into the most passive non-resistants imaginable, and let the offenders have unlimited scope to commit all the robberies, cruelties and murders they pleased; would as many lives have been sacrificed, or as much real misery have been experienced by the human race, as have actually resulted from the general method of self-preservation, by personal conflict and resistance of injury with injury? He must be a bold man who affirms it.[45]

What is most interesting about Ballou's argument is that it is, in essence, an empirical one. His claim is not the more typical pacifist claim that there is some principle that directly forbids the use of force even in cases of self-defense. His assertion is rather that the consequences of regarding the use of force as appropriate in self-defensive situations have been disastrous—or, more exactly,

[45]Ballou, "Christian Non-Resistance," in *Nonviolence in America: A Documentary History*, 31, 38–39 (S. Lynd ed. 1966).

worse precisely in terms of the preservation of human life than would have been the case if the use of force even in such circumstances were always deemed impermissible.

It is very difficult to know what to make of such an argument. In particular, it is more difficult than it may appear at first to state the argument coherently. What precisely is Ballou's thesis? Perhaps he is saying something like this: The principle that force may justifiably be used in cases of self-defense tends to be misapplied in practice. Persons almost inevitably tend to overestimate the imminence and severity of a threat of violence to themselves. They use force prematurely and in excess under an invocation of the doctrine of self-defense. And if this is true of persons generally, it is probably even truer of countries in their relations with other countries. The answer, therefore, is to induce persons and countries to forego the resort to force even in cases of self-defense.

This argument is something of a paradox. If everyone were to accept and consistently to act upon the principle that force ought never to be used, even in cases of self-defense, then there would be nothing to worry about. No one would ever use force at all, and we really would not have to worry about misapplications of the principle of self-defense.

But Ballou's appeal is to persons to give up the principle of self-defense even if others have not renounced even the aggressive resort to force. In other words, Ballou's argument is one for unilateral rather than bilateral pacifism, and that is precisely what makes it so hard to accept. As I have said, Ballou's thesis appears to be an empirical one. He appears to concede that if only some persons renounce the doctrine of self-defense they certainly do not thereby guarantee their own safety from attack. Innocent persons in this position may very well be killed by those who use force freely. Ballou seems to be saying that while this is so, the consequences have been still worse where self-defense has not been abandoned. But there is just no reason to suppose that unilateral pacifism if practiced by an unspecified group of persons would have resulted in fewer rather than more deaths.[46]

Perhaps, though, this is not what Ballou really has in mind. Perhaps instead the main thrust of his argument is as follows: People generally agree that force should not be used except in self-defense. But the evidence indicates that this principle is usually misapplied. Hence, a partial pacifism, restricted to the use of force only in cases of self-defense, is illusory and unsound. Even if all

[46]Still another argument against unilateral pacificism is, of course, that there are evils other than the destruction of lives. Suppose, for example, that unilateral pacifism would result in fewer death but in substantially greater human slavery. It is by no means clear that such would be a morally preferable state of affairs.

323

countries agreed never to use force except in self-defense, they would still be so prone to construe the behavior of other countries as imminently threatening that wars would be prevalent and the consequences horrendous. This is the reason why even self-defense cannot be permitted as an exception to pacifism. Everyone and every country should, therefore, renounce self-defense as the one remaining exception to pacifism.

Again there is an element of paradox to the argument. Suppose it looks to country Y as though country X is about to attack it. Ballou would say country Y should not, under the principle of self-defense, prepare to fight back. Of course, if all countries do follow the principle of never using force except in self-defense, this makes good sense because country Y can rely on the fact that country X will not attack first. So there is no need to eliminate the defense of self-defense. But what if country X should in fact attack? Here Ballou's advice is that country Y should still not respond because of the likelihood of misapplying the doctrine of self-defense. Once again the case is simply not convincing. In any particular case it just might be that the doctrine would not be misapplied and that the consequences of not defending oneself would in fact be less desirable than those of resorting to self-defensive force.

In short, the case against a limited doctrine of self-defense cannot, I think, be plausibly made out on grounds such as those urged by Ballou. Although a world without war would doubtless be a better one, it is by no means clear that unilateral abandonment of the doctrine of self-defense would have such beneficial consequences. If there is an argument against war, it must rest on something other than the harms inherent in the doctrine of self-defense.

4

The strongest argument against war is that which rests upon the connection between the morality of war and the death of innocent persons. The specter of thermonuclear warfare makes examination of this point essential; yet the problem was both a genuine and an urgent one in the pre-atomic days of air warfare, particularly during the Second World War.

The argument based upon the death of innocent persons goes something like this: Even in war innocent persons have a right to life and limb that should be respected. It is no less wrong and no more justifiable to kill innocent persons in war than at any other time. Therefore, if innocent persons are killed in a war, that war is to be condemned.

The argument can quite readily be converted into an attack upon all modern war. Imagine a thoroughly unprovoked attack upon another country—an attack committed, moreover, from the worst of motives and for the most despicable of ends. Assume too, for the moment, that under such circumstances there is nothing immoral about fighting back and even killing those who are attacking. Nonetheless, if in fighting back innocent persons will be killed, the defenders will be acting immorally. However, given any war fought today, innocent persons will inevitably be killed. Therefore, any war fought today will be immoral.

There are a variety of matters that require clarification before the strength of this argument can be adequately assessed. In particular, there are four questions that must be examined: (1) What is meant by "innocence" in this context? (2) Is it plausible to suppose that there are any innocents? (3) Under what circumstances is the death of innocent persons immoral? (4) What is the nature of the connection between the immorality of the killing of innocent persons and the immorality of the war in which this killing occurs?

It is anything but clear what precisely is meant by "innocence" or "the innocent" in an argument such as this. One possibility would be that all noncombatants are innocent. But then, of course, we would have to decide what was meant by "noncombatants." Here we might be tempted to claim that noncombatants are all those persons who are not in the army—not actually doing the fighting; the combatants are those who are. There are, however, serious problems with this position. For it appears that persons can be noncombatants in this sense and yet indistinguishable in any apparently relevant sense from persons in the army. Thus, civilians may be manufacturing munitions, devising new weapons, writing propaganda, or doing any number of other things that make them indistinguishable from many combatants vis-à-vis their relationship to the war effort.

A second possibility would be to focus upon an individual's causal connection with the attempt to win the war rather than on his status as soldier or civilian. On this view only some noncombatants would be innocent and virtually no combatants would be. If the causal connection is what is relevant, meaningful distinctions might be made among civilians. One might distinguish between those whose activities or vocations help the war effort only indirectly, if at all, and those whose activities are more plausibly described as directly beneficial. Thus the distinctions would be between a typical grocer or a tailor on the one hand, and a worker in an armaments plant on the other. Similarly, children, the aged, and the infirm would normally not be in a position to play a role causally connected in this way with the waging of war.[47]

There are, of course other kinds of possible causal connections. In particular, someone might urge that attention should also be devoted to the existence of a causal connection between the individual's civic behavior and the war effort. Thus, for example, a person's voting behavior, or the degree of his political opposition to the government, or his financial contributions to the war effort might all be deemed to be equally relevant to his status as an innocent.

Still a fourth possibility, closely related to those already discussed, would be that interpretation of innocence concerned with culpability rather than causality per se. On this view a person would properly be regarded as innocent if he could not fairly be held responsible for the war's initiation or conduct. Clearly, the notion of culpability is linked in important ways with that of causal connection, but they are by no means identical. So it is quite conceivable, for example, that under some principles of culpability many combatants might not be culpable and some noncombatants might be extremely culpable, particularly if culpability were to be defined largely in terms of state of mind and enthusiasm for the war. Thus, an aged or infirm person who cannot do very much to help the war effort but is an ardent proponent of its aims and objectives might be more culpable (and less innocent in this sense) than a conscriptee who is firing a machine gun only because the penalty for disobeying the command to do so is death.[48]

[47]For a fuller development of this point see Ford, "The Morality of Obliteration Bombing," 5 *Theological Studies* 261, 280–286 (1944).

[48]This discussion hardly exhausts the possible problems involved in making clear the appropriate notion of innocence. I have not, for example, discussed at all the view that culpability is linked with the *cause* for which a war is fought. On this view, innocence might turn much more on the question of which side a person was on than on his connection with or responsibility for waging the war. I do not think this sense of innocence is intended by those who condemn wars that involve the deaths of innocent persons.

Similarly, I have avoided completely a number of difficulties inherent in the problem of culpability for the behavior of one's country. To what degree does the denial of access to adequate information about the war excuse one from culpability in supporting it? Are children who are taught that their country is always right to be regarded as innocents even though they act on this instruction and assiduously do what they can to aid the war effort? To what degree does the existence of severe penalties for political opposition render ostensibly culpable behavior in fact innocent?

All of these questions arise more directly in connection with the issue of individual responsibility for the behavior of one's country and oneself in time of war. This issue is, as I have indicated, beyond the scope of this Article. As is apparent, however, a number of the relevant considerations are presented once the problem of the death of innocent persons is raised.

But we need not propose an airtight definition of "innocence" in order to answer the question of whether, in any war, there will be a substantial number of innocent persons involved. For irrespective of which sense or senses of innocence are ultimately deemed most instructive or important, it does seem clear that there will be a number of persons in any country (children are probably the clearest example) who will meet any test of innocence that is proposed.

The third question enumerated earlier is: Under what circumstances is the death of innocent persons immoral? One possible view is that which asserts simply that it is unimportant which circumstances bring about the death of innocent persons. As long as we know that innocent persons will be killed as a result of war, we know all we need to know to condemn any such war.

Another, and perhaps more plausible, view is that which regards the death of innocent persons as increasingly unjustifiable if it was negligently, recklessly, knowingly, or intentionally brought about. Thus, if a country engages in acts of war with the intention of bringing about the death of children, perhaps to weaken the will of the enemy, it would be more immoral than if it were to engage in acts of war aimed at killing combatants but which through error also kill children.[49]

A different sort of problem arises if someone asks how we are to differentiate the death of children in war from, for example, the death of children that accompany the use of highways or airplanes in times of peace. Someone might, that is, argue that we permit children to ride in cars on highways and to fly in airplanes even though we *know* that there will be accidents and that as a result of these accidents innocent children will die. And since we know this to be the case, the situation appears to be indistinguishable from that of engaging in acts of war where it is known that the death of children will be a direct, although not intended, consequence.

I think that there are three sorts of responses that can be made to an objection of this sort. In the first place, in a quite straightforward sense the highway does not, typically, cause the death of the innocent passenger; the careless driver or the defective tire does. But it is the intentional bombing of the heavily populated city that does cause the death of the children who live in the city.

In the second place, it is one thing to act where one knows that

[49]There is a substantial body of literature on the problem of the intentionality of conduct in time of war. Discussion has focused chiefly on the plausibility of the Catholic doctrine of "double" or "indirect" effect. See, e.g., P. Ramsey, *supra* note 13, at 46–59; Anscombe, *supra* note 43, at 57–59; Ford, *supra* note 47, at 289, 290–298.

certain more or less identifiable persons will be killed (say, bombing a troop camp when one knows that those children who live in the vicinity of the camp will also be killed), and quite another thing to engage in conduct in which all one can say is that it can be predicted with a high degree of confidence that over a given period of time a certain number of persons (including children) will be killed. The difference seems to lie partly in the lack of specificity concerning the identity of the persons and partly in the kind of causal connection involved.

In the third place, there is certainly a difference in the two cases in respect to the possibility of deriving benefits from the conduct. That is to say, when a highway is used, one is participating in a system or set of arrangements in which benefits are derived from that use (even though risks, and hence costs, are also involved). It is not easy to see how a similar sort of analysis can as plausibly be proposed in connection with typical acts of war.

The final and most important issue that is raised by the argument concerning the killing of the innocent in time of war is that of the connection between the immorality of the killing of innocent persons and the immorality of the war in which this killing occurs. Writers in the area often fail to discuss the connection.

Miss Anscombe puts the point this way:"[I]t is murderous to attack [the innocent] or make them a target for an attack which [the attacker] judges will help him toward victory. For murder is the deliberate killing of the innocent, whether for its own sake or as a means to some further end."[50] And Father John Ford, in a piece that certainly deserves to be more widely known outside of theological circles, puts the point several different ways: At one place he asserts that noncombatants have a right to live, even in wartime;[51] and at another place he says that "to take the life of an innocent person is always intrinsically wrong";[52] and at still a third place: "[E]very Catholic theologian would condemn as intrinsically immoral the direct killing of innocent noncombatants."[53]

Now, leaving aside the question of whether Miss Anscombe has defined murder correctly and leaving aside the question of whether Father Ford's three assertions are equivalent expressions, the serious question that does remain is what precisely they mean to assert about the intentional killing of innocent persons in time of war.

There are two very different ambiguities in their statements

[50]Anscombe, *supra* note 43, at 49.
[51]Ford, *supra* note 47, at 269.
[52]Id. at 272.
[53]Id. at 273.

that have to be worked out. In the first place, we have to determine whether the immorality in question is in their view "absolute" or in some sense "prima facie." And in the second place, we should ask whether the immorailty in question is in their view to be predicated of the particular act of intentional killing or of the entire war. To elaborate briefly in turn on each of these two ambiguities: Suppose someone were to claim that it is immoral or wrong to lie. He might mean any one of at least three different things: (1) He might mean that it is *absolutely* immoral to lie. That is to say, he might be claiming that there are no circumstances under which one would be justified in telling a lie and that there are no circumstances under which it would, morally speaking, be better to lie than to tell the truth. (2) Or he might even mean that it is prima facie immoral to lie. That is to say, he might be claiming that, absent special, overriding circumstances, it is immoral to lie. On this view, even when these special, overriding circumstances do obtain so that an act of lying is justifiable, it still involves some quantum of immorality. (3) The third possibility is that he might mean that, typically, lying is wrong. As a rule it is immoral to lie, but sometimes it is not. And when it is not, there is nothing whatsoever wrong or immoral about telling a lie.

For the purposes of the present inquiry the differences between (2) and (3) are irrelevant;[54] the difference between a position of absolute immorality and either (2) or (3) are not. The question of the killing of the innocents should similarly fit into the foregoing categories and identical conclusions should obtain, although to some degree the differences among these views and the plausibility of each are affected by the type of activity under consideration. Thus, the absolutist view, (1), may seem very strange and unconvincing when applied to lying or promise-keeping; it may seem less so, though, when applied to murder or torture. Similarly (3) may seem quite sensible when predicated of lying or promise-keeping but patently defective when applied to murder or torture.

In any event the case at hand is that of murder. It is likely that Father Ford and Miss Anscombe mean to assert an absolutist view here — that there are no circumstances under which the intentional killing of innocent persons, even in time of war, can be justified. It is always immoral to do so.[55] At least their arguments are

---

[54] For discussion of the differences between these two positions in other contexts see Wasserstrom, "The Obligation To Obey the Law," 10 *U.C.L.A.L. Rev.* 780, 783–785 (1963).
[55] I offer this interpretation because the language typically used seems to support it. For example, Miss Anscombe says: "Without understanding of this principle [of double effect], anything can be — and is wont to be — justified, and the Chris-

phrased in absolutist terms. If this is the view that they intend to defend, it is, I think, a hard one to accept. This is so just because it ultimately depends upon too complete a rejection of the relevance of consequences to the moral character of action. It also requires too rigid a dichotomy between acts and omissions. It seems to misunderstand the character of our social life to claim that, no matter what the consequences, the intentional killing of an innocent person could never be justifiable—even, for example, if a failure to do so would bring about the death of many more innocent persons.

This does not, of course, mean that the argument from the death of the innocent is either irrelevant or unconvincing. It can be understood to be the very convincing claim that the intentional or knowing killing of an innocent person is always prima facie (in sense (2)) wrong. A serious evil is done every time it occurs. Moreover, the severity of the evil is such that there is strong presumption against its justifiability. The burden, and it is a heavy one, rests upon anyone who would seek to justify behavior that has as a consequence the death of innocent persons.

The second question concerns what we might call the "range" of the predication of immorality. Even if we were to adopt the absolutist view in respect to the killing of the innocent, it would still remain unclear precisely what it was that was immoral. The narrowest view would be that which holds that the particular action—for instance, the intentional killing of a child—is immoral and unjustified. A broader view would be one that holds that the side that engages in such killing is conducting the war immorally. But this too could mean one of two different things.

A moderate view would be that if one is helpless to prevent the death of the innocent, it is appropriate to weigh such a result against such things as the rightness of the cause for which the war is being fought, the offensive or defensive character of the war, and so on. While there is nothing that can justify or excuse the killing of a particular innocent, this does not necessarily mean that, on balance, the total participation in the war by the side in question is to be deemed absolutely immoral and unjustifiable.

A more extreme view would hold that the occurrence of even

<hr />

tian teaching *that in no circumstances may one commit murder, adultery, apostasy (to give a few examples) goes by the board.* These absolute prohibitions of Christianity by no means exhaust its ethic; there is a large area where what is just is determined partly by a prudent weighing up of consequences. But the prohibitions are bedrock, and without them the Christian ethic goes to pieces." Anscombe, *supra* note 43, at 57–58 (emphasis added). And it is also consistent with what I take to be the more general Catholic doctrine on the intentional taking of "innocent" life—the absolute prohibition against abortion on just this ground.

a single instance of immorality makes the entire act of fighting the war unjustifiable. Thus, the murder of innocent persons is absolutely immoral in not one but two quite different senses.

My own view is that as a theoretical matter an absolutist position is even less convincing here. Given the number of criteria that are relevant to the moral assessment of any war and given the great number of persons involved in and the extended duration of most wars, it would be false to the complexity of the issues to suppose that so immediately simple a solution were possible.

But having said all this, *the practical*, as opposed to the theoretical, thrust of the argument is virtually unabated. If wars were conducted, or were likely to be conducted, so as to produce only the occasional intentional killing of the innocent, that would be one thing. We could then say with some confidence that on this ground at least wars can hardly be condemned out of hand. Unfortunately, though, mankind no longer lives in such a world and, as a result, the argument from the death of the innocent has become increasingly more convincing. The intentional, or at least knowing, killing of the innocent on a large scale became a practically necessary feature of war with the advent of air warfare. And the genuinely indiscriminate killing of very great numbers of innocent persons is the dominant legacy of the birth of thermonuclear weapons. At this stage the argument from the death of the innocent moves appreciably closer to becoming a decisive objection to war. For even if we reject, as I have argued we should, both absolutist interpretations of the argument, the core of truth that remains is the insistence that in war, no less than elsewhere, the knowing killing of the innocent is an evil that throws up the heaviest of justificatory burdens. My own view is that in any major war that can or will be fought today, none of those considerations that can sometimes justify engaging in war will in fact come close to meeting this burden. But even if I am wrong, the argument from the death of the innocent does, I believe, make it clear both where the burden is and how unlikely it is today to suppose that it can be honestly discharged.

ethics and
nuclear deterrence

douglas lackey

The Strategic Arms Limitation Agreement signed by President Nixon in Moscow in May 1972 was universally and rightly hailed as a step toward peace. The principal clauses of the agreement limit the construction of antimissile systems, and these systems are the only devices within the scope of conceivable technology that can fend off a nuclear attack. In effect, the United States and the Soviet Union have agreed upon mutual defencelessness; each side has acknowledged, as practically a permanent condition, the ability of the other to attack and destroy it if it wishes. At the same time, this mutual guarantee of ability to attack carries with it a guarantee of the ability to *counterattack;* each side, if attacked first, can destroy the other with a counterstrike emanating from nuclear submarines surviving the initial attack.[1] Though this state

[1]My opinion about the ability of nuclear submarines to survive a nuclear attack may seem akin to optimism about the Maginot Line. But I leave it to the reader to construct a plan to neutralize 30 cruising missile submarines. First, they must be located, which is technologically impossible at present. Then they must be destroyed, which is at present very difficult. And all this must be accomplished *simultaneously,* since, if just *one* submarine survives, it can annihilate any nation not protected by an antimissile system. Some plans have been suggested for seeding the oceans with mines, but it is very unlikely that magnetic mines could affix themselves to the 30th submarine before they were detected on the 1st. A slightly more plausible suggestion would be to interrupt the military communications system with dummy messages luring all the opponent's submarines into traps. But the small likelihood that such a scheme would succeed, coupled with the dev-

of affairs is hardly utopian, it is a distinct improvement over the previous delicate balance of terror. If both sides are guaranteed the ability to counterattack, neither side, barring accidents and assuming the usual desire for self-preservation, will attack the other. For the first time since the introduction of intercontinental missiles in the early 1960s, the major powers have achieved stable deterrence.

Though the present strategic balance is an improvement over past uncertainties, this gives us no cause to believe that it is the best possible arrangement. For an indefinite period, to preserve this balance, the United States and the Soviet Union must spend large sums on armaments, endure the risk of nuclear accidents, face the possibility that any minor disagreement may escalate into a nuclear war, and maintain an attitude sufficiently bellicose to assure the other side that destruction will swiftly and surely follow upon attack. My purpose in this paper is to examine the extent to which we can rest content with the present strategic *détente*. There are two sorts of criticism possible: first, the utilitarian one that this policy will not produce the best consequences for the world over all the practical alternatives; second, the sterner criticism that our policy is intrinsically abhorrent and ought to be abandoned simply because of what it is. I shall take up each criticism in turn.

1. A UTILITARIAN CRITIQUE

Utilitarian critiques are always future-oriented; given the world as it is *now*, with the weapons that actually exist on both sides, which policy will produce the best future results? This prevents retroactive criticisms of past military decisions; and though they

---

astating effects of its probable failure, would prevent anyone but a madman from acting upon it. No military or strategic authority today questions the ability of nuclear submarines to survive nuclear attack, and this optimism stands in striking contrast to pessimistic critics in the 1930s who noted the impotence of the Maginot Line against air attacks. (See, for example, Bertrand Russell's *Which Way to Peace*, ch. 2.)

To test the solidity of the present stalemate, consider the strategic impact of the MIRVs (multiple, independently targeted, reentry vehicles) with which our Minuteman and Poseidon missiles are presently being equipped. This device enables up to ten warheads, each targeted to a different location, to be placed on a single ballistic missile! Under normal conditions, an offensive device like this would give immediate victory to the side that first developed it. But suppose, for example, that the United States develops the MIRV first, possesses no antimissile system, and decides to launch a devastating attack on the Soviet Union. However powerful this offensive thrust, *some* Russian submarines would survive, and the United States would be defenseless against their counterattack. Without an antimissile system, the MIRV is strategically worthless; yet construction of it in this country proceeds apace, lest the Russians get it first.

provide an interesting compendium of missed opportunities and mental lapses, the errors of the 1960s will not concern us here. The costs of the *present* policy (by present policy I mean the policy to maintain force levels at least as high as they now are, subject to the limitations of the SALT I agreement) have already been indicated. *First*, there is the enormous cost of maintaining and operating the present American weapons systems. (Notice that we cannot include present interest on loans taken to develop these systems; that is a critique of *past* action). *Second*, there is the enormous cost of the maintaining and operating of the corresponding arsenal in the Soviet Union. It is not unfair, I believe, to include costs of Soviet arms as part of the utilitarian cost of American policy, even though Americans do not decide whether Russia shall arm. "Cost" in a utilitarian calculation is cost to the human race, and each agent is responsible for such costs as can reasonably be predicted to follow from his policies. It is reasonable to predict, judging from what we know of the Soviet Union and its leadership, that if we maintain our present armament, the Russians will maintain theirs; and also reasonable to predict that if we acted differently as regards the level of arms, the Russians would also. Hence their expenditures should be charged against our policy. By parity of reasoning, the Russian policy must include among its costs the money that Americans, in all their rhetorical fury, can reasonably be predicted to spend in response to Russian armaments. But this would be relevant to a critique of Russian policy, and I am here concerned only with our own. *Third*, since the weapons of destruction exist and are very complex, there is a chance that systems will malfunction and some or all of the world be destroyed by accident. The malfunction may be due to mechanical failure, as is described in the book *Fail Safe*, or to human failure, as is depicted in the movie *Dr. Strangelove*. Though the chances of such accidents are considerably less than they were, say, in October of 1960, when an American nuclear attack was almost ordered against Russia in response to radar signals that had bounced off the moon, the possibility of either sort of failure is still quite real. For reasons quite analogous to those given above as regards the financial burden of armaments, the possibility of malfunction in Russian systems must be charged against our policy, just as much as the possibility of malfunction in American systems. Even though the Russian systems are not supervised by us, they exist in response to ours and their possible malfunctions are concomitants of our policies. Russian expenses and Russian risks are hidden costs of our policies usually ignored even by liberal critics.

The financial burden of armaments is certain; accidental nu-

Douglas Lackey

clear war is just a possibility. In estimating the value of current defence policy one must subtract some factor for the possibility of accidental war. This factor will be, estimated by the usual methods, the product of the chance of war and the disutility of this result. Though the chance of accidental war is slight, it is not negligible when Russian malfunctions are also considered; and since the disutility of nuclear war is great, the total subtraction from the value of the present policy on this ground alone should be substantial. *Fourth,* since the weapons of destruction exist, there is always the possibility that they will be *deliberately* used, if the leaders of one nation deem some provocation sufficient. The subtraction for this factor, as with the third, is achieved by multiplying the chance that some conflict will escalate to nuclear war by the disutility of that war, which is considerable.

The "gains" that can be attributed to the present policy are said to be threefold. First, the certainty of an American counterattack deters the Russians from launching a nuclear attack on the United States in order to gain some end. To the extent that such attacks are deterred, the world gains and not just the United States. Second, the ability of the United States to launch a devastating counterattack vitiates all Russian attempts to use threats of attack as a regular instrument of policy. If the United States could not attack, the Soviet Union could blackmail the United States at every point, threatening destruction if concessions be not made. Third, if the United States retains its capacity to counterattack, then it has the option, in *extreme* situations, of threatening to attack even though attack is suicidal. Though the Soviet leaders know that any attack is unlikely, they cannot be *certain* that the American leaders will *not* go to war over the issue concerned; and accordingly such threats by the United States will not be totally without effect. President Kennedy used such threats, successfully, to secure the removal of Russian missiles from Cuba. In short, the maintenance of our present military capacity reduces the risk of attack and blackmail, and occasionally can be used to secure goals of policy.

Each of these three "gains" must be carefully analyzed. First, it is claimed that American armaments "reduce the threat of Russian attack." The superficial appeal of this claim disappears when we raise the question: Reduce the chances of attack *relative to what?* Certainly it reduces the chances of attack relative to some anti-Communist fantasy in which the leaders of the Soviet Union daily plot the conquest of the United States. But such fantasies are incredible and it is madness to praise a present policy because it is better than some imaginary evil. The fact is that with the present policy there is a certain chance of war, which can be calculated by combining the possibility of accidental war with the possibility of deliberate attack; and this is an evil of the policy which can only be justified on the grounds that all other policies on balance do even worse.

The same criticism applies to the second "plus" of our deterrence policy: it prevents nuclear blackmail. Our policy can "prevent" nuclear blackmail only if there *is* nuclear blackmail to be prevented. But there is little evidence that either side is prone to blackmail of this sort. On the Russian side, the military tradition is either to act or not to act: threatening to act is not a standard feature of Russian policy. The Soviets did not *threaten* to invade Hungary and Czechoslovakia; they simply invaded them. They did not threaten to attack us if we intercepted their ships steaming toward Cuba in 1962; they merely stopped them. As for the United States, the use of nuclear threats was eschewed in the Acheson era, when there was often something worth blackmailing; and in the Dulles era, though the nuclear sabers were often rattled as a general display, they remained preternaturally still during the Hungarian invasion, the most provocative Soviet act of the 1950s. During this period the United States could have attacked Russia at any time with relative impunity, yet it did not even threaten to attack. In short, the major powers are not given to nuclear blackmail.[2] If this blackmail problem ever does arise, it will arise in the context of nuclear *terrorists*—revolutionary kamikazes with nuclear devices—against whom the threat of counterattack is useless. The true situation is that with the present policy there is not a "reduction" in the chance of nuclear blackmail but rather a set chance of blackmail given present conditions, and no argument has yet been provided that this chance is less than the chance that one would have in all other alternative policies.

The third "plus" of present policy is that if we possess strength we can negotiate from strength—gaining ends we could not attain otherwise. (The latest variant on this theme is the reiterated argument of the present administration that we must first increase armaments in order to facilitate negotiations to decrease them.) This third plus may be a plus from the perspective of those who make American policy, but it can hardly be considered a plus for humanity in general. "To negotiate from strength" is a euphemism for the making of threats; the making of threats increases the

[2]Interestingly enough, one of the few persons who ever publicly advocated the use of nuclear blackmail was Bertrand Russell, who recommended in 1948 that the threat of nuclear attack be used to force the Russians to accept the Baruch-Lilienthal plan for the internationalization of atomic weapons. If a nuclear war ever does break out, Russell will have been proved right in his suggestion, but no one will remember it.

chance of nuclear war. The great disutility of this result outweighs any gains that might result from "negotiating from strength," even if (as is unlikely) the negotiations are aimed at a moral result. In summary, then, even if the present policy results in more good than evil,[3] it is not demonstrated that it results in more good on balance than all alternative policies.

Of the alternative policies, the one that most clearly challenges the present policy of seeking bilateral arms reductions while maintaining the arms race is the policy of gradual unilateral disarmament. The most plausible unilateral disarmament policy at present would be this: first, to cease all nuclear testing; to declare a moratorium on armaments research; to deactivate the implementation of MIRV; to withdraw our strategic air bases from Spain, Thailand, Formosa, etc.; and to phase out all Minuteman missiles and sites. All of this would be merely Stage I, since it would leave the strategic balance completely unimpaired, so long as the Soviet Union built no ABM and the United States retained its fleet of missile submarines. Each one of these steps should be accompanied by requests that similar steps be taken by the Soviet Union, but compliance by the Soviet Union should not be considered a precondition for any of the American initiatives.

Stage II of the disarmament procedure should be as follows: the United States should announce that it will not counterattack if attacked by the Soviet Union and shall progressively deactivate its nuclear submarines, down to a point in which the ability of the United States to reply to a Russian attack would be considerably reduced.[4] At the same time, the United States should undertake extensive steps to increase Soviet–American trade, in such areas as exploit the natural specializations of the respective countries.

The consequences of this alternative policy would be, at a minimum, a reduction of the chance of accidental and escalated nuclear war, relative to the present policy, and the diversion of American capital and intellect into enterprises more likely to increase the economic health of the nation.[5] In addition, it is highly

[3]Strictly speaking, "an increase in expected value."
[4]The reader may wonder why I consider it preferable to deactivate nuclear submarines rather than transfer them to an international agency. The reason I consider this undesirable is that American nuclear submarines are now ultimately responsible to civilian authority, and the tradition of military subservience to civilian authority is stronger in the United States than in most of the United Nations. Transfer of submarines to an international agency with no tradition of obedience would substantially increase chances of a nuclear *coup d'etat*.
[5]The argument that increased military expenditures are needed to preserve economic vitality is completely bogus. The world's two strongest and fastest developing economies—West Germany's and Japan's—are the economies of nations who have spent least for armaments, among major advanced nations, since 1945.

likely that a reduction in the American level of armaments would lead to a reduction in Russian armaments, since one principal rationale for the Russian maintenance of these arms is the threat of American attack.

This leaves the question of "nuclear blackmail." If the United States enters into extensive economic arrangements with Russia, provided that these arrangements are not exploitative but based on a national specialization, the Soviet Union would have no cause to blackmail the United States, since an injury to a trading partner is an injury to oneself. Furthermore, the Soviet Union can ill-afford to alienate the United States, even if the United States lacks nuclear arms, since the United States holds the balance of power, both military and economic, between the Soviet Union and China, who are at present, enemies by geography, by history, and by ideology. In short, though the possibility of nuclear blackmail exists if the United States abandons its armaments, there is little likelihood that there would be such blackmail; and, in my opinion, the small chance of this bad result is far outweighed by the decreased chance of accidental or deliberate nuclear war.

The policy that I recommend bears some resemblance to suggested policies of national pacifism in the 1930s. Since these policies were discredited by events, it is important to see that the problems of the 1970s are significantly different from those of the 1930s. The principal tension of the 1930s was between Germany and other states, and Germany possessed the most advanced military technology. The principal tension of the 1970s and 1980s will be between the advanced countries and the underdeveloped countries, within which the population bomb will explode. In short, tension in the 1930s was between strong and strong; in the 1980s it will be between strong and weak. The underdeveloped countries do not stand to the world on the same military basis that Germany stood to the rest of Europe. Furthermore, in the 1930s, Germany and Italy were infected with an ideology that contained self-fulfilling prophecies of the inevitability of war. There is no force in the contemporary scene that corresponds to fascism. Neither ideology of democracy nor the ideology of capitalism preach the inevitability of war, and in the ideology of communism, though there will be inevitable war between *classes*, there need be no inevitable war between *nations*, especially war by socialist states against capitalist states, who will be defeated not by external invasion but internal contradictions. There is no nation at present which simultaneously has the power, the desire, or the need to go to war.

Historical predictions are a risky business, and the policy of unilateral disarmament may appear unduly risky, even when its probable positive effects are considered. But if disarmament increases the risk of conquest, continued armament increases the risk of war; and of these two, the latter is the more serious, especially if the welfare of the entire world is considered and not the special national interests of the United States.

II. PRISONER'S DILEMMA DENIED

A critic of the preceding section might argue that the whole proof hangs upon an overly generous interpretation of Russian intentions. "One can argue," a defender of armaments might retort, "that the United States has a moral obligation to disarm if the Soviet Union is also willing to disarm, since mutual disarmament benefits everyone. But if the Soviet Union does not disarm, no argument based on probabilities or expected values should compel us to disarm and open ourselves to conquest. Calculation of probabilities of historical events is mere guesswork, but no guesswork is involved in the judgment that Russian conquest of an armed United States is not possible but Russian conquest of a disarmed United States is a real possibility. The proper way to evaluate the strategic situation is to forget spurious probabilities and to use game-theoretic methods. In the strategic game, the disarming of the United States gives the Russians a move which simple logic compels them to take and which is disaster for us."

I would be willing, if pressed, to defend the probabilistic approach to deterrence theory, because I believe that the case for unilateral disarmament can be successfully made without spurious precision. In the preceding section, for example, I claimed that the chance of accidental war resulting from present policies is small but not negligible, and this degree of precision, which is not very great but all that the argument needs, can be supported by empirical evidence. But if a game-theoretic analysis is desired, I shall not shrink from providing one, since these analyses have their independent merits.

In a game-theoretic analysis of strategy, each opponent is viewed as having choices between various policies and payoffs are assigned to each opponent after all simultaneously make some choice of policy. In the deterrence situation as we now find it, in which each opponent knows that a first strike is suicidal, the main policy choices are "disarming unilaterally" or "remaining at an arms level equal to one's opponents." Symbolizing "retaining

arms" as A and "disarming unilaterally" as D, the game matrix
for deterrence looks like this:

	A	D	
A			USA
D			

USSR

Now, if both countries disarm, neither will attack the other, neither
risks accidental war, and neither wastes resources on armaments;
and if both countries maintain arms at present levels, neither will
deliberately attack the other, but both risk accidental war, and both
pay for armaments. Obviously the payoff figures for the D–D game
should be higher than the payoff figures for the A–A game, and
the payoff figures should be equal for each player in each case; for
example:

	A	D	
A	−10, −10		USA
D		0, 0	

USSR

(Left-hand payoffs to USA, right-hand payoffs to USSR; scale of
payoffs is arbitrary.)

This leaves us the difficulty of assigning the payoffs for the
D–A games. A critic of disarmament might say that if one country
is disarmed while the other remains armed, this is a tremendous
advantage to the armed nation, which can do as it wills, and a tremendous disadvantage to the disarmed nation, which must suffer
what it must. Accordingly, the disarmament critic sets the payoff
for the armed country (against disarmed) very high, higher than
the payoff for being armed (against armed); and he sets the payoff
for the disarmed country (against armed) very low, lower than the
payoff for being disarmed (against disarmed); for example:

	A	D	
A	−10, −10	10, −20	USA
D	−20, 10	0, 0	

USSR

which is an instance of the game pattern known as the Prisoner's

340

Douglas Lackey

Dilemma. Having got this far, the critic of disarmament will argue: "The USSR will either arm or disarm. If the Soviet Union arms, it is preferable (−10 to −20) for the USA to arm; and if the Soviet Union disarms, then it is preferable (10 to 0) for the USA to arm. Therefore, whatever the Soviet Union does, it is preferable for the United States to remain armed.

This is the sort of reasoning that generates arms races, and arms races are admitted on all sides to be regrettable. The difficulty is to find a flaw in this reasoning that will allow one to escape from an arms race once one is caught up in it. There have been numerous attempts, by philosophers and peace-oriented game theoreticians, to demonstrate that the policy of disarmament is rational, or moral, in the Prisoner's Dilemma situation, but all these attempts have been unconvincing. My own feeling is that the main mistake is not in the disarmament critic's reasoning once the Prisoner's Dilemma is established, but in the reasoning that assigns the payoffs so as to create the Dilemma. If one considers nuclear arms only, then it is not a tremendous advantage to be armed when your so-called opponent is disarmed. Nuclear arms are expensive; they may blow up in your face; and they cannot be used for a war of aggrandizement, since when used against an enemy they destroy the spoils. The only serviceable use of nuclear arms is to destroy an opponent who threatens you; and if your opponent is disarmed, he is no threat. In short, I deny that the Prisoner's Dilemma is the correct model to use in analysis of the present deterrence situation; the real world, I believe, looks more like this:

	A	D
A	−10, −10	−8, −2
D	−2, −8	0, 0

If *this* matrix is the correct mirror of reality, then game-theoretic analysis shows that the strategy of disarmament is preferable whether one's "opponent" is disarmed or armed.

III. A DEONTOLOGICAL CRITIQUE

Suppose that for some reason or lack of reason the Soviet Union launches a nuclear first strike against the United States. Even under these conditions it would be clearly immoral for the United States to retaliate in kind against the Soviet Union, since retaliation by the United States would result in the death of millions of innocent people, for no higher purpose than useless revenge. The

341

present policy of deterrence requires preparations for such retaliation and threats and assurances by us that it will be forthcoming if the United States is attacked. Indeed, if our deterrent is to remain credible, the response of the United States to attack should be semiautomatic. Defenders of armaments justify all the preparations on the grounds that they will prevent an attack *on us;* if retaliation is ever needed, they say, the system has already failed. Now, a Russian attack against the United States would be at least as immoral as our retaliation against the Russians. So one aspect of the moral problem of deterrence is this: Is one justified in *threatening* to do something which is immoral, if the reasoned intention behind one's threat is to prevent something immoral from occurring?

Let us consider some analogous situations.

(1) It would be immoral to kill a man in order to prevent default on a debt, even if one had no intention of killing the man at all, so long as he pays the debt. Indeed, it is immoral to threaten to kill a man in order to pay a debt, even if one has no intention of killing him under any circumstances, including nonpayment of the debt. In this case at least, threatening evil is not justified by good results or an increased chance of good results. Perhaps this lack of justification derives from the inherent wrongfulness of such threats of violence or from the bad results that would follow if everyone regularly made threats of this sort—whatever the cause, the good results that *actually* follow from the threat[6] do not justify it; even, I would say, in a state of nature containing no judicial system. (2) It might be objected that this example is unfair because the stakes in question are not high enough. Would it be equally immoral to threaten to kill Jones if the intention of the threat is to prevent Jones from doing murder himself, and if the threat will *be* carried out only when Jones actually does murder? This, perhaps, is the way deterrence theorists view the present strategic *détente.* It must be admitted that in this situation the threat to kill is not *obviously* immoral. Indeed, anyone who recommends capital punishment for convicted murderers is allowing that such threats, if tempered by due process of law, are *not* immoral.

The difficulty with this example is that it does not truly reflect the structure of our present nuclear policy. Our policy is not to threaten a potential *murderer* with death in order to prevent him from murdering, and to execute *him* when he actually does murder, but rather to threaten *someone else* with death in order to prevent a potential murderer from attacking and to execute *someone else* when the murderer actually strikes. An American counterattack

[6]This includes the actual increased chance that the debt will be paid.

would be directed against the Russian people, and it is not the Russian people who would be ordering an attack on the American people. Similarly, if leaders in the United States ordered an attack on Russia, the Russian counterattack would fall on the American people and not on the leaders who ordered the attack.[7] In the present *détente*, the leaders of each side hold the population of the other hostage, and threaten to execute the hostages if the opposing *leaders* do not meet certain conditions. The proper moral examples, then, with which to analyze the *détente* should be examples of hostage-taking. (3) Suppose that the Hatfields and the McCoys live in an area sufficiently rural that disputes cannot be settled by appeal to a higher authority. For various reasons, the two families take a dislike to each other. Each family, let us assume, possesses hand grenades that could destroy the other family completely; and against these hand grenades there is no adequate defense. Each family, in what it considers to be a defensive move, kidnaps a child from the family of the other and holds it hostage. Each side wires its hostage to a device which will explode and kill the hostage if there is any loud noise nearby — such as the noise of a grenade attack or, what is not likely but still *possible*, the accidental explosion of the captors' own grenades or the sounding of a nearby clap of thunder. This example, I believe, fairly represents the present policies of deterrence.

A defender of Hatfield foreign policy might justify himself as follows: "We have no intention of killing the McCoy child, unless, of course, we are attacked. If we are attacked, we must kill him automatically (or else lose the credibility of this deterrent); but we feel that it is very unlikely that, under these conditions, any attack will occur. True, there is some small chance that the child will die by accident, but this is only a *small* chance, and so we have good reason to believe that this will not happen. At the same time, the presence of the hostage reduces the chance that the McCoys will attack, relative to the chances of attack if we had taken no hostage. If the child dies, we cannot be blamed, since we had good reason to believe that he would not, and if he lives, we are to be commended for adopting a policy which has in fact prevented an attack."

The moral reply here is obvious: the Hatfields have no *right* to seize the McCoy child, whatever dubious advantages they gain

---

[7]I am assuming that the Russian and American peoples cannot be held responsible for the decisions of their leaders. For the Russians, this is surely the case; for Americans, who live in a relatively more democratic nation, the issue is more debatable. Still, whatever fraction of responsibility the American people would bear for an attack on Russia, it would hardly be sufficient to justify punishing millions of Americans with injury and death.

by seizing him. True they only *threaten* to kill him, but threatening to kill him increases the chance of his being killed, and they have no right to increase these chances. The moral repulsiveness of the Hatfield policy derives from its abuse of the innocent for dubious ends. Deterring the McCoys in this manner is like deterring one's neighbors from running into you on the road by seizing their children and tying them to the front bumper of your car.[8] If everyone did this, accidents might decrease and, on balance, more lives saved than lost. Perhaps it could be predicted that the chances of a single child dying on a car bumper are slight; perhaps, by a miracle, no child would die.[9] Whatever the chances and whatever the gains, no one could claim the right to use a single child in this way. Yet it seems that the present American policy uses the entire Russian population in just this manner. In the preceding section I argued that our deterrence policy does not produce the best results when all alternative policies are considered. These examples show that even if the policy *did* produce the best results, it still ought not to be adopted.

(4) The key step in the preceding criticism is that the Hatfields have no right to increase the chances of the McCoy child dying, and analogously the United States has no right to increase the chances of the Russian populations dying. The threat is illicit if the threat is real. This leads to the interesting possibility that the threat is licit if it is fraudulent. Suppose that the United States *says* that it will counterattack if the Soviet Union attacks and gives every indication that it will counterattack (missile silos are constructed, submarines cruise the oceans, etc.); but, in fact, unknown to anyone except the highest officials in the government, all the American warheads are disarmed and simply cannot go off. In this case the United States does not threaten, but merely *seems* to threaten to counterattack. If the chance of Russian attack is decreased, such a plan would have good results without the intrinsic repulsiveness of the present policy.

But this plan has practical and moral flaws. The practical flaw is that the bogus threat will not serve as a deterrent unless the Soviet Union *does* discover that, according to the usual analysis, the chances of war will be greatly increased. So, it is not obvious that this plan gives good results, since one must balance the decreased chance of war (if the Soviet Union respects the deterrent) against the increased chance of war (if the Soviet Union discovers that the deterrent is bogus). Furthermore, if this plan is successfully put into effect and the Soviet Union does not have a similar

---

[8]This example is in Paul Ramsey, *Modern War and the Christian Conscience.*
[9]This miracle, in reference to nuclear weapons, we have seen since 1945.

plan of its own, the bogus-warhead plan will result in high and wasteful Soviet expenditures and in an increased chance of accidental or deliberate attack from the Soviet side.

The chances of nuclear war have diminished considerably since the early 1960s;[10] our policies now are safer than they were then. But these improvements should not blind us to the inherent abhorrence of the present policies and the dangers that they pose. Mutual deterrence is neither rational, nor prudent, nor moral, compared to other policies that are not beyond the power of rational men.

[10]In the early 1960s, the American public overestimated the chance that nuclear war would occur. In the early 1970s, I believe that the public underestimates the chance that nuclear war will occur, and public interest in this issue is nil. But it is a good thing that this mistake is common, since lack of expectation that nuclear attacks will occur lessens the chance that nuclear accidents will be interpreted as hostile acts. In the strange world of nuclear deterrence, ignorance may bring bliss.

pacifism:
a philosophical
analysis

jan narveson

Several different doctrines have been called "pacifism," and it is impossible to say anything cogent about it without saying which of them one has in mind. I must begin by making it clear, then, that I am limiting the discussion of pacifism to a rather narrow band of doctrines, further distinctions among which will be brought out below. By "pacifism," I do *not* mean the theory that violence is evil. With appropriate restrictions, this is a view that every person with any pretensions to morality doubtless holds: Nobody thinks that we have a right to inflict pain wantonly on other people. The pacifist goes a very long step further. *His* belief is not only that violence is evil but also that it is morally wrong to use force to resist, punish, or prevent violence. This further step makes pacifism a radical moral doctrine. What I shall try to establish below is that it is in fact, more than merely radical—it is actually incoherent because self-contradictory in its fundamental intent. I shall also suggest that several moral attitudes and psychological views which have tended to be associated with pacifism as I have defined it do not have any necessary connection with that doctrine. Most pro-

From *Ethics*, vol. 75 (1965). Rewritten for this volume, including the insertion of part of a subsequent article, "Is Pacifism Consistent?," from *Ethics*, vol. 78 (1968).

ponents of pacifism, I shall argue, have tended to confuse these different things, and that confusion is probably what accounts for such popularity as pacifism has had.

It is next in order to point out that the pacifistic attitude is a matter of degree, and this in two respects. In the first place, there is the question: How much violence should not be resisted, and what degree of force is one not entitled to use in resisting, punishing, or preventing it? Answers to this question will make a lot of difference. For example, everyone would agree that there are limits to the kind and degree of force with which a particular degree of violence is to be met: we do not have a right to kill someone for rapping us on the ribs, for example, and yet there is no tendency toward pacifism in this. We might go further and maintain, for example, that capital punishment, even for the crime of murder, is unjustified without doing so on pacifist grounds. Again, the pacifist should say just what sort of a reaction constitutes a forcible or violent one. If somebody attacks me with his fists and I pin his arms to his body with wrestling holds which restrict him but cause him no pain, is that all right in the pacifist's book? And again, many non-pacifists could consistently maintain that we should avoid, to the extent that it is possible, inflicting a like pain on those who attempt to inflict pain on us. It is unnecessary to be a pacifist merely in order to deny the moral soundness of the principle, "an eye for an eye and a tooth for a tooth." We need a clarification, then, from the pacifist as to just how far he is and is not willing to go. But this need should already make us pause, for surely the pacifist cannot draw these lines in a merely arbitrary manner. It is his reasons for drawing the ones he does that count, and these are what I propose to discuss below.

The second matter of degree in respect of which the pacifist must specify his doctrine concerns the question: Who ought not to resist violence with force? For example, there are pacifists who would only claim that they themselves ought not to. Others would say that only pacifists ought not to, or that all persons of a certain type, where the type is not specified in terms of belief or non-belief in pacifism, ought not to resist violence with force. And finally, there are those who hold that everyone ought not to do so. We shall see that considerations about this second variable doom some forms of pacifism to contradiction.

My general program will be to show that (1) only the doctrine that everyone ought not to resist violence with force is of philosophical interest among those doctrines known as "pacifism"; (2) that doctrine, if advanced as a moral doctrine, is logically untenable; and (3) the reasons for the popularity of pacifism rest on failure to see exactly what the doctrine is. The things which pacifism wishes to accomplish, insofar as they are worth accomplishing, can be managed on the basis of quite ordinary and conservative moral principles.

Let us begin by being precise about the kind of moral force the principle of pacifism is intended to have. One good way to do this is to consider what it is intended to deny. What would non-pacifists, which I suppose includes most people, say of a man who followed Christ's suggestion and, when unaccountably slapped, simply turned the other cheek? They might say that such a man is either a fool or a saint. Or they might say, "It's all very well for him to do that, but it's not for me"; or they might simply shrug their shoulders and say, "Well, it takes all kinds, doesn't it?" But they would *not* say that a man who did that ought to be punished in some way; they would not even say that he had done anything wrong. In fact, as I have mentioned, they would more likely than not find something admirable about it. The point, then, is this: The non-pacifist does *not* say that it is your *duty* to resist violence with force. The non-pacifist is merely saying that there's nothing wrong with doing so, that one has every right to do so if he is so inclined. Whether we wish to add that a person would be foolish or silly to do so is qu te another question, one on which the non-pacifist does not *need* to take any particular position.

Consequently, a genuine pacifist cannot merely say that we may, if we wish, prefer not to resist violence with force. Nor can he merely say that there is something admirable or saintly about not doing so, for, as pointed out above, the non-pacifist could perfectly well agree with that. He must say, instead, that, for whatever class of people he thinks it applies to, there is something positively wrong about meeting violence with force. He must say that, insofar as the people to whom his principle applies resort to force, they are committing a breach of moral duty—a very serious thing to say. Just how serious, we shall ere long see.

Next, we must understand what the implications of holding pacifism as a moral principle are, and the first such implication requiring our attention concerns the matter of the size of the class of people to which it is supposed to apply. It will be of interest to discuss two of the four possibilities previously listed, I think. The first is that in which the pacifist says that only pacifists have the duty of pacifism. Let us see what this amounts to.

If we say that the principle of pacifism is the principle that all and only pacifists have a duty of not opposing violence with force, we get into a very odd situation. For suppose we ask ourselves, "Very well, which people are the pacifists then?" The answer will have to be "All those people who believe that pacifists have the duty not to meet violence with force." But surely one could believe that a certain class of people, whom we shall call "pacifists," have the duty not to meet violence with force without believing that one ought not, oneself, to meet violence with force. That is to say, the "principle" that pacifists ought to avoid meeting violence with force, is circular: It presupposes that one already knows who the pacifists are. Yet this is precisely what that statement of the principle is supposed to answer! We are supposed to be able to say that anybody who believes that principle is a pacifist; yet, as we have seen, a person could very well believe that a certain class of people called "pacifists" ought not to meet violence with force without believing that he himself ought not to meet violence with force. Thus everyone could be a "pacifist" in the sense of believing that statement and yet no one believes that he *himself* (or anyone in particular) ought to avoid meeting violence with force. Consequently, pacifism cannot be specified in that way. A pacifist must be a person who believes either that he himself (at least) ought not to meet force with force or that some larger class of persons, perhaps everyone, ought not to meet force with force. He would then be believing something definite, and we are then in a position to ask why.

Incidentally, it is worth mentioning that when people say things such as "Only pacifists have the duty of pacifism," "Only Catholics have the duties of Catholicism," and, in general, "Only X-ists have the duties of X-ism" they probably are falling into a trap which catches a good many people. It is, namely, the mistake of supposing that what it *is* to have a certain duty is to *believe* that you have a certain duty. The untenability of this is parallel to the untenability of the previously mentioned attempt to say what pacifism is. For, if having a duty is believing that you have a certain duty, the question arises, "*What* does such a person believe?" The answer that must be given if we follow this analysis would then be, "He believes that he believes that he has a certain duty"; and so on, ad infinitum.

On the other hand, one might believe that having a duty does not consist in believing that one has and yet believe that only those people really have the duty who believe that they have it. But in that case, we would, being conscientious, perhaps want to ask the question, "Well, *ought* I to believe that I have that duty, or oughtn't I?" If you say that the answer is "Yes," the reason cannot be that you already do believe it, for you are asking whether you *should*. On the other hand, the answer "No" or "It doesn't make any difference—it's up to you," implies that there is really no reason for doing the thing in question at all. In short, asking whether I ought to believe that I have a duty to do x, is equivalent to asking whether I should *do x*. A person might very well believe that he ought to do x but be wrong. It might be the case that he really ought *not* to do x; in that case the fact that he believes he ought to do x, far from being a reason why he ought to do it, is a reason for us to point out his error. It also, of course, presupposes that he has some reason other than his belief for thinking it is his duty to do x.

Having cleared this red herring out of the way, we must consider the view of those who believe that they themselves have a duty of pacifism and ask ourselves the question: What general kind of reason must a person have for supposing a certain type of act to be *his* duty, in a moral sense? Now, one answer he might give is that pacifism as such is a duty, that is, that meeting violence with force is, as such, wrong. In that case, however, what he thinks is not merely that *he* has this duty, but that *everyone* has this duty.

Now he might object, "Well, but no; I don't mean that everyone has it. For instance, if a man is defending, not himself, but *other* people, such as his wife and children, then he has a right to meet violence with force." Now this, of course, would be a very important qualification to his principle and one of a kind which we will be discussing in a moment. Meanwhile, however, we may point out that he evidently still thinks that, if it weren't for certain more important duties, everyone would have a duty to avoid meeting violence with force. In other words, he then believes that, other things being equal, one ought not to meet violence with force. He believes, to put it yet another way, that if one does meet violence with force, one must have a special excuse or justification of a moral kind; then he may want to give some account of just which excuses and justifications would do. Nevertheless, he is now holding a general principle.

Suppose, however, he holds that no one *else* has this duty of pacifism, that only he himself ought not to meet force with force, although it is quite all right for others to do so. Now if this is what our man feels, we may continue to call him a "pacifist," in a somewhat attenuated sense, but he is then no longer holding pacifism as a *moral* principle or, indeed, as a principle at all.[1] For now his disinclination for violence is essentially just a matter of taste. I like pistachio ice cream, but I wouldn't dream of saying that other people have a duty to eat it; similarly, this man just doesn't *like* to meet force with force, although he wouldn't dream of insisting

[1] Compare, for example, K. Baier, *The Moral Point of View* (Ithaca: Cornell University Press, 1958), p. 191.

that others act as he does. And this is a secondary sense of "paci-fism," first, because pacifism has always been advocated on moral grounds and, second, because non-pacifists can easily have this same feeling. A person might very well feel squeamish, for exam-ple, about using force, even in self-defense, or he might not be able to bring himself to use it even if he wants to. But none of these has anything to do with asserting pacifism to be a duty. Moreover, a mere attitude could hardly license a man to refuse military serv-ice if it were required of him, or to join ban-the-bomb crusades, and so forth. (I fear, however, that such attitudes have sometimes caused people to do those things.)

And, in turn, it is similarly impossible to claim that your sup-port of pacifism is a moral one if your position is that a certain selection of people, but no one else, ought not to meet force with force, even though you are unprepared to offer any reason what-ever for this selection. Suppose, for example, that you hold that only the Arapahoes, or only the Chinese, or only people more than six feet high have this "duty." If such were the case, and no rea-sons offered at all, we could only conclude that you had a very pe-culiar attitude toward the Arapahoes, or whatever, but we would hardly want to say that you had a moral principle. Your "prin-ciple" amounts to saying that these particular individuals happen to have the duty of pacifism just because they are the individuals they are, and this, as Bentham would say, is the "negation of all principle." Of course, if you meant that somehow the property of being over six feet tall *makes* it your duty not to use violence, then you have a principle, all right, but a very queer one indeed unless you can give some further reasons. Again, it would not be possible to distinguish this from a sheer attitude.

Pacifism, then, must be the principle that the use of force to meet force is wrong *as such*, that is, that nobody may do so unless he has a special justification.

There is another way in which one might advocate a sort of "pacifism," however, which we must also dispose of before getting to the main point. One might argue that pacifism is desirable as a tactic: that, as a matter of fact, some good end, such as the reduc-tion of violence itself, is to be achieved by "turning the other cheek." For example, if it were the case that turning the other cheek caused the offender to break down and repent, then that would be a very good reason for behaving "pacifistically." If uni-lateral disarmament causes the other side to disarm, then certainly unilateral disarmament would be a desirable policy. But note that its desirability, if this is the argument, is due to the fact that peace is desirable, a moral position which anybody can take, pacifist or no, plus the purely contingent fact that this policy causes the other side to disarm, that is, it brings about peace.

And, of course, that's the catch. If one attempts to support pacifism, because of its probable effects, then one's position depends on what the effects are. Determining what they are is a purely empirical matter, and, consequently, one could not possibly be a pacifist as a matter of pure principle if his reasons for supporting pacifism are merely tactical. One must, in this case, submit one's opinions to the governance of fact.

It is not part of my intention to discuss matters of fact, as such, but it is worthwhile to point out that the general history of the human race certainly offers no support for the supposition that turning the other cheek always produces good effects on the aggressor. Some aggressors, such as the Nazis, were apparently just "egged on" by the "pacifist" attitude of their victims. Some of the S.S. men apparently became curious to see just how much torture the victim would put up with before he began to resist. Furthermore, there is the possibility that, while pacifism might work against some people (one might cite the British, against whom pacifism in India was apparently rather successful—but the British are comparatively nice people), it might fail against others (e.g., the Nazis).

A further point about holding pacifism to be desirable as a tactic is that this could not easily support the position that pacifism is a *duty*. The question whether we have no *right* to fight back can hardly be settled by noting that not to fight back might cause the aggressor to stop fighting. To prove that a policy is a desirable one because it works is not to prove that it is *obligatory* to follow it. We surely need considerations a good deal less tenuous than this to prove such a momentous contention as that we have no *right* to resist.

It appears, then, that to hold the pacifist position as a genuine, full-blooded moral principle is to hold that nobody has a right to fight back when attacked, that fighting back is inherently evil, as such. It means that we are all mistaken in supposing that we have a right of self-protection. And, of course, this is an extreme and extraordinary position in any case. It appears to mean, for instance, that we have no right to punish criminals, that all of our machinery of criminal justice is, in fact, unjust. Robbers, murderers, rapists, and miscellaneous delinquents ought, on this theory, to be let loose.

Now, the pacifist's first move, upon hearing this, will be to claim that he has been misrepresented. He might say that it is only one's *self* that one has no right to defend, and that one may legitimately fight in order to defend other people. This qualification cannot be made by those pacifists who qualify as conscientious objectors, of course, for the latter are refusing to defend their fellow citizens and not merely themselves. But this is comparatively trivial when we contemplate the next objection to this amended version of the theory. Let us now ask ourselves what it is about attacks on *other* people which could possibly justify *us* in defending them, while we are not justified in defending ourselves? It cannot be the mere fact that they are other people than ourselves, for, of course, everyone is a different person from everyone else, and if such a consideration could ever of itself justify anything at all it could also justify anything whatever. That mere difference of person, as such, is of no moral importance, is a presupposition of anything that can possibly pretend to be a moral theory.

Instead of such idle nonsense, then, the pacifist would have to mention some specific characteristic which every *other* person has which we lack and which justifies us in defending them. But this, alas, is impossible, for, while there may be some interesting difference between *me* on the one hand and everyone else on the other, the pacifist is not merely addressing himself to me. On the contrary, as we have seen, he has to address himself to everyone. He is claiming that each person has no right to defend himself, although he does have a right to defend other people. And, therefore, what is needed is a characteristic which distinguishes *each* person from everyone else, and not just *me* from everyone else— which is plainly self-contradictory.

Again, then, the pacifist must retreat in order to avoid talking nonsense. His next move might be to say that we have a right to defend all those who are not able to defend themselves. Big, grown-up men who are able to defend themselves ought not to do so, but they ought to defend mere helpless children who are unable to defend themselves.

This last, very queer theory could give rise to some amusing logical gymnastics. For instance, what about groups of people? If a group of people who cannot defend themselves singly can defend themselves together, then when it has grown to that size ought it to stop defending itself? If so, then every time a person *can* defend someone else, he would form with the person being defended a "defensive unit" which was able to defend itself, and thus would by this very presence debar himself from making the defense. At this rate, no one will ever get defended, it seems: The defenseless people by definition cannot defend themselves, while those who can defend them would enable the group consisting of the defenders and the defended to defend themselves, and hence they would be obliged not to do so.

Such reflections, however, are merely curious shadows of a much more fundamental and serious logical problem. This arises when we begin to ask: But why should even defenseless people be defended? If resisting violence is inherently evil, then how can it suddenly become permissible when we use it on behalf of other people? The fact that they are defenseless cannot possibly account for this, for it follows from the theory in question, that everyone ought to put himself in the position of people who are defenseless by refusing to defend himself. This type of pacifist, in short, is using the very characteristic (namely, being in a state of not defending oneself which he wishes to encourage in others as a reason for denying it in the case of those who already have it (namely, the defenseless). This is surely inconsistent.

To attempt to be consistent, at least, the pacifist is forced to accept the characterization of him at which we tentatively arrived. He must say that no one ought ever to be defended against attack. The right of self-defense can be denied coherently only if the right of defense, in general, is denied. This in itself is an important conclusion.

It must be borne in mind, by the way, that I have not said anything to take exception to the man who simply does not wish to defend himself. So long as he does not attempt to make his pacifism into a principle, one cannot accuse him of any inconsistency, however much one might wish to say that he is foolish or eccentric. It is solely with moral principles that I am concerned here.

We now come to the last and most fundamental problem of all. If we ask ourselves what the point of pacifism is, what gets it going, so to speak, the answer is, of course, obvious enough: opposition to violence. The pacifist is generally thought of as the man who is so much opposed to violence that he will not even use it to defend himself or anyone else. And it is precisely this characterization which I wish to show is morally inconsistent.

To begin with, we may note something which at first glance may seem merely to be a matter of fact, albeit one which should worry the pacifist, in our latest characterization of him. I refer to the commonplace observation that, generally speaking, we measure a man's degree of opposition to something by the amount of effort he is willing to put forth against it. A man could hardly be said to be dead set against something if he is not willing to lift a finger to keep it from going on. A person who claims to be completely opposed to something yet does nothing to prevent it would ordinarily be said to be a hypocrite.

As facts, however, we cannot make too much of these. The pacifist could claim to be willing to go to any length, short of violence, to prevent violence. He might, for instance, stand out in the cold all day long handing out leaflets (as I have known some to do), and this would surely argue for the sincerity of his beliefs.

But would it really?

Let us ask ourselves, one final time, what we are claiming when we claim that violence is morally wrong and unjust. We are, in the first place, claiming that a person *has no right* to indulge in it, as such (meaning that he has no right to indulge in it, *unless* he has an overriding justification). But what do we mean when we say that he has no right to indulge in it? Violence, of the type we are considering, is a two-termed affair: one does violence *to* somebody, one cannot simply "do violence." It might be oneself, of course, but we are not primarily interested in those cases, for what makes it wrong to commit violence is that it harms the people to whom it is done. To say that it is wrong is to say that those to whom it is done have a right *not* to have it done to them. (This must again be qualified by pointing out that this is so only if they have done nothing to merit having that right abridged.)

Yet what could that right to their own security, which people have, possibly consist in if not a right at least to be protected from whatever violence might be offered them? But lest the reader think that this is a gratuitous assumption, note carefully the reason why having a right involves having a right to be defended from breaches of that right. It is because the prevention of infractions of that right is precisely what one has a right to when one has a right at all. A right just *is* a status justifying preventive action. To say that you have a right to X but that no one has any justification whatever for preventing people from depriving you of it, is self-contradictory. If you claim a right to X, then to describe some action as an act of depriving you of X, is logically to imply that its absence is one of the things that you have a right to.

Thus far it does not follow logically that we have a right to use force in our own or anyone's defense. What does follow logically is that one has a right to whatever may be necessary to prevent infringements of his right. One might at first suppose that the universe *could* be so constructed that it is never necessary to use force to prevent people who are bent on getting something from getting it.

Yet even this is not so, for when we speak of "force" in the sense in which pacifism is concerned with it, we do not mean merely physical "force." To call an action a use of force is not merely to make a reference to the laws of mechanics. On the contrary, it is to describe whatever is being done as being a means to the infliction on somebody of something (ordinarily physical) which he does not want done to him; and the same is true for "force" in the sense in which it applies to war, assault and battery, and the like.

The proper contrary of "force" in this connection is "rational persuasion." Naturally, one way there *might* be of getting somebody not to do something he has no right to do is to convince him he ought not to do it or that it is not in his interest to do it. But it is inconsistent, I suggest, to argue that rational persuasion is the only morally permissible method of preventing violence. A pragmatic reason for this is easy enough to point to: Violent people are too busy being violent to be reasonable. We cannot engage in rational persuasion unless the enemy is willing to sit down and talk; but what if he isn't? One cannot contend that every human being can be persuaded to sit down and talk before he strikes, for this is not something we can determine just by reasoning; it is a question of observation. But these points are not strictly relevant anyway, for our question is not the empirical question of whether there is some handy way which can always be used to get a person to sit down and discuss moral philosophy when he is about to murder you. Our question is: *If* force is the only way to prevent violence in a given case, is its use justified *in that case?* This is a purely moral question which we can discuss without any special reference to matters of fact. And, moreover, it is precisely this question which we should have to discuss with the would-be violator. The point is that if a person can be rationally persuaded that he ought not to engage in violence, then precisely what he would be rationally persuaded of if we were to succeed would be the proposition that the use of force is justifiable to prevent him from doing so. For note that if we were to argue that only rational persuasion is permissible as a means of preventing him, we would have to face the question: Do we mean *attempted* rational persuasion, or *successful* rational persuasion, that is, rational persuasion which really does succeed in preventing him from acting? Attempted rational persuasion might fail (if only because the opponent is unreasonable), and then what? To argue that we have a right to use rational persuasion which also succeeds (i.e., we have a right to its success as well as to its use) is to imply that we have a right to prevent him from performing the act. But this, in turn, means that, if attempts at rational persuasion fail, we have a right to the use of force. Thus what we have a right to, if we ever have a *right* to anything, is not merely the use of rational persuasion to keep people from depriving you of the thing to which you have the right. We do indeed have a right to that, but we also have a right to anything else that might be necessary (other things being equal) to prevent the deprivation from occurring. And it is a logical truth, not merely a contingent one, that what *might* be necessary is *force*. (If merely saying something could miraculously deprive someone of the ability to carry through a course of action, then those speech-acts would be called a type of force, if a very mysterious one. And we could properly begin to oppose their use for precisely the same reasons as we now oppose violence.)

What this all adds up to, then, is that *if* we have any rights at all, we have a right to use force to prevent the deprivation of the thing to which we are said to have a right. But the pacifist, of *all* people, is the one most concerned to insist that we do have some rights, namely, the right not to have violence done to us. This is logically implied in asserting it to be a duty on everyone's part to avoid violence. And this is why the pacifist's position is self-contradictory. In saying that violence is wrong, one is at the same time saying that people have a right to its prevention, by force if necessary. Whether and to what extent it may be necessary is a question of fact, but, since it is a question of fact only, the moral right to use force on some possible occasions is established.[2]

We now have an answer to the question. How much force does a given threat of violence justify for preventive purposes? The answer, in a word, is "Enough." That the answer is this simple may at first sight seem implausible. One might suppose that some elaborate equation between the aggressive and the preventive force is needed: the punishment be proportionate to the crime. But this is a misunderstanding. In the first place, prevention and punishment are not the same, even if punishment is thought to be directed mainly toward prevention. The punishment of a particular crime logically cannot prevent *that* instance of the crime, since it presupposes that it has already been performed; and punishment need not involve the use of any violence at all, although law-enforcement officers in some places have a nasty tendency to assume the contrary. But preventive force is another matter. If a man threatens to kill me, it is desirable, of course, for me to try to prevent this by the use of the least amount of force sufficient to do the job. But I am justified even in killing him *if* necessary. This

[2]This basic argument may be compared with a view of Kant's, to be found in the *Rechtslehre*, translated under the title *Metaphysical Elements of Justice* by J. Ladd, Library of Liberal Arts, pp. 35–36 (Introduction, D).

much, I suppose, is obvious to most people. But suppose his threat is much smaller: suppose that he is merely pestering me, which is a very mild form of aggression indeed. Would I be justified in killing him to prevent this, under any circumstances whatever?

Suppose that I call the police and they take out a warrant against him, and suppose that when the police come, he puts up a struggle. He pulls a knife or a gun, let us say, and the police shoot him in the ensuing battle. Has my right to the prevention of his annoying me extended to killing him? Well, not exactly, since the immediate threat in response to which he is killed is a threat to the lives of the policemen. Yet my annoyer may never have contemplated real violence. It is an unfortunate case of unpremeditated escalation. But this is precisely what makes the contention that one is justified in using enough force to do the job, whatever amount that may be, to prevent action which violates a right less alarming than at first sight it seems. For it is difficult to envisage a reason why extreme force is needed to prevent mild threats from realization except by way of escalation, and escalation automatically justifies increased use of preventive force.

The existence of laws, police, courts, and more or less civilized modes of behavior on the part of most of the populace naturally affects the answer to the question of how much force is necessary. One of the purposes of a legal system of justice is surely to make the use of force by individuals very much less necessary than it would otherwise be. If we try to think back to a "state of nature" situation, we shall have less difficulty envisaging the need for large amounts of force to prevent small threats of violence. Here Hobbes's contention that in such a state every man has a right to the life of every other becomes understandable. He was, I suggest, relying on the same principle as I have argued for here: that one has a right to use as much force as necessary to defend one's rights, which include the right of safety of person.

And needless to say, my arguments here do not give us any reason to modify the obviously vital principle that if force should be necessary, then one must use the least amount of it compatible with maintaining the rights of those being protected. There is, for example, no excuse for sending armed troops against unarmed students to contain protest marches and demonstrations.

I have said that the duty to avoid violence is only a duty, other things being equal. We might arrive at the same conclusion as we have above by asking the question: Which "other things" might count as being unequal? The answer to this is that whatever else they may be, the purpose of preventing violence from being done is necessarily one of these justifying conditions. That the use of force is never justified to prevent initial violence being done to one logically implies that there is nothing wrong with initial violence. We cannot characterize it as being wrong if preventive violence is not simultaneously being characterized as justifiable.

We often think of pacifists as being gentle and idealistic souls, which in its way is true enough. What I have been concerned to show is that they are also confused. If they attempt to formulate their position using our standard concepts of rights, their position involves a contradiction: Violence is wrong, *and* it is wrong to resist it. But the right to resist is precisely what having a right of person is, if it is anything at all.

Could the position be reformulated with a less "commital" concept of rights? I do not think so. It has been suggested[3] that the pacifist need not talk in terms of this "kind" of rights. He can affirm, according to this suggestion, simply that neither the aggressors nor the defenders "have" rights to what they do, that to affirm their not having them is simply to be against the use of force, without this entailing the readiness to use force if necessary to protect the said rights. But this will not do I believe. For I have not maintained that having a right, or believing that one has a right, entails a *readiness* to defend that right. One has a perfect right not to resist violence to oneself if one is so inclined. But our question has been whether self-defense is justifiable, and not whether one's belief that violence is wrong entails a willingness or readiness to use it. My contention has been that such a belief does entail the justifiability of using it. If one came upon a community in which no sort of violence was ever resisted and it was claimed in that community that the non-resistance was a matter of conscience, we should have to conclude, I think, not that this was a community of saints, but rather that this community lacked the concept of justice—or perhaps that their nervous systems were oddly different from ours.

No position can ever be shown to contain a contradiction if we allow its upholder to interpret his language in any manner he chooses. Perhaps some pacifists have convinced themselves that to have a right is nothing more than to possess a certain peculiar non-natural property. I don't know. But what is this to the present subject? The language which the pacifist employs is not his private property, and his theories, if he should happen to have any, about the proper logical analysis of that language, are not entitled to any *special* hearing when we come to discuss what he is saying in it. What I want to know is: Is it anything but verbal hocus-pocus to affirm that we *have rights* but to deny that they ought ever to be

[3] I owe this suggestion to my colleague, Leslie Armour.

defended? If a right isn't an entitlement to protection, then is it anything at all? This, I think, is the pacifist's dilemma. He would like to live in a world utterly at peace. So would most of us. But we do not, and so the question is, what to do about it? The pacifist's way is, as it were, to make Munich the cornerstone of our moral lives. We will act (or is that the right word here?) as if there were no violence anywhere, and then, hopefully, there will come a time when magic prevails and there is no more of it. By that time, the circle will no doubt also have been squared and infinity encompassed. But the rest of us, meanwhile, will wonder what has become of that supposed right to peace which we thought the pacifist was allowing us when we see him standing by, protesting at the top of his lungs, to be sure, but not *doing* anything about it, in the presence of violence by others.

It might be useful here to sum up the pacifist's problem, as I see it. To maintain the pacifist doctrine, I contend that one of the following three statements must be denied:

1. To will the end (as morally good) is to will the means to it (at least prima facie).
2. Other things being equal, the lesser evil is to be preferred to the greater.
3. There are no "privileged" moral persons: No person necessarily has a different status, counts for more or less than another as such, in matters of morals.

I claim, what might be denied, that all of these may be defended on purely logical or "meta-ethical" grounds and that in any case the pacifist seems to be committed to them. He is committed to (1) because his objection to violence is that it produces suffering, unwanted pain, in the recipients. As far as I know, no pacifist objects to football or Indian leg-wrestling among consenting parties. He is committed to (2) because he holds that to inflict suffering is the greatest of evils and that *this* is why the claims of non-violence take precedence to those of, say, justice (if these are really different). And he is committed to (3) by virtue of his claiming to address this doctrine to everyone, on general moral grounds. But these three principles among them imply, as far as I can see, both the commitment to force when it is necessary to prevent more violence and also the conception of a right as an entitlement to defense. And they therefore leave pacifism, as a moral doctrine, in a logically untenable position.

7

SUICIDE
AND
DEATH

the morality
and rationality
of suicide*

richard b. brandt

"Suicide" is conveniently defined, for our purposes, as doing something which results in one's death, either from the intention of ending one's life or the intention to bring about some other state of affairs (such as relief from pain) which one thinks it certain or highly probable can be achieved only by means of death or will produce death. It may seem odd to classify an act of heroic self-sacrifice on the part of a soldier as suicide. It is simpler, however, not to try to define "suicide" so that an act of suicide is always irrational or immoral in some way; if we adopt a neutral definition like the above we can still proceed to ask when an act of suicide in that sense is rational, morally justifiable, and so on, so that all evaluations anyone might wish to make can still be made.

The literature in anthropology makes clear that suicide has been evaluated very differently in different societies; and philosophers in the Western tradition have been nearly as divergent in

From Richard B. Brandt, "The Morality and Rationality of Suicide," from *A Handbook for the Study of Suicide*, edited by Seymour Perlin. Copyright © 1975 by Oxford University Press, Inc. Reprinted by permission.

*This paper was written while a Fellow at the Center for Advanced Study in the Behavioral Sciences, and also a Special Fellow in the Department of Health, Education and Welfare.

their evaluative views of it. I shall not attempt to review these evaluations. What I shall do is analyze the problem, and appraise some conclusions, from the point of view of contemporary philosophy. Some readers may think that to do this is merely to state another moral prejudice, but I am optimistic enough to believe that as they read on they will be convinced that this is not the case, and that contemporary philosophical thought has moved to a new level of sophistication on this issue as on many others.

I wish to discuss three questions. First, when is it rational, from the point of view of an agent's own welfare, for him to commit suicide? Second, when is it objectively right or wrong, morally, for an agent to take his own life? Third, if an agent takes his own life when it was objectively wrong for him to do so, when may we think that his action was morally blameworthy (or, if we like a theological term, sinful)? What these questions mean, and how they differ, must be explained as we go along. I shall discuss them, however, in reverse order, moving from what seems to me the least important question (listed third above) to the most important one (listed first above).

1. THE MORAL BLAMEWORTHINESS OF SUICIDE

In former times the question whether suicide is sinful was of great interest because the answer to it was considered relevant to how the agent would spend eternity. At present the practical issue is not great, although a normal funeral service may be denied a person judged to have committed suicide sinfully. The chief practical issue at present seems to be that persons may disapprove morally of a decedent for having committed suicide, and his friends or relatives may wish to defend his memory against moral charges. The practical issue does not seem large, but justifies some analysis of the problem.

The question whether an act of suicide was sinful or morally blameworthy is not apt to arise unless it is already believed that the agent morally ought not to have done it; this question will be examined in the following section. But sometimes we do believe that an agent ought morally not to have committed suicide: for instance, if he really had very poor reason for doing so, and his act foreseeably had catastrophic consequences for his wife and children. At least, let us suppose that we do so believe. In that case we might still think that the act was hardly morally blameworthy or sinful if, say, the agent was in a state of great emotional turmoil at the time. We might then say that, although what he did was wrong, his action is *excusable*, just as in the criminal law it may be decided that, although a person broke the law, he should not be punished because he was *not responsible*, e.g., was temporarily insane, did what he did inadvertently, and so on.

The foregoing remarks assume that to be morally blameworthy (or sinful) on account of an act is one thing, and for the act to be wrong is another. But, if we say this, what after all does it *mean* to say that a person is morally blameworthy on account of an action? We cannot say there is agreement among philosophers on this matter, but I suggest the following account as being safe from serious objection: "X is morally blameworthy on account of an action A" may be taken to mean "X did A, and X would not have done A had not his character been in some respect below standard; and in view of this it is fitting or justified for X to have some disapproving attitudes including remorse toward himself, and for some other persons Y to have some disapproving attitudes toward X and to express them in behavior." Traditional thought would include God as one of the "other persons" who might have and express disapproving attitudes. Another possible view would include only the justifiability of critical or disapproving attitudes toward a person on account of his action; one could then go on to say that such attitudes *are* justified if and only if the act would not have occurred but for the agent's character being below standard in some respect. I shall, however, adopt the former view.

In case the foregoing definition does not seem obviously correct, it is worthwhile pointing out that it is usually thought that an agent is not blameworthy or sinful for an action unless it is a *reflection on him;* the definition brings this fact out and makes clear why—that it would not have occurred but for a defect of character.

It may be thought that the above definition introduces terms as obscure as the one we are defining (e.g., "character" and "below standard"), and it is true these need explanation which cannot be provided here. But I think we are able to move more easily with them than with the original term; the definition is really clarifying. For instance, if someone charges that a suicide was sinful, we now properly ask, "What defect of character did it show?" Some writers have claimed that suicide is blameworthy because it is *cowardly;* and since being cowardly is generally conceded to be a defect of character, if an act of suicide is admitted to be both objectively wrong and also cowardly, the claim to blameworthiness is made out, if the above definition is correct. Of course, most people would hesitate to call taking one's own life (e.g., falling on one's sword) exactly a cowardly act; and there will certainly be controversy about which acts are cowardly and which are not. But at least we can see part of what has to be done to make a charge of blameworthiness valid.

The most interesting question is the general one: Which types of suicide in general are ones which, even if objectively wrong (in a sense to be explained below), are not sinful or blameworthy? Or, in other words, When is a suicide *morally excused* even if it is objectively wrong? We can at least identify some types of cases. (1) Suppose I *think* I am morally bound to commit suicide because I have a terminal illness and continued medical care will ruin my family financially. Suppose, however, that I am mistaken in this belief, and that suicide in such circumstances is not right. But surely I am not morally blameworthy; for I may be doing, out of a sense of duty to my family, what I would personally prefer not to do and is hard for me to do. What defect of character might my action show? Suicide from a genuine sense of duty is not blameworthy, even when the moral conviction in question is mistaken. (2) Suppose that I commit suicide when I am temporarily of unsound mind, either in the sense of the M'Naghten rule that I do not know that what I am doing is wrong, or of the Durham rule that, owing to a mental defect, I am substantially unable to do what is right. Surely any suicide in an unsound state of mind is morally excused. (3) Suppose I commit suicide when I could not be said to be temporarily of unsound mind, but simply because I am not myself. For instance, I may be in an extremely depressed mood. Now a person may be in a highly depressed mood, and commit suicide on account of being in that mood, when there is nothing the matter with his character—or, in other words, his character is not in any relevant way below standard. What are other examples of being "not myself," which might be states of a person responsible for his committing suicide, and which would or might render the suicide excusable even if wrong? Being frightened; being distraught; being in almost any highly emotional frame of mind (anger, frustration, disappointment in love); perhaps just being terribly fatigued. So there are at least three types of suicide which are morally excused even if objectively wrong.

The main point is this. Mr. X may commit suicide and it may be conceded that he ought not to have done so. But it is another step to show that he is sinful, or morally blameworthy, for having done so. To make out that further point, it must be shown that his act is attributable to some substandard trait of character. So Mrs. X after the suicide can concede that her husband ought not to have done what he did, but point out that it is no reflection on him. The distinction, unfortunately, is often overlooked, particularly by Catholic writers. St. Thomas, who recognizes the distinction in some places, seems blind to it in his discussion of suicide.

2. WHEN SUICIDE IS MORALLY JUSTIFIED, OR OBJECTIVELY RIGHT

It is clear, then, that even when a suicide is objectively wrong, the person may not be reprehensible, or sinful, on account of what he did. This state of affairs is possible, of course, only because an act being objectively wrong is one thing, and a person being morally blameworthy or sinful on account of it is another.

Let us now consider our second topic: when a suicide is objectively right or morally justified.

A good many philosophers and social scientists will be sceptical whether anything helpful can be said on this topic, on the assumption, which has been popular in the past thirty years, that there can be no knowledge about such matters, and that moral statements are merely expressions of the attitudes of the speaker. (Such persons doubtless have already been feeling unhappy while reading the preceding section.) I hope, however, for better things, and expect to say something convincing on the central question.

It may be clarifying for the reader if I say at the outset that what I mean by "is objectively wrong" or "is morally unjustified" is "would be prohibited by the set of moral rules which a rational person would prefer to have current or subscribed to in the consciences of persons in the society in which he expected to live a whole life, as compared with any other set of moral rules or none at all." This definition is controversial, and nothing in the following argument will turn on it, but it may be helpful to the reader to have my cards on the table.

First, I wish to clear away some confusions which have beset discussions of our question. The distinctions I am about to make are no longer controversial, and can be accepted by sceptics on the fundamental issues as well as by anyone else.

Persons who say suicide is morally wrong must be asked which of two positions they are affirming: Are they saying that every act of suicide is wrong, *everything considered?* Or are they merely saying that there is always *some* moral obligation—doubtless of serious weight—not to commit suicide, so that very often suicide is wrong, although it is possible that there are *countervailing considerations* which in particular situations make it right or even a moral duty? It is quite evident that the first position is absurd; only the second has a chance of being defensible.

In order to get clear what is wrong with the first view, we may begin with an example. Suppose an Army pilot's single-seater plane goes out of control over a heavily populated area; he has the choice of staying in the plane and bringing it down where it will do little damage but at the cost of certain death for himself, and of bailing out and letting the plane fall where it will, very possibly killing a good many civilians. Suppose he chooses to do the former, and so, by our definition, commits suicide. Does anyone want to say that his action is morally wrong? Even Immanuel Kant, who opposed suicide in all circumstances, apparently would not wish to say that it is; he would in fact say that this act is not one of suicide, for, he says, "It is no suicide to risk one's life against one's enemies, and even to sacrifice it, in order to preserve one's duties toward oneself."[1] St. Thomas, in his discussion, may seem to say it would be wrong, for he says, "It is altogether unlawful to kill oneself," admitting as an exception only the case of being under special command of God. But in fact St. Thomas would say that the act is right because the basic intention of the pilot was to save the lives of civilians, and whether an act is right or wrong is a matter of the basic intention.[2] The charitable interpretation of St. Thomas is to assert that he recognizes that in this case there are two obligations, one to spare the lives of innocent civilians and the other not to destroy one's own life, and that of the two

---

[1] *Lectures on Ethics*, New York, Harper Torchbook, 1963, p. 150.

[2] See St. Thomas Aquinas, *Summa Theologica*, Second Part of the Second Part, Q. 64, Art. 5. In Article 7, he says: "Nothing hinders one act from having two effects, only one of which is intended, while the other is beside the intention. Now moral acts take their species according to what is intended, and not according to what is beside the intention, since this is accidental as explained above (Q. 43, Art. 3: I.–II., Q. 1, Art. 3, ad 3)."

Mr. Norman St. John-Stevas, the most articulate contemporary defender of the Catholic view, writes as follows:

> Christian thought allows certain exceptions to its general condemnation of suicide. That covered by a particular divine inspiration has already been noted. Another exception arises where suicide is the method imposed by the State for the execution of a just death penalty. A third exception is *altruistic* suicide, of which the best known example is Captain Oates. Such suicides are justified by invoking the principle of double effect. The act from which death results must be good or at least morally indifferent; some other good effect must result; the death must not be directly intended or the real means to the good effect; and a grave reason must exist for adopting the course of action. (*Life, Death and the Law*, Bloomington, Ind., Indiana University Press, 1961, pp. 250–251.)

Presumably the Catholic doctrine is intended to allow suicide when this is required for meeting strong moral obligations; whether it can do so consistently depends partly on the interpretation given to "real means to the good effect." Readers interested in pursuing further the Catholic doctrine of double effect and its implications for our problem should read Philippa Foot, "The Problem of Abortion and the Doctrine of Double Effect," (*The Oxford Review*, no. 5, Trinity 1967, pp. 5–15). [Reprinted in this volume, pp. 59–70.]

obligations the former is the stronger, and therefore the action is right.

In general, we have to admit that there are things there is some moral obligation to avoid which, on account of other morally relevant considerations, it is sometimes right or even morally obligatory to do. There may be some obligation to tell the truth on every occasion, but there are surely many cases in which the consequences of telling the truth would be so catastrophic that one is obligated to lie. To take simple cases: Should one always tell an author truthfully how one evaluates his book, or tell one's wife truthfully whether she looks attractive today? The same again, for promises. There seems to be some moral obligation to do what one has promised (with some exceptions); but if one can keep a trivial promise only at serious cost to another (e.g., keep an appointment only by failing to give aid to someone injured in an accident), it is surely obligatory to break the promise.

The most that the moral critic of suicide could hold, then, is that there is *some* moral obligation not to do what one knows will cause one's death; but he surely cannot say there are no circumstances in which there are obligations to do things which in fact will result in one's death—obligations so strong that it is at least right, and possibly morally obligatory, to do something which will certainly result in one's own death. Possibly those who argue that suicide is immoral do not intend to contest this point, although if so they have not expressed themselves very clearly.

If this interpretation is correct, then in principle it would be possible to argue that, in order to meet my obligation to my family, I might take my own life, as the only course of action which could avoid catastrophic hospital expenses, in a terminal illness. I suspect critics may not concede this point, but *in principle* it would seem they must admit arguments of this type; the real problem is comparing the weights of the obligation to extend my own life and of the obligation to see to the future welfare of my family.

The charitable interpretation of critics of suicide on moral grounds, then, is to attribute to them the view that there is a strong moral obligation not to take one's own life, although this obligation may be overmatched by some other obligations, say to avoid causing the death of others. Possibly the main point they would wish to make is that it is never right to take one's own life *for reasons of one's own personal welfare*, of any kind whatsoever. From here on, I shall construe the position in this way. Some of the arguments used to support the immorality of suicide, however, are so strong that if they were supportable at all, they would prove that suicide is *never* moral.

What reasons have been offered for believing that there is a strong moral obligation to avoid suicide, which cannot be over-weighed by any consideration of personal welfare? I shall discuss the main arguments briefly in a common-sense way.

The first arguments may be classified as *theological*. St. Augustine and others urged that the Sixth Commandment ("Thou shalt not kill") prohibits suicide, and that we are bound to obey a divine commandment. To this reasoning one might first reply that it is arbitrary exegesis of the Sixth Commandment to assert that it was ever intended to prohibit suicide. The second reply is that if there is not some consideration which shows on the merits of the case that suicide is morally wrong, God had no business prohibiting it. Doubtless some will object to this point, and I must confess that I think that it is merely quaint to appeal to the Commandments in a serious moral discussion in the Twentieth Century. But anyone interested can find my more serious defense of this objection elsewhere.[3] A second type of theological argument with wide support was accepted by John Locke, who wrote:

> ... Men being all the workmanship of one omnipotent and infinitely wise Maker; all the servants of one sovereign Master, sent into the world by His order and about His business; they are His property, whose workmanship they are made to last during His, not one an-other's pleasure. . . . Every one . . . is bound to preserve himself, and not to quit his ·station wilfully. . . .[4]

And Kant:

> We have been placed in this world under certain conditions and for specific purposes. But a suicide opposes the purpose of his Creator; he arrives in the other world as one who has deserted his post; he must be looked upon as a rebel against God. So long as we remember the truth that it is God's intention to preserve life, we are bound to regulate our activities in conformity with it. . . . This duty is upon us until the time comes when God expressly commands us to leave this life. Human beings are sentinels on earth and may not leave their posts until relieved by another beneficent hand.[5]

Unfortunately, however, even if it is granted that it is the duty of human beings to do what God commands or intends them to do, more argument is required to show that God does *not* permit human beings to quit this life when their own personal welfare would

[3]R. B. Brandt, *Ethical Theory*, Englewood Cliffs, N.J., Prentice-Hall, Inc., 1959, pp. 61–82.
[4]John Locke, *Two Treatises of Government*, chap. 2.
[5]Immanuel Kant, *Lectures on Ethics*, Harper Torchbook, 1963, p. 154.

Richard B. Brandt

be maximized by so doing. How does one draw the requisite inference about the intentions of God? The difficulties and contradictions in arguments to reach such a conclusion are discussed at length and perspicaciously by David Hume in his essay "On Suicide," and in view of the unlikelihood that readers will need to be persuaded about these, I shall merely refer the interested to that essay.[6]

A second group of arguments may be classed as arguments *from natural law*. St. Thomas says:

> It is altogether unlawful to kill oneself, for three reasons. First, because everything naturally loves itself, the result being that everything naturally keeps itself in being, and resists corruptions so far as it can. Wherefore suicide is contrary to the inclination of nature, and to charity whereby every man should love himself. Hence suicide is always a mortal sin, as being contrary to the natural law and to charity.

Here St. Thomas ignores two obvious points. First, it is not obvious why a human being is morally bound to do what it has some inclination to do. (St. Thomas did not criticize chastity.) Second, while it is true that most human beings do feel a strong urge to live, the human being who commits suicide obviously feels a stronger inclination to do something else. The "inclination" of the deliberate suicide is not to cling to life, but to do something else instead. It is as natural for a human being to dislike, and to take steps to avoid, say, great pain, as it is to cling to life. A somewhat similar argument by Immanuel Kant may seem better. In a famous passage Kant writes: The maxim of a person who commits suicide

> ... is "From self-love I make it my principle to shorten my life if its continuance threatens more evil that it promises pleasure." The only further question to ask is whether this principle of self-love can become a universal law of nature. It is then seen at once that a system of nature by whose law the very same feeling whose function is to stimulate the furtherance of life should actually destroy life would contradict itself and consequently could not subsist as a system of nature. Hence this maxim cannot possibly hold as a universal law of nature and is therefore entirely opposed to the supreme principle of all duty.[7]

[6]This essay was first published in 1783, and appears in collections of Hume's works. For an argument similar to Kant's, see also St. Thomas, *Summa Theologica*, II, II, Q. 64, Art. 5.
[7]I. Kant, *The Fundamental Principles of the Metaphysics of Morals*, translated by H.J. Paton, London, The Hutchinson Group, 1948, chap. 2. First German edition in 1785.

371

What Kant finds contradictory is that the motive of self-love (interest in one's own long-range welfare) should sometimes lead one to struggle to preserve one's life, but at other times to end it. But where is the contradiction? One's circumstances change; and, if the argument of the following section is correct, one sometimes maximizes one's own long-range welfare by trying to stay alive, but at other times by bringing about one's demise. So, if one's consistent motive is to maximize one's long-term welfare, sometimes (usually) one will do one thing; but sometimes one may do another.

A third group of arguments, a form of which goes back at least to Aristotle, has a more modern and convincing ring. These are arguments to show that, in one way or another, a suicide necessarily does harm to other persons, or to society at large. Some of these arguments are farfetched. Aristotle says that the suicide treats the *state* unjustly.[8] Partly following Aristotle, St. Thomas says: "Every man is part of the community, and so, as such, he belongs to the community. Hence by killing himself he injures the community."[9] Blackstone held that a suicide is an offense against the king "who hath an interest in the preservation of all his subjects," perhaps following Judge Brown in 1563, who argued that suicide cost the king a subject——"he being the head has lost one of his mystical members."[10] The premise of such arguments is, as Hume pointed out, obviously mistaken in many instances. It is true that Freud would perhaps have injured society had he not finished his last book (as he did), instead of committing suicide to escape the pain of throat cancer. But surely there have been many suicides whose demise was not a noticeable loss to society; an honest man could only say that in many instances society was better off without them.

It need not be denied that suicide is often injurious to other persons, especially the family of a suicide. Clearly it sometimes is. But we should notice what this fact establishes. Suppose we admit, as generally would be done, that there is some obligation not to perform any action that will probably or certainly be injurious to other people, the strength of the obligation being dependent on various factors, notably the seriousness of the expected injury. Then there is *some* obligation not to commit suicide, when that act would probably or certainly be injurious to other people——a conclusion which will probably not be disputed. But, as we have already seen, there are many cases of some obligation to do some-

[8]Aristotle, *Nicomachaean Ethics,* bk. 5, chap. 10, p. 1138a.
[9]Loc. cit.
[10]Blackstone, *Commentaries,* IV: 189; Brown in *Hales v. Petit,* I Plow. 253, 75 E.R. 387 (C.B. 1563). Both cited by Norman St. John-Stevas, op. cit., p. 235.

thing, but which nevertheless are *not* cases of a duty to do that thing, *everything considered.* So it *could* sometimes be quite justi-fied morally to commit suicide, even if the act will do some harm to someone. Must a man with a terminal illness undergo excru-ciating pain because his death will cause his wife sorrow—when she will be caused sorrow a month later anyway, when he is dead of natural causes? So, to repeat, the fact that someone has some obligation not to commit suicide when that act will probably in-jure other persons does not imply that, everything considered, it is wrong for him to do it. Moreover, the fact that there is some obligation not to commit suicide when it will probably injure others does not show that suicide *as such* is something there is some obligation to avoid. It is not proved that there is an obliga-tion to avoid suicide as such. There is an obligation to avoid in-juring others and to avoid suicide when it will probably injure others; but this is very different from showing that suicide *as such* is something there is some obligation to avoid, in all instances.

Is there any way in which we could give a sound argument, convincing to the modern mind, establishing that there is (or is not) *some moral obligation* to avoid suicide *as such,* an obligation of course which might be overriden by other obligations in some or many cases? (Captain Oates might have a moral obligation not to commit suicide as such, but his obligation not to stand in the way of his comrades getting to safety might have been so strong that, everything considered, he was justified in leaving the polar camp and allowing himself to freeze to death.)

To give all the argument which would make an answer to this question convincing would take a great deal of space. I shall there-fore simply state one answer to it which seems plausible to some contemporary philosophers and which I suspect will seem plausi-ble to the reader. Suppose it could be shown that it would maxi-mize the long-run welfare of everybody affected if people were taught that there is a moral obligation to avoid suicide—so that people would be motivated to avoid suicide just because they thought it wrong (would have anticipatory guilt feelings at the very idea), and so that other people would be inclined to disap-prove persons who commit suicide unless there were some excuse (such as those mentioned in the first section). One might ask: How could it maximize utility to mould the conceptual and motivational structure of persons in this way? To which the answer might be: Feeling in this way might make persons who are impulsively in-clined to commit suicide in a bad mood, or a fit of anger or jeal-ousy, take more time to deliberate; hence, some suicides that have bad effects generally might be prevented. In other words, it might be a good thing in its effects for people to feel about suicide in the way they feel about breach of promise or injuring others, just as it might be a good thing for people to feel a moral obligation not to smoke, or to wear seat belts. I do not say this *would* be a good thing; all I am saying is that *if* it could be made out to be welfare-maximizing for people's consciences to trouble them at the very thought of suicide (etc.), then I would think that there is some moral obligation not to commit this act. I am not at all sure, in fact, whether it *would* be welfare-maximizing for people to have negative moral feelings about suicide as such; maybe what is needed is just for them to have negative moral feelings about injuring others in some way, and perhaps negative moral feelings about failing to deliberate adequately about their own welfare, before taking any serious and irrevocable course of action. It might be that negative moral feelings about suicide as such would stand in the way of courageous action by those persons whose welfare really is best served by suicide, and whose suicide is, in fact, the best thing for everybody concerned. One piece of information highly relevant to what ought to be "taught-into" the consciences of people in this regard is why people do commit suicide and how often the general welfare (and especially their own welfare) is served by so doing. If among those people who commit suicide who are intellectually able to weigh pros and cons are usually ones who commit suicide in a depression and do not serve anybody's welfare by so doing, then that would be a point in favor of teaching people that suicide is wrong as such.

3. WHETHER AND WHEN SUICIDE IS BEST OR RATIONAL FOR THE AGENT

We come now to a topic which, for better or worse, strikes me as of more considerable practical interest: whether and when suicide is the rational or best thing for a person, from the point of view of his own welfare. If I were asked for advice by someone contemplating suicide, it is to this topic, I believe, that I would be inclined primarily to address myself. Some of the writers who are most inclined to affirm that suicide is morally wrong are quite ready to believe that from the agent's own selfish point of view suicide would sometimes be the best thing for him, but they do not discuss the point in any detail. I should like to get clear when it is and when it is not. Not that we can hope to get any simple conclusions applicable to everybody. What I hope to do is produce a way of looking at the matter which will help an individual see whether suicide is the best thing for *him* from the point of view of his own welfare—or whether it is the best thing for someone being advised, from the point of view of that person's welfare.

It is reasonable to discuss this topic under the restriction of two assumptions. First, I assume we are trying to decide between a *successful* suicide attempt, and no attempt. A person might try to commit suicide and succeed only in blinding himself. I am assuming that we need not worry about this possibility, so that the alternative is between producing death and continuing life roughly as it now is. The second assumption I am making is that when a person commits suicide, he is dead; that is, we do not consider that killing himself is only a way of expediting his departure to a blissful or extremely unpleasant afterlife. I shall assume there is *no* afterlife. I believe that at the present time potential suicides deliberate on the basis of both these assumptions, so that in making them I am addressing myself to the real problem as prospective suicides see it. What I want to produce is a fresh and helpful way of looking at their problem.

The problem, I take it, is a choice between future world-courses: the world-course which includes my demise, say, an hour from now, and several possible ones which contain my demise at a later point. We cannot have precise knowledge about many features of the latter group of world-courses. One thing I can't have precise knowledge about is how or when I shall die if I do not commit suicide now. One thing is certain: it will be sometime, and it is almost certain that it will be before my one-hundredth birthday. So, to go on the rational probabilities, let us look up my life expectancy at my present age from the insurance tables, making any corrections that are called for in the light of full medical information about my present state of health. If I do not already have a terminal illness, then the choice, say, is between a world-course with my death an hour from now, and several world-courses with my death, say, twenty years from now. The problem, I take it, is to decide whether the expectable utility to me of some possible world-course in which I go on for another twenty years is greater than or less than the expectable utility to me of the one in which my life stops in an hour. One thing to be clear about is: we are not choosing between death and immortality. We are choosing between death now and death some (possibly short) finite time from now.

Why do I say the choice is between *world*-courses and not just a choice between future life-courses of the prospective suicide, the one shorter than the others? The reason is that one's suicide has some impact on the world (and one's continued life has some im-

375

pact on the world), and that how the rest of the world is will often make a difference to one's evaluation of the possibilities. One *is* interested in things in the world other than just one's self and one's own happiness. For instance, one may be interested in one's children and their welfare, or in one's future reputation, or the contribution one might make to the solution of some problems, or in the publication of a book one is finishing with its possible clarifying effects on the thinking of a profession, and so on.

What is the basic problem for evaluation? It is the choice of the expectably *best* world-course. One way of looking at the evaluation, although in practice we cannot assign the specific numbers it is suggested we assign is this: We compare the suicide world-course with the continued-life world-course (or several of them), and note the features with respect to which they differ. We then assign numbers of these features, representing their utility to us if they happen, and then multiplying this utility by a number which represents the probability that this feature will occur. (Suppose I live, and am certain that either P or Q will occur, and that it is a 50:50 chance which; then I represent this biography as containing the sum of the utility of P multiplied by one-half and the utility of Q multiplied by one-half.) We then sum these numbers. The sum will represent the expectable utility of that world-course to us. The world-course with the highest sum is the one that is rationally chosen. But of course it is absurd to suppose that we can assign these numbers in actual fact; what we can actually do is something in a sense simpler but less decisive.

If we look at the matter in this way, we can see that there is a close analogy between an analysis of the rationality of suicide, and a firm's analysis of the rationality of declaring bankruptcy and going out of business. In the case of the firm, the objectives may be few and simple, and indeed for some boards of directors the only relevant question is: Will the stockholders probably be better off, or worse off, financially, if we continue or if we declare insolvency? More likely the question considered will be a bit more complex, since an enlightened firm will at least wonder what will happen to its officers and employees and customers and even possibly the general public if it goes out of business, and how their utilities will be affected. There is also another difference: When the firm goes out of business, none of the people involved goes out of business (unless some officer, etc., kills himself).

Perhaps a closer analogy, if we want an analogy, to this choice between world-courses is the choice between a life-course in which I get twelve hours' sleep tonight, and one in which I do some one (the best) of the various possibilities open to me. The

Richard B. Brandt

difference between the cases is that, to make the analogy more exact, I have to ignore the fact that I shall waken.

Since, as I have suggested, we cannot actually assign numbers in the way suggested, so as to compare expectable utilities, what then *is* the basic question we can and should answer, in order to determine which world-course is best, from the point of view of our own welfare? Certainly the question has to do with what we do or shall, or under certain circumstances would, *want* to happen, or want not to happen. But it is not just a question of what we prefer *now*, doubtless with some clarification of the other possibilities being considered. The reason for this is that we know that our preferences change, and the preferences of tomorrow (assuming we can know something about them) are just as legitimately taken into account in deciding what to do now as the preferences of today. The preferences of any future day have a right to an equal vote as to what we shall do now; there is no reason for giving special weight to today's preference, since any reason that can be given today for weighing heavily today's preference can be given tomorrow for weighing heavily tomorrow's preference. So, given this symmetry of reasons, the preferences of any time-stretch have a rational claim to an equal vote. Now the importance of that fact is this: we often know quite well that our desires, aversions, and preferences are going to be very different after a short span of time, from what they now are. When a person is in a state of despair—perhaps brought about by a rejection in love, or by discharge from a long-held position—nothing but the thing he cannot have seems desirable; everything else is turned to ashes. Yet we know quite well that the passage of time may reverse all this; after a time the grass may look green again and things in the world that are available to us will look attractive. So, if we were to go on the preferences of today, when the emotion of despair seems more than we can stand, we might find death preferable to life; but if we allow for the preferences of the weeks and years ahead, when many goals will be enjoyable and attractive, we might find life much preferable to death. So, if a choice, or what is best, is to be determined by what we want not only now but later (and later desires on an equal basis with the present)—as it should be—then what is the best or preferable world-course will often be quite different from what it would be if the choice, or what is best for one, were fixed by one's desires and preferences now. It may be hard to look to the future and see what one's attitudes are likely to be, but that is necessary if one's evaluation is to be rational.

Of course, if one commits suicide there are no future desires or aversions which may be compared with present ones, and which should be allowed an equal vote in deciding what is best. In that respect the status of the course of action which results in death is different from any other course of action we may undertake.

I do not wish to suggest the rosy possibility that it is often or always reasonable to believe that next week I shall be more interested in living than I am today, if today I take a dim view of continued existence. Quite on the contrary, when a person is seriously ill the probabilities are that he will continue to feel worse until sedations become so extensive that he is incapable of emotional reaction toward anything, one way or the other. Thus sometimes when on the basis of today's attitudes I must say that I prefer death to life, I shall find no reason to think that tomorrow the preference order will be reversed—rather, if anything, I can know that tomorrow I shall prefer death to life more strongly. When this situation obtains, I may do better by choosing the world-course which contains my own life-span as short as possible.

The argument is often used—and it may as well be introduced in this connection as any other—that one can never be *certain* what is going to happen, and hence one is never rationally justified in doing anything as drastic as taking one's life. And it is true that certainties are hard to find in this life; they do not exist even in the sciences, if we are strict about it. Unfortunately for the critic who makes use of this line of argument, it works both ways. I might say, when I am very depressed about my life, that the one thing I am certain of is that I am now very depressed and prefer death to life, and there is only some probability that tomorrow I shall feel differently; so, one might argue that if one is to go only by certainties, I had better end it now. No one would take this seriously. We always have to live by probabilities, and make our estimates as best we can. People sometimes argue that one should not commit suicide in order to escape excruciating pain because a miraculous cure for one's terminal disease might be found tomorrow. And it is true that such a cure could, as a matter of logical possibility, be found tomorrow. But if everyone had argued in that way in the past hundred years, all of them would have waited until the bitter end and suffered excruciating pain; the line of argument that ignores probabilities and demands certainty would not have paid off in the past, and there is no reason to think it will pay off much better in the future. Indeed, if the thought were taken generally that probabilities should be ignored when they are short of certainty, in practical decisions, it can be demonstrated that the policy for action *cannot* pay off. A form of much the same argument is the assertion that if you are alive tomorrow you can always decide to end it all then, if you want to; whereas if you are dead tomorrow, you cannot then decide that it is better to live. The factual point is correct, of course. But the argument has practical bearing only if there is some reason to think that tomorrow you might want to live; and sometimes it is as nearly certain as matters of this sort can be, that you will not. It is true, of course, that one can always bear another day; so why not put it off? This argument, of course, can be used for every day, with the result that one never takes action. One would think that, as soon as it is clear beyond reasonable doubt not only that death is now preferable to life, but also that it will be every day from now until the end, the rational thing is to act promptly.[11]

Let us not pursue the question whether it is rational for a person with a painful terminal illness to commit suicide; obviously it is. However, the issue seldom arises, and few patients of this sort do so. With such patients matters get worse only slowly so that no particular time seems the one calling for action; they are so heavily sedated that it is impossible for the mental processes of decision leading to action to occur; or else they are incapacitated in a hospital and the very physical possibility of ending their lives is not available. Let us leave this gruesome topic and turn to the practically more important problem: whether it is rational for persons to commit suicide for some other reason than painful terminal physical illness. Most persons who commit suicide do so, apparently, because they face some nonphysical problem which depresses them beyond their ability to bear. It is to them that the above point, about the rational necessity of taking into account attitudes one will have next week, is primarily addressed.

If we look over a list of the problems that bother people, and some of which various writers have regarded as good and sufficient reasons for ending life, one finds (in addition to serious illness) things like the following: some event which has made one feel ashamed or has cost one loss of prestige and status; reduction to poverty as compared with former affluence; the loss of a limb or of physical beauty; the loss of sexual capacity; some event which makes it seem impossible that one will achieve things by which

---

[11]A patient who announces such a decision to his physician may expect amazement and dismay. The patient should not forget, however, that except for the area of the physical sciences his physician is likely to be almost a totally ignorant man, whose education has not proceeded beyond high school. The physician is not a reliable source of information about anything but the body.

Physicians are also given to rosy prognoses about the absence of pain in a terminal illness. The writer once had some bone surgery, and after a night of misery listened to a morning radio program entitled "The Conquest of Pain," in which hearers were assured that the medical profession had solved the problem of pain and that they need not give a second thought to this little source of anxiety.

one sets store; loss of a loved one; disappointment in love; the infirmities of increasing age. It is not to be denied that such things can be serious blows to one's prospects of happiness.

In deciding whether, everything considered, one prefers a world-course containing one's early demise as compared with one in which this is postponed to its natural terminus, there are various plain errors to be avoided—errors to which a person is especially prone when he is depressed. Let us forget for a moment the relevance to the decision of preferences that we may have tomorrow, and concentrate on some errors which may infect our preference as of today, and for which correction or allowance must be made.

In the first place, depression, like any severe emotional experience, tends to primitivize one's intellectual processes. It restricts the range of one's survey of the possibilities. One thing that a rational person will do is compare the world-course containing his suicide with his *best* alternative. But his best alternative is precisely a possibility he may overlook if, in a depressed mood, he thinks only of how badly off he is and does not contemplate plans of action which he has not at all considered. If a person is disappointed in love, it is possible to adopt a vigorous plan of action which carries a good chance of acquainting him with someone he likes at least as well; and if old age prevents one from continuing the tennis games with one's favorite partner, it is possible to learn some other game which provides the joys of competition without the physical demands.

There is another insidious influence of a state of depression, on one's planning. Depression seriously affects one's judgment about probabilities. A person disappointed in love is very likely to take a dim view of himself, his prospects, and his attractiveness; he thinks that, because he has been rejected by one person, he will probably be rejected by anyone who looks desirable to him. In a less gloomy frame of mind he would make, quite correctly, different estimates. Part of the reason for such gloomy probability estimates is that depression tends to repress one's memory evidence which supports a non-gloomy prediction. Thus a rejected lover tends to forget all the cases in which he has elicited enthusiastic response from ladies in relation to whom he has been the one who has done the rejecting. Thus his pessimistic self-image is based upon a highly selected, and pessimistically selected, set of data. Even when he is reminded of the data, however, he is apt to resist an optimistic inference. Even if he knows enough about the logic of inductive inference to know that the rational thing to do is project the frequency of past experiences into the future, bas-

Richard B. Brandt

ing one's estimate of the probability of a future event on the frequency of that event in the past, he is apt, doubtless sometimes with some reason, to reject the conclusion, for instance, on the ground that past experiences are unrepresentative and cannot be relied upon for a prognosis of the future. Obviously, however, there is such a thing as a reasonable and correct prognosis on the basis of an accurate account of past experience, and it is the height of irrationality not to estimate the future on that basis.

Another kind of distortion of the look of future prospects is not a result of depression, but is quite normal. Events distant in the future feel small, just as objects distant in space look small. The prospect of them does not have the effect on motivational processes that it would have if it were of an event in the immediate future. Rat-psychologists call essentially this fact the "goal-gradient" phenomenon; a rat, for instance, will run faster toward a food-box when he is close enough so that he can actually see it, and does not do as well when he can only represent it in some nonperceptual way, as presumably he does in the early stages of a maze. Similarly, a professor will accept an invitation to give a lecture or read a paper a year ahead, which he would not dream of accepting only a month ahead; the vision of the work involved somehow does not seem as repellent at the greater distance. Everyone finds it hard to do something disagreeable now, even for the sake of something more seriously important at a future date; the disagreeable event now tends to be postponed, unless one makes one's self attend to the importance of the event which is thereby jeopardized. In the case of a person who has suffered some misfortune, and whose situation now is an unpleasant one, this phenomenon of the reduction of the motivational size of events more distant in time has the effect that present unpleasant states are compared with probable future pleasant ones, as it were by looking at the future ones through the wrong end of binoculars. The future does not elicit motivation, desire, or preference in relation to its true size. So, at the time of choice, future good things are apt to play less of a role than is their due. A rational person will, of course, make himself see the future in its proper size, and compensate for this feature of human psychology.

Another serious source of error in estimating the potential value to us of possible future outcomes of various courses of action is the very method we sometimes must use, and naturally tend to use, in determining how much we do or will want them or like them when they occur. It is true that sometimes we can and do rely on memory; we can recall, with something less than perfect reliability, how much we enjoyed certain situations in the past (but sometimes we must correct projections from these recollections by information about how we have changed as persons with the effect that we may be able to meet these situations better or worse —say, a night's camping out—and enjoy them more or less, in future). But most frequently what we do, and sometimes the only thing we can do, is simply imagine as vividly as we can what a certain situation would be like, and notice whether it now seems attractive, whether we are now drawn toward it and enthusiastic about it, or not. Unfortunately the reliability of this subjective test, as an indicator of how much we shall want or enjoy a certain kind of thing tomorrow is seriously affected by the frame of mind in which we make it. Something which in fact we should much like in the future may utterly fail to stir us or even repel us, in a depressed or disappointed frame of mind; its favorable features either escape attention or simply fail to set the motivational machinery into motion which would make it seem attractive. Just as the sight of a good steak leaves us cold when we have just finished a hearty meal (presumably because chemical processes in the hypothalamus desensitize the relevant nervous channels or at any rate block the stimuli from having their ordinarily arousing effects), so the percept of a charming woman and *a fortiori* the mere thought of her will not elicit enthusiastic response from the rejected lover. Sorrow or depression simply shuts off or turns down the motivational machinery on which we customarily rely for deciding whether we will want, or enjoy having, certain things. Except, of course, the thing about which we are depressed; with it, the process is reversed. If there is something we have lost, or are debarred from getting, those of its features which normally strike us as unpleasant or unfavorable are excluded from attention or at any rate lose their repulsive force; whereas a halo is cast upon the features of the object which have been liked or wanted, rather as if the good features were now seen under a microscope and appear much larger than in real life. Why this should be so is not obvious. But even rats, it has been shown, will run harder for something which they have been frustrated in getting, than they run in ordinary circumstances. There is something about being frustrated in getting something which makes it look much better than it ordinarily does.

It is obvious that if we are trying to determine whether we now prefer, or shall later prefer, the outcomes in one world-course to the outcomes of another (and this is leaving aside the question of the weight of the votes of preferences at a later date), we have to take into account these infirmities of our "sensing" machinery. To say this does not tell us what to do about it, since to know that the machinery is out of order is not to tell us what results it would give us if it were working. One maxim of many wise people is to refrain from making important decisions in a stressful frame of mind; and one of the "important" decisions one might make is surely suicide. But, if decisions have to be made, at least one can make one's self recall, as far as possible, how one reacted to outcomes like the ones now to be assessed, on occasions in the past when one was in a normal frame of mind. Such reactions, however rough and defective in reliability, are at least better than the feeble pulses of sensing machinery which is temporarily out of order.

Most suicides which are irrational seem to be suicides of a moment of despair. What should be clear from the above is that a moment of despair should be, if one is seriously contemplating suicide, a moment of reassessment of one's goals and values, a reassessment which the individual must realize is very difficult to make objectively, because of the very quality of his depressed frame of mind. Let us consider in an example what form such a reassessment might take, based on a consideration of the "errors" we have been considering.

Suppose the president of a company is ousted in a reorganization and, to make matters as bad as possible, let us suppose he has made unwise investments so that his income from investments is small and, to cap it off, his wife has eloped with another man. His children are already grown, and he is too old to hope for election to a comparable position in another business. So his career and his home life are gone. Here we have the makings of a suicide. Let us suppose his pessimistic estimates are right: that there is no comparable future open to him in business, and that his wife is really gone. The prospect is one of uninteresting employment, if any; loneliness and no affection from a wife; moving from a luxurious home into a modest apartment; inability to entertain his friends in the manner to which he has been accustomed; and so on. Is all this bearable?

Obviously the man has to find a new mode of life. If he is an interesting man he can count on finding a woman with whom he can be close and who can mean as much to him as his wife actually did; or he may even find that he can become close to several persons of real interest, possibly resulting in an experience enriched beyond his imagination, as compared with the confines of traditional married life. The matter of career is more serious. Even Kant, who condemned suicide in all cases, says (inconsistently, I think) that a man unjustly convicted of a crime, who was offered a choice between death and penal servitude, would certainly, if honorable, "choose death" rather than "the galleys. A man of inner worth does not shrink from death; he would die rather than live as an object of contempt, a member of a gang of scoundrels in the galleys." Kant may have been right about what it is rational to do, in this extreme instance. Would death be better for the ex-president of a company, than accepting a job, let us say, as a shoe salesman? There are some compensations in the latter. An intelligent man might find himself interested in engaging in conversation a variety of customers from all walks of life. He can try out his psychological knowledge by devices to play on the vanity of women as a motivation for buying expensive shoes. The prospect might seem unattractive. But, if he wants to be rational, he will not fail to get a full view of the various things about the job which he might enjoy—or which he might enjoy, after a time, when he had got over contrasting them with a past career which is no longer open to him. He will hopefully not forget that as a shoe salesman he will not require sleeping pills because of company problems which he cannot get off his mind. If he understands human nature and his own, he may be able to see that while this job is not as desirable as the post he lost, after a time he can enjoy it and be happy in it and find life worth living. Other reflections which this man may have, relevant to his initial impulse to end it all, will come to mind—applications of the distinctions made above.

At this point David Hume was not his usual perspicuous self—nor was Plato before him.[12] For Hume speaks of the propriety of suicide for one who leads a hated life, "loaded with pain and sickness, with *shame and poverty*."[13] Pain and sickness are one thing; they cannot be enjoyed and cannot be escaped. But shame and poverty are another matter. For some situations Hume might be right. But Hume, accustomed as he was to the good things of life, was too short with shame and poverty; a life which he would classify as one of shame and poverty might be a happy life, inferior to Hume's life style, but still preferable to nothing.

A decision to commit suicide may in certain circumstances be a rational one. But a person who wants to act rationally must take into account at least the various possible "errors" mentioned above, and make appropriate rectifications in his initial evaluations.

4. THE ROLE OF OTHER PERSONS

We have not been concerned with the law, or its justifiability, on the matter of suicide; but we may note in passing that for a long

[12] *The Laws*, Bk. IX.
[13] Loc. cit.

Richard B. Brandt

time in the Western world suicide was a felony, and in many states attempted suicide is still a crime. It is also a crime to aid or encourage a suicide in many states; one who makes a lethal device available for a suicidal attempt may be subject to a prison sentence— including physicians, if they provide a lethal does of sedatives.[14]

The last-mentioned class of statutes raises a question worth our consideration: what are the moral obligations of other persons toward those who are contemplating suicide? I ignore questions of their moral blameworthiness, and of what it is rational for them to do from the point of view of personal welfare, as being of secondary concern. I have no doubt that the question of personal interest is important particularly to physicians who may not wish to risk running afoul of the law; but this risk is, after all, something which partly determines what is their moral obligation, since moral obligation to do something may be reduced by the fact that it is personally dangerous to do it.[15]

The moral obligation of other persons toward one who is contemplating suicide is an instance of a general obligation to render aid to those in serious distress, at least when this can be done at no great cost to one's self. I do not think this general principle is seriously questioned by anyone, whatever his moral theory; so I feel free to assume it as a premise. Obviously the person contemplating suicide is in great distress of some sort; if he were not, he would not be considering seriously terminating his life.

How great a person's obligation is to one in distress depends on a number of factors. Obviously a person's wife, daughter, and close friend have special obligations to devote time to helping this sort of person—to going over his problem with him, to think it through with him, etc.—which others do not have. But that anyone in this kind of distress has a moral claim on the time of anyone who knows the situation (unless there are others more responsible who are already doing what should be done) is obvious.

What is there an obligation to do? It depends, of course, on the situation, and how much the second person knows about the situation. If the individual has decided to terminate his life if he can, and it is clear that he is right in this decision, then, if he needs

[14]For a proposal for American law on this point see the Model Penal Code, Proposed Official Draft, The American Law Institute, 1962, pp. 127–128; also Tentative Draft No. 9, p. 56.
[15]The law can be changed, and one of the ways in which it gets changed is by responsible people refusing to obey it and pointing out how objectionable it is on moral grounds. Some physicians have shown leadership in this respect, e.g., on the matter of dispensing birth control information and abortion laws. One wishes there were more of this.

385

help in executing the decision, there is a moral obligation to give him help. If it is sleeping pills he needs, then they should be obtained for him. On this matter a patient's physician has a special obligation, from which all his antiquated talk about the Hippo-cratic oath does not absolve him. It is true that there are some damages one cannot be expected to absorb, and some risks which one cannot be expected to take, on account of the obligation to render aid. But the cowardice and lack of social responsibility of some physicians can be excused only by conviction of a charge of ignorance.

On the other hand, if it is clear that the individual should not commit suicide, from the point of view of his own welfare, or if there is a presumption that he should not (when the only evidence is that a person is discovered unconscious, with the gas turned on), it would seem to be the individual's obligation to intervene, and prevent the successful execution of the decision, see to the availability of competent psychiatric advice and temporary hos-pitalization, if necessary. Whether one has a right to take such steps when a clearly sane person, after careful reflection over a period of time, comes to the conclusion that an end to his life is what is best for him and what he wants, is very doubtful, even when one thinks his conclusion a mistaken one; it would seem that a man's own considered decision about whether he wants to live must command respect, although one must concede that this could be debated.

The more interesting role in which a person may be cast, however, is that of adviser. It is often important to one who is contemplating suicide to go over his thinking with another, and to feel that a conclusion, one way or the other, has the support of a respected mind. One thing one can obviously do, in rendering the service of advice, is to discuss with the person the various types of issue discussed above, made more specific by the concrete circumstances of his case, and help him find whether, in view, say, of the damage his suicide would do to others, he has a moral obligation to refrain, and whether it is rational or best for him, from the point of view of his own welfare, to take this step or adopt some other plan instead.

To get a person to see what is the rational thing to do is no small job. Even to get a person, in a frame of mind when he is seriously contemplating (or perhaps has already unsuccessfully attempted) suicide, to recognize a plain truth of fact may be a major operation. If a man insists, "I am a complete failure," when it is obvious that by any reasonable standard he is far from that, it may be tremendously difficult to get him to see the fact. The relaxing quiet of a hospital room may be a prerequisite of ability to think clearly and weigh facts with some perspective.

But there is another job beyond that of getting a person to see what is the rational thing to do; that is to help him *act* rationally, or *be* rational, when he has conceded what would be the rational thing.

How either of these tasks may be accomplished effectively may be discussed more competently by an experienced psychiatrist than by a philosopher. But it may not be inappropriate to point out that sometimes an adviser can *cure* a man's problem, in the course, or instead, of giving advice what to do about it. Loneliness and the absence of human affection (especially from the opposite sex) are states which exacerbate any other problems; disappointment, reduction to poverty, etc., seem less impossible to bear in the presence of the affection of another. Hence simply to be a friend, or to find someone a friend, may be the largest contribution one can make either to helping a person be rational or see clearly what is rational for him to do; this service may make one who was contemplating suicide feel that there is no longer a future for him which it is impossible to face.

suicide

r. f. holland

I am concerned with the subject as an ethico-religious problem. Is suicide all right or isn't it; and if it isn't, why not?

The question should not be assumed to be susceptible of an answer in the way the question whether arsenic is poisonous is susceptible of an answer (which would be *the* answer to the question). Moreover in the case of arsenic the question what it is, and the question whether it is poisonous, are separable questions: you can know that arsenic is poisonous without having analysed its nature. But to know or believe that suicide is objectionable *is* to have analysed its nature or construed its significance in one way rather than another. So let us not ask at the outset whether suicide is objectionable as though we already knew perfectly well what it was (which we don't), but let us rather approach the problem by asking what it might *mean* to commit suicide—or simply, What *is* suicide? I do not think it is just one thing and I do not expect to get very far with the question.

Durkheim, whose book on suicide is one of the classics of sociology, seems to me not to have understood what suicide is. He believed that in order to avoid being prejudiced the enquirer into human behaviour should never go by what people think ("the confused impressions of the crowd") but should make comparisons and look for the common properties of actions as a botanist or

From *Talk of God*, Royal Institute of Philosophy Lectures, volume 2, 1967–1968. London: Macmillan, 1969. Reprinted by permission of St. Martin's Press and Macmillan & Co., Ltd. (London and Basingstoke).

zoologist distinguishes objective common properties among flowers and fruits, fish and insects.[1] Durkheim thought it a condition of the possibility of investigation that systems of human behaviour should be capable of being identified and classified as one thing or another quite independently of any reference to the agents' ideas. And since intentions involve ideas, he declined to allow that the question whether a man was a suicide could be settled in the negative by the discovery that he did not intend to take his life:

> . . . If the intention of self-destruction alone constituted suicide, the name suicide could not be given to facts which, despite apparent differences, are fundamentally identical with those always called suicide and which could not be otherwise described without discarding the term. The soldier facing certain death to save his regiment does not wish to die, and yet is he not as much the author of his death as the manufacturer or merchant who kills himself to avoid bankruptcy? This holds true for the martyr dying for his faith, the mother sacrificing herself for her child, etc. Whether death is accepted merely as an unfortunate consequence, but inevitable given the purpose, or is actually itself sought and desired, in either case the person renounces existence, and the various methods of doing so can be only varieties of a single class.[2]

On this account of the matter it looks as if we have to say that a man who exposes himself to mortal danger, for whatever reason and whatever the circumstances, is exposing himself to suicide. Well, why not? Isn't it enough that the man should know what he is doing?

> The common quality of all these possible forms of supreme renunciation is that the determining act is performed advisedly; that at the moment of acting the victim knows the certain result of his conduct, no matter what reason may have led him to act thus. . . . We may say then conclusively: the term *suicide is applied to all cases of death resulting directly or indirectly from a positive or negative act of the victim himself which he knows will produce this result.*[3]

Durkheim here ignores the problem of how the investigator, especially one who is supposed to be collecting data in the spirit of a botanist, can judge whether or not a man knows what he is doing. And in trying to make the applicability of the term "suicide" to martyrdom turn upon this, he simply begs the question of *what* it

[1] *Suicide* (trans. Spaulding and Simpson) (London, 1952), pp. 41–42.
[2] Ibid., p. 43.
[3] Ibid., p. 44.

is that the martyr is doing; for of this we are only entitled to say thus far that he goes to his death.

Though the martyr may go willingly to a death which he foresees, it is a death which has been decided upon for him first by someone else. Whether he now makes things easy or difficult for the decider is hardly to the point. He might accept the decision as justice and so in a way concur with it, assisting its implementation out of duty, as Socrates did. Socrates took the cup of hemlock and drank it, and thereby might be said strictly to have died by his own hand. Yet even this cannot make a man a suicide, given the fact that his death was not decreed by him. In the case of the mother who dies while rescuing her child from a blazing building, the death is not decided upon at all, inevitable though her action might cause it to be. Similarly with the soldier facing certain death to save his regiment, of whom Durkheim remarks that he does not wish to die. He would not necessarily be a suicide even if he did wish to die—to die well or just to die. For to wish that death might come, to hope that it will soon come, is still not to decree that one shall die. Socrates had a wish for death and thought it his business as a philosopher to "practice dying";[4] but not to practise suicide, which he said should be committed by no one.[5]

However I can imagine an objector insisting that there is a logical entailment which I have not got round between "Socrates knowingly and deliberately drank the poison" and "Socrates killed himself, i.e., was a suicide." One way of meeting this objection would be to accept the entailment and invoke the idea that in killing himself a man may be at the same time doing something else. Thus in killing himself by taking hemlock Socrates was also doing something else which belonged to the role of a state prisoner and formed part of the procedure for judicial execution in Athens. And the additional factor makes (so it might be said) a radical difference to the ethico-religious status of the self-slaughter. But although this has an illuminating sound the illumination is spurious because the alleged entailment between Socrates' taking of the hemlock and his committing suicide is non-existent. Taking hemlock does not, in the context of an Athenian judicial execution, amount to slaughtering oneself: in this circumstance it is no more an act of suicide than the condemned man's walk to the scaffold in our society.

If the suggestion be that Socrates was a man bent on self-destruction to whom the advent of his execution came in handy, then that is a different matter. But I should think the innuendo im-

[4] *Phaedo*, 64A.
[5] *Phaedo*, 62A.

possible to account for save as a misinterpretation of the fact that Socrates did in a certain sense wish to die. Hence he was able to take the poison gladly as the fulfilment of his wish. However, anyone construing that wish as a pointer towards suicide would be taking it for something other than it was through failing to relate it to its surrounds.

Though he did not go in for theology, Socrates thought it well said that mortals are the chattels of the Gods.[6] "Wouldn't you be angry," he went on, "if one of your chattels should kill itself when you had not indicated that you wanted it to die?" Socrates, then, did not wish to die before it was time for him to die. He did not wish to run away from anything. And it certainly cannot be said of him that he wished to die because he found no sense in living. On the contrary the sense he found in living was what on the one hand made him reject suicide and on the other hand enabled him to look on death, whenever it should come, as something to be welcomed rather than feared; hence it enabled him to die courageously. To put this another way, the sense he made of death and the sense he made of life were one and the same. A man who decides to commit suicide because he sees no sense in living cannot from this point of view be said to contemplate anything sensible in regard to his situation, for his death must be just as senseless to him as his life.

In contrast with the kind of objection that Socrates had against suicide, some of the objections to be heard against it are only of an external or accidental nature. For instance one reason, and it is a moral reason, which a man contemplating suicide might give for refraining is the fact that he has a wife and children who depend on him. However this consideration would be no more a reason against suicide than it would be a reason against his walking out on them and declining to return, so we do not learn from this example whether or not the suicide itself is especially objectionable. It would be likewise with the case of an army officer who cannot pay his gambling debts, so he wants to commit suicide, for which there are precedents anyway; but then he reflects that this would be a reprehensible thing to do because if he kills himself there will be no chance of the debts ever being repaid, whereas his duty is to try to work them off. The objection would be much the same if he were inclined to go off to live in Rhodesia under an assumed name.

I once read of an officer with gambling debts who confusedly thought he had a moral reason, not against, but in favour of shooting himself. The note he left behind contained a remark to the

[6] *Phaedo*, 62B.

effect that he was choosing death rather than dishonour (at the time of writing he had not yet been found out). Now the great maxim of the military ethic, "death rather than dishonour," is exemplified by the conduct of the sentry who declines to leave his post when he could run away to safety but stays and carries out his duty although the consequence of doing so is death. Here the death and the dishonour are genuine alternatives—if he escapes the first he incurs the second, and if he embraces the first he avoids the second. But the case of the gambling officer is not like that at all. So far from being an alternative to the disgrace incurred by his inability to pay the debts, his death by suicide is rather a consequence of that disgrace. What he ends up with is both the death and the dishonour. There might or might not have been a way out of the dishonour had he stayed alive, but at least it is clear that killing himself is no way out of it. As Socrates observes in the *Phaedo*, death is not an escape from everything: if it were, it would indeed be a boon to the wicked.[7]

There are situations, though the gambling officer's is not one of them and neither is the sentry's, in which the only way of choosing death rather than dishonour would be to kill oneself—for instance if it is dishonourable to be taken captive and the only way of avoiding capture is to kill oneself. In just this situation Greek heroes fell upon their swords. However in regard to dishonour there is a distinction to be drawn between doing and suffering. The captured hero suffers his dishonour in being treated as a slave: he does not in his loss of freedom *do* anything dishonourable. He would therefore have been exhorted by Socrates not to commit suicide but to accept what comes, for Socrates believed that harm befell a man through his doing evil rather than through his suffering it.[8]

The choice before the hero on the eve of his capture is, one might say, between suicide and *indignity*. Opting for the former he chooses both nobly and rationally according to a thoroughly serious conception. For a man who is truly a hero cannot consent to live otherwise than as a hero; and above all the servile life is not open to him. Now if a Christian were to make that choice. . . . But then you see for a Christian it could not possibly be *that* choice. The status of the alternatives would not be the same although the Christian also might be described as choosing between suicide and indignity. However, in his case opting for the indignity would not be ignoble, while opting for the suicide would amount to consigning himself to damnation.

[7] *Phaedo*, 107C.
[8] *Gorgias*, 469B.

Let us now try to explore the idea of a choice between suicide and dishonour not in the sense of suffering but of doing something terrible. Compare the Greek hero with a modern spy who on his impending capture kills himself by swallowing a pill which has been supplied for use in this emergency. I am supposing that he swallows the pill not because of the possible consequences of the capture for himself but because he knows that under torture he will inevitably betray the secrets of his comrades and his country. Though I cannot imagine Socrates saying to a man in this predicament that he must not commit suicide, there is something he might have said to him earlier, namely that anyone who is concerned about his soul should beware of engaging in this sort of spying. For it is to enter into an institution the ethics of which require that in a certain eventuality you poison yourself; and the poisoning is not transformed into something other than suicide by the institutional role as it was in Socrates' own case by the role of being a condemned man in process of execution. Still, the fact that the spy's suicide is committed as an act of self-sacrifice gives it a very different flavour from the deed of the financier who does away with himself when his empire starts to totter. The financier "can't take it." This is also true, though on a much deeper level, of the Greek hero, who unlike the financier dies nobly. The hero commits suicide because there is something he cannot accept for himself, namely captivity. But the spy (in this particular variant out of many possible cases) is concerned solely with the good of others. Because of this one would like to deny that his is the spirit of a suicide. The difficulty is that he has supposedly entered the spying profession, which is a suicidal game, with his eyes open: he was not compelled to enter into it. But this consideration also means that his case fails to provide me with exactly the example I was looking for: I wanted an example of a completely forced choice between suicide and the doing of something morally terrible.

It might be held by a religious person that no man is ever forced to make such a choice; that it is something a good God would never inflict on a human being. But whether or not it be religiously imaginable, it is logically possible and I can depict a case where there will be no question of the agent's having voluntarily let himself in for the outcome by postulating that he suffers and knows that he suffers from a congenital form of mental instability, as a result of which he is overtaken from time to time by irresistible impulses towards something very horrible, such as raping children. Getting himself locked up is no solution, either because no one will listen to him or because no mental hospital is secure enough to contain him during one of his fits; and his fits come upon him without warning. So he decides to kill himself.

At first it may seem possible to argue that this man is not a suicide. For does he not belong to the category of those who are called upon to sacrifice their lives for the safety of others? Most often in such cases the order of events is: salvation of the imperilled followed by death of the saver, as in shipwrecks, when the men who have made possible the escape of others are trapped on board; or else the two events are concomitant, as at a grenade-throwing practice when one of the grenades is dropped and there is no time to throw it clear, whereupon an N.C.O. falls on the grenade and with his body shields the others from its effects. Either way, what the saver here decrees is another's salvation, with the unavoidable consequence of a death for himself which he does not decree. If, as with my imaginary maniac, the saver's own death has to take place first in order that the peril to others should be averted, the characterisation of what is decreed can remain exactly the same as before. To put it another way, all the man really does is to preserve someone else and his death is encompassed as a consequence of this. The peculiarity of the case is that the death has to be encompassed first and is thus an instance of an effect preceding its cause.

But now I fear that the argument has overreached itself; not in positing an effect that precedes its cause, which I should accept here as a coherent conception, but in gliding over the fact that the man's death is not encompassed *for* him——he encompasses it directly himself. This is manifestly a doing and not a suffering; hence it was false to claim that "all he really does is to preserve someone else." That is not all, for he kills himself.

A comparable example, not this time from the imagination, is that of the explorer, Captain Oates. On the day before his death Oates had said that he could not go on and had proposed that the the rest of the party should leave him in his sleeping bag. "That we could not do," says Scott, whose account of the upshot is as follows:

> He slept through the night before last, hoping not to wake; but he woke in the morning—yesterday. It was blowing a blizzard. He said, "I am just going outside and may be some time." He went out into the blizzard and we have not seen him since. . . . We knew that poor Oates was walking to his death, but although we tried to dissuade him, we knew it was the act of a brave man and an English gentleman.[9]

What Oates decreed was that his hard-pressed companions should

[9]*Scott's Last Expedition* (London, 1935), vol. i, p. 462.

be relieved of an encumbrance: of this there can be little doubt. He had borne intense suffering for weeks without complaint (Scott tells us) but remained cheerful right to the end. The sentiment that he was entitled to quit, or that anyway he was going to quit, never entered into it. Accordingly I want to deny he was a suicide, as I should have liked to do in the case of the maniac. And there is a feature of Oates's case that enables me to persist in my denial beyond the point to which I could take it in the other case. For if someone objects, "But he killed himself," in regard to the maniac there was no answer, but in Oates's case I can say, "No; the blizzard killed him." Had Oates taken out a revolver and shot himself I should have agreed he was a suicide.

We are back again at the distinction between doing and suffering, which here as elsewhere is fraught with difficulty. For if a man puts his head on a railway line and claims "I'm not going to kill myself, the train will do it," I shall reject that as a sophistical absurdity; yet I do not consider it absurd to claim that the blizzard killed Oates. But then of course neither is it absurd to claim that he killed himself by going out into the blizzard. And there is much to be said for a description that is midway between the two: "He let the blizzard kill him." To call one of these descriptions the right one is to say little more than "That's how I look at it."

Still I do not look at it arbitrarily when I say that Oates was killed by the blizzard. The indirectness of what he did in relation to the onset of his death and the entrance of time as a factor are features of the case which help to put it for me in this perspective. Yet do not time and a certain indirectness enter in as factors when a man puts his head on a railway line? They enter in, but not to the same effect because of the difference in the spirit and in the surroundings of what is done. That the blizzard is a natural phenomenon is something that makes a difference. To be sure, a man who out of sorrow drowns himself might also perhaps be said to expose himself to a natural phenomenon, but again the context and the spirit of it are different. Oates simply walks away from his companions—and in the act of doing so becomes exposed to the blizzard: he needs to put distance between himself and them and he cannot do so in any other way. He is concerned only with their relief. And he is well on the way towards death already. Such are the features of the case which in combination make it possible, though not obligatory, to say of him unsophistically what would naturally be said of a martyr, namely that he goes to his death.

The great divide among attitudes towards suicide lies between those in whose eyes this possibility is of special significance and those to whom it would not matter whether a man like Oates were held to be no suicide, or a suicide but an honourable one. The former are upholders of a religious ethics and I should call them that even though they might entertain no theological beliefs and never even mention a deity: the latter I should call humanists.

I am not suggesting that from the standpoint of an ethics untinged with religion it would have been exactly the same if Oates had shot himself. For it would have been ugly, unpleasant and messy, and hence a course to be rejected out of fastidiousness or consideration for the feelings of his companions. From the religiously ethical standpoint, however, the rejection of that course would be bound up with ideas of a different kind, about a man's relations to his life and destiny, or in other words about the soul.

Schopenhauer remarked that if there are any moral arguments against suicide they lie very deep and are not touched by ordinary ethics.[10] An ordinary ethics is for instance one in which the idea of prudence looms large, as it did for Aristotle, or which speaks, as Kant did, about the duty of self-preservation. Schopenhauer saw something vulgar in the idea of duties to oneself no matter what were deemed to be their foundation. But Kant spoke in a different vein when he called suicide the extreme point along the line of *crimina carnis* and when he drew attention to the element of disdain for the world in Stoicism ("leave the world as you might leave a smoky room").[11] Both of these latter considerations of Kant connect with the point which Schopenhauer took to be central about suicide, namely that it is a phenomenon of strong assertion of will.[12] The real reason why suicide must be condemned, Schopenhauer said, had to do with self-conquest. In this idea he was at one with Socrates and not far distant from the Christian religion. A Christian perhaps might speak, not so much of conquering, but rather of dying to the self, and the most spiritual expression of the idea for him would be in prayer—particularly in such a prayer as "Thy will, not mine, be done."

The sanctity of life is an idea that a religious person might want to introduce in connection with suicide, but if he left the matter there he would be representing suicide as objectionable in the same way and to the same degree as murder. It is only when he thinks of life as a gift that the difference starts to emerge. For the murderer does not destroy a gift that was given *to him;* he destroys something which was given to someone else but which happens to have got in his way. This argues his crime to be from the stand-

[10]*Foundation of Morals.*
[11]*Lectures on Ethics: Suicide.*
[12]*World as Will and Idea,* § 69.

396

point of ordinary ethics worse than that of the suicide, of whom at least it may be said that it was his own affair. On the other hand the suicide, unlike the murderer, is—religiously speaking— necessarily an ingrate; and the ingratitude here is of no ordinary kind, for it is towards his Creator, the giver of life, to whom every- thing is owed. That the destruction of a life should at the same time be the act of extreme ingratitude towards the giver of a life accounts for the special horror attaching to parricide, against which there is something like the same religious feeling as there is against suicide: as if these were two different ways of getting as close as possible to deicide. Or perhaps rather it is parricide which symbolises the destruction of God and suicide the destruc- tion of the universe. Thus G. K. Chesterton: "The man who kills a man, kills a man. The man who kills himself, kills all men; as far as he is concerned he wipes out the world."[13] Chesterton took himself there to be expressing the spirit of *all* suicides and in that he was mistaken. But there is no doubt that when a substitute for the end of the world is called for, suicide is the only possible one:

> Dressed in flowing white robes, 26 people sat tense and silent in an upper room of a London house. Leader of the strange group was middle-aged solicitor Peter Shanning. He had given up practising law after experiencing what he called "an amazing series of dreams." He claimed it had been revealed to him that the world would come to an end on July 23rd, 1887, at 3 p.m. Shanning spent five years travelling the country and preaching. He gained 25 believers and they bought a house in north London. On the fatal day, they were gathered in a room, watching the clock ticking towards 3 p.m. Shan- ning sat quietly praying. Three o'clock came—and went. It wasn't the end of the world. But it was the end of Shanning. After his fol- lowers had left in bewilderment, he shot himself dead. (From a fea- ture in a popular weekly paper.)

The fact that there is about suicide a kind of terribleness that ordinary, i.e., non-religious, ethics fails to touch is a weakness in ordinary ethics not only from the standpoint of religion but from the standpoint of philosophy. However, there is from the stand- point of philosophy a weakness to be discerned in the religious conception of suicide also. For according to the religious concep- tion, all suicides are (unless their minds are unsound) guilty of an identical offence and separated from non-suicides by the same gulf; so that it does not really matter what kind of a suicide a man is so long as he is one.

[13]*Orthodoxy: The Flag of the World* (London, 1909).

Now this principle of equal disvalue, as it might be called, is manifestly objectionable to the non-religious conscience, which will either wish to remain silent in the face of suicide or else will wish to attribute to it an enormous range of disvalue, and also sometimes value, in a gamut that resists compression and runs from the squalid and mindless suicides of playboys or film starlets through the pitiful suicides of the oppressed and rejected, the anguished and maddened suicides of those goaded beyond endurance, the Stoic suicides and the heroic suicides, and thence to the self-sacrificial suicides, terminating with cases that religion would doubtless not classify as suicide at all. Ordinary ethics, however, will see no point in any alternative classification because it can descry variety in suicide where religion neglects it. And in this discrimination philosophy must side with ordinary ethics. For philosophy is a distinction-drawing business which emphasises differences and focuses the mind on variant possibilities.

Consider for just a moment some of the alternative possibilities inherent in the case of the gambling officer I mentioned earlier, who thought he was choosing death rather than dishonour. The point was then that suicide could not be the kind of escape he thought it was. But suppose he realised that there were no possibility of escape from the dishonour anyway. If so, he could divide through by the dishonour and consider whether it might not be as well for him to commit suicide in order to put an end to his misery. If that were the idea, it could be objected on the one hand that the misery might pass and on the other hand that, even supposing it did not, the idea of being put out of one's misery is below human dignity and appropriate rather to dogs and horses.

However, it might not be simply a matter of his wanting to put himself out of his misery but rather that he has got himself into an impossible situation. And this is different, for it is now being supposed that the incurring of the dishonour means he can no longer carry on his life as a soldier. This possibility is closed to him, yet no other life is conceivable: soldiering *is* his life. The morality of the society, and the military ethic in particular, might well in all seriousness prescribe suicide for just this type of case.

On this interpretation, the suicide of the gambling officer has come to resemble that of an American journalist named Wertenbaker, who developed cancer in middle age and whose story has been told by his wife. Here too it was not, or not simply, a question of the man's inability to stand misery, but of his finding it impossible to carry on living as the kind of creature he had become. A difference between the two cases is that the officer's life,

unlike the journalist's, becomes impossible as the result of something he himself did, and this consideration would be capable of
affecting the outcome in more than one way. For on the one hand
the knowledge that he has made a mess of his life through his own
fault might drive a man to suicide out of sheer self-hatred ("he
could murder himself"; and so he does). On the other hand he
might be willing to abide by the consequences of his own folly
out of a sense of equity which would not be there to sustain him
if he thought he were the victim of a cruel and arbitrary fate. Not
that Wertenbaker entertained this thought; he wrote as follows:

> Problem with death is to recognise the point at which you can die
> with all your faculties, take a healthy look at the world and people
> as you go out of it. Let them get you in bed, drug you or cut you, and
> you become sick and afraid and disgusting, and everybody will be
> glad to get rid of you. It shouldn't be such a problem if you can re-
> member how it was when you were young. You wouldn't give up
> something for instance to add ten years to your life. All right, don't
> ask for them now. You wouldn't give up drinking and love-making
> and eating—and why should you have given them up? Nothing is
> ever lost that has been experienced and it can all be there at the mo-
> ment of death—if you don't wait too long.[14]

What Wertenbaker saw no sense in was prolonging his life
beyond a certain point, living on as something different from what
he had been before, as a squalid pain-wracked thing, a dying man.
It cannot be said that he found life meaningless. Rather, the meaning he found in life was such as to justify, to give him a reason for,
doing away with himself in a certain circumstance.

In relation to the example of Wertenbaker, Chesterton's words
about wiping out the world have little grip. Wertenbaker did not
want to throw back the world in its creator's face—and not just
because he had no belief in a creator either: if he had been offered his life over again he would have taken it gladly.

But all of it? No, not all of it: he was not prepared to accept *the
whole* of the life that had been given him. Instead he despaired of
it, despaired of the existence of any power to sustain him in his
predicament. That he should have reviled what his life had become was understandable. The trouble was he did not love what
he reviled; he had not "this primary and supernatural loyalty to
things."

The last few words of that religiously ethical comment are

[14]Lael Tucker Wertenbaker, *Death of a Man* (New York, 1950), p. 10.

Chesterton's again and they help to make clear the point of the passage I quoted before.[15] But still I do not see how they could be expected to influence a man like Wertenbaker, who after all had his own kind of loyalty to things.

[15]His remark about the suicide wiping out of the world might otherwise seem to be no more than a solipsistic muddle.

death

thomas nagel

"The syllogism he had learnt from Kiesewetter's logic: 'Caius is a man, men are mortal, therefore Caius is mortal,' had always seemed to him correct as applied to Caius, but certainly not as applied to himself. . . . What did Caius know of the smell of that striped leather ball Vanya had been so fond of?"

Tolstoy, *The Death of Ivan Ilyich*

If, as many people believe, death is the unequivocal and perma- nent end of our existence, the question arises whether it is a bad thing to die. There is conspicuous disagreement about the matter: some people think death is dreadful; others have no objection to death *per se*, though they hope their own will be neither prema- ture nor painful.

Those in the former category tend to think those in the latter are blind to the obvious, while the latter suppose the former to be prey to some sort of confusion. On the one hand it can be said that life is all one has, and the loss of it is the greatest loss one can sustain. On the other hand it may be objected that death deprives this supposed loss of its subject, and that if one realizes that death is not an unimaginable condition of the persisting person, but a mere blank, one will see that it can have no value whatever, posi- tive or negative.

This essay, in shortened form, originally appeared in volume IV, no. 1 of *Nous*, a quarterly journal published by Wayne State University Press, Detroit, Michigan, and is used with the publisher's permission. The shorter version was read at a meeting of the Western Division of the American Philosophical Association in St. Louis, May 9, 1970.

Since I want to leave aside the question whether we are, or might be, immortal in some form, I shall simply use the word "death" and its cognates in this discussion to mean *permanent* death, unsupplemented by any form of conscious survival. I wish to consider whether death is in itself an evil; and how great an evil, and of what kind, it might be. This question should be of interest even to those who believe that we do not die permanently, for one's attitude toward immortality must depend in part on one's attitude toward death.

Clearly if death is an evil at all, it cannot be because of its positive features, but only because of what it deprives us of. I shall try to deal with the difficulties surrounding the natural view that death is an evil because it brings to an end all the goods that life contains.[1] An account of these goods need not occupy us here, except to observe that some of them, like perception, desire, activity, and thought, are so general as to be constitutive of human life. They are widely regarded as formidable benefits in themselves, despite the fact that they are conditions of misery as well as of happiness, and that a sufficient quantity of more particular evils can perhaps outweigh them. That is what is meant, I think, by the allegation that it is good simply to be alive, even if one is undergoing terrible experiences. The situation is roughly this: There are elements which, if added to one's experience, make life better; there are other elements which, if added to one's experience, make life worse. But what remains when these are set aside is not merely *neutral:* it is emphatically positive. Therefore life is worth living even when the bad elements of experience are plentiful, and the good ones too meager to outweigh the bad ones on their own. The additional positive weight is supplied by experience itself, rather than by any of its contents.

I shall not discuss the value that one person's life or death may have for others, or its objective value, but only the value it has for the person who is its subject. That seems to me the primary case, and the case which presents the greatest difficulties. Let me add only two observations. First, the value of life and its contents does not attach to mere organic survival: almost everyone would be indifferent (other things equal) between immediate death and immediate coma followed by death twenty years later without reawakening. And second, like most goods, this can be multiplied by time: more is better than less. The added quantities need not be temporarily continuous (though continuity has its social advantages). People are attracted to the possibility of long-term sus-

[1] As we shall see, this does not mean that it brings to an end all the goods that a man can possess.

pended animation or freezing, followed by the resumption of conscious life, because they can regard it from within simply as a *continuation* of their present life. If these techniques are ever perfected, what from outside appeared as a dormant interval of three hundred years could be experienced by the subject as nothing more than a sharp discontinuity in the character of his experiences. I do not deny, of course, that this has its own disadvantages. Family and friends may have died in the meantime; the language may have changed; the comforts of social, geographical, and cultural familiarity would be lacking. Nevertheless these inconveniences would not obliterate the basic advantage of continued, though discontinuous, existence.

If we turn from what is good about life to what is bad about death, the case is completely different. Essentially, though there may be problems about their specification, what we find desirable in life are certain states, conditions, or types of activity. It is *being* alive, *doing* certain things, having certain experiences, that we consider good. But if death is an evil, it is the *loss of life*, rather than the state of being dead, or nonexistent, or unconscious, that is objectionable.[2] This asymmetry is important. If it is good to be alive, that advantage can be attributed to a person at each point of his life. It is a good of which Bach had more than Schubert, simply because he lived longer. Death, however, is not an evil of which Shakespeare has so far received a larger portion than Proust. If death is a disadvantage, it is not easy to say when a man suffers it.

There are two other indications that we do not object to death merely because it involves long periods of nonexistence. First, as has been mentioned, most of us would not regard the *temporary* suspension of life, even for substantial intervals, as in itself a misfortune. If it develops that people can be frozen without reduction of the conscious lifespan, it will be inappropriate to pity those who are temporarily out of circulation. Second, none of us existed before we were born (or conceived), but few regard that as a misfortune. I shall have more to say about this later.

The point that death is not regarded as an unfortunate *state* enables us to refute a curious but very common suggestion about the origin of the fear of death. It is often said that those who object to death have made the mistake of trying to imagine what it is like to *be* dead. It is alleged that the failure to realize that this task is logically impossible (for the banal reason that there is nothing to imagine) leads to the conviction that death is a mysterious and therefore terrifying prospective *state*. But this diagnosis is evi-

[2]It is sometimes suggested that what we really mind is the process of *dying*. But I should not really object to dying if it were not followed by death.

dently false, for it is just as impossible to imagine being totally unconscious as to imagine being dead (though it is easy enough to imagine oneself, from the outside, in either of those conditions). Yet people who are averse to death are not usually averse to unconsciousness (so long as it does not entail a substantial cut in the total duration of waking life).

If we are to make sense of the view that to die is bad, it must be on the ground that life is a good and death is the corresponding deprivation or loss, bad not because of any positive features but because of the desirability of what it removes. We must now turn to the serious difficulties which this hypothesis raises, difficulties about loss and privation in general, and about death in particular.

Essentially, there are three types of problem. First, doubt may be raised whether *anything* can be bad for a man without being positively unpleasant to him: specifically, it may be doubted that there are any evils which consist merely in the deprivation or absence of possible goods, and which do not depend on someone's *minding* that deprivation. Second, there are special difficulties, in the case of death, about how the supposed misfortune is to be assigned to a subject at all. There is doubt both as to *who* its subject is, and as to *when* he undergoes it. So long as a person exists, he has not yet died, and once he has died, he no longer exists; so there seems to be no time when death, if it is a misfortune, can be ascribed to its unfortunate subject. The third type of difficulty concerns the asymmetry, mentioned above, between our attitudes to posthumous and prenatal nonexistence. How can the former be bad if the latter is not?

It should be recognized that if these are valid objections to counting death as an evil, they will apply to many other supposed evils as well. The first type of objection is expressed in general form by the common remark that what you don't know can't hurt you. It means that even if a man is betrayed by his friends, ridiculed behind his back, and despised by people who treat him politely to his face, none of it can be counted as a misfortune for him so long as he does not suffer as a result. It means that a man is not injured if his wishes are ignored by the executor of his will, or if, after his death, the belief becomes current that all the literary works on which his fame rests were really written by his brother, who died in Mexico at the age of 28. It seems to me worth asking what assumptions about good and evil lead to these drastic restrictions.

All the questions have something to do with time. There certainly are goods and evils of a simple kind (including some pleasures and pains) which a person possesses at a given time simply in virtue of his condition at that time. But this is not true of all the things we regard as good or bad for a man. Often we need to know his history to tell whether something is a misfortune or not; this applies to ills like deterioration, deprivation, and damage. Sometimes his experiential *state* is relatively unimportant—as in the case of a man who wastes his life in the cheerful pursuit of a method of communicating with asparagus plants. Someone who holds that all goods and evils must be temporarily assignable states of the person may of course try to bring difficult cases into line by pointing to the pleasure or pain that more complicated goods and evils cause. Loss, betrayal, deception, and ridicule are on this view bad because people suffer when they learn of them. But it should be asked how our ideas of human value would have to be constituted to accommodate these cases directly instead. One advantage of such an account might be that it would enable us to explain *why* the discovery of these misfortunes causes suffering—in a way that makes it reasonable. For the natural view is that the discovery of betrayal makes us unhappy because it is bad to be betrayed—not that betrayal is bad because its discovery makes us unhappy.

It therefore seems to me worth exploring the position that most good and ill fortune has as its subject a person identified by his history and his possibilities, rather than merely by his categorical state of the moment—and that while this subject can be exactly located in a sequence of places and times, the same is not necessarily true of the goods and ills that befall him.[3]

These ideas can be illustrated by an example of deprivation whose severity approaches that of death. Suppose an intelligent person receives a brain injury that reduces him to the mental condition of a contented infant, and that such desires as remain to him can be satisfied by a custodian, so that he is free from care. Such a development would be widely regarded as a severe misfortune, not only for his friends and relations, or for society, but also, and primarily, for the person himself. This does not mean that a contented infant is unfortunate. The intelligent adult who has been *reduced* to this condition is the subject of the misfortune. He is the one we pity, though of course he does not mind his condition—there is some doubt, in fact, whether he can be said to exist any longer.

The view that such a man has suffered a misfortune is open to the same objections which have been raised in regard to death. He does not mind his condition. It is in fact the same condition he

[3]It is certainly not true in general of the things that can be said of him. For example, Abraham Lincoln was taller than Louis XIV. But when?

was in at the age of three months, except that he is bigger. If we did not pity him then, why pity him now; in any case, who is there to pity? The intelligent adult has disappeared, and for a creature like the one before us, happiness consists in a full stomach and a dry diaper.

If these objections are invalid, it must be because they rest on a mistaken assumption about the temporal relation between the subject of a misfortune and the circumstances which constitute it. If, instead of concentrating exclusively on the oversized baby before us, we consider the person he was, and the person he *could* be now, then his reduction to this state and the cancellation of his natural adult development constitute a perfectly intelligible catastrophe.

This case should convince us that it is arbitrary to restrict the goods and evils that can befall a man to nonrelational properties ascribable to him at particular times. As it stands, that restriction excludes not only such cases of gross degeneration, but also a good deal of what is important about success and failure, and other features of a life that have the character of processes. I believe we can go further, however. There are goods and evils which are irreducibly relational; they are features of the relations between a person, with spatial and temporal boundaries of the usual sort, and circumstances which may not coincide with him either in space or in time. A man's life includes much that does not take place within the boundaries of his body and his mind, and what happens to him can include much that does not take place within the boundaries of his life. These boundaries are commonly crossed by the misfortunes of being deceived, or despised, or betrayed. (If this is correct, there is a simple account of what is wrong with breaking a deathbed promise. It is an injury to the dead man. For certain purposes it is possible to regard time as just another type of distance.) The case of mental degeneration shows us an evil that depends on a contrast between the reality and the possible alternatives. A man is the subject of good and evil as much because he has hopes which may or may not be fulfilled, or possibilities which may or may not be realized, as because of his capacity to suffer and enjoy. If death is an evil, it must be accounted for in these terms, and the impossibility of locating it within life should not trouble us.

When a man dies we are left with his corpse, and while a corpse can suffer the kind of mishap that may occur to an article of furniture, it is not a suitable object for pity. The man, however, is. He has lost his life, and if he had not died, he would have continued to live it, and to possess whatever good there is in living.

If we apply to death the account suggested for the case of dementia, we shall say that although the spatial and temporal locations of the individual who suffered the loss are clear enough, the misfortune itself cannot be so easily located. One must be content just to state that his life is over and there will never be any more of it. That *fact*, rather than his past or present condition, constitutes his misfortune, if it is one. Nevertheless if there is a loss, someone must suffer it, and *he* must have existence and specific spatial and temporal location even if the loss itself does not. The fact that Beethoven had no children may have been a cause of regret to him, or a sad thing for the world, but it cannot be described as a misfortune for the children that he never had. All of us, I believe, are fortunate to have been born. But unless good and ill can be assigned to an embryo, or even to an unconnected pair of gametes, it cannot be said that not to be born is a misfortune. (That is a factor to be considered in deciding whether abortion and contraception are akin to murder.)

This approach also provides a solution to the problem of temporal asymmetry, pointed out by Lucretius. He observed that no one finds it disturbing to contemplate the eternity preceding his own birth, and he took this to show that it must be irrational to fear death, since death is simply the mirror image of the prior abyss. That is not true, however, and the difference between the two explains why it is reasonable to regard them differently. It is true that both the time before a man's birth and the time after his death are times when he does not exist. But the time after his death is time of which his death deprives him. It is time in which, had he not died then, he would be alive. Therefore any death entails the loss of *some* life that its victim would have led had he not died at that or any earlier point. We know perfectly well what it would be for him to have had it instead of losing it, and there is no difficulty in identifying the loser.

But we cannot say that the time prior to a man's birth is time in which he would have lived had he been born not then but earlier. For aside from the brief margin permitted by premature labor, he *could* not have been born earlier: anyone born substantially earlier than he was would have been someone else. Therefore the time prior to his birth is not time in which his subsequent birth prevents him from living. His birth, when it occurs, does not entail the loss to him of any life whatever.

The direction of time is crucial in assigning possibilities to people or other individuals. Distinct possible lives of a single person can diverge from a common beginning, but they cannot converge to a common conclusion from diverse beginnings. (The latter would represent not a set of different possible lives of one individual, but a set of distinct possible individuals, whose lives have identical conclusions.) Given an identifiable individual, countless possibilities for his continued existence are imaginable, and we can clearly conceive of what it would be for him to go on existing indefinitely. However inevitable it is that this will not come about, its possibility is still that of the continuation of a good for him, if life is the good we take it to be.[4]

We are left, therefore, with the question whether the nonrealization of this possibility is in every case a misfortune, or whether it depends on what can naturally be hoped for. This seems to me the most serious difficulty with the view that death is always an evil. Even if we can dispose of the objections against admitting misfortune that is not experienced, or cannot be assigned to a definite time in the person's life, we still have to set some limits on *how* possible a possibility must be for its nonrealization to be a misfortune (or good fortune, should the possibility be a bad one). The death of Keats at 24 is generally regarded as tragic; that of Tolstoy at 82 is not. Although they will both be dead forever, Keats's death deprived him of many years of life which were allowed to Tolstoy; so in a clear sense Keats's loss was greater (though not in the sense standardly employed in mathematical comparison between infinite quantities). However, this does not prove that Tolstoy's loss was insignificant. Perhaps we record an objection only to evils which are gratuitously added to the inevitable; the fact that it is worse to die at 24 than at 82 does not imply that it is not a terrible thing to die at 82, or even at 806. The question is whether we can regard as a misfortune any limitation,

---

[4]I confess to being troubled by the above argument, on the ground that it is too sophisticated to explain the simple difference between our attitudes to prenatal and posthumous nonexistence. For this reason I suspect that something essential is omitted from the account of the badness of death by an analysis which treats it as a deprivation of possibilities. My suspicion is supported by the following suggestion of Robert Nozick. We could imagine discovering that people developed from individual spores that had existed indefinitely far in advance of their birth. In this fantasy, birth never occurs naturally more than 100 years before the permanent end of the spore's existence. But then we discover a way to trigger the premature hatching of these spores, and people born who have thousands of years of active life before them. Given such a situation, it would be possible to imagine *oneself* having come into existence thousands of years previously. If we put aside the question whether this would really be the same person, even given the identity of the spore, then the consequence appears to be that a person's birth at a given time *could* deprive him of many earlier years of possible life. Now while it would be cause for regret that one had been deprived of all those possible years of life by being born too late, the feeling would differ from that which many people have about death. I conclude that something about the future *prospect* of permanent nothingness is not captured by the analysis in terms of denied possibilities. If so, then Lucretius's argument still awaits an answer.

like mortality, that is normal to the species. Blindness or near-blindness is not a misfortune for a mole, nor would it be for a man, if that were the natural condition of the human race.

The trouble is that life familiarizes us with the goods of which death deprives us. We are already able to appreciate them, as a mole is not able to appreciate vision. If we put aside doubts about their status as goods and grant that their quantity is in part a function of their duration, the question remains whether death, no matter when it occurs, can be said to deprive its victim of what is in the relevant sense a possible continuation of life.

The situation is an ambiguous one. Observed from without, human beings obviously have a natural lifespan and cannot live much longer than a hundred years. A man's sense of his own experience, on the other hand, does not embody this idea of a natural limit. His existence defines for him an essentially open-ended possible future, containing the usual mixture of goods and evils that he has found so tolerable in the past. Having been gratuitously introduced to the world by a collection of natural, historical, and social accidents, he finds himself the subject of a *life*, with an indeterminate and not essentially limited future. Viewed in this way, death, no matter how inevitable, is an abrupt cancellation of indefinitely extensive possible goods. Normality seems to have nothing to do with it, for the fact that we will all inevitably die in a few score years cannot by itself imply that it would not be good to live longer. Suppose that we were all inevitably going to die in *agony* — physical agony lasting six months. Would inevitability make *that* prospect any less unpleasant? And why should it be different for a deprivation? If the normal lifespan were a thousand years, death at 80 would be a tragedy. As things are, it may just be a more widespread tragedy. If there is no limit to the amount of life that it would be good to have, then it may be that a bad end is in store for us all.

the makropulos case: reflections on the tedium of immortality

bernard williams

This essay started life as a lecture in a series 'on the immortality of the soul or kindred spiritual subject'.[1] My kindred spiritual subject is, one might say, the mortality of the soul. Those among previous lecturers who were philosophers tended, I think, to discuss the question whether we are immortal; that is not my subject, but rather what a good thing it is that we are not. Immortality, or a state without death, would be meaningless, I shall suggest; so, in a sense, death gives the meaning to life. That does not mean that we should not fear death (whatever force that injunction might be taken to have, anyway). Indeed, there are several very different ways in which it could be true at once that death gave the meaning to life and that death was, other things being equal, something to be feared. Some existentialists, for instance, seem to have said that death was what gave meaning to life, if anything did, just because it was the fear of death that gave meaning to life; I shall not follow

Reprinted from *Problems of the Self* by Bernard Williams by permission of Cambridge Press. © Cambridge University Press 1973.

[1] At the University of California, Berkeley, under a benefaction in the names of Agnes and Constantine Foerster. I am grateful to the Committee for inviting me to give the 1972 lecture in this series.

them. I shall rather pursue the idea that from facts about human desire and happiness and what a human life is, it follows both that immortality would be, where conceivable at all, intolerable, and that (other things being equal) death is reasonably regarded as an evil. Considering whether death can reasonably be regarded as an evil is in fact as near as I shall get to considering whether it should be feared: they are not quite the same question.

My title is that, as it is usually translated into English, of a play by Karel Čapek which was made into an opera by Janaček and which tells of a woman called Elina Makropulos, *alias* Emilia Marty, *alias* Ellian Macgregor, alias a number of other things with the initials 'EM', on whom her father, the Court physician to a sixteenth-century Emperor, tried out an elixir of life. At the time of the action she is aged 342. Her unending life has come to a state of bordeom, indifference and coldness. Everything is joyless; 'in the end it is the same', she says, 'singing and silence'. She refuses to take the elixir again; she dies; and the formula is deliberately destroyed by a young woman among the protests of some older men.

EM's state suggests at least this, that death is not necessarily an evil, and not just in the sense in which almost everybody would agree to that, where death provides an end to great suffering, but in the more intimate sense that it can be a good thing not to live too long. It suggests more than that, for it suggests that it was not a peculiarity of EM's that an endless life was meaningless. That is something I shall follow out later. First, though, we should put together the suggestion of EM's case, that death is not necessarily an evil, with the claim of some philosophies and religions that death is necessarily not an evil. Notoriously, there have been found two contrary bases on which that claim can be mounted: death is said by some not to be an evil because it is not the end, and by others, because it is. There is perhaps some profound temperamental difference between those who find consolation for the fact of death in the hope that it is only the start of another life, and those who equally find comfort in the conviction that it is the end of the only life there is. That both such temperaments exist means that those who find a diagnosis of the belief in immortality, and indeed a reproach to it, in the idea that it constitutes a consolation, have at best only a statistical fact to support them. While that may be just about enough for the diagnosis, it is not enough for the reproach.

Most famous, perhaps, among those who have found comfort in the second option, the prospect of annihilation, was Lucretius, who, in the steps of Epicurus, and probably from a personal fear of death which in some of his pages seems almost tangible, addresses himself to proving that death is never an evil. Lucretius has two basic arguments for this conclusion, and it is an important feature of them both that the conclusion they offer has the very strong consequence—and seems clearly intended to have the consequence—that, for oneself at least, it is all the same whenever one dies, that a long life is no better than a short one. That is to say, death is never an evil in the sense not merely that there is no-one for whom dying is an evil, but that there is no time at which dying is an evil—sooner or later, it is all the same.

The first argument[2] seeks to interpret the fear of death as a confusion, based on the idea that we shall be there after death to repine our loss of the *praemia vitae,* the rewards and delights of life, and to be upset at the spectacle of our bodies burned, and so forth. The fear of death, it is suggested, must necessarily be the fear of some experiences had when one is dead. But if death is annihilation, then there are no such experiences: in the Epicurean phrase, when death is there, we are not, and when we are there, death is not. So, death being annihilation, there is nothing to fear. The second argument[3] addresses itself directly to the question of whether one dies earlier or later, and says that one will be the same time dead however early or late one dies, and therefore one might as well die earlier as later. And from both arguments we can conclude *nil igitur mors est ad nos, neque pertinent hilum*—death is nothing to us, and does not matter at all.[4]

The second of these arguments seems even on the face of things to contradict the first. For it must imply that if there *were* a finite period of death, such that if you died later you would be dead for less time, then there *would* be some point in wanting to die later rather than earlier. But that implication makes sense, surely, only on the supposition that what is wrong with dying consists in something undesirable about the condition of being dead. And that is what is denied by the first argument.

More important than this, the oddness of the second argument can help to focus a difficulty already implicit in the first. The first argument, in locating the objection to dying in a confused objection to being dead, and exposing that in terms of a confusion with being alive, takes it as genuinely true of life that the satisfaction of desire, and possession of the *praemia vitae,* are good things. It is not irrational to be upset by the loss of home, children, possessions—what is irrational is to think of death as, in the relevant sense, *losing* anything. But now if we consider two lives, one very

[2]*de Rerum Natura* III, 870 *seq,* 898 *seq.*
[3]Ibid., 1091.
[4]Ibid., 830

short and cut off before the *praemia* have been acquired, the other fully provided with the *praemia* and containing their enjoyment to a ripe age, it is very difficult to see why the second life, by these standards alone, is not to be thought better than the first. But if it is, then there must be something wrong with the argument which tries to show that there is nothing worse about a short life than a long one. The argument locates the mistake about dying in a mistake about consciousness, it being assumed that what commonsense thinks about the worth of the *praemia vitae* and the sadness of their (conscious) loss is sound enough. But if the *praemia vitae* are valuable; even if we include as necessary to that value consciousness that one possesses them; then surely getting to the point of possessing them is better than not getting to that point, longer enjoyment of them is better than shorter, and more of them, other things being equal, is better than less of them. But if so, then it just will not be true that to die earlier is all the same as to die later, nor that death is never an evil—and the thought that to die later is better than to die earlier will not be dependent on some muddle about thinking that the dead person will be alive to lament his loss. It will depend only on the idea, apparently sound, that if the *praemia vitae* and consciousness of them are good things, then longer consciousness of more *praemia* is better than shorter consciousness of fewer *praemia*.

Is the idea sound? A decent argument, surely, can be marshalled to support it. If I desire something, then, other things being equal, I prefer a state of affairs in which I get it from one in which I do not get it, and (again, other things being equal) plan for a future in which I get it rather than not. But one future, for sure, in which I would not get it would be one in which I was dead. To want something, we may also say, is to that extent to have reason for resisting what excludes having that thing: and death certainly does that, for a very large range of things that one wants.[5] If that is right, then for any of those things, wanting something itself gives one a reason for avoiding death. Even though if I do not succeed, I will not know that, nor what I am missing, from the perspective of the wanting agent it is rational to aim for states of affairs in which his want is satisfied, and hence to regard death as something to be avoided; that is, to regard it as an evil.

It is admittedly true that many of the things I want, I want

---

[5]Obviously the principle is not exceptionless. For one thing, one can want to be dead: the content of that desire may be obscure, but whatever it is, a man presumably cannot be *prevented* from getting it by dying. More generally, the principle does not apply to what I elsewhere call *non-I desire*: for an account of these, see 'Egoism and Altruism', pp. 260 *seq*. They do not affect the present discussion, which is within the limits of egoistic rationality.

only on the assumption that I am going to be alive; and some people, for instance some of the old, desperately want certain things when nevertheless they would much rather that they and their wants were dead. It might be suggested that not just these special cases, but really all wants, were conditional on being alive; a situation in which one has ceased to exist is not to be compared with others with respect to desire-satisfaction — rather, if one dies, all bets are off. But surely the claim that all desires are in this sense conditional must be wrong. For consider the idea of a rational forward-looking calculation of suicide: there can be such a thing, even if many suicides are not rational, and even though with some that are, it may be unclear to what extent they are forward-looking (the obscurity of this with regard to suicides of honour is an obscurity in the notion of shame). In such a calculation, a man might consider what lay before him, and decide whether he did or did not want to undergo it. If he does decide to undergo it, then some desire propels him on into the future, and *that* desire at least is not one that operates conditionally on his being alive, since it itself resolves the question of whether he is going to be alive. He has an unconditional, or (as I shall say) a *categorical* desire.

The man who seriously calculates about suicide and rejects it, only just has such a desire, perhaps. But if one is in a state in which the question of suicide does not occur, or occurs only as total fantasy — if, to take just one example, one is happy — one has many such desires, which do not hang from the assumption of one's existence. If they did hang from that assumption, then they would be quite powerless to rule out that assumption's being questioned, or to answer the question if it is raised; but clearly they are not powerless in those directions — on the contrary they are some of the few things, perhaps the only things, that have power in that direction. Some ascetics have supposed that happiness required reducing one's desires to those necessary for one's existence, that is, to those that one has to have granted that one exists at all; rather, it requires that some of one's desires should be fully categorical, and one's existence itself wanted as something necessary to them.

To suppose that one can in this way categorically want things implies a number of things about the nature of desire. It implies, for one thing, that the reason I have for bringing it about that I get what I want is not merely that of avoiding the unpleasantness of not getting what I want. But that must in any case be right — otherwise we should have to represent every desire as the desire

414

to avoid its own frustration, which is absurd.

About what those categorical desires must be, there is not much of great generality to be said, if one is looking at the happy state of things: except, once more against the ascetic, that there should be not just enough, but more than enough. But the question might be raised, at the impoverished end of things, as to what the minimum categorical desire might be. Could it be *just* the desire to remain alive? The answer is perhaps 'no'. In saying that, I do not want to deny the existence, the value, or the basic necessity of a sheer reactive drive to self-preservation: humanity would certainly wither if the drive to keep alive were not stronger than any perceived reasons for keeping alive. But if the question is asked, and it is going to be answered calculatively, then the bare categorical desire to stay alive will not sustain the calculation—that desire itself, when things have got that far, has to be sustained or filled out by some desire for something else, even if it is only, at the margin, the desire that future desires of mine will be born and satisfied. But the best insight into the effect of categorical desire is not gained at the impoverished end of things, and hence in situations where the question has actually come up. The question of life being desirable is certainly transcendental in the most modest sense, in that it gets by far its best answer in never being asked at all.

None of this—including the thoughts of the calculative suicide—requires my reflection on a world in which I never occur at all. In the terms of 'possible worlds' (which can admittedly be misleading), a man could, on the present account, have a reason from his own point of view to prefer a possible world in which he went on longer to one in which he went on for less long, or—like the suicide—the opposite; but he would have no reason of this kind to prefer a world in which he did not occur at all. Thoughts about his total absence from the world would have to be of a different kind, impersonal reflections on the value *for the world* of his presence or absence: of the same kind, essentially, as he could conduct (or, more probably, not manage to conduct) with regard to anyone else. While he can think egoistically of what it would be for him to live longer or less long, he cannot think egoistically of what it would be for him never to have existed at all. Hence the sombre words of Sophocles[6] 'Never to have been born counts highest of all . . .' are well met by the old Jewish reply—'how many are so lucky? Not one in ten thousand'.

[6]*Oedipus at Colonus* 1224, seq.

Lucretius' first argument has been interestingly criticised by Thomas Nagel,[7] on lines different from those that I have been following. Nagel claims that what is wrong with Lucretius' argument is that it rests on the assumption that nothing can be a misfortune for a man unless he knows about it, and that misfortunes must consist in something nasty *for* him. Against this assumption, Nagel cites a number of plausible counter-instances, of circumstances which would normally be thought to constitute a misfortune, though those to whom they happen are and remain ignorant of them (as, for instance, certain situations of betrayal). The difference between Nagel's approach and mine does not, of course, lie in the mere point of whether one admits misfortunes which do not consist of or involve nasty experiences: anyone who rejects Lucretius' argument must admit them. The difference is that the reasons which a man would have for avoiding death are, on the present account, grounded in desires—categorical desires—which he has; he, on the basis of these, has reason to regard possible death as a misfortune to be avoided, and we, looking at things from his point of view, would have reason to regard his actual death as his misfortune. Nagel, however, if I understand him, does not see the misfortune that befalls a man who dies as necessarily grounded in the issue of what desires or sorts of desires he had; just as in the betrayal case, it could be a misfortune for a man to be betrayed, even though he did not have any desire not to be betrayed. If this is a correct account, Nagel's reasoning is one step further away from Utilitarianism on this matter than mine,[8] and rests on an independent kind of value which a sufficiently Utilitarian person might just reject; while my argument cannot merely be rejected by a Utilitarian person, it seems to me, since he must if he is to be consistent, and other things being equal, attach disutility to any situation which he has good reason to prevent, and he certainly has good reason to prevent a situation which involves the non-satisfaction of his desires. Thus, granted categorical desires, death has a disutility for an agent, although that disutility does not, of course, consist in unsatisfactory experiences involved in its occurrence.

The question would remain, of course, with regard to any given agent, whether he had categorical desires. For the present argument, it will do to leave it as a contingent fact that most people do: for they will have a reason, and a perfectly coherent reason,

[7]'Death', *Nous* IV.1 (1970), pp. 73 *seq.* Reprinted with some alterations in Rachels ed., *Moral Problems.*

[8]Though my argument does not in any sense imply Utilitarianism; for some further considerations on this, see the final paragraphs of this paper.

to regard death as a misfortune, while it was Lucretius' claim that no-one could have a coherent reason for so regarding it. There may well be other reasons as well; thus Nagel's reasoning, though different from the more Utilitarian type of reason I have used against Lucretius, seems compatible with it and there are strong reasons to adopt his kind of consideration as well. In fact, further and deeper thought about this question seems likely to fill up the apparent gap between the two sorts of argument; it is hard to believe, for one thing, that the supposed contingent fact that people have categorical desires can really be as contingent as all that. One last point about the two arguments is that they coincide in not offering—as I mentioned earlier—any considerations about worlds in which one does not occur at all; but there is perhaps an additional reason why this should be so in the Utilitarian-type argument, over and above the one it shares with Nagel's. The reason it shares with Nagel's is that the type of misfortune we are concerned with in thinking about X's death is X's misfortune (as opposed to the misfortunes of the state or whatever); and whatever sort of misfortune it may be in a given possible world that X does not occur in it, it is not X's misfortune. They share the feature, then, that for anything to be X's misfortune in a given world, then X must occur in that world. But the Utilitarian-type argument further grounds the misfortune, if there is one, in certain features of X, namely his desires; and if there is no X in a given world, then *a fortiori* there are no such grounds.

But now—if death, other things being equal, is a misfortune; and a longer life is better than a shorter life; and we reject the Lucretian argument that it does not matter when one dies; then it looks as though—other things always being equal—death is at any time an evil, and it is always better to live than die. Nagel indeed, from his point of view, does seem to permit that conclusion, even though he admits some remarks about the natural term of life and the greater misfortune of dying in one's prime. But wider consequences follow. For if all that is true, then it looks as though it would be not only always better to live, but better to live always, that is, never to die. If Lucretius is wrong, we seem committed to wanting to be immortal.

That would be, as has been repeatedly said, with other things equal. No-one need deny that since, for instance, we grow old and our powers decline, much may happen to increase the reasons for thinking death a good thing. But these are contingencies. We might not age; perhaps, one day, it will be possible for some of us not to age. If that were so, would it not follow then that, more life being *per se* better than less life, we should have reason so far as that went (but not necessarily in terms of other inhabitants) to live for ever? EM indeed bears strong, if fictional witness against the desirability of that; but perhaps she still laboured under some contingent limitations, social or psychological, which might once more be eliminated to bring it about that really other things were equal. Against this, I am going to suggest that the supposed contingencies are not really contingencies; that an endless life would be a meaningless one; and that we could have no reason for living eternally a human life. There is no desirable or significant property which life would have more of, or have more unqualifiedly, if we lasted for ever. In some part, we can apply to life Aristotle's marvellous remark about Plato's Form of the Good:[9] 'nor will it be any the more good for being eternal: that which lasts long is no whiter than that which perishes in a day'. But only in part; for, rejecting Lucretius, we have already admitted that more days may give us more than one day can.

If one pictures living for ever as living as an embodied person in the world rather as it is, it will be a question, and not so trivial as may seem, of what age one eternally is. EM was 342; because for 300 years she had been 42. This choice (if it was a choice) I am personally, and at present, well disposed to salute—if one had to spend eternity at any age, that seems an admirable age to spend it at. Nor would it necessarily be a less good age for a woman: that at least was not EM's problem, that she was too old at the age she continued to be at. Her problem lay in having been at it for too long. Her trouble was it seems boredom: a boredom connected with the fact that everything that could happen and make sense to one particular human being of 42 had already happened to her. Or, rather, all the sorts of things that could make sense to one woman of a certain character; for EM has a certain character, and indeed, except for her accumulating memories of earlier times, and no doubt some changes of style to suit the passing centuries, seems always to have been much the same sort of person.

There are difficult questions, if one presses the issue, about this constancy of character. How is this accumulation of memories related to this character which she eternally has, and to the character of her existence? Are they much the same kind of events repeated? Then it is itself strange that she allows them to be repeated, accepting the same repetitions, the same limitations—indeed, *accepting* is what it later becomes, when earlier it would not, or even could not, have been that. The repeated patterns of personal relations, for instance, must take on a character of being

[9] *Ethica Nicomachea* 1096[b] 4.

inescapable. Or is the pattern of her experiences not repetitious in this way, but varied? Then the problem shifts, to the relation between these varied experiences, and the fixed character: how can it remain fixed, through an endless series of very various experiences? The experiences must surely happen to her without really affecting her; she must be, as EM is, detached and withdrawn.

EM, of course, is in a world of people who do not share her condition, and that determines certain features of the life she has to lead, as that any personal relationship requires peculiar kinds of concealment. That, at least, is a form of isolation which would disappear if her condition were generalised. But to suppose more generally that boredom and inner death would be eliminated if everyone were similarly becalmed, is an empty hope: it would be a world of Bourbons, learning nothing and forgetting nothing, and it is unclear how much could even happen.

The more one reflects to any realistic degree on the conditions of EM's unending life, the less it seems a mere contingency that it froze up as it did. That it is not a contingency, is suggested also by the fact that the reflections can sustain themselves independently of any question of the particular character that EM had; it is enough, almost, that she has a human character at all. Perhaps not quite. One sort of character for which the difficulties of unending life would have less significance than they proved to have for EM might be one who at the beginning was more like what she is at the end: cold, withdrawn, already frozen. For him, the prospect of unending cold is presumably less bleak in that he is used to it. But with him, the question can shift to a different place, as to why he wants the unending life at all; for, the more he is at the beginning like EM is at the end, the less place there is for categorical desire to keep him going, and to resist the desire for death. In EM's case, her boredom and distance from life both kill desire and consist in the death of it; one who is already enough like that to sustain life in those conditions may well be one who had nothing to make him want to do so. But even if he has, and we conceive of a person who is stonily resolved to sustain for ever an already stony existence, his possibility will be of no comfort to those, one hopes a larger party, who want to live longer because they want to live more.

To meet the basic anti-Lucretian hope for continuing life which is grounded in categorical desire, EM's unending life in this world is inadequate, and necessarily so relative to just those desires and conceptions of character which go into the hope. That is very important, since it is the most direct response, that which should have been adequate if the hope is both coherent and what it initially seemed to be. It also satisfied one of two important conditions which must be satisfied by anything which is to be adequate as a fulfilment of my anti-Lucretian hope, namely that it should clearly be *me* who lives for ever. The second important condition is that the state in which I survive should be one which, to me looking forward, will be adequately related, in the life it presents, to those aims which I now have in wanting to survive at all. That is a vague formula, and necessarily so, for what exactly that relation will be must depend to some extent on what kind of aims and (as one might say) prospects for myself I now have. What we can say is that since I am propelled forward into longer life by categorical desires, what is promised must hold out some hopes for those desires. The limiting case of this might be that the promised life held out some hope just to that desire mentioned before, that future desires of mine will be born and satisfied; but if that were the only categorical desire that carried me forward into it, at least this seems demanded, that any image I have of those future desires should make it comprehensible to me how in terms of my character they could be my desires.

The second condition, the EM kind of survival failed, on reflection, to satisfy; but at least it is clear why, before reflection, it looked as though it might satisfy the condition — it consists, after all, in just going on in ways in which we are quite used to going on. If we turn away now from EM to more remote kinds of survival, the problems of those two conditions press more heavily right from the beginning. Since the major problems of the EM situation lay in the indefinite extension of one life, a tempting alternative is survival by means of an indefinite series of lives. Most, perhaps all, versions of this belief which have actually existed have immediately failed the first condition: they get nowhere near providing any consideration to mark the difference between rebirth and new birth. But let us suppose the problem, in some way or another, removed; some conditions of bodily continuity, minimally sufficient for personal identity, may be supposed satisfied. (Anyone who thinks that no such conditions could be sufficient, and requires, for instance, conditions of memory, may well find it correspondingly difficult to find an alternative for survival in this direction which both satisfies the first requirement, of identity, and also adequately avoids the difficulties of the EM alternative.) The problem remains of whether this series of psychologically disjoint lives could be an object of hope to one who did not want to die. That is, in my view, a different question from the question of whether it will be him — which is why I distinguished originally two different requirements to be satisfied. But it is a question; and even if the first requirement be supposed satisfied, it is exceedingly unclear that the second can be. This will be so, even if one were to accept the idea, itself problematical, that one could have reason to fear the future pain of someone who was merely bodily continuous with one as one now is.[10]

There are in the first place certain difficulties about how much a man could consistently be allowed to know about the series of his lives, if we are to preserve the psychological disjointness which is the feature of this model. It might be that each would in fact have to seem to him as though it were his only life, and that he could not have grounds for being sure what, or even that, later lives were to come. If so, then no comfort or hope will be forthcoming in this model to those who want to go on living. More interesting questions, however, concern the man's relation to a future life of which he did get some advance idea. If we could allow the idea that he could fear pain which was going to occur in that life, then we have at least provided him with one kind of reason which might move him to opt out of that life, and destroy himself (being recurrent, under conditions of bodily continuity, would not make one indestructible). But physical pain and its nastiness are to the maximum degree independent of what one's desires and character are, and the degree of identification needed with the later life to reject that aspect of it is absolutely minimal. Beyond that point, however, it is unclear how he is to bring this later character and its desires into a relation to his present ones, so as to be satisfied or the reverse with this marginal promise of continued existence. If he can regard this future life as an object of hope, then equally it must be possible for him to regard it with alarm, or depression, and—as in the simple pain case—opt out of it. If we cannot make sense of his entertaining that choice, then we have not made sense of this future life being adequately related to his present life, so that it could, alternatively, be something he might want in wanting not to die. But can we clearly make sense of that choice? For if we— or he—merely wipe out his present character and desires, there is nothing left by which he can judge it at all, at least as something *for him*; while if we leave them in, we—and he—apply something irrelevant to that future life, since (to adapt the Epicurean phrase), when they are there, it is not, and when it is there, they are not. We might imagine him considering the future prospects, and agreeing to go on if he found them congenial. But that is a muddled picture. For whether they are congenial to him as he is

[10]One possible conclusion from the dilemma discussed in 'The Self and the Future'. For the point, mentioned below, of the independence of physical pain from psychological change, see p. 54 [of *Problems of the Self*].

now must be beside the point, and the idea that it is not beside the point depends on carrying over into the case features that do not belong to it, as (perhaps) that he will remember later what he wanted in the earlier life. And when we admit that it is beside the point whether the prospects are congenial, then the force of the idea that the future life could be something that he *now* wanted to go on to, fades.

There are important and still obscure issues here,[11] but perhaps enough has been said to cast doubt on this option as coherently satisfying the desire to stay alive. While few will be disposed to think that much can be made of it, I must confess that out of the alternatives it is the only one that for me would, if it made sense, have any attraction — no doubt because it is the only one which has the feature that what one is living at any given point is actually *a life*. It is singular that those systems of belief that get closest to actually accepting recurrence of this sort seem, almost without exception, to look forward to the point when one will be released from it. Such systems seem less interested in continuing one's life than in earning one the right to a superior sort of death.

The serial and disjoint lives are at least more attractive than the attempt which some have made, to combine the best of continuous and of serial existence in a fantasy of very varied lives which are nevertheless cumulatively effective in memory. This might be called the *Teiresias* model. As that case singularly demonstrates, it has the quality of a fantasy, of emotional pressure trying to combine the uncombinable. One thing that the fantasy has to ignore is the connexion, both as cause and as consequence, between having one range of experiences rather than another, wishing to engage in one sort of thing rather than another, and having a character. Teiresias cannot have a character, either continuously through these proceedings, or cumulatively at the end (if there were to be an end) of them: he is not, eventually, a person but a phenomenon.

In discussing the last models, we have moved a little away from the very direct response which EM's case seemed to provide to the hope that one would never die. But perhaps we have moved not nearly far enough. Nothing of this, and nothing much like this, was in the minds of many who have hoped for immortality; for it was not in this world that they hoped to live for ever. As one might say, their hope was not so much that they would never die

---

[11] For a detailed discussion of closely related questions, though in a different framework, see Derek Parfit, 'Personal Identity', *Philosophical Review*, LXXX (1971), pp. 3–27.

as that they would live after their death, and while that in its turn can be represented as the hope that one would not really die, or, again, that it was not really oneself that would die, the change of formulation could point to an after-life sufficiently unlike this life, perhaps, to earth the current of doubt that flows from EM's frozen boredom.

But in fact this hope has been and could only be modelled on some image of a more familiar untiring or unresting or unflagging activity or satisfaction; and what is essentially EM's problem, one way or another, remains. In general we can ask, what it is about the imaged activities of an eternal life which would stave off the principle hazard to which EM succumbed, boredom. The Don Juan in Hell joke, that heaven's prospects are tedious and the devil has the best tunes, though a tired fancy in itself, at least serves to show up a real and (I suspect) a profound difficulty, of providing any model of an unending, supposedly satisfying, state or activity which would not rightly prove boring to anyone who remained conscious of himself and who had acquired a character, interests, tastes and impatiences in the course of living, already, a finite life. The point is not that for such a man boredom would be a tiresome consequence of the supposed states or activities, and that they would be objectionable just on the utilitarian or hedonistic ground that they had this disagreeable feature. If that were all there was to it, we could imagine the feature away, along no doubt with other disagreeable features of human life in its present imperfection. The point is rather that boredom, as sometimes in more ordinary circumstances, would be not just a tiresome effect, but a reaction almost perceptual in character to the poverty of one's relation to the environment. Nothing less will do for eternity than something that makes boredom *unthinkable*. What could that be? Something that could be guaranteed to be at every moment utterly absorbing? But if a man has and retains a character, there is no reason to suppose that there is anything that could be that. If, lacking a conception of the guaranteedly absorbing activity, one tries merely to think away the reaction of boredom, one is no longer supposing an improvement in the circumstances, but merely an impoverishment in his consciousness of them. Just as being bored can be a sign of not noticing, understanding or appreciating enough, so equally not being bored can be a sign of not noticing, or not reflecting, enough. One might make the immortal man content at every moment, by just stripping off from him consciousness which would have brought discontent by reminding him of other times, other interests, other possibilities. Perhaps, indeed, that is what we have already done, in a more tempting way, by picturing him just now as at every moment totally absorbed—but that is something we shall come back to.

Of course there is in actual life such a thing as justified but necessary boredom. Thus—to take a not entirely typical example—someone who was, or who thought himself, devoted to the radical cause might eventually admit to himself that he found a lot of its rhetoric excruciatingly boring. He might think that he ought not to feel that, that the reaction was wrong, and merely represented an unworthiness of his, an unregenerate remnant of intellectual superiority. However, he might rather feel that it would not necessarily be a better world in which no-one was bored by such rhetoric and that boredom was, indeed, a perfectly worthy reaction to this rhetoric after all this time; but for all that, the rhetoric might be necessary. A man at arms can get cramp from standing too long at his post, but sentry-duty can after all be necessary. But the threat of monotony in eternal activities could not be dealt with in that way, by regarding immortal boredom as an unavoidable ache derived from standing ceaselessly at one's post. (This is one reason why I said that boredom in eternity would have to be *unthinkable*.) For the question would be unavoidable, in what campaign one was supposed to be serving, what one's ceaseless sentry-watch was for.

Some philosophers have pictured an eternal existence as occupied in something like intense intellectual enquiry. Why that might seem to solve the problem, at least for them, is obvious. The activity is engrossing, self-justifying, affords, as it may appear, endless new perspectives, and by being engrossing enables one to lose oneself. It is that last feature that supposedly makes boredom unthinkable, by providing something that is, in that earlier phrase, at every moment totally absorbing. But if one is totally and perpetually absorbed in such an activity, and loses oneself in it, then as those words suggest, we come back to the problem of satisfying the conditions that it should be me who lives for ever, and that the eternal life should be in prospect of some interest. Let us leave aside the question of people whose characteristic and most personal interests are remote from such pursuits, and for whom, correspondingly, an immortality promised in terms of intellectual activity is going to make heavy demands on some theory of a 'real self' which will have to emerge at death. More interesting is the content and value of the promise for a person who *is*, in this life, disposed to those activities. For looking at such a person as he now is, it seems quite unreasonable to suppose that those activities would have the fulfilling or liberating character that they do have for him, if they were in fact all he could do or conceive of doing. If they are genuinely fulfilling, and do not operate (as they can) merely as a compulsive diversion, then the ground and shape of the satisfactions that the intellectual enquiry offers him, will relate to *him*, and not just to the enquiry. The *Platonic introjection*, seeing the satisfactions of studying what is timeless and impersonal as being themselves timeless and impersonal, may be a deep illusion, but it is certainly an illusion.

We can see better into that illusion by considering Spinoza's thought, that intellectual activity was the most active and free state that a man could be in, and that a man who had risen to such activity was in some sense most fully individual, most fully himself. This conclusion has been sympathetically expounded by Stuart Hampshire, who finds on this point a similar doctrine in Spinoza and in Freud:[12] in particular, he writes '[one's] only means of achieving this distinctness as an individual, this freedom in relation to the common order of nature, is the power of the mind freely to follow in its thought an intellectual order'. The contrast to this free intellectual activity is 'the common condition of men that their conduct and their judgements of value, their desires and aversions, are in each individual determined by unconscious memories'—a process which the same writer has elsewhere associated with our having any character at all as individuals.[13]

Hampshire claims that in pure intellectual activity the mind is most free because it is then least determined by causes outside its immediate states. I take him to mean that rational activity is that in which the occurrence of an earlier thought maximally explains the occurrence of a later thought, because it is the rational relation between their contents which, granted the occurrence of the first, explains the occurrence of the second. But even the maximal explanatory power, in these terms, of the earlier thought does not extend to total explanation: for it will still require explanation why this thinker on this occasion continued on this rational path of thought at all. Thus I am not sure that the Spinozist consideration which Hampshire advances even gives a very satisfactory sense to the *activity* of the mind. It leaves out, as the last point shows, the driving power which is needed to sustain one even in the most narrowly rational thought. It is still further remote from any notion of creativity, since that, even within a theoretical context, and certainly in an artistic one, precisely implies the origination of ideas which are not fully predictable in terms of the content of

[12]*Spinoza and the Idea of Freedom,* reprinted in *Freedom of Mind* (Oxford: Clarendon Press, 1972), pp. 183 *seq;* the two quotations are from pp. 206–207.
[13]*Disposition and Memory, Freedom of Mind,* pp. 160 *seq;* see especially pp. 176–177.

existing ideas. But even if it could yield one sense for 'activity', it would still offer very little, despite Spinoza's heroic defence of the notion, for *freedom*. Or—to put it another way—even if it offered something for freedom of the intellect, it offers nothing for freedom of the individual. For when freedom is initially understood as the absence of 'outside' determination, and in particular understood in those terms as an unquestionable *value*, my freedom is reasonably not taken to include freedom from my past, my character and my desires. To suppose that those are, in the relevant sense, 'outside' determinations, is merely to beg the vital question about the boundaries of the self, and not to prove from premises acceptable to any clear-headed man who desires freedom that the boundaries of the self should be drawn round the intellect. On the contrary, the desire for freedom can, and should, be seen as the desire to be free in the exercise and development of character, not as the desire to be free of it. And if Hampshire and others are right in claiming that an individual character springs from and gets its energies from unconscious memories and unclear desires, then the individual must see them too as within the boundaries of the self, and themselves involved in the drive to persist in life and activity.

With this loss, under the Spinozist conception, of the individual's character, there is, contrary to Hampshire's claim, a loss of individuality itself, and certainly of anything that could make an eternity of intellectual activity, so construed, a reasonable object of interest to one concerned with individual immortality. As those who totally wish to lose themselves in the movement can consistently only hope that the movement will go on, so the consistent Spinozist—at least on this account of Spinozism—can only hope that the intellectual activity goes on, something which could be as well realised in the existence of Aristotle's prime mover, perhaps, as in anything to do with Spinoza or any other particular man.

Stepping back now from the extremes of Spinozist abstraction, I shall end by returning to a point from which we set out, the sheer desire to go on living, and shall mention a writer on this subject, Unamuno, whose work *The Tragic Sense of Life*[14] gives perhaps more extreme expression than anyone else has done to that most basic form of the desire to be immortal, the desire not to die.

> I do not want to die—no, I neither want to die nor do I want to want to die; I want to live for ever and ever and ever. I want this 'I' to live—this poor 'I' that I am and that I feel myself to be here

[14]*Del sentimiento trágico de la vida*, translated by J. E. Crawford Flitch (London: 1921). Page references are to the Fontana Library edition, 1962.

and now, and therefore the problem of the duration of my soul, of my own soul, tortures me.[15]

Although Unamuno frequently refers to Spinoza, the spirit of this is certainly far removed from that of the 'sorrowful Jew of Amsterdam'. Furthermore, in his clear insistence that what he desperately wants is this life, the life of this self, not to end, Unamuno reveals himself at equal removes from Manicheanism and from Utilitarianism; and that is correct, for the one is only the one-legged descendant of the other. That tradition—Manichean, Orphic, Platonic, Augustinian—which contrasts the spirit and the body in such a sense that the spiritual aims at eternity, truth and salvation, while the body is adjusted to pleasure, the temporary, and eventual dissolution, is still represented, as to fifty per cent, by secular Utilitarianism: it is just one of the original pair of boots left by itself and better regarded now that the other has fallen into disrepair. Bodies are all that we have or are: hence for Utilitarianism it *follows* that the only focus of our arrangements can be the efficient organisation of happiness. Immortality, certainly, is out, and so life here should last as long as we determine —or eventually, one may suspect, others will determine—that it is pleasant for us to be around.

Unamuno's outlook is at the opposite pole to this and whatever else may be wrong with it, it salutes the true idea that the meaning of life does not consist either in the management of satisfactions in a body or in an abstract immortality without one. On the one hand he had no time for Manicheanism, and admired the rather brutal Catholic faith which could express its hopes for a future life in the words which he knew on a tombstone in Bilbao:[16]

Aunque estamos in polvo convertidos
en Ti, Señor, nuestra esperanza fía,
que tornaremos a vivir vestidos
con la carne y la piel que nos cubria.

At the same time, his desire to remain alive extends an almost incomprehensible distance beyond any desire to continue agreeable experiences:

For myself I can say that as a youth and even as a child I remained unmoved when shown the most moving pictures of hell, for even then nothing appeared quite so horrible to me as nothingness itself.[17]

[15]Ibid., p. 60.
[16]Ibid., p. 79
[17]Ibid., p. 28

The most that I have claimed earlier against Lucretius is not enough to make that preference intelligible to me. The fear of sheer nothingness is certainly part of what Lucretius rightly, if too lightly, hoped to exorcise; and the *mere* desire to stay alive, which is here stretched to its limit, is not enough (I suggested before) to answer the question, once the question has come up and requires an answer in rational terms. Yet Unamuno's affirmation of existence even through limitless suffering[18] brings out something which is implicit in the claim against Lucretius. It is not necessarily the prospect of pleasant times that create the motive against dying, but the existence of categorical desire, and categorical desire can drive through both the existence and the prospect of unpleasant times.

Suppose, then, that categorical desire does sustain the desire to live. So long as it remains so, I shall want not to die. Yet I also know, if what has gone before is right, that an eternal life would be unliveable. In part, as EM's case originally suggested, that is because categorical desire will go away from it: in those versions, such as hers, in which I am recognisably myself, I would eventually have had altogether too much of myself. There are good reasons, surely, for dying before that happens. But equally, at times earlier than that moment, there is reason for not dying. Necessarily, it tends to be either too early or too late. EM reminds us that it can be too late, and many, as against Lucretius, need no reminding that it can be too early. If that is any sort of dilemma, it can, as things still are and if one is exceptionally lucky, be resolved, not by doing anything, but just by dying shortly before the horrors of not doing so become evident. Technical progress may, in more than one direction, make that piece of luck rarer. But as things are, it is possible to be, in contrast to EM, *felix opportunitate mortis*— as it can be appropriately mistranslated, lucky in having the chance to die.

---

[18]An affirmation which takes on a special dignity retrospectively in the light of his own death shortly after his courageous speech against Millán Astray and the obscene slogan '¡Viva la Muerte!' See Hugh Thomas, *The Spanish Civil War* (Harmondsworth: Pelican, 1961), pp. 442–444.

about the
contributors

G. E. M. ANSCOMBE is Professor of Philosophy at Cambridge University. She has done important work in many areas of philosophy, and is the author of *Intention* (1957).

RICHARD B. BRANDT is Professor of Philosophy at the University of Michigan. He has written *Hopi Ethics* (1954), *Ethical Theory* (1959), and many well-known papers on moral philosophy.

R. S. DOWNIE, Professor of Philosophy at the University of Glasgow, is the author of *Roles and Values* (1971) and the co-author, with Elizabeth Telfer, of *Respect for Persons* (1969).

R. M. DWORKIN is Professor of Jurisprudence at Oxford University and Lecturer in Law at the Yale Law School. He has written many important papers on law and the philosophy of law.

PHILIPPA FOOT teaches philosophy at the University of California at Los Angeles and at Oxford. She is the author of numerous influential papers on moral philosophy, and the editor of *Theories of Ethics* (1967).

H. L. A. HART, formerly Professor of Jurisprudence at Oxford, is the author of *The Concept of Law* (1961) and *Law, Liberty and Morality* (1963). *Punishment and Responsibility* (1968) is a collection of some of Professor Hart's essays.

R. F. HOLLAND, Professor of Philosophy at the University of Leeds, has written on a variety of philosophical issues and is the editor of the series *Studies in Philosophical Psychology*.

WILLIAM KNEALE, formerly White's Professor of Moral Philosophy at Oxford, is the author of *Probability and Induction* (1949), and co-author, with Martha Kneale, of *The Development of Logic* (1962).

DOUGLAS LACKEY teaches philosophy at Baruch College of the City University of New York. He has edited Bertrand Russell's *Essays in Analysis* (1973) and he is a contributor to *Assassination* (1974), edited by Harold Zellner.

J. R. LUCAS is Fellow of Merton College at Oxford. He is the author of *The Principles of Politics* (1966), *The Freedom of the Will* (1970), and other works.

THOMAS NAGEL is Professor of Philosophy at Princeton University. He is the author of *The Possibility of Altruism* (1970) and many papers on ethics and the philosophy of mind.

JAN NARVESON teaches philosophy at the University of Waterloo in Canada. His book *Morality and Utility* (1967) is a detailed study of utilitarian ethics.

PAUL RAMSEY is Harrington Spear Paine Professor of Religion at Princeton. He is the author of *The Patient as Person* (1970), *Fabricated Man* (1970), and other books.

JOHN RAWLS is Professor of Philosophy at Harvard University. His major work is *A Theory of Justice* (1971).

BETTY ROSZAK is co-editor, with Theodore Roszak, of *Masculine/Feminine: Readings in Sexual Mythology and the Liberation of Women* (1969).

SARA RUDDICK teaches philosophy at the New School for Social Research. She has contributed to the *Canadian Journal of Philosophy* and to *Language and Philosophy* (1969), edited by Sidney Hook.

PETER SINGER is Senior Lecturer in Philosophy at La Trobe University in Australia. He is the author of *Democracy and Disobedience* (1973), and his book *Animal Liberation* will soon be published by New York Review Books.

JUDITH JARVIS THOMSON is Professor of Philosophy at the Massachusetts Institute of Technology. She has written on a variety of philosophical issues, and she is co-editor, with Gerald Dworkin, of *Ethics* (1968).

RICHARD WASSERSTROM is Professor of Philosophy and Law at the University of California at Los Angeles. He is the author of *The Judicial Decision* (1961), and many papers on the philosophy of law; and he is the editor of *War and Morality* (1970) and *Morality and the Law* (1971).

ROGER WERTHEIMER, who teaches philosophy at the City University of New York, is the author of *The Significance of Sense* (1972).

BERNARD WILLIAMS is Professor of Philosophy at Cambridge. He is the author of *Morality: An Introduction to Ethics* (1972). *Problems of the Self* (1973) is a collection of Professor Williams' essays.

selected
bibliography

This bibliography is intended simply to provide the reader with some references to additional work on the subjects of the essays contained in this book. It is not meant to be exhaustive.

1. SEX

Atkinson, Ronald, *Sexual Morality*. New York: Harcourt Brace Jovanovich, 1966.

Fletcher, Joseph, *Moral Responsibility*. Philadelphia: Westminster, 1967. Chs. 5–8.

Hart, Harold (ed.), *Sexual Latitude: For and Against*. New York: Hart, 1971.

Heron, Alastair (ed.), *Towards a Quaker View of Sex*. London: Friends Home Service Committee, 1964. Excerpts reprinted in Gibson Winter (ed.), *Social Ethics*, New York: Harper & Row, 1968.

Kardiner, Abram, *Sex and Morality*. Indianapolis, Ind.: Bobbs-Merrill, 1954.

Ramsey, Paul, "On Taking Sexual Responsibility Seriously Enough," *Christianity and Crisis*, vol. 23 (1964). Reprinted in Gibson Winter (ed.), *Social Ethics*, New York: Harper & Row, 1968.

Russell, Bertrand, *Marriage and Morals*. New York: Liveright, 1929.

Sex and Morality: A Report to the British Council of Churches. Philadelphia, Pa.: Fortress, 1966.

Storr, Anthony, *Sexual Deviation*. Harmondsworth, Middlesex: Penguin Books, 1964.

Whiteley, C. H. and W. M., *Sex and Morals*. London: B. T. Batsford, 1967.
Wilson, John, *Logic and Sexual Morality*. Harmondsworth, Middlesex: Penguin Books, 1965.

2. ABORTION

Brody, Baruch, "Abortion and the Law," *The Journal of Philosophy*, vol. 68 (1971).
Brody, Baruch, "Abortion and the Sanctity of Human Life," *American Philosophical Quarterly*, vol. 10 (1973).
Brody, Baruch, "Thomson on Abortion," *Philosophy and Public Affairs*, vol. 1 (1973).
Callahan, Daniel, *Abortion: Law, Choice, and Morality*. New York: Macmillan, 1970.
Church Assembly Board for Social Responsibility, *Abortion: An Ethical Discussion*. London: Church Information Office, 1965.
Cooke, Robert E., et al., *The Terrible Choice: The Abortion Dilemma*. New York: Bantam, 1968.
Feinberg, Joel (ed.), *The Problem of Abortion*. Belmont, Cal.: Wadsworth, 1973. Contains a useful bibliography.
Finnis, John, "The Rights and Wrongs of Abortion," *Philosophy and Public Affairs*, vol. 2 (1973).
McCormick, Richard A., "Past Church Teaching on Abortion," *Proceedings of the Catholic Theological Society of America*, vol. 23 (1968).
Margolis, Joseph, "Abortion," *Ethics*, vol. 84 (1973).
Noonan, John T., Jr. (ed.), *The Morality of Abortion: Legal and Historical Perspectives*. Cambridge: Harvard University Press, 1970.
Rosen, Harold (ed.), *Abortion in America*. Boston: Beacon, 1967.
St. John-Stevas, Norman, *The Right to Life*. London, 1963.
Thomson, J. J., "Rights and Deaths," *Philosophy and Public Affairs*, vol. 2 (1973).
Tooley, Michael, "Abortion and Infanticide," *Philosophy and Public Affairs*, vol. 2 (1972).
Who Shall Live? Man's Control Over Birth and Death. A Report Prepared for the American Friends Service Committee, New York: Hill & Wang, 1970. Contains a useful bibliography.
Williams, Glanville, *The Sanctity of Life and the Criminal Law*. New York: Knopf, 1968. Chs. 5–6.

3. PREJUDICE AND DISCRIMINATION

Blackstone, William T. (ed.), *The Concept of Equality*. Minneapolis, Minn.: Burgess, 1969.

Brandt, Richard B. (ed.), *Social Justice*. Englewood Cliffs, N.J.: Prentice-Hall, 1962.

Cowan, J. L., "Inverse Discrimination," *Analysis*, vol. 33 (1972).

Godlovitch, Roslind, "Animals and Morals," *Philosophy*, vol. 46 (1971).

Godlovitch, S. and R., and Harris, J. (eds.), *Animals, Men, and Morals*. London: Taplinger, 1972.

Mothersill, Mary, "Notes on Feminism," *The Monist*, vol. 57, no. 1 (1973). This issue of *The Monist* is devoted to Women's Liberation, and contains other articles on the same subject.

Nagel, Thomas, "Equal Treatment and Compensatory Discrimination," *Philosophy and Public Affairs*, vol. 2 (1973).

Nickel, James W., "Discrimination and Morally Relevant Characteristics," *Analysis*, vol. 33 (1972).

Roszak, Betty and Theodore (eds.), *Masculine/Feminine*. New York: Harper & Row, 1969.

4. CIVIL DISOBEDIENCE

Bedau, H. A., "On Civil Disobedience," *The Journal of Philosophy*, vol. 58 (1961).

Bedau, H. A. (ed.), *Civil Disobedience: Theory and Practice*. New York: Pegasus, 1969.

Brown, Stuart M., Jr., "Civil Disobedience," *The Journal of Philosophy*, vol. 58 (1961).

Cohen, Carl, *Civil Disobedience*. New York: Columbia University Press, 1971.

Cohen, Carl, "Civil Disobedience and the Law," *Rutgers Law Review*, vol. 21 (1966).

Cohen, Marshall, "Liberalism and Disobedience," *Philosophy and Public Affairs*, vol. 1 (1973).

Hook, Sidney, "Social Protest and Civil Disobedience," in Paul Kurtz (ed.), *Moral Problems in Contemporary Society*. Englewood Cliffs, N.J.: Prentice-Hall, 1968.

Hughes, Graham, "Civil Disobedience and the Political-Question Doctrine," *New York University Law Review*, vol. 43 (1968).

Keeton, Morris, "The Morality of Civil Disobedience," *Texas Law Review*, vol. 43 (1965).

Malament, David, "Selective Conscientious Objection and the *Gillette* Decision," *Philosophy and Public Affairs*, vol. 1 (1972).

Singer, Peter, *Democracy and Disobedience*. Oxford: Oxford University Press, 1973.

Spitz, David, "Democracy and the Problem of Civil Disobedience," *American Political Science Review*, vol. 48 (1954).

Thalberg, Irving, "Philosophical Problems of Civil Disobedience," *Scientia*, vol. 101 (1966).

Walzer, Michael, "The Obligation to Disobey," *Ethics*, vol. 77 (1967).

Wasserstrom, Richard A., "The Obligation to Obey the Law," *U.C.L.A. Law Review*, vol. 10 (1963).

Weingartner, Rudolf H., "Justifying Civil Disobedience," *Columbia Forum*, vol. 9 (1966).

5. PUNISHMENT

Acton, H. B. (ed.), *The Philosophy of Punishment*. London: Macmillan, 1969. Contains a helpful bibliography.

Armstrong, K. G., "The Retributivist Hits Back," *Mind*, vol. 70 (1961).

Baier, Kurt, "Is Punishment Retributive?" *Analysis*, vol. 16 (1955).

Bedau, H. A. (ed.), *The Death Penalty in America*. Garden City, N.Y.: Doubleday, 1964.

Doyle, James F., "Justice and Legal Punishment," *Philosophy*, vol. 42 (1967).

Ewing, A. C., *The Morality of Punishment*. London: Routledge & Kegan Paul, 1929.

Ezorsky, Gertrude (ed.), *Philosophical Perspectives on Punishment*. Albany, N.Y.: State University of New York Press, 1972. Contains a useful bibliography.

Flew, Antony, "The Justification of Punishment," *Philosophy*, vol. 29 (1954).

Hart, H. L. A., *Punishment and Responsibility*. Oxford: Oxford University Press, 1968.

Honderich, T., *Punishment: The Supposed Justifications*. New York: Harcourt Brace Jovanovich, 1970.

Mabbott, J. D., "Punishment," *Mind*, vol. 58 (1939).

Mundle, C. W. K., "Punishment and Desert," *Philosophical Quarterly*, vol. 4 (1954).

Quinton, Anthony M., "On Punishment," *Analysis*, vol. 14 (1954).

Raab, Francis V., "A Moralist Looks at the Durham and M'Naghton Rules," *Minnesota Law Review*, vol. 46 (1961).

Rawls, John, "Two Concepts of Rules," *The Philosophical Review*, vol. 64 (1955).

Smart, Alwynne, "Mercy," *Philosophy*, vol. 43 (1968).

Squires, J. E. R., "Blame," *Philosophical Quarterly*, vol. 18 (1968).

6. WAR

Bennett, John C. (ed.), *Nuclear Weapons and the Conflict of Conscience*. New York: Scribner, 1962.

Brandt, R. B., "Utilitarianism and the Rules of War," *Philosophy and Public Affairs*, vol. 1 (1972).

Freud, Sigmund, "Reflections Upon War and Death," in *Character and Culture*. New York: Collier, 1963.

Fried, Morton; Harris, Marvin; and Murphy, Robert (eds.), *War*. Garden City, N.Y.: Natural History Press, 1967.

Ginsberg, Robert (ed.), *The Critique of War*. Chicago: Regnery, 1969. Includes a useful bibliography.

Hare, R. M., "Rules of War and Moral Reasoning," *Philosophy and Public Affairs*, vol. 1 (1972).

Nagel, Thomas, "War and Massacre," *Philosophy and Public Affairs*, vol. 1 (1972).

Ramsey, Paul, *The Just War*. New York: Scribner, 1968.

Somerville, John, "Democracy and the Problem of War," in Paul Kurtz (ed.), *Moral Problems in Contemporary Society*. Englewood Cliffs, N.J.: Prentice-Hall, 1968.

Stein, Walter (ed.), *Nuclear Weapons: A Catholic Response*. New York: Sheed & Ward, 1961.

Wasserstrom, Richard, "The Relevance of Nuremberg," *Philosophy and Public Affairs*, vol. 1 (1971).

Wasserstrom, Richard A. (ed.), *War and Morality*. Belmont, Cal.: Wadsworth, 1970. Includes a useful bibliography.

Walzer, Michael, "World War II: Why Was This War Different?" *Philosophy and Public Affairs*, vol. 1 (1971).

Wells, Donald A., "How Much Can 'The Just War' Justify?" *The Journal of Philosophy*, vol. 66 (1969).

Wells, Donald A., *The War Myth*. New York: Pegasus, 1967.

7. SUICIDE

Alvarez, A., *The Savage God*. New York: Random House, 1972.

Douglas, Jack D., *The Social Meanings of Suicide*. Princeton, N.J.: Princeton University Press, 1967.

Durkheim, Emile, *Suicide*. New York: Free Press, 1951.

Hume, David, "Of Suicide," in *Essays: Moral, Political, and Literary*. Oxford: Oxford University Press, 1963.

Kant, Immanuel, "Suicide," *Lecture on Ethics*. New York: Harper & Row, 1963.

Landsberg, P. L., *The Experience of Death and the Moral Problem of Suicide*. London: Rockliff, 1963.

St. John-Stevas, Norman, *Life, Death, and the Law*. Bloomington, Ind.: Indiana University Press, 1961. Ch. 6.

Shneidman, Edwin S., and Farberow, Norman L. (eds.), *Clues to Suicide*. New York: McGraw-Hill, 1968.

Sprott, S. E., *The English Debate on Suicide*. LaSalle, Ill.: Open Court, 1961.

Stengel, Erwin, *Suicide and Attempted Suicide*. Harmondsworth, Middlesex: Penguin, 1964.

Voltaire, "Of Suicide," in *Candide and Other Writings*. New York: Modern Library, 1956.

Williams, Glanville, *The Sanctity of Life and the Criminal Law*. New York: Knopf, 1968. Ch. 7.

8. DEATH

Choron, Jacques, *Death and Western Thought*. New York: Collier, 1963.

Ewin, R. E., "What Is Wrong with Killing People?" *The Philosophical Quarterly*, vol. 22 (1972).

Feifel, Herman (ed.), *The Meaning of Death*. New York: McGraw-Hill, 1959.

Fletcher, Joseph, *Morals and Medicine*. Boston: Beacon Press, 1960.

Freud, Sigmund, "Reflections Upon War and Death," *Character and Culture*. New York: Collier, 1963.

Fulton, Robert (ed.), *Death and Identity*. New York: Wiley, 1965.

Goodrich, T., "The Morality of Killing," *Philosophy*, vol. 44 (1969).

Henson, Richard, "Utilitarianism and the Wrongness of Killing," *The Philosophical Review*, vol. 80 (1971).

Hinton, John, *Dying*. Harmondsworth, Middlesex: Penguin, 1967.

Kubler-Ross, Elisabeth, *On Death and Dying*. New York: Macmillan, 1969.

Labby, Daniel H. (ed.), *Life or Death: Ethics and Options*. Seattle, Wash.: University of Washington Press, 1968.

Lamont, Corliss, "The Crisis Called Death," in Paul Kurtz (ed.), *Moral Problems in Contemporary Society*. Englewood Cliffs, N.J.: Prentice-Hall, 1968.

Landsberg, P. L., *The Experience of Death and the Moral Problem of Suicide*. London: Rockliff, 1963.

Lepp, Ignace, *Death and Its Mysteries*. Toronto: Macmillan, 1968.

Natanson, Maurice, "Humanism and Death," in Paul Kurtz (ed.), *Moral Problems in Contemporary Society*. Englewood Cliffs, N.J.: Prentice-Hall, 1968.

Scott, Nathan A. (ed.), *The Modern Vision of Death*. Richmond, Va.: John Knox, 1967.

Toynbee, Arnold, et al., *Man's Concern with Death*. New York: McGraw-Hill, 1968.

Who Shall Live? Man's Control Over Birth and Death. A Report Prepared for the American Friends Service Committee. New York: Hill & Wang, 1970. Contains a useful bibliography.

Williams, Glanville, *The Sanctity of Life and the Criminal Law*. New York: Knopf, 1968.

75 76 77 78 9 8 7 6 5 4 3 2 1